Strategic Public Relations Management

Planning and Managing Effective Communication Programs

LEA's COMMUNICATION SERIES
Jennings Bryant/Dolf Zillmann, General Editors

Selected titles in Public Relations (James Grunig, Advisory Editor) include:

Culbertson/Chen • International Public Relations:
A Comparative Analysis

Dozier/Grunig/Grunig • Manager's Guide to Excellence
in Public Relations and Communication Mangement

Fearn-Banks • Crisis Communications: A Casebook Approach

Grunig • Excellence in Public Relations and Communication
Management

Kelly • Effective Fund-Raising Management

Kunczik • Images of Nations and International Public Relations

Ledingahm/Bruning • Public Relations as Relationship
Management: A Relational Approach to the Study and Practice
of Public Relations

Lerbinger • The Crisis Manager: Facing Risk and Responsibility

Spicer • Organizational Public Relations: A Political Perspective

For a complete list of titles in LEA's Communication Series, please contact Lawrence Erlbaum Associates, Publishers.

Strategic Public Relations Management
Planning and Managing Effective Communication Programs

Erica Weintraub Austin
Bruce E. Pinkleton
Washington State University

LAWRENCE ERLBAUM ASSOCIATES, PUBLISHERS

2001   Mahwah, New Jersey   London

Lawrence Erlbaum Associates, Inc., Publishers
10 Industrial Avenue
Mahwah, NJ 07430

Cover design by Kathryn Houghtaling Lacey

Library of Congress Cataloging-in-Publication Data

Austin, Erica Weintraub.
  Strategic public relations management : planning and
effective communication programs / Erica Weintraub
Austin, Bruce E. Pinkleton.
    p. cm.
Includes bibliographical references and index.
ISBN 0-8058-3159-2 (cloth : alk. paper) — ISBN
0-8058-3160-6 (pbk. : alk. Paper)
    1. Public relations—Management.   I. Pinkleton,
Bruce E. II. Title.
HD59 .A97 2000
659.2—dc21
                                              00-034758
                                              CIP

Books published by Lawrence Erlbaum Associates are printed
on acid-free paper, and their bindings are chosen for strength
and durability.

Printed in the United States of America
10 9 8 7 6 5 4 3 2

To our families
Bruce, Jimmy, and Noah
Chris, Lauren, and Brett

Contents

3 Elements of the Campaign Recipe   27

4 Determining Research Needs: Developing   45
the Research Plan

II. GATHERING USEFUL DATA
FOR STRATEGIC GUIDANCE

5 Research Decisions and Data Collection   71

Appendixes

References   379

Author Index   387

Subject Index   391

Preface

We decided to write this book in 1995 when we attended the national Public Relations Society of America convention in Seattle. The sessions on measurement and evaluation were standing room only, and many conversations in the hallways focused on the same issues. Meanwhile, discussions in the trade press about the need to improve results have increased steadily over the past 10 years. We have been getting calls from organizations wanting research who have never seen the need for it before. We have had alumni reporting back to us about how valuable their course work in research and planning was for them and their organizations. Both experience and observation have taught us that research and strategic planning are powerful tools.

ACKNOWLEDGMENTS

In this book, we have tried to put together lessons learned from both applied and academic experience. We have been privileged to learn from many excellent teachers including Chuck Atkin, Steve Chaffee, June Flora, Gina Garramone, Randall Murray, and Don Roberts. We are indebted to Jim Grunig, whose input, advice, and encouragement were critical factors in the completion of this book. We also owe many thanks to our students, who have taught us well over the past 10 years.

There are a number of other people whose special efforts have helped us make this book happen. We would like to thank the director of the Edward R. Murrow School of Communication, Alexis Tan, for helping us develop the confidence and expertise necessary to complete this project, and for providing support in every way he can. We also have deeply appreciated the help and humor of our colleague, Julie

Andsager, who has done everything from listening to us whine to typing references. Talented graduate student Yuki Fujioka provided valuable feedback on a key chapter. A number of other graduate and undergraduate students have helped with research, including Tracy Lee Clarke, Heather Crandall, Kris Fortman, Petra Guerra, Lisa Laughter, and Bill Wisniewski.

We also have greatly benefited from the help of professionals, including Glen Cameron, University of Missouri; H. Stewart Elway, Elway Research, Inc., Ned Hubbell, Michigan State University (retired); Sara Labberton, KVO Public Relations; Walter Lindenmann, Ketchum Public Relations (retired); Edward Maibach, Porter Novelli; Norman Nager, California State University-Fullerton; Louis Richmond, Richmond Public Relations; Scott Simms, Conkling, Fiskum & McCormick; and Collin Tong, Washington State University. We also would like to thank the Puget Sound Chapter of the Public Relations Society of America, which invited us to try our ideas on them and then provided us with critical and enthusiastic feedback. Thanks also to The Institute for Public Relations Research and Education for financial support, and to Christopher Knaus who made that support possible. We have also appreciated the helpfulness of editor Linda Bathgate and production manager Robin Weisberg of Lawrence Erlbaum Associates throughout the publication process.

We are grateful for the advice and support of Stan and Rodelle Weintraub, who have written many more books than we ever will and make it look easy. Finally, although it sounds trite it is no less true that our families' unselfish support has made this book possible. The magnitude of this project required us to work many late nights and weekends, and we occasionally sacrificed scout meetings, basketball practices, and other family activities to stay on schedule. Writing this book has been great, but the best part is being able to go home now.

—*Erica Weintraub Austin*
—*Bruce E. Pinkleton*

The Need for Strategic Public Relations Management

Strategic public relations planning and research techniques have evolved into the most powerful tools available to public relations practitioners. Today's competitive business environment increasingly puts pressure on communication managers to demonstrate in a measurable way how the results from public relations programs benefit the organizations they serve. Practitioners well prepared to use the tools available to them can enjoy bigger budgets, more autonomy in decision making, and greater support from management. Managers relying on an intuitive model of public relations practice based on their knowledge of media markets and a well-developed network of contacts, however, tend to have less credibility, enjoy less autonomy, receive lower priority, and suffer greater risk of cost cutting that threatens job security.

SURVIVING AMID FIERCE COMPETITION

The increasingly competitive business and social environment makes it critical for public relations managers to understand how to apply public relations planning, research, and program-evaluation practices that help ensure success and accountability. Research-based public relations practices enable managers to solve complex problems, set and achieve or exceed goals and objectives, track the opinions and beliefs of key publics, and employ program strategies with confidence

1

they will have the intended results. Although the use of research in public relations management cannot guarantee program success, it allows practitioners to maximize their abilities and move beyond creative reactions to scientific management. A more strategic management style can help control the ways a situation will develop and the outcomes practitioners achieve in those situations.

Consider the following scenarios in which communication professionals can use research-based planning to develop effective strategies for solving a problem and demonstrate program success:

Community relations. You are the public affairs director for the largest employer in a community. The local media have been running stories about problems at the company, claiming management has lost sight of its unique role in the community. The board of directors wants a clear understanding of public perceptions of the company. It also wants to develop new programs that will better serve the community and improve community relations. You are not convinced the company needs to establish new programs as much as it needs to support its existing programs. How do you determine the opinions and attitudes of community members toward the company? How do you measure community perceptions of existing programs, as well as community interest in new programs?

Special events planning and promotion. You are the manager of a performing arts coliseum. The coliseum has lost money on several events over the past 2 years and now is threatened by competition from a new community theater scheduled for construction in 2 years. Coliseum management and its board of directors sense they are out of touch with the community and are unsure how to address the situation. How can management determine community programming interests and begin to reorient itself to the needs and desires of community members without wasting valuable resources?

Political campaign. You are the campaign manager for a state senatorial candidate. The mostly rural district has 75,000 registered voters, many of whom work as farmers or in farming-related businesses and industries. The election is 3 months away, and the candidates are engaged in a close contest. How do you track changes in voters' perceptions of your candidate as the election nears?

Nonprofit. You are a public relations practitioner at a small, nonprofit organization. Your new assignment is to rescue a local special event with a troubled history. The event, sponsored by the local chamber of commerce, is supposed to raise money for your organization while attracting visitors to your community who patronize local businesses. Last year's event was a disaster, however, despite a strong media relations effort. Because of low attendance, the organization barely broke even on the event, and local businesses have lost interest in participating next year as sponsors. How do you find out what went wrong and make next year's event a success?

Development. You are a senior development officer at a major university. Development has become increasingly important as state budgets have dwindled. The university is making preparations for the largest development campaign in its history. Unfortunately, students let their partying get out of hand after a big football win over cross-state rivals, and the fracas attracts national media attention. You are concerned the negative media attention will significantly hinder university development efforts. You need to understand the opinions and attitudes of key publics to develop a quick plan that will allow you to respond in an effective manner. How do you determine the responses of donors and nondonors to news of the altercation?

Public relations practitioners face problems like these on a regular basis.

STRATEGIC VERSUS TACTICAL DECISION MAKING

Research helps practitioners get accurate information quickly at a relatively low cost to aid them in sophisticated planning and problem solving such as this every day. When practitioners respond to organizational problems and challenges by engaging in media relations campaigns, they typically respond tactically instead of strategically. Tactical decision making can allow public relations programs and campaigns to drift aimlessly, lacking direction or purpose. Practitioners often use media clips as the basis for program accountability in this instance, but the benefits of clip-based evaluation are limited. It is impossible, for example, for practitioners to determine message effects on targeted audiences' opinions, attitudes, or behavior using clips. Practitioners find their ability to solve organizations' problems through such a response also severely limited because no basis exists for determining the extent of a problem or evaluating the results of their programs. Finally, organizations can become frustrated in their attempts to adapt to changing internal and external environments because practitioners have no basis for understanding and accomplishing the steps necessary to successfully address or accommodate stakeholders' opinions. The result is that practitioners' success may be limited. They typically end up in a defensive position with external and internal audiences, having no basis for effectively communicating the benefits of their campaigns and programs to organizational management.

When practitioners respond to problems and challenges strategically instead of tactically, they have a much greater likelihood of helping organizations meet their challenges, solve or avoid protracted problems, and adjust to the expectations of key stakeholders in mutually beneficial ways. Research and planning are not simple remedies for every organizational problem. No amount of research or planning, for example, can rescue an organization from the consequences of its own poor performance. Nevertheless, practitioners' use of research, planning, and evaluation contribute to an informed organizational decision-making process with a greater likelihood of success. When practitioners use these tools, their programs and campaigns can have clear goals that direct program implementation. Practitioners can use formative research to find initial benchmarks for goals and objectives, and to determine campaign strategy. Practitioners using tactics purposefully and selectively can communicate the benefits of public relations campaigns and programs to organizational management more easily. Ultimately, practitioners have the opportunity to enjoy greater success at placing their organizations in stable, mutually beneficial relationships with key stakeholders.

As Cutlip, Center, and Broom (2000) noted, public relations is a management function that identifies, establishes, and maintains mutually beneficial relationships between an organization and the publics on whom its success or failure depends. This definition and many others like it, although simple on their face, actually suggest a complex set of processes. For public relations practitioners to operate as managers, for example, they cannot simply input the decisions made by others in an organization. They need to assert themselves as members of what is commonly called the dominant coalition, those with the authority to make decisions and set policy. In other words, they need to lead organizations and not just act as "service providers." Dozier, Grunig, and Grunig (1995) stated, "Just as communication flows one way, so too does influence" (p. 77). What Dozier et al. meant by this is that service providers implement decisions made by others instead of influencing organizational decision making. As a result, practitioners operating as service providers commonly are limited to advocating organizational viewpoints. This prevents them from helping the organization build and maintain long-term relationships that ensure long-term organizational success, which requires some adjustment to public perceptions and needs.

THE OFTEN MISUNDERSTOOD ROLE OF PUBLIC RELATIONS

Public relations practices encompass a broad range of activities that can lead to confusion about how it differs from marketing and advertising. The goals of each differ in important ways. Advertising focuses on selling products to consumers through controlled placement of paid media messages, a narrow and specific role. Marketing, including integrated marketing communications, often uses public relations techniques to sell products and services. The marketing role is broader than that of advertising but still focuses on consumers rather than on all the key publics of an organization. Public relations, on the other hand, strives to help organizations develop and preserve the variety of relationships that ensure long-term success, which is broader than those of advertising or marketing. These stakeholders can include consumers but also includes government regulators, community members, shareholders, members of the media, and employees. Therefore, although public relations techniques often are employed in marketing and advertising, it is more appropriate for organizational management to treat public relations as the umbrella under which other activities including marketing and advertising occur.

Many practitioners struggle with the fact that this is difficult to put into practice, and they often find their role misunderstood. A survey of New York chapter members of the Public Relations Society of America (PRSA), for example, found that 92% believed that most people do not understand what public relations is (APR Pros,@ 1998). Public relations also suffers from low credibility. In the New York survey, 93% of the professionals enjoyed their work, and 68% were proud of their field, but 67% believed the field did not have a good image, and 65% believed they were not as respected as members of other professions. This image problem was supported by a recent credibility study undertaken by PRSA, which found the public relations specialist ranked almost at the bottom of a list of approximately 50 professions (Public Relations Society of America, 1999).

It could seem that public relations' image problem stems from its reputation as being a "velvet ghetto" (Cline & Toth, 1993, p. 184), rather than from unsatisfactory practitioner performance. Women dominate the public relations field, and even though they perform more tasks at the managerial level than men do, they tend to earn less than men in the field (Cline & Toth, 1993). In addition, more women still perform tasks at a tactical level while operating as managers (Toth & Grunig, 1993), which could contribute to the devaluation of women and of public relations. We believe, however, that managers—whether male or female—can enhance their status and perhaps also their salaries by adopting a more research-based, strategic management style.

To improve their stature within organizations and among a broad range of publics, public relations professionals must take a planned, strategic approach to their programs and problem solving. When operating as subordinates instead of organizational leaders, practitioners implement decisions made by others instead of contributing to organizational decision making. In short, they work at a tactical level. As leading experts continue to emphasize, communication specialists who operate as technicians cannot effectively build public consensus or position an organization on issues of strategic importance (e.g., Broom & Dozier, 1990; Dozier et al., 1995; "Keys," 1998; "M&As," 1998; "Personal competency," 1998; "Reputation," 1994).

USING RESEARCH TO ENHANCE THE CREDIBILITY OF PUBLIC RELATIONS

One reason communication specialists experience frustration and insufficient credibility appears to lie in how they conduct and apply research. A national survey of 300 professionals in 1996 assessing their research practices found managers in a double bind (Austin, Pinkleton, & Dixon, in press; Pinkleton, Austin, & Dixon, 1999). Professionals reported clients and CEOs as enthusiastic about research, but reluctant about providing the budget to pay for it. Meanwhile, the more the managers performed a specific type of research, the less they valued it, and the more they valued a particular research method, the less they employed it. As shown in Table 1.1, practitioners relied most

TABLE 1.1
Use and Value of Research Measures
Among Public Relations Practitioners

	Mean for Use (Rank)	Mean for Perceived Value (Rank)
Advertising equivalency	3.71 (9)	3.37 (9)
Volume of media pickups	5.43 (2)	4.57 (8)
Favorable media treatment	5.35 (3)	4.96 (7)
Media coverage	5.47 (1)	5.19 (5)
Changes in awareness	4.95 (4)	5.64 (4)
Changes in knowledge	4.85 (5)	5.90 (2)
Changes in attitudes	4.74 (6)	5.77 (3)
Changes in sales	4.07 (8)	5.08 (6)
Changes in behavior	4.64 (7)	6.02 (1)

Note. All measures on 7-point scales, with 1 indicating less use or value and 7 indicating more use or value.

on measures of volume of media pickups and tracking of media coverage, which they found the least beneficial. On the other hand, practitioners relied least on measures of changes in awareness, knowledge, attitudes, sales, and behavior, which they found the most valuable. The results also showed that the professionals almost uniformly embraced research as vital for proving that public relations programs are effective, but less than half agreed that research is accepted as an important part of public relations. A 1995 PRSA survey also found that 92% believed research was talked about more than used (Public Relations Society of America, 1995). Finally, although 68% of practitioners attending a seminar on PR measurement said they do evaluations, only 23% said their research was providing useful results ("The New," 1999). This pattern of results suggests that constraints prevent communication professionals from doing enough research, or at least enough of the type of research that clients and senior executives find compelling. In response, *PR Reporter* proclaimed measurement and evaluation as the field's top issue for the year 2000 ("To Start," 2000).

Moving from a tactical approach to a strategic management style requires skillful use of research and planning techniques. Recent discussions among senior public relations practitioners at professional meetings and in the trade press have consistently emphasized the need for managers to demonstrate forward thinking by anticipating instead of reacting to problems and opportunities. In an increasingly crowded and complex media and social environment, practitioners need to design innovative programs they can prove will work. Gaining autonomy and the support and confidence of clients and upper management for their ideas requires several things. These include the ability to provide evidence supporting the need for communication programs, reasons why proposed strategies will work, and evidence at the end of a program that the program has indeed worked. In short, strategic public relations management demands a set of abilities that require competence in planning principles, research methods, communication theory, and effective communication presentation skills.

ORGANIZATION OF THE BOOK

Part I of this book presents a framework for planning that managers can apply to guide decision making. Chapter 2 addresses the development of the mission statement, problem statement, and situation analysis, all of which form the basis for program development. Chapter 3 introduces the elements of the strategic planning process, which include goals, objectives, strategies, and tactics. Chapter 4 focuses on how to determine research needs and develop a research plan to gather information that will help practitioners plan their program.

Part II addresses when and how to do research for public relations planning and evaluation. Chapter 5 covers basic issues to consider when developing research plans. Chapter 6 introduces the range of informal methods available to the communication manager, while chap. 7 provides some detail on how to conduct focus groups. Chapter 8 introduces the range of formal methods commonly used in communication research, and chap. 9 covers the nuances of survey research specifically. Chapter 10 provides the basics of sampling using terms and concepts accessible to those uninitiated in social science methods. Chapter 11 focuses on how to construct questionnaires that provide trustworthy and useful information, and chap. 12 discusses how to collect and analyze questionnaire data.

Part III explains how communication theory can assist the manager in strategic planning. Chapter 13 introduces public relations and communication theory and demonstrates its relevance to daily practice. Chapter 14 covers the range of theories available to help managers develop effective program strategies, and chap. 15 boils decades of research into a set of principles and applications for practical use.

Part IV discusses how to present a persuasive case for public relations programming, with chap. 16 explaining the elements of a public relations proposal and providing a set of writing and presentation tips.

Experts in public relations seem to agree that public relations practitioners have the most success when they operate from a research-based, strategic management style. As a result, this book provides professionals and advanced public relations students with the information they need to engage in strategic public relations management. Communication specialists who apply these skills should secure a place for public relations at the leadership level in organizational decision making.

A FRAMEWORK FOR PLANNING

Where the Strategic Manager Begins: Taking Stock

Management by Objectives
The Accountable Manager
The Mission Statement
The Problem Statement
The Situation Analysis
Sources of Information
Final Thoughts

For public relations practitioners trained more as writers rather than as social scientists, the new bottom-line-oriented environment presents a major challenge. Organizations want cost-effective results. Many public relations practitioners argue that the cultivation of relationships is a fuzzy business, difficult to document with numbers. The result: Public relations positions become vulnerable to corporate "restructuring."

The best insurance against cost cutters, and the best way to gain credibility and mobility in management, is to adopt what Broom and Dozier (1990) called the *scientific management* approach. This approach does not discount the importance of creativity and communication skills, but it does put them into an *effects-oriented* context. Say a hospital wants to open a new wing in the hope that it will increase business. For a hospital, this is a touchy subject: It doesn't want to appear greedy to take advantage of people's bad news and emergencies. Moreover, the promotion budget is probably limited because many hospitals are struggling to keep up with increasing medical costs and decreasing insurance reimbursements. Hospitals also do not want to appear wasteful, particularly if financed publicly. How can the hospital increase business without causing offense, and without spending too much or appearing unseemly?

In what Nager and Allen (1984) called *traditional public relations*, the communication manager would come up with creative ideas for communication vehicles such as brochures and advertisements according to the budget and staffing available. Should we use two-color or four-color? Glossy or matte? The manager's decision making would focus on what looks best, sounds best, and works within the budget.

The scientific manager, on the other hand, would begin with a different set of questions: Why do we need this new wing? To whom are we targeting this campaign? How much increased traffic do we need, and how much is realistic to expect? What will motivate people to take advantage of this new service? The *bottom line*: What goal should we set for this campaign?

The effects emphasis is *goal oriented*, lending itself to the bottom-line perspective of most organizations. Once you know what you must accomplish, you can focus your efforts more efficiently and to greater effect. The two major components of the scientific management approach are planning and research.

MANAGEMENT BY OBJECTIVES

The most common planning tool used by communication managers is known as *management by objectives* (MBO). MBO is an effects-oriented process for developing what are essentially campaign "recipes." If you write an easy-to-follow recipe, and you have skilled personnel in your kitchen, you can have confidence that you will cook up a successful campaign. Just like writing a recipe, however, MBO requires that you make strategic decisions about what you want to serve (a meal or just a dessert), how many you want to serve (your definition of bottom-line success), whom you expect for dinner (your publics), and when they will arrive (your deadline). You can adjust the ingredients according to your budget. Not every recipe for chocolate cake needs Belgian chocolate, and not every campaign will need glossy, four-color brochures. But just as you would not leave flour out of a bread recipe, the MBO approach can help you identify which campaign ingredients cannot be compromised. Moreover, the MBO approach can provide the hard evidence and persuasive reasoning you will need to convince your key decision makers that the campaign ingredients you identify as essential really are essential. In short, the MBO approach gives the communication manager credibility, flexibility, and control.

The MBO approach sounds easy but frequently confuses managers because practitioners often have an incomplete understanding of the elements that go into MBO recipe building. If you've ever wondered what the difference is between a goal and an objective, you have a lot of company. Definitions of goals and objectives are rarely provided, even in public relations textbooks. This chapter should make those distinctions clear.

THE ACCOUNTABLE MANAGER

Let's begin by comparing the communication manager's role in traditional and scientific management approaches. As discussed by Nager and Allen (1984), the bottom line of communication programs differs fundamentally. Traditional practitioners do lots of communication activities, but they may have a piecemeal perspective. For example, they may produce newsletters, brochures, news releases, and an occasional special event without much thought to how each news story or communication piece serves a specific and an overall purpose. MBO practitioners, on the other hand, have lots of goals they plan to accomplish. Their perspective is more holistic. As a result, everything MBO managers do has a clear, effects-oriented purpose. Because they organize their activities according to a results perspective, they can show the need and the effectiveness of each effort more readily than traditional practitioners can. Each newsletter, brochure, news release, and special event serves a clear purpose that is part of a larger framework.

The MBO manager, or scientific manager, focuses on six activities. As summarized by Ehling (1985), these include:

1. *Conceptualization.* A leader must hold the big picture and be able to identify and organize the smaller elements to fit that larger picture. The goal is to identify specific tasks and responsibilities that need to be fulfilled to maintain mutually beneficial relationships between an organization and the publics on which its success depends, such as budgeting, goal setting, strategic planning, organizing, administering, and evaluating (notice these elements constitute Tasks 2–6).

2. *Monitoring.* Monitoring is, in other words, research. The scientific manager will do much issue tracking to stay ahead of emerging trends and on top of potential crises. The goal is to anticipate and evaluate opportunities and challenges that arise out of the organization's interactions and relationships with other organizations and society.

3. *Planning.* The manager must be able to build the recipes that will guide the organization through the opportunities and challenges identified in the monitoring process. The goal is to ensure the achievement of measurable results that fulfill needs identified in the monitoring process.

4. *Organization and Coordination.* The manager must make effective use of available resources. These include budget and person-

nel within the organization as well as opportunities for cooperative partnerships with other organizations that can help them achieve mutually beneficial results. The goal is the effective and efficient implementation of strategies for the communication programs developed in the planning process.

   5. *Administration.* The manager must fulfill the promises made in the planning process. The manager will supervise the programs to activate and adjust communication programs. Nothing ever goes exactly according to plan, because resources and the environment continue to change, so the manager must maintain motivating, creative leadership throughout the implementation of each program. The goal is the fulfillment of communication program goals on budget and on deadline.

   6. *Evaluation.* The scientific manager remains accountable. Every communication activity must have a clear purpose and an anticipated result. The manager must show results and an ability to use program successes and failures as part of the monitoring process, to develop even more effective future programs. The goal is the accountability, credibility, and guidance to make future communication programs even more successful.

TABLE 2.1
Tasks and Goals of the MBO Manager

Task	Relation to Four-Step PR Process Elements	Goal
Conceptualization	Defining the PR problem	To identify tasks and responsibilities to be fulfilled for maintenance of long-term relationships
Monitoring	Defining the PR problem	To anticipate and evaluate opportunities and challenges
Planning	Planning and programming	To ensure achievement of measurable results that fulfill identified needs
Organization and Coordination	Planning and programming	To implement effective and efficient strategies
Administration	Taking action and communicating	To fulfill program goals on budget and on deadline
Evaluation	Evaluating the program	To demonstrate accountability and credibility, and to provide guidance for future programming

The MBO recipe-building process, then, parallels the four-step public relations process familiar to many practitioners (Cutlip et al., 2000). The first step is *defining the public relations problem*. The definitional process helps the manager identify the effects campaigns need to accomplish. This encompasses Roles 1 and 2. The second step is *planning and programming*. At this point the manager develops the campaign recipe in detail. This encompasses Roles 3 and 4. The third step is *taking action and communicating*, or implementing the program which encompasses Role 5. In the fourth step, *evaluating the program*, the manager identifies program successes and failures for accountability and future use. This encompasses Role 6.

With the manager's roles and planning process identified, we turn to the products the manager will use and produce at each stage. These are the key elements of the recipe the manager must develop. The elements include (a) a mission statement, (b) a problem statement, (c) situation analysis, (d) goals, (e) objectives, (f) strategies, and (g) tactics.

THE MISSION STATEMENT

We can think of these elements as a pyramid (Fig. 2.1), for which the mission statement forms the base. Everything we do must show clear relevance to the organization's mission. A *mission statement* is the statement of philosophy and purpose for an organization. Every orga-

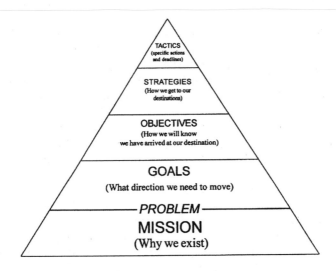

FIG. 2.1.   The strategic planning pyramid. The organization's mission forms the basis for strategic planning. Decisions at each level of the pyramid depend on the decisions made on the underlying levels.

nization should have one, so your first step as a manager is to get a copy, and, if one does not exist, to develop one. Mission statements can take a lot of time and effort to develop and can stretch for pages. The communication manager needs some sort of summary, however, to guide the daily activities of everyone connected with your organization. Everyone should have a clear idea of why your organization exists, beyond "to make money"—something along the lines of an abstract or point summary. The Robert Mondavi Winery, for example, has developed a one-line "vision statement" that appears in every voice-mail message from the CEO, in all statements to analysts, in most official statements, and at the beginning of most formal presentations to employees. The statement, "We will be the preeminent fine wine producer in the world," drives all strategic planning. Development of the deceptively simple statement required input from all employees to make sure they would buy into it. The senior management drafted a statement and met with 6 to 10 groups of 15 to 20 employees to discuss and evaluate the statement. A second draft based on their comments was tested the same way, resulting in the final version.

Displaying the mission statement prominently on internal and external communication pieces ensures that everyone with whom the organization has a relationship will have a clear understanding of what the company has on its list of priorities. Unfortunately, many companies fail to do this. Because the mission statement provides the organization's justification for existence, communication managers can effectively justify their existence as a department and as individual staff members by showing how communication programs enhance the organization's mission. Using the mission statement, you can show how the public relations department's activities are central to the organization's success. No longer is public relations marginalized, and the result is that public relations departments become much less vulnerable to the budget axe.

The mission statement should identify the products the organization produces, the services it provides, and the types of relationships it strives to cultivate. A regional charter airline such as Champion Air in the Minneapolis area focuses on "surpassing the expectations of our customers," reflecting its specialist status, whereas a discount passenger airline such as Southwest Airlines focuses on "low fares, lots of flights, and the friendliest service in the sky." Northwest Airlines, with a global focus, aims to make the travel experience "the most convenient, most enjoyable, and safest possible," with attention to establishing new routes and implementing electronic services. Airborne Express, meanwhile, delivers packages not people, and so its mission is "to provide businesses customized distribution solutions at lower cost than the competition."

Because public relations is the construction and maintenance of mutually beneficial relationships, the mission statement provides the guidelines for all planning and monitoring. In particular, it enables the manager to produce the *problem statement*. To do so, the manager must address two key questions: How do you know a problem when you see one, and what is a problem statement?

A *problem* occurs when the organization encounters something in its environment or in its relationships with key publics that threatens its ability to fulfill its mission. The hospital, for example, may have encountered new insurance rules on maternity hospitalization that cut in half the number of days patients may stay following a healthy birth free of complications. The average stay in 1996 was down to about 1 day, after shrinking from 2 weeks to 1 week to 3 days to 2 days. Clearly, this trend threatens the hospital's ability to maintain a healthy bottom line. This does not give the communication manager anything substantive to guide planning, however. "We need to make more money" provides no clues to identify which ways of making money are appropriate for the hospital, nor does it provide any reason why key publics inside and outside the organization should feel motivated to care whether the hospital makes its money. The manager needs to know the *philosophy and purpose* of the organization—its mission—to guide planning and to build mutually beneficial relationships.

So, what is the mission of a hospital and how does the reduction in insurance coverage for maternity care threaten this mission? The mission may be to provide high-quality care for the community. Some hospitals also will have a research-related mission or a teaching-related mission, as shown in Sidebar 2.1. These statements help the communication manager identify publics and activities that are appropriate.

THE PROBLEM STATEMENT

If the mission statement represents the organization's foundational guiding document for all of its operations, the *problem statement* becomes the communication manager's foundational document to guide a communication campaign. The problem statement summarizes the key elements of the issue or opportunity and how it relates to the organization's ability to fulfill its mission. The problem statement is concise and specific, much like the lead of a news story. According to Kendall (1996), it should be 18 to 25 words, phrased in a simple subject-verb-object construction. Kendall noted that, in some cases, the problem statement may be more appropriately considered an "opportunity" statement. Armed with no information other than the problem statement, a manager still should be able to at least rough out some ideas for a successful campaign.

SIDEBAR 2.1.
Hospital Mission Statements, 1999

A mission statement should identify the products the organization produces, the services it provides, and the types of relationships it strives to cultivate. Note that statements differ according to the type and size of community served, the affiliation of the hospital, and the emphasis of the hospital on training, community outreach, or a specialized type of medicine.

University/Teaching

The University Hospital, Cincinnati:

To strive to provide care of the highest quality to all persons seeking treatment in our facilities. This includes a blend of human concern and clinical expertise, while promoting excellence in education, research, and technological progress.

New York University Medical Center, New York University School of Medicine:(from the original statement, 50 years ago)

The training of physicians, the search for new knowledge, and the care of the sick. The three are inseparable. Medicine can be handed on to succeeding generations only by long training in the scientific methods of investigation and by the actual care of patients.... Our current interpretation of this statement is that the appropriate teaching medicine and the training of physicians must be accomplished in a setting of excellence at the highest level of human achievement. With this understanding, we strive to provide a rich environment for scholarship, research, and patient care where the faculty understands that the students, as our successors, should not merely replace, but surpass.

St. Francis Health System, Pittsburgh, Pennsylvania:

1) to establish and maintain a hospital for the care of persons suffering from illnesses or disabilities, without distinction as to their religious beliefs, race, national origin, age, sex, handicap or economic status; 2) to carry on educational activities related to rendering care to the sick and injured or the promotion of health; 3) to encourage research related to health care; 4) to participate, as far as circumstances may warrant, in any activity intended to promote individual and community health.

Urban Community/Teaching

Detroit Medical Center:

Committed to improving the health of the population served by providing the highest quality health care services in a caring and efficient manner.

Together, with Wayne State University, the DMC strives to be the region's premier health care resource through a broad range of clinical services; the discovery and application of new knowledge; and the education of practitioners, teachers and scientists.

Detroit Receiving Hospital:

Committed to being one of the nation's premier emergency, trauma, critical care and ambulatory center providing high quality services to all patients within the communities services, regardless of the person's religious, racial or ethnic identification or economic status. In collaboration with Wayne State University, Detroit Receiving strives to provide leadership in the education and training of health care professionals and in the development of new diagnostics and treatment modalities that enhance the quality of life.

Saint Joseph Hospital, Denver, Colorado, owned by the Sisters of the Charity of Leavenworth, Kansas:

To provide a continuum of healthcare services—ambulatory through tertiary—in partnership with the medical staff. The hospital, which is sponsored by the Sisters of Charity of Leavenworth and operates under the direction of the Health Services Corporation, intends to provide these services in a healing environment which meets the physical, emotional, and spiritual needs of its patients and their families, other visitors, donors, and employees. Superior service and fiscal and environmental responsibility are cornerstones of the excellent care Saint Joseph Hospital strives to provide to residents of the Rocky Mountain Region. The hospital is committed to providing graduate medical education, to caring for the medically indigent, to improving community health, and to continuing its leadership role in Colorado healthcare.

Regional/Suburban

Medina General Hospital, Medina, Ohio:

The leader in providing ethical quality care for the individual and in promoting a healthy community.

Jefferson General Hospital, Port Townsend, Washington:

To provide quality, cost-effective medical care and health services to residents and visitors of Eastern Jefferson County and adjacent areas.

St. Elizabeth's Hospital, Belleville, Illinois, Hospital Sisters of the Third Order of Saint Francis:

To minister to those in need of healthcare in response to God's call to serve each other, especially the poor. In the performance of its mission, St. Elizabeth's Hospital will foster the values of love, compassion, com-

(continues)

petence, and reverence for life. St. Elizabeth's Hospital is committed to performing its mission through ecumenical cooperation with other healthcare providers and the community, whenever possible.

Rural Community/Regional

Clearwater Valley Hospital and Clinics, Inc., Orofino, Idaho (North Central Idaho):

Providing competent, compassionate health and wellness services in an environment which enhances human worth. The mission is accomplished through the implementation of the values *respect, hospitality, justice, and stewardship.* The Hospital and Clinics are committed to witness God's love for all people, with a special concern for the poor and powerless.

Mary Lanning Memorial Hospital, nonprofit regional health center in South Central Nebraska:

Committed to a tradition of excellence through leadership in the provision of quality medical services and health education for the people of South Central Nebraska.

Specialist

Glenrose Rehabilitation Hospital, Edmonton, Alberta, Canada:

To work with our patients and their families as they meet the challenges of disability and seek fulfillment in their lives; share knowledge and experience with those who are involved in the process of rehabilitation; engage in research to advance knowledge and contribute to rehabilitation practice in the community at large.

Mary Freed Bed Hospital & Rehabilitation Center, Grand Rapids, Michigan:

To provide people with disabilities the opportunity to achieve independence through rehabilitation. We seek excellence through innovation, leadership, and advocacy.

Children's Hospital and Health Center, San Diego, California:

To restore, sustain, and enhance the health and developmental potential of children.

Women's Hospital, Baton Rouge, Louisiana:

To create opportunities that improve the health status of women and infants.

The problem statement comprises six elements (see Fig. 2.2):

1. What is the problem, issue or opportunity? The problem may be one of reputation, of financial difficulty, of declining membership, or of impending legislation, for example.
2. Where is this problem occurring? This may represent an internal problem, a regional issue, national issue, or international issue.
3. When did this become a problem? Perhaps you have tackled an issue that always has been a problem, or perhaps you have been asked to address a problem that is getting better, or worse, or is cyclical.
4. How did this become a problem? Your problem may have developed because of a lack of awareness, or because of poor product quality, or because of ineffective customer or member relations.
5. For whom is it a problem? Your problem most likely does not affect everyone in the world, but instead involves certain key publics with whom your organization's relationship is threatened.
6. Why is this a problem? In other words, how does this threaten the organization's ability to fulfill its mission? This answers the "so what" question, or why management and key publics should care about this issue in the first place. If your problem has no easily identifiable "why," you probably will find it difficult to get key decision makers in your organization to buy into the need for your campaign.

FIG. 2.2. Elements of the problem statement. A statement of the public relations problem is incomplete unless it includes all six of the elements portrayed.

Your problem statement, in short, provides the justification and the framework for your campaign, all in one or two sentences.

THE SITUATION ANALYSIS

Frequently the communication manager receives a request to develop a campaign based on an initial issue statement that contains few of the elements necessary for a complete problem definition. To develop a complete problem statement usually requires formative research to flesh out the details. These details are known as the *situation analysis*.

The situation analysis is a detailed explanation of the opportunities and challenges (sometimes called opportunities and "threats") that exist within the organization and in its environment (see Table 2.2). Sometimes the analysis of opportunities and challenges is called SWOT analysis, for strengths, weaknesses, opportunities, and threats. The terminology may differ, but it means the same thing: The manager needs to find out as much as possible about the problem, the relevant publics, and the environment.

A situation analysis usually begins with the problem statement, followed by a discussion of the history of the problem and how it conflicts with the organization's mission. The situation analysis then includes a discussion of the relevant publics, as well as a discussion of opportunities that should help solve the problem and challenges that could pose barriers. Assumptions should be made clear, and all assertions should be backed up with evidence—data, theory, management and communication principles, expert sources, and so on. The situation analysis represents everything you have been able to find out about the problem. It shows your familiarity with the organization, its publics, the environment, and the problem. It also helps you identify what additional information you may need to design a successful campaign.

TABLE 2.2
Opportunity/Challenge Planning Box

Location Situation	Internal	External
Opportunities	Internal Opportunities (strengths)	External Opportunities (opportunities)
Challenges	Internal Challenges (weaknesses)	External Challenges (threats)

The situation analysis makes it possible for the communication team to develop hypotheses, or hunches, about possible causes and solutions for your problem. You may conclude from your analysis that a problem initially presented as poor communication is an informed lack of public support for a company's vision. On the other hand, research might reveal that an apparent lack of support stems from the noisy complaints of a small minority, with the majority unaware of the issue but ready to mobilize on the organization's behalf. These discoveries will affect the type of communication program an organization designs.

SOURCES OF INFORMATION

The development of a situation analysis requires a thorough understanding of the issue or problem, the client organization, the environment, and the relevant publics. Original research often is necessary, such as surveys and focus groups, but library research and an examination of organizational records also can provide important information. The communication manager's ability to solve a problem depends on available resources (such as time and funding), available expertise, political realities, and the reasons for the problem. The manager's challenge, therefore, is to gather as much background information as possible, as quickly as possible, to determine the scope of the problem as well as the challenges and opportunities that will affect problem solving. Forces for or against change exist both within an organization and outside in the political and social environment. Along with the internal and external factors, the practitioner may find Hubbell's Helpful Questions useful, developed from the lessons of Ned Hubbell, director (retired), Project Outreach, Michigan Education Association, as a set of questions to ask before beginning to plan (see Sidebar 2.2).

Internal Factors

Often an organization attributes its problems to outside forces (the media are a favorite target for blame), but the communication manager should begin to understand the problem by developing an understanding of the organization itself. Important types of information include the organization's mission, its decision-making and operating structure, its evolution and history, and its culture. Sources of information include the following:

- written documents such as mission statements, charters, and by-laws;

F. Does the agency have any allies? If so, who?
G. Are there important neutral parties to be considered?
H. What additional factors are impacting competitive posture?

VI. SITUATION ANALYSIS (TRENDS)

A. What are the perceived key changes taking place outside of the organization?
B. What are the perceived key changes taking place within the organization?
C. What issues are emerging in the industry? How will these impact the agency?
D. Are there broad social trends impacting the agency?
E. Are there any developing innovations within the industry that may impact the agency? Is the agency working on any innovations?
F. Are agency funding sources secure?

- biographical statements of key members of the organization;
- descriptions of products and services;
- records regarding budgets, expenditures, staffing levels;
- records regarding business policies and procedures;
- published documents such as annual reports and newsletters;
- specific records related to the problem, such as memos;
- records regarding organizational calendars of events;
- decision makers and other staff knowledgeable about the issue;
- existing surveys or other research of internal publics;
- web sites and records related to web use.

External Factors

Sources of information outside the organization can provide an understanding of opportunities and challenges that the organization needs to anticipate or that it has encountered in the past. Important types of information include publics who come in contact with the organization, information networks linking individuals inside and outside the organization, portrayals of the organization by key individuals and the media, and information about political, social, economic, and environmental issues that can affect the organization's ability to control an issue. Sources of information include:

- consumer and trade publications in which the organization or the issue is mentioned;
- publications in which competing organizations or issue positions are mentioned;

- records of broadcast news coverage of the organization or the issue;
- records of internet sites relevant to the organization or issue;
- individuals and organizations that favor or criticize the organization or its stance on the issue (sometimes an organization has lists of key contacts, friends, or critics);
- individuals at key media outlets who cover the organization or the issue;
- calendars of events for the community and other relevant regions;
- existing surveys of relevant publics from national, regional, or specialized sources;
- lists of relevant government agencies and key contacts that deal with the organization and relevant issues;
- records of relevant government regulations that are pending, current, and repealed.

FINAL THOUGHTS

Once existing background information has been reviewed, the communication manager can assess the situation more effectively. The exercise of drafting the problem statement can reveal information gaps that require further investigation. Only when all of the elements of a problem statement can be written with specifics can the manager determine appropriate strategy.

A significant part of program planning, as a result, depends on research. The manager's confidence in the effectiveness of a program plan, and the manager's ability to demonstrate accountability to a client, increases with each bit of relevant information obtained. Public relations programs exist in an environment filled with uncertainty and variables that managers simply cannot control. The better the manager's understanding of all elements of the situation, the more control—or at least predictability—the manager will have over the result of a communication program.

❦ 3 ❦

Elements of the Campaign Recipe

Goals
Objectives
Strategies
Tactics
The Strategic Planning Ladder
Initiating the Planning Process
Final Thoughts

Once public relations managers have performed precampaign research they can revise the problem statement and situation analysis and go on to design the campaign. Keep in mind that change is constant, so all planning documents must respond to changes in resources, context, and available information. The manager will revise a problem statement if research demonstrates the initial problem diagnosis overstates, understates, or misstates the problem. Similarly, managers can revise the situation analysis as the situation changes. It follows that the campaign plan, too, may require adjustment occasionally. If, however, you have done thorough precampaign research, the campaign plan rarely will need a major change.

GOALS

The campaign plan includes at least four levels of information, all presented in writing. The first is the *goal*. A goal is a conceptual statement of what you plan to achieve. The goal is essentially a set of statements that together negate the problem. For example, if the problem for an organization is a lack of awareness, the goal will focus on increasing awareness. If the problem is a lack of credibility, the goal will focus on increasing credibility. If the problem is a lack of volunteer involvement, a series of goals may focus on new volunteer recruitment, increasing involvement among existing volunteers, and increasing opportunities for volunteer activity. Managers can provide clients with long-term or short-term goals, depending on the context of a program or campaign.

A goal statement includes the following elements:

1. *The word "to."* This signals the reader that an action statement will follow. It also demonstrates a results orientation. Both of these characteristics make goals easy for busy clients and CEOs to understand quickly.

2. *An active verb.* This demonstrates that a proposed communication plan will have specific effects. The verb should reflect an effect rather than an action. In other words, the goal should not promise to do something such as disseminate newsletters; instead, it should promise to accomplish something, such as improving customer loyalty. Appropriate verbs include increase, decrease, and maintain. Occasionally, others are appropriate, such as initiate or eliminate.

3. *A conceptual, quantifiable statement of the desired outcome.* This specifies what will be changed and by how much. The focus may be on outcomes such as knowledge, beliefs, opinions, behaviors, sales figures, membership figures, or donation levels. This signals the reader how the manager plans to measure success. As a result, this outcome must be quantifiable in some way. For example, levels of employee satisfaction may be quantified in terms of a combination of sick time, complaints, longevity, work quality, and self-reported opinions. Each proposed measure on its own may not adequately represent "employee satisfaction," but as a group they seem appropriate. Each proposed measure will become a stated objective of the campaign. Increasing levels of employee satisfaction, therefore, can be the focus of a goal statement. Each goal should focus on only one outcome. A program designed to change several outcomes should state each outcome as a separate goal.

4. *Identification of relevant target publics.* Not only should the client see at a glance what is to be changed, but the client also should know among whom it will change. A single communication campaign cannot promise to improve a company's reputation among every individual in the world, so the manager should offer some parameters. This will guide the development of strategy, which will tend to differ depending on the target public.

For example, Blockbuster and CIM, Inc., created a Silver Anvil Award-winning campaign to launch video sales of the *Titanic* movie. The Silver Anvil Award is awarded annually by the Public Relations So-

TABLE 3.1
Active Verbs Appropriate for Goals and Objectives

Address	Enhance	Persuade	Supply
Administer	Enlarge	Plan	Systematize
Analyze	Enlist	Position	Tabulate
Approve	Establish	Prepare	Teach
Arrange	Evaluate	Present	Tell
Assign	Examine	Preside	Trace
Attain	Expand	Protect	Track
Authorize	Finish	Provide	Train
Build	Gain	Publish	Verify
Calculate	Generate	Raise	Write
Catalog	Govern	Reassure	
Communicate	Group	Recommend	
Complete	Guide	Record	
Conceive	Hire	Recruit	
Conduct	Identify	Rectify	
Confine	Implement	Reduce	
Contract	Improve	Regain	
Control	Increase	Release	
Convince	Index	Remove	
Coordinate	Inform	Request	
Correct	Initiate	Require	
Create	Institute	Research	
Decide	Interview	Reshape	
Decrease	Investigate	Retain	
Delegate	Justify	Review	
Demonstrate	Keep	Revise	
Design	Locate	Schedule	
Develop	Maintain	Secure	
Diminish	Make	Select	
Direct	Moderate	Sort	
Disapprove	Motivate	Start	

(Continues)

29

TABLE 3.1 (Continued)		
Distribute	Negotiate	Stimulate
Document	Notify	Straighten
Draft	Obtain	Strengthen
Earn	Organize	Submit
Educate	Outline	Summarize
Employ	Overcome	Supervise

ciety of America to honor public relations programs that incorporate sound research, planning, execution, and evaluation. Goals for the *Titanic* campaign included, "to capitalize on consumers' fascination with the *Titanic* to attract customers to Blockbuster Video stores" and "to generate media coverage of Blockbuster's guaranteed availability of *Titanic*."

OBJECTIVES

Although these Blockbuster goals are not *measurable*, they are *quantifiable*. In other words, they cannot count "capitalizing on consumers' fascination with the *Titanic*," which is an idea, but they can count things that represent that idea, such as the number of people who come to Blockbuster as a result of a *Titanic* promotion. They cannot count "media coverage," per se, but they can count the number of articles, column inches, or minutes broadcast that mention the movie and Blockbuster together. Nager and Allen (1984) wrote that it helps to think of a goal as a *directional statement*, such as planning to "go north" You cannot ever "arrive" at "north," because north is an idea, a concept. It is relative to where you are now, or where you used to be, or where you will be some other time. So you have to supply some context if you want to turn the direction into some sort of destination so that you will be able to say, "I have arrived!" You can go north from someplace, and you can go specific places located in a northerly direction, but to know you have done it right, you need to give yourself some checkpoints. You need to know where you are starting out—known in communication campaigns as the *baseline*—and you need to know where you want to end up—known as the *objective*.

If the goal has promised to "improve employee morale," the manager will have created a directional statement, but will not yet have any concrete destinations to guide campaign planning and provide accountability. You never will arrive at "improving morale." You can,

TABLE 3.2
Active Verbs Appropriate for Objectives

Administer	Finish	Reduce
Approve	Gain	Regain
Assign	Generate	Request
Attain	Hire	Retain
Authorize	Implement	Schedule
Catalog	Improve	Secure
Complete	Increase	Select
Conduct	Institute	Start
Create	Interview	Submit
Decrease	Locate	Tabulate
Develop	Make	
Distribute	Obtain	
Draft	Present	
Earn	Provide	
Employ	Publish	
Enlarge	Raise	
Enlist	Record	
Establish	Recruit	

Note.   You can insert a number after each verb to indicate a specific, measurable amount of change.

however, find things to measure that will represent improvements in morale, just as you can find cities that represent north. These things that you measure—your destinations—will serve as your objectives.

In the Blockbuster example, the outcomes for the goals include connecting use of Blockbuster stores with the *Titanic* movie and connecting media coverage of the movie with its availability at Blockbuster. The manager cannot count either of these outcomes. To quantify these ideas, such as media coverage, you might count the number of news stories that contain references to both the movie and the video store. Or you might count the number of on-air promotions and contests connecting the movie and its availability at Blockbuster. To measure high visibility, you might count the number of news stories that make the front page of the entertainment section of the newspaper, or you might be satisfied with the number of stories that make it into the news at all.

All of these would be *measurable outcomes*, or destinations, for your image and visibility campaign.

An objective, then, is a measurable destination that represents the achievement of a campaign goal. Much confusion exists regarding objectives, most likely because several types of objectives exist. Many communication managers, for example, write conceptual statements (goals) and call them objectives. A true objective, however, is specific and measurable, stating not what the campaign will do, but rather what a campaign will accomplish. Three types of objectives exist.

Global objectives focus on general program outcomes. They summarize the overall effect of a campaign. For example, a global objective might be to obtain the necessary legislative support to enable a company to proceed with a planned expansion. Although concrete—the expansion either proceeds or doesn't—the objective does not specify the details that have to be in place for the expansion to take place. For example, the company needs to have enough sympathetic legislators win election or re-election in the next election. In addition, someone has to write and introduce the legislation. Advocacy groups with alternative views need to be persuaded or countered. These process-oriented or task-oriented outcomes are known as *intermediate objectives*. Finally, the campaign may state *terminal objectives*, which provide specific measurable or observable results to the campaign, measured by behaviors or actions, such as at least 51 senators voting for the passage of a particular bill.

An objective must include the following elements:

1. *The word "to."* Again, this signals that a promise of accountability follows.

2. *An active verb.* As before, this indicates that something specific will happen as a result of the public relations program.

3. *The "criterion outcome" or measurable destination.* This puts the focus on a concrete "operationalization" of the idea presented in a goal. This outcome must be measurable or reliably observable. Each objective should focus on a single criterion outcome, which means that several objectives may correspond to quantify a single goal statement. The wording of the criterion outcome should make clear what measurement technique is required for accountability. For example, an objective promising "to increase self-reported confidence in the institution" by a certain amount requires a survey; an objective pledging "to increase the number of participants in professional development seminars by 20%" requires an attendance record.

4. *The relevant target public.* Some objectives, such as those focused on raising awareness, may not be relevant to all target publics in a campaign. Therefore, to avoid overpromising, specify which objectives relate to which publics.

5. *The amount of change expected.* This critical piece of information distinguishes the objective from the goal by providing concrete verification of goal attainment. This can take the form of a number or a percentage. The amount of designated change should be ambitious enough to require real improvement, but realistically attainable. Stating too high a level can impress a client in a pitch meeting but can make a competent campaign look like a failure. Understating the level can lead a client to think the campaign will be a sham and not worth the investment. As a result, objectives are difficult to write. However effective the campaign strategies may be, the objectives ultimately determine whether a campaign is a success or a failure.

How much change is necessary or realistic can be determined only through research and still may require the best judgment of the communication manager. In addition, objectives sometimes require negotiation, particularly when they are chosen on the basis of political judgments or intuition instead of on the basis of research. Sometimes clients impose minimum levels of change, and sometimes these levels may not be realistic. The Washington State Legislature, for example, determined in 1997 that all state universities had to improve student retention and graduation rates by specified amounts. The universities knew they would not be able to achieve the amounts. Ironically, the ability to achieve some of the stated objectives, such as cutting time to graduation, would be compromised by increases in enrollment and retention, which were the focus of other objectives. The university administrators knew that many students drop out or change institutions because they are struggling, and so keeping them from leaving would probably hurt overall time-to-graduation rates. The universities' challenge, as a result, was to make their best effort to achieve the stated objectives while acquiring evidence to convince the legislators that alternative objectives would be more appropriate. Although the universities had to sacrifice some state funding because they failed to meet the original objectives, they were successful in guiding the legislature to more reasonable objectives during the next legislative session.

6. *A target date or deadline.* This seals the promise of accountability and is an essential element of the objective.

Note how concrete and specific the objective is. Many managers find objectives discomfiting because they represent a clear promise. They state in no uncertain terms what will be accomplished and by when. The obvious danger is promising too much. The manager, however, has only two viable alternatives: make promises that can be kept or make no promises. Because promises provide accountability, they make or break your reputation. To make no promises in a bottom-line oriented environment potentially keeps public relations marginalized and powerless. As a result, the only choice for the successful communication manager is to make promises that can be kept. The only way to do this—to determine realistic objectives—is through research. Blockbuster was able to set objectives and develop strategy based on continuing market research of theater attendance and video sales, customers' video rental and purchase habits, the usefulness of incentives, and the attraction of "being among the first" to buy the movie. It also used the movie attendance research to determine the target audience, which was dominated by young females. More sample outcomes appear in Table 3.3.

TABLE 3.3
Examples of Communication Program Outcomes
(From 1999 Silver Anvil Award Winners)

- To reduce curbside disposal of grassclippings by 5%.
    Puget Sound Environmental Quality Agencies with Elgin DDB

- To move the major media from a 3 to 1 negative position to at least a 50 to 50 position in 6 months.
    Internet Council of Registrars (CORE) with the Gable Group

- To obtain permission from the town to rebuild.
    Oak Tree Dairy Farm with Epoch 5

- To transition 900 existing customers to the new program; to attract 4,100 new users before opening the Lanes.
    San Diego Association of Governments with Frank Wilson & Associates, Inc.

- To generate 500 new calls to the Fund's 800 number to increase the prospect base needed to achieve targeted growth.
    Colorado Student Obligation Bond Authority with Kostka Gleason Communications, Inc.

- To get North Americans actively involved in home fire safety by encouraging them to develop a home fire escape plan and practice it collectively on October 7 at 6 p.m.
    National Fire Protection Association

Objectives Drive Evaluation

Every objective, if written properly, necessitates some form of evaluation and dictates the form the evaluation should take. In the case of Blockbuster's *Titanic* promotional campaign, some of the objectives included the following:

- to develop a promotion/special event that attracts at least 500,000 customers to Blockbuster throughout the United States and encourages them to purchase or rent *Titanic* at Blockbuster sooner than at other video stores;
- to obtain at least $2 million in free media exposure for Blockbuster during the launch;
- to determine how many customers came to Blockbuster stores as a result of the *Titanic* promotion. (Blockbuster was able to count the number of people who attended the special midnight launch of *Titanic* video sales, including the number who lined up around the block ahead of time. Blockbuster counted the average transaction amount during the sale, which increased 321% over that of a normal business day. It also did research, which established that nearly 50% of consumers who purchased the movie during the event would not have done so if the store hours had not been extended. To determine how much media coverage was worth, Blockbuster applied a formula to the print and video coverage of the event, which it estimated at $9 million.)

The Importance of Coordinating Objectives With Evaluation

As an example of coordinating objectives with evaluation, the American Medical Women's Association (AMWA) and Fleishman Hillard, Inc., teamed up to increase awareness, diagnosis, and treatment of thyroid disease. The campaign took place in response to figures indicating that more than half of the estimated 13 million Americans with thyroid disease, most of whom are women, remain undiagnosed. Untreated, thyroid disease can cause cholesterol problems, osteoporosis, and infertility. Meanwhile, a simple blood test can detect the disease, and treatment is straightforward. As a result, the AMWA and Fleishman Hillard's stated objective was to increase the number of women being tested for thyroid disease by at least 10% in the first 15 months of the campaign. This objective dictated that campaign success would depend on tracking figures of women tested for thyroid disease. The campaign documented an increase of more than 40% in the number of women tested. The campaign included other measures of success as well, such as the number of total prescriptions of thyroid treatment medication, which increased by 10%, and indicated that more women were being treated for thyroid disease.

The campaign had several associated results as well. More than 6,600 individuals were screened during local market screening events, at a rate of over 300 people per hour. The AMWA and Fleishman Hillard achieved exposure to over 100 million people with media coverage that included national coverage on television shows such as *Good Morning America*, CNN, FOX, and MSNBC; national coverage in print venues such as the Associated Press, *USA Today*, *The Washington Post*, and several magazines; and local print and broadcast coverage in various markets. A television public service announcement was broadcast 3,800 times, reaching an estimated 128 million viewers. A radio public service announcement reached an estimated 40 million listeners. The campaign also brought the issue to the attention of Congress through invited testimony and visits to four key Congress members' home districts. These achievements, however striking, would not in themselves demonstrate campaign success as promised. If the stated objective promises behavior change in the form of increased blood tests, success must be measured in those terms.

It may seem unfair that a campaign might achieve results but still seem like a failure if the ultimate objective is not met. This makes it especially useful to include intermediate and terminal objectives along with global objectives for a campaign. In the case of the thyroid disorder campaign, an appropriate global objective would be to track treatment of thyroid disease and the incidences of related osteoporosis, cholesterol problems, and birth defects, which the campaign managers documented. An appropriate terminal objective would be to increase testing, which the campaign planners documented. Appropriate intermediate objectives would include media impressions, congressional hearings, and local screening successes, which they also documented. Even if the ultimate campaign objectives had not been met, the campaign managers would be able to show that progress had been made and that future efforts might have more striking results. Indeed, the success of the thyroid campaign led to a campaign expansion that attracted the collaboration of additional health organizations.

STRATEGIES

Apparent success depends on how objectives are stated. Actual success depends on the competent use of appropriate *strategy*. If the goal represents the direction we plan to go, and the objective represents destinations at which we plan to arrive, then strategies represent how we plan to get there. A strategy is a statement of the communication themes or vehicles that will be used to accomplish a specific objective. It represents an overall plan of action that will tie together each action taken to implement the campaign. The communication manager constructs strategies based on the following elements:

1. *Available data.* This includes the situation analysis and all the research that has gone into creating it. It also includes the manager's knowledge from previous experience with an organization and with communication campaigns. In the case of the thyroid campaign, available data included research by Fleishman Hillard with consumers, healthcare professionals, media, managed care organizers, professional societies, and consumer groups. It found that only 30% of women had been tested for thyroid disease in 1996, that nearly 90% of people did not know that thyroid problems could do things such as elevate cholesterol levels, and that although half of all women experienced three or more symptoms associated with a thyroid disorder 75% of them did not discuss the symptoms with a doctor.

2. *Communication and public relations principles.* This includes knowledge of the public relations function and its parameters. Fleishman Hillard knew it could help by boosting public awareness, bringing the issue to the attention of Congress, and promoting testing among individuals at risk (women). It had expertise in all of these areas of promotion.

3. *Communication and persuasion theories.* The body of knowledge in the social sciences can provide you with the ability to make hypotheses, or likely informed guesses, about the types of strategies that will accomplish the stated objective and be relevant to a situation. Social science theories are essentially explanations of how and why things happen the way they do. In short, theories can tell you how people are likely to react to your campaign and why.

In the case of the thyroid campaign, Fleishman Hillard realized that the problem was a lack of awareness instead of active resistance to testing. People demonstrated they did not know much about the importance of the thyroid gland, its effects, or how easy it was to diagnose and treat thyroid problems. As a result, Fleishman Hillard knew it needed to build knowledge. It also knew from persuasion theories that people are more likely to take action if they understand the relevance of an issue and if they can see that taking action is both easy and effective. As a result, Fleishman Hillard developed three related strategies:

1. Build consumer knowledge, particularly among women, about the thyroid gland's function and effect on the body.
2. Humanize thyroid disease by demonstrating its effect on quality of life and risks to long-term health.
3. Demonstrate the ease and simplicity of a sensitive thyroid stimulating hormone (TSH) test to detect thyroid dysfunction.

TACTICS

These strategies, of course, are ideas for guidance instead of a list of actions to implement. They are, in fact, counterparts to goals, which are ideas about campaign results. The communication campaign, therefore, also must include an action counterpart to the objective. These are called *tactics* and are the tasks that must be accomplished to achieve a stated objective. The tactics are the specifics of your recipe. They are, essentially, job assignments. Tactics include the following:

- the task;
- the responsible parties for completing the task;
- deadline for completion of the task.

Tactics include the development of specific communication vehicles, such as public service announcements, logos, brochures, training materials, and special events. For Fleishman Hillard, the tactics included the development of an engaging theme, the identification of a celebrity spokesperson (Gail Devers, the Olympic Gold Medalist who had previously suffered with undiagnosed thyroid problems for 3 years), the development of high-profile events that attract both national and local media coverage, the implementation of special events such as a VIP breakfast to bring the spokesperson and physicians together with key members of Congress, a free TSH testing event on Capitol Hill, and more. Each stated tactic related to a specific strategy, which was designed to achieve a stated objective, which demonstrated the accomplishment of a stated goal.

THE STRATEGIC PLANNING LADDER

As the thyroid campaign illustrates, the campaign plan becomes a tightly organized set of specific tasks that put carefully selected strategies into action to accomplish stated objectives that represent organization goals that enable an organization to achieve its mission. To

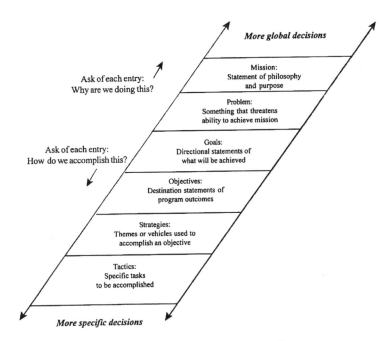

FIG. 3.1. The strategic planning ladder. How the mission, problem statements,
goals, objectives, strategies, and tactics relate to one another.

make sure all elements of the campaign plan are necessary and appropriate, it helps to think of the progression of specificity as a ladder.
When going up the ladder, such as considering the appropriateness of
a tactic, ask "why are we doing this?" In other words, does every action
have a stated purpose?

The answer to the why question for a tactic should be a strategy. The
answer for a strategy should be an objective. The answer for an objective should be a goal, and the answer for a goal should be the problem,
to which the answer is the mission. Why do we need to produce a brochure? Because we need to provide information to potential applicants
to spark their interest and gain their confidence. Why do we need an informational campaign? Because we need to increase applications from
this target public by 30%. Why do we need to increase applications?
Because we want to increase representation from this target public in
our program. Why do we want to increase their representation? Because our organization strives to serve the entire community, and they
have not been represented in the same proportion in which they exist
in the community.

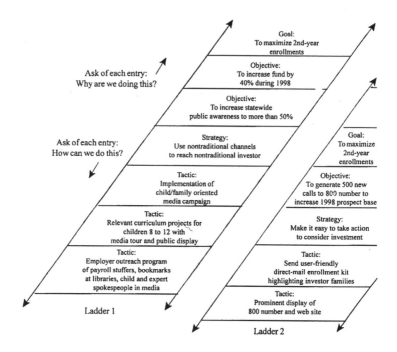

FIG. 3.2. The strategic planning ladder. Examples of how goals, objectives, strategies, and tactics relate to one another as demonstrated by the "Educate Our Kids" campaign implemented by the Colorado Student Obligation Fund with Kostka Gleason Communications, Inc. in 1998. A communication program may have a number of interrelated "ladders."

In reverse, going down the ladder, the manager should ask "how will we accomplish this?" To solve a problem requires a goal statement. To achieve the goal requires objectives. To meet the objectives requires a strategy, and each strategy requires tactics to put it into action. How can we increase representation of the target public in our program? We can increase the number of applications by the next deadline date. How can we increase the applications? We can develop an information campaign targeting interested community members from the target group. How can we implement the campaign? Among other things, we can develop brochures.

INITIATING THE PLANNING PROCESS

The public relations program plan represents the culmination of much research, analysis, and expertise. Sometimes it can be difficult to determine where to begin the planning process. Client representatives may have nonspecific or conflicting ideas, and public relations personnel may have varying interests in and interpretations of the issue as well. As a result, it can be useful to begin the planning process with an old-fashioned brainstorming session. Several brainstorming techniques exist. One especially effective strategy is called story boarding.

Story boarding, originally developed by the Walt Disney Corp. to design *Steamboat Willie*, is a highly visible, highly interactive way of gathering and sorting ideas. Story boarding refers to the process of creating the story that will guide strategic planning. In effect, it is a way to approach the process of analyzing the situation and identifying the strengths and opportunities that will inform decision making. Besides helping participants work through a problem, the technique provides a mechanism for tracking the decision-making process so others can see how collaborators arrived at a final decision. This gives confidence to participants who can be reminded of the factors that produced a decision, and it adds credibility to the decisions made because they are based on evidence clearly presented.

Managers can use story boards for four purposes:

1. *Planning* is used to outline the steps required to reach a specific result, such as preparing for a special event.
2. *Idea* is used to develop a concept or a theme for a specific purpose.
3. *Communication* is used to determine who needs to know something, what they need to know, and how best to interact with them.
4. *Organization* is used to determine who will take responsibility for designated tasks, and how to work together as departments, individuals, or organizations to accomplish a plan.

Story boarding uses a "creative thinking" process to guide brainstorming. The process includes three stages of idea generation, critical review, and consensus building to create a shared vision of a plan. It is a little like a focus group, requiring a facilitator to guide discussion and encourage freedom of thought. During the idea-generation stage, participants offer ideas for issues such as the who, what, where, when, why, and how of a problem; the identification of important target publics, opportunities, and constraints for a campaign; and the creation of campaign themes. Each idea is noted on an index card, which gets pinned or taped onto walls or tackable surfaces. During critical review, the group sifts through ideas to organize, refine, and prioritize them. Finally, during consensus building, the participants try to arrive at an agreement for the plan, idea, communication strategy, or organization. The rules for the creative thinking process include the following:

- the more ideas, the better;
- no criticism;
- hitchhiking is good (triggering ideas from others' ideas);
- spelling does not count;
- handwriting does not count;
- one idea per "card";
- "yell out" each idea during brainstorming.

This technique helped the state of Washington develop a campaign focused on alcohol abuse prevention that required the cooperation of a wide spectrum of individuals from organizations with various agendas and perspectives. Representatives from the Department of Alcohol and Substance Abuse (DASA), the Governor's budgeting office, the state liquor control board, the public schools, higher education, and other organizations all gathered to determine how to focus the campaign and how to assign responsibilities. Beginning from the DASA's stated goal, to "teach that alcohol is a drug," participants shared their personal experience, knowledge of research, and awareness of practical constraints such as how to ensure the cooperation of important stakeholders. The discussion gradually identified an agreed-upon target group: parents of children younger than the usual age of first experimentation. From there, the group developed an action plan for developing benchmark and formative research, which led to development of campaign materials.

The research for the campaign included a statewide survey of parents with children between the ages of 3 and 10 that would serve as a benchmark for later evaluation and would provide useful information for media relations activities. It also included a series of focus groups used to test the proposed message strategies.

The goal of the campaign was to educate parents of young children about talking to their kids about alcohol at an early age. A process goal was to equip parents with the knowledge and awareness that they can be the most significant source of help in influencing their children's attitudes and behavior toward responsible drinking habits. Objectives included distributing 100,000 informational brochures to parents over a 2-year period, increasing awareness of the "alcohol is a drug" message among Washington parents by 10% each year over a 2-year period, securing statewide media commitments to run $250,000 of pro bono advertising in support of the campaign each year, increasing by 10% the number of Washington parents who rank alcohol use by kids as a "serious problem," and increasing by 10% the awareness of "the harmful effects of alcohol use by children."

The strategy for the campaign included the development of a multiyear, multimedia statewide campaign focusing on increasing parents' knowledge that alcohol is a drug and that they can be the most powerful deterrent and source of help to their children regarding potential alcohol use. The strategy also included securing cooperative funding sources to sustain the campaign for two years; to maintain high visibility through the use of public relations and media relations activities throughout the campaign; and to coordinate all campaign activities at state, county, and local levels to ensure a successful launch.

The nine primary tactics for the campaign included implementing the statewide surveys; developing three distinctly different conceptual treatments of the "alcohol is a drug" theme; obtaining commitments from magazines, newspapers, newsletters, television stations, and radio stations; developing a poster and a parent guide; and securing co-op partners.

The campaign achieved its objectives, distributing 103,265 informational brochures to parents over a 2-year period, increasing awareness from 53% to 62% (an increase of 17%), and securing over $250,000 of pro bono advertising in support of the campaign. The campaign did not greatly increase the percentage of Washington parents who were "extremely concerned" about alcohol use by kids and considered it a "serious problem," which already was at 45% and averaged 5.8 on a 7-point scale. The number of parents who mentioned alcohol as the "most used drug" by children increased by 13%, rising from 46% to 52% among parents who recalled the campaign. The postcampaign survey demonstrated that 72% of parents saw or heard one of the public service advertisements produced for the campaign.

FINAL THOUGHTS

The DASA campaign embodied all of the essential elements of scientific program planning, from the development of the situation analysis at the beginning of the campaign to the demonstration of accountability at the end of the campaign. The use of careful research and a clear plan ensured that every campaign tactic fulfilled a necessary strategy and that every strategy responded to a desired objective. Every objective realized a relevant goal, and the goals took aim at the problem of underage drinking. The clarity of the MBO process makes it easy for an outside observer to understand the purpose of the campaign, the reasons for actions taken in pursuit of campaign goals, and the results achieved at campaign's end. The MBO technique cannot guarantee success for the practitioner, but the focus it provides will make success a more likely outcome. Because of its overt emphasis on accountability, the MBO technique also makes an achievement impossible to dismiss.

4

Determining Research Needs: Developing the Research Plan

Now you know that you need to develop an effective public relations plan, and that to do this you need to develop strategies that will achieve stated objectives. To arrive at this plan, a public relations manager needs to apply what Lloyd Kirban, executive vice president and director of research for Burson-Marsteller in New York (Broom & Dozier, 1990, p. 21), called "informed creativity." The role of research is to focus brainstorming, confirm or disconfirm hunches, and help fine-tune your strategies.

THE ROLE OF RESEARCH

Because the strategic manager is goal oriented, the decision to do research depends on its relevance to program goals and an organization's mission. In other words, research should be goal oriented, like

45

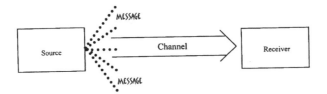

FIG. 4.1. A simplified model of communication. The linear model is useful for its portrayal of the basic elements in the communication process. Chapter 13 discusses important limitations of this model as a representation of the communication process.

the program plan itself. "Doing research" may seem intimidating to those without a social science background, but research spans a range of activities, many of which managers do instinctively. What does it mean to do research, and what are the goals of research? Research is systematic listening used in an attempt to reduce uncertainty. The goal of research is to gain maximum control of the things that can be controlled, and maximum understanding of the things that cannot be controlled.

Examine a simple model of the communication process and consider what elements we can control and what elements we cannot control. This varies with the context in which a manager works, but communication research has demonstrated that, overall, managers have the most control over the *source*, and the least control over the *receiver*. With the use of paid advertising, the manager can control the source, the message, and the channel. Public relations messages, however, often must go through "gatekeepers," or people between the original source and the ultimate message recipient. These include editors, reporters, and opinion leaders, among others. As a result, you may have control over who your initial source will be, such as the CEO of a corporation, and you can agree with your source on a message, but you can lose control quickly as the message goes through gatekeepers and evolves. Your best hope for control, therefore, is to gain a thorough understanding of everything that might affect the dissemination, evolution, and interpretation of your key messages.

THE BENEFITS OF RESEARCH

Research offers benefits that can help the strategic manager develop the understanding necessary to design and maintain successful public relations programs. First, research can help managers make sense of the increasing fragmentation of audiences in global, multimedia communication environments. Research can probe attitudes, identify opinion leaders, and help determine appropriate timing for actions and messages.

Second, research can help keep top-level management from losing touch with important stakeholders from which they may become insulated. According to the "homophily" principle (Rogers & Kincaid, 1981), people tend to exchange ideas most frequently among those who share similar characteristics, such as beliefs, values, education, and social status. Without extra effort, therefore, management can lose touch with nonmanagement employees, as well as with other stakeholders. Homophily refers to the degree to which pairs of individuals who interact share similarities, which tend to help them understand each other and value each other's perspectives. Because effective public relations focuses on relationship building, it is important for stakeholders who depend on each other to understand and respect each other; two-way communication is essential to effective public relations. One survey found that 24% of unionized companies that used attitude surveys to gather information from employees suffered strikes, while 48% of those who had not done opinion research suffered strikes. Among all companies surveyed, 64% of those that suffered strikes had not performed survey research in the past year. Monsanto, for example, discovered through a benchmarking survey of employees that the employees were suffering from information overload. In response, the company consolidated 22 newsletters into one, and made more use of E-mail, less use of video and audio media, and more use of face-to-face communication. The company also adopted an open communication policy that fostered trust on the premise that trust increases productivity. Following the changes, a new survey showed that 80% of employees felt they were getting good information, exceeding their objective of at least 50%.

Third, research can help confirm whether complaints about an organization are widespread beliefs or whether they represent the impressions of a vocal minority that holds little credibility with key stakeholders. It also can prevent organizations from wasting effort on nonexistent issues. For example, the American Dairy Association (ADA) knows from recent research that it does not need to do a multimillion dollar campaign to dissuade Americans from thinking cheese is an unsuitable lunch food because of its fat content. A recent survey of 1,002 respondents demonstrated that cheese already was the most common food chosen for lunch, that the top reason for choosing it was its taste, and that eating nutritiously was the second highest priority (after taking a break) at lunchtime (American Dairy Association, 1999). Because "low in fat" was one of the top two factors cited by respondents as making a meal nutritious, the ADA could safely conclude that fat in cheese was not preventing people from putting it into their lunch boxes. In fact, because no cheese-fat-lunch connection seemed to exist in public opinion, implementing a campaign acknowledging the connection could create a problem where none had existed before.

Fourth, research can guide strategy so that funds and efforts are spent wisely. Research can reduce the cost of a campaign and, as a result, can enhance the credibility of the public relations professionals with top management. An organization may find that a mass mailing, besides being expensive, is less effective than a few targeted, customized contacts. Editors commonly grouse that they receive many shotgun style news releases that go straight into the garbage because the releases do not show immediate relevance to their readers or viewers.

Fifth, research can help prevent unintended effects. A firm called Successful Marketing Strategies found out the hard way, when a "tease and deliver" promotional strategy for a high-tech product backfired. The promotion for the product, which was designed to save data from accidental destruction on diskettes, included a mailing to trade publication editors, in a plain brown envelope, which featured a note that read, "Who's been shooting [name of publication] readers?" A decal of a bullet hole appeared on the outside of the envelope, which was hand addressed to 50 editors and reporters without any return address. A second mailing, 2 days later, was stamped CASE FILE 7734 and had a card that read, "Who's been shooting [name of publication] readers in the foot?" The answer, inside the fold-out card, was that they were shooting themselves in the foot by not having the product to protect their data. Had the firm done advance research on the target public, it would have learned that several editors had received bona fide threats in the past, which made them sensitive to this sort of mailing. Had the firm done pretesting, it might have caught the typo on the first mailing (leaving out "in the foot") that increased the perception of real threat. It also might have discovered that editors receiving the anonymous mailing might call in the FBI or the Postal Service to investigate, which happened. Fortunately, the company managed to assuage the nerves of most editors through individual follow-up contacts and ended up with a lot of attention for the product. The firm learned, however, that public relations professionals need to consider the perspective of the people who will receive their messages to make sure messages will be received as intended. As Settles (1989) wrote, "Success in public relations comes from the ability to incorporate the lessons learned from past mistakes into bold future steps" (p. 39). To the extent the manager can catch mistakes in the pretesting stage, fewer lessons will have to be learned the hard way.

Sixth, research can provide facts on which objectives for accountability can be based. Baseline data on consumer attitudes or behavior, for example, are necessary to demonstrate change after a campaign is finished. NewsEdge Corp. demonstrated that a campaign to address high employee turnover following a merger of three competing companies reduced turnover from 40% to 6%, earning the company a Platinum PR Honorable Mention from *PR News*.

SPECIFIC RESEARCH FUNCTIONS

As a manager, you will consider three types of research in planning: formative research, program research, and summative (or evaluation) research. Formative research provides data and perspective to guide campaign creation. Program research guides the implementation of the program to ensure that strategies have the intended effects instead of unintended, counter-productive effects. Summative research provides data to evaluate the success of a public relations program based on the achievement of stated objectives.

More specifically, research can help strategic planning in six key areas:

1. *Problem identification.* First, research can show whether a problem suspected to exist truly does exist. It also can help identify where the problem is, when the problem occurs, or when it developed.
2. *Problem effects or implications.* Research can demonstrate how big a problem is, as well as for whom it poses difficulties.
3. *Strategic direction.* Research can suggest ways to communicate effectively about a problem and actions to solve the problem.
4. *Strategy testing.* Research methods as diverse as focus groups and surveys can be used to test creative strategies to make sure they work as anticipated. Some companies now monitor their reputation through the use of chat rooms, mail lists, and news groups.
5. *Evaluation of results.* Research can provide accountability to help public relations practitioners prove program impact by demonstrating program results that confirm success.

ELEMENTS OF A RESEARCH PLAN

Research plans, like public relations plans, are vital to the success of public relations programs. Because they too are goal oriented, they help keep strategic planning on track, on time, and within budget. A research plan includes an explanation of research needs; research goals; research objectives; hypotheses or hunches; and research questions to guide data collection and analysis, help propose research strategies, and prompt a discussion of how the results will be used. Your organization may develop its own template for a research plan, but one model that includes all of the important elements appears in Table 4.1.

TABLE 4.1
Elements of the Research Plan

Title Page
(Include client's name, agency name, date, and title)

I. Research Needs

- Problem statement
- Situation analysis

   –the issue (problem statement)

   –what is known about the client and the issue
   (internal and external opportunities and challenges)

   –assumptions

   –information needs (questions)

   length: usually 2 to 4 pages

II. Research Goals (What are you trying to find out?)

- Formal statement of research goals
- Further explanation of each goal, as needed

   length: usually 1 page or less

III. Research Objectives (How you will find out, and by when?)

- Formal statement objectives

   length: usually 1 page or less

IV. Hypotheses (Hunches, etc.)

- Anticipated answers to questions
- Reasoning for answer anticipated

   length: usually 1 to 2 pages

V. Research Strategies

- Explanation of methodology, sampling
- Operationalization of concepts (How ideas will be measured?)
- Procedures for data analysis

   length: usually 2 to 4 pages

VI. Expected Uses of the Results

- What will be done with the information gained
   (Market segmentation, theme development, strategy development)

   length: usually 1 page or less

DETERMINING RESEARCH NEEDS

To develop a research plan, you must determine your research needs. Your initial situation analysis can help you do this. What do you know about the problem, the situation, your opportunities, and your constraints? What do you need to know?

For everything you think you know, test whether you have evidence to confirm that your information is correct. You use many types of evidence, ranging from experts' observations to survey or sales data. The more scientific your data, the more convincing it will be, and the more it can be trusted. More specifically, you can consider the following as evidence:

1. Public relations principles, laws and professional guidelines can provide guidance for procedural and ethical issues.

2. Communication and persuasion theories are scientifically tested ideas about how and why things happen the way they do. Theories do not provide hard and fast rules about how things work. The way social science works, a theory cannot be proven right; it only can be proven wrong.

3. Expert observations can provide some validation, particularly at the brainstorming stage, but they are not as unimpeachable as hard data from surveys, sales, spreadsheets, or experiments. Quotes from individuals with high credibility and relevance to the situation are most useful.

4. Quantitative data can include survey data, sales figures, content analysis, results of experiments, budget histories, formal tracking data from web sites, customer service calls, and so on.

5. Qualitative data can include focus groups, interviews, field observations, informal tracking of communication among stakeholders, and so on. These tend to be most useful at the brainstorming stage.

You may find that some of your ideas about the problem are based on assumptions instead of on hard evidence. If possible, test the veracity of these assumptions. For example, service organizations frequently assume that poor attendance, low subscriptions, or low registrations reflect a poor reputation that requires improvement. Upon further research, however, organizations may find that their problems stem from low awareness instead of from negative attitudes, requiring a public relations program different from what a reputation management program would entail. The reverse also is true.

DETERMINING AND UNDERSTANDING
TARGET PUBLICS

You want to know as much as possible about target publics. First you need to identify and, perhaps, prioritize them. This process is called *segmentation*. Then you need to understand more deeply their interests, their needs, their concerns, their beliefs, and their behaviors.

Your *target publics* are subcategories of your *stakeholders*. Stakeholders are those who should care and be involved, or those who can be affected by or who can affect your program. Since public relations focuses on the development and maintenance of mutually beneficial relationships, ask yourself who benefits from your organization's activities, directly and indirectly, and on whom does your organization depend to achieve stated goals, both in the short term and in the long term. Who belongs in your problem statement? You can segment publics by various characteristics. These include the following:

1. *Demographics*. These include common census-type categories, such as age, gender, race or ethnicity, education level, occupation, family size, marital status, income, geographic location, political party, and religion.

2. *Psychographics*. These include personality and attitudinal characteristics, including values, beliefs, and lifestyle. These characteristics can help you identify who holds hopes, fears and interests that most help or hinder your public relations and organizational goals.

3. *Sociographics*. A wide variety of categories can be called sociographics, but they tend to focus on behaviors and characteristics common to an easily identified group of people. Broom and Dozier (1990) summarized several sociographic categories of value to public relations professionals, including the following:

- Covert power. This represents an attempt to discover who holds indirect power over persons who may more directly affect your program's success. For example, an administrative assistant holds a great deal of covert power over a busy executive who relies on the assistant to screen calls and help prioritize schedules. Family members also hold covert power over many business decisions, and certainly over purchasing decisions. Marketers refer to the power of children in sales as the "nag factor."
- Position. This represents an attempt to identify occupations or leadership positions that make individuals important stakeholders and depends greatly on the context in which you work. For example, lobbyists, journalists, legislators, union represen-

tatives, PTA officers, and teachers all can act as opinion leaders with wide-ranging effects in certain situations.

- Reputation. Sometimes people who influence others' opinions and behaviors cannot be categorized neatly into occupations or positions but can be identified by other stakeholders. For example, particular older peers may influence the extent to which younger schoolchildren embrace a recycling or health-promotion campaign. People in a community may identify individuals who have credibility over a zoning issue by virtue of their social ties or community activism.
- Organizational membership. A special interest group will care who is a member and who is not. It is important to identify who is a member of competing or complementary organizations that can be of assistance to your program directly or indirectly. When the Seattle Sheraton wanted to gain the business of corporate executives, for example, it determined on which organizations the executives served as board members. Targeting its community service activities to these organizations helped the Sheraton cement ties with these important decision makers.
- Role in decision process. Decisions often are made in incremental steps by a combination of individuals and committees. Gaining support at each step can require different strategies.

4. *Behaviors.* Purchasing patterns and attendance histories can provide useful information about who is using your organization's services, who might use them, who has rejected them, and so on.

5. *Communication behaviors.* These include latent (inactive but relevant) and active publics. You need to determine levels of awareness and the extent to which individuals care or don't care about your organization and its activities. These characteristics are likely to affect how they react to information about your organization. Grunig and Hunt (1984) suggested three measures to determine activity:

- Problem recognition. This represents the extent to which publics sense that a problem exists. If they see no problem, they will not be "active" or interested in the issue. Their level of recognition will affect the extent to which they seek to process information related to the issue.
- Constraint recognition. This represents the degree to which individuals believe they have the ability to affect an issue or situation. They may see constraints, or impediments, that limit their ability to change a situation or participate in an activity. If they do not feel they can participate or make a difference, they will be less likely to make an effort to think extensively about the issue.

- Level of involvement. This represents the degree to which individuals feel a connection between a situation or issue and themselves. The more they believe an issue can affect them, the more likely they are to take an active interest. Less involved individuals take a more passive approach.

Grunig proposed four types of publics: (a) those active on all relevant issues, (b) those apathetic on all relevant issues, (c) those active on issues only if they involve most people in a relevant population, and (d) those active only on a single issue. More recently ("Grunig's Paradigm," 1998), Grunig suggested that stakeholders can be divided into three segments, depending on their level of "excitement" or interest in an issue. The groups include:

- *long haul types*, deeply interested in a topic and its ramifications;
- *special interest types*, concerned only about certain elements of a topic, such as how a newly proposed school building will affect their property taxes;
- *hot button types*, interested only by elements that spark emotional debate, such as gun control.

DETERMINING PROGRAM OUTCOMES

You need to identify what your program outcomes will be, as well as whether you need to evaluate *intermediate outcomes* along with *ultimate outcomes*. Motivating some sort of behavioral outcome helps public relations demonstrate bottom-line value. Often, however, a number of intermediate steps are required before you can achieve that final outcome. For example, a campaign to promote donations for the hungry could find it difficult to gain people's attention, particularly if the campaign takes place at a time other than the Christmas season, when donation activity tends to be high. Holding an event attractive to a public potentially interested in the issue could encourage them to bring a donation (even a single can of food). Once present at the event, they can be encouraged to make additional donations or to become a member of the sponsoring organization. Attendance would be an intermediate behavior, can donations would be a second intermediate behavior, and memberships would be the ultimate behavior.

TESTING COMMUNICATION CHANNELS

You need to know as much as possible about the potential channels of communication available for your public relations program. Some channels will be more expensive, or more time consuming, or more efficient, or will reach different audiences. People who are more interested will go to more trouble to get information about an issue, but an organization frequently must assume that target publics are not interested or at best are easily distracted by competing messages and priorities. This may vary depending on your market and the publics with whom you wish to communicate. The National Cancer Institute has developed a helpful chart of mass media channel characteristics that can serve as a general guide.

To choose effective communication vehicles, you need to assess the following:

1. *Credibility.* This refers to the extent to which the target publics trust the source of your messages, believe the source is unbiased, and believe the source is competent or expert in the topic under discussion.
2. *Reach and exposure frequency.* Is it easy for the target publics to gain access to information via this channel? How much exposure can you achieve?
3. *Efficiency.* You need to consider relative cost (in advertising called "cost per thousand") against relative benefits. Costs include production and distribution costs in terms of monetary investments, and time and staff requirements. To what extent can you reach target audiences versus other audiences less critical to your program?
4. *Control.* You need to determine to what extent the content and distribution of the message can be managed, and to what extent control is important for the public relations program. In crisis situations, companies often buy advertising to get their messages out without any filters. In other cases, a lack of control is preferred because of the increased credibility for a message that appears as editorial copy instead of as a purchased advertisement.
5. *Flexibility.* This refers to the extent to which the target publics can gain access to the message in a way convenient to them. The Internet, for example, provides users with the flexibility to review as much information as they wish whenever they wish, as opposed to having to wait to learn about a topic until the 11:00 news.
6. *Context.* This refers to the environment in which a message is presented, such as in the middle of a sports or entertainment program, during the news, or on the ceiling of a subway train.

TABLE 4.2
Characteristics of Mass Media Channels

Medium	Target Publics	PSA Placement Opportunities	Contextual Advantages and Limitations	Appropriateness for Emotional or Information-Dense Messages	Reach	Style of Use	Expense
Television	Potentially largest and widest range, but not always at times when PSAs most likely broadcast. Unintended audiences also likely exposed.	Expensive for paid placement. Unpaid placements often infrequent, at poor time slots.	Can combine information with entertainment. Message may be obscured by commercial clutter.	Better for simple, entertaining messages than for complex details. Can visually demonstrate a behavior.	Can reach low income and other audiences not as likely to turn to specialized sources.	Viewers often pay little attention. Viewers must be present when message aired unless motivated to record a program. Direct-mail videocassettes possible.	PSAs can be expensive to produce and distribute with competitive production values. Feature placement requires contacts.
Radio	Various formats offer more opportunity for targeting. Usually reach fewer people than with TV.	Paid placement of pro-social ads relatively inexpensive. Many others competing for free exposure.	Opportunity for direct audience involvement via call-in shows.	Audio alone may make message less intrusive. Audio alone requires simple message content.	Can reach audiences not at home and in emergency conditions. Useful for spreading quickly changing information in a crisis.	Generally passive consumption. Exchange with audience possible, but target audience must be there when aired.	Live copy very flexible and inexpensive. PSAs must fit station format. Feature placement requires contacts.

Channel						
Magazines	Can more specifically target to market segments.	Have no requirement for PSA use; PSAs more difficult to place.	Can explain complex issues in some depth.	Print may lend itself to factual, detailed message delivery.	Audience can clip, contemplate material. Requires literacy.	Easier to give thoughtful attention to material. May pass on to another. Can read at convenience.	Public service ads inexpensive to produce. Ad or article placement can be time consuming.
Newspapers	Can reach broad audiences rapidly. Best for more involved audiences.	PSAs relatively rare. Paid placement usually necessary.	Can convey issues more thoroughly than on TV or in radio and faster than through magazines. Feature placement possible.	Print lends itself to more factual, detailed, rational delivery.	Easy audience access to in-depth issue coverage. Requires literacy.	Short life of newspaper limits rereading, sharing with others.	Small papers may take public service ads, welcome news briefs. Coverage demands a newsworthy item.
Internet	Best for reaching highly involved information seekers but also can reach browsers if listed conveniently on search engines.	PSA placement on others' sites unlikely, but coordination with relevant sites can create links between sites to facilitate visits.	Can explain issues in brief but also can provide almost unlimited depth. Complete reports can be made available electronically. Bypasses traditional gatekeepers.	A user-friendly home page can help attract low-involved users. Inside pages can provide more depth.	Provides convenient access to information but depends on literacy and computer access.	Interactive use is possible.	Simple web sites easy and inexpensive to produce, but sophisticated sites quite costly to maintain.

Note. Adapted from *Making Health Communication Programs Work: A Planner's Guide*. U.S. Department of Health and Human Services, NIH Publication #89-1493. Rockville, MD: 1989.

You want to be able to predict how a message will be received by those you wish to receive it. To do this you need to know how your target public feels about your organization, and possible information sources, and how their attitudes relate to specific message strategies you might employ. Keep in mind that you need to be able to anticipate the extent to which unintended recipients may have access to your message and how their reactions may affect your program goals. You don't want to have to remove your product from the shelves, as one company did in at least one region, because of serious unintended effects. In the case of the cereal company, the promotion on the cereal box invited children to get the prize (a cookie shaped like a person and named Wendell Cookie) out of the box in several silly ways. These included, "Tell a good elephant joke. When you hear Wendell laughing, you'll know where he is," but also included, "Call the fire department. Tell them to rescue a guy from your cereal box." Unfortunately, some children took the admonition to call the fire department seriously, resulting in costly calls to 911 that required authorities to respond.

You also don't want to pull costly advertising, as did the Ad Council and Connect for Kids, a child advocacy initiative of the Benton Foundation, when humor in their ad campaign disparaged other child advocates. The copy in the ad called school board members "boogerheads," attracting nationwide protest from school boards and superintendents for being disrespectful in a campaign that was intended to promote respect ("Humor Backfires," 1999).

TESTING MESSAGES

The Center for Substance Abuse Prevention has developed a helpful guide for avoiding problems in message development ("Avoiding Common Errors," 1990). They recommend checking to make sure messages are clear, accurate, and relevant. Clarity means checking whether the target public might interpret a message in a way other than, especially opposite to, what was intended. Mixed messages may appear to include contradictions. Pretesting can help the message designer avoid confusion.

Accuracy means making sure factual statements are correct and based on solid, verifiable evidence. Taking information out of context can change its meaning so that it no longer can be considered accurate. Unfortunately, many "facts" spread over the Internet without the benefit of fact checkers and editors, and they sometimes end up in print in credible media. Be careful to verify information independently such that the original source can be traced and checked. Second-hand information should not be considered real information. According to Kogan Page, Ltd., creators of a Corporate Communication Handbook

("Culling Lessons," 1998), the lack of accurate information is one of the three most important characteristics of a crisis. Supplying accurate information, therefore, can be one of the most effective tools for defusing a crisis.

Relevance means making sure the intended receivers will pay attention to the message. Messages must appeal to their values and interests, and communicate in a language they use and understand. Porter Novelli, for example, found that calling obesity a "disease" instead of a "condition" made overweight individuals more receptive to messages about an antiobesity drug. Attempts to use current slang and dialects can backfire and require careful pretesting.

TESTING INFORMATION SOURCES

When testing a message, it is imperative to test the credibility of the source. Research can guide you as you consider who should serve as information sources for your public relations program messages. Sources must be credible, expert and relevant, and—you hope—interesting. To the social scientist, credibility includes various elements, but in general it simply means that people will find the source trustworthy. Public relations issues often boil down to a lack of trust. Expertise means the person seems knowledgeable about the topic. Relevant means that the target public will relate well to the person. Teenagers, for example, often would rather hear from another teenager than from an authority figure. In a crisis, even if the public relations officer is knowledgeable about company policies and plans, and even if the officer has a credible reputation among journalists, the most relevant source still is the CEO, because the CEO is the person in charge.

One way of testing credibility is to have the moderator of a focus group, a semistructured group interview, ask what participants would think of a message if the sponsor were a commercial advertiser, or a religious organization of some type, or the government, or a local chamber of commerce. A clear, accurate, and relevant message from a source perceived as untruthful, biased, or incompetent can backfire. As chap. 15 explains, credibility is one of the most important requirements for effective communication and, when necessary, for persuasion.

DEVELOPING RESEARCH STRATEGIES

A myriad of approaches are available for tackling a problem and developing a complete situation analysis. Each approach explained here offers a slightly different emphasis; so, depending on the context, one or a combination of these techniques may be most appropriate.

It has been said that asking "why is this happening?" five times in a series reveal the cause of a problem, which may initially be obscured. This technique, called the Five WHYs, is especially useful when a problem is difficult to understand or particularly unusual. For example, when a large piece of the Jefferson Monument in Washington, DC, fell off, threatening the safety of visitors and creating a public relations worry, the Five WHYs traced the problem as follows.

The observation was that acid rain appeared to be eroding the monument, causing it to crumble. This suggested that a shelter might need to be built to protect it, which would be an expensive and potentially unattractive solution. But why was the erosion also evident on the inside of the monument, where rain would not be a factor?

WHY #1. This erosion was traced to the strong soap used to clean the monument daily, combined with jet fumes from the nearby National Airport. Why was it necessary to do so much more cleaning than at other monuments in the area?

WHY #2. It was pigeon droppings that required the extra cleaning. Why were pigeon droppings such a problem at this location?

WHY #3. An infestation of spiders that pigeons find especially tasty had occurred. Why was there an infestation of spiders?

WHY #4. Spiders were finding a bounty of midge eggs to eat, which they loved. Why were there midge eggs?

WHY #5. Midges live in the reeds in the backwaters of the Potomac River, which runs near the monument. At sunset, they swim and mate and lay their eggs, but they can get distracted by bright lights, which they love.

The solution was to turn on the lights by the monument one hour later. It was inexpensive, effective, and not unattractive (Geistfeld, 1995)!

Whatever strategy you use while researching an issue, this example nicely illustrates a tactic useful for delving into the heart of a problem. Some specific types of research strategies include the following:

1. *Communications audit.* According to Kendall (1996), an audit examines, describes, and evaluates the status of a designated program. A communications audit examines the vehicles through which messages are sent and received from stakeholders. The audit requires:

- identifying the relevant internal and external publics;

- collecting data from designated publics, using methods such as interviews, focus groups, and surveys to determine their use of communication vehicles, as well as their impression of the vehicles and of the organization;
- analyzing current programs, personnel, and materials used for communication;
- Examining trends, opportunities, and challenges relevant to the organization.

The audit, which can focus on the public relations department or on the organization as whole, culminates in recommendations for action. Just as financial audits occur regularly, communication audits also should take place on a regular basis. Because audits are broad based, they can help address specific problems but audits also can help guide more global, long-term planning.

2. *Social responsibility audit.* This is a more specific form of the communications audit. Kendall (1996) recommended a social responsibility audit as an examination of an organization's performance related to corporate citizenship. As described by Kendall, the social responsibility audit focuses on factors that affect the organization, rather than on publics and communication activities. The social responsibility audit involves:

- identifing issues that have social or civic implications;
- ranking the issues based on when the issue will affect the organization, the extent to which its effects will be direct or indirect, and the significance of the issue to the organization;
- examining which departments can affect or will be affected by the issues;
- developing possible responses.

3. *Reputation audit* ("Can Value," 1996). Reputation is so important that it may be helpful to quantify. A reputation audit can provide a situation analysis focused on reputation. The audit involves:

- an identity analysis, which is essentially a communications audit;
- an image analysis, to determine how the organization is perceived by key constituencies via surveys;
- a coherence analysis, to compare the desired identity with the perceived identity.

4. *GAP research.* The gap method uses a series of four questions to ask target publics to perform their own diagnosis of an organization's strengths and weaknesses ("Gap Research," 1994). The questions include the following:

- On a scale (such as 1–9), how would you rate us on ...?
- Why did you give that rating? (This could evolve into the five WHYs.)
- Knowing the organization as you do, how good could we get if we really tried (on the same scale as used for question 1)?
- What would we have to do to get there?

The gap method is a way to perform focused brainstorming with a variety of stakeholders. Sometimes a more sophisticated analysis is unnecessary.

5. *Co-orientation research.* This is a perspective especially appropriate to public relations problems because of its focus on relationships. According to co-orientation theory, successful communication depends on accurate perceptions from all parties involved, with ultimate success defined as consensus. In the case of a controversy, an organization can ask the following questions:

- What does the organization think about X?
- What does the organization think the public thinks about X?
- What does the public think the organization thinks about X?
- What does the public think about X?

By asking these four questions, the public relations manager can determine the extent to which the problem is one of true disagreement or one of perceived agreement or disagreement. Co-orientation, as a result, is a good way to diagnose the potential for miscommunication that can hurt attempts at building consensus and damage an organization's reputation. According to Broom and Dozier (1990), the most common public relations audit involves establishing an organization's view on an issue, determining the target public's view on the issue, and determining the distance between the two views. This type of audit, however, does not account for the extent to which these views may be based on misperceptions of the other party's views or intentions. The co-orientation model accounts for both actual disagreement and perceived disagreement, which makes it a more powerful strategic planning tool. Co-orientation analysis determines actual agreement, perceived agreement,

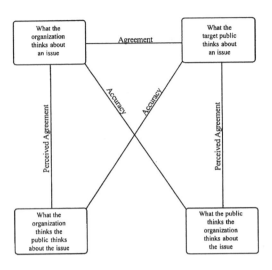

FIG. 4.2.   The co-orientation model. The achievement of agreement, accuracy, and perceived agreement constitute *consensus*, which is the ideal outcome for public relations.

and accuracy. True consensus cannot occur until both parties agree and know they agree.

DEVELOPING REALISTIC RESEARCH PROPOSALS

It may appear that an organization can perform unlimited types of research endlessly. Clearly, organizations cannot afford the time and expense involved. As a result, the development of a research plan also requires an examination of constraints and priorities that can guide the type and extent of research pursued. The manager needs to prioritize research needs and appropriate research methods, because the ideal research will never take place. Some mysteries will remain unsolved, and good research often raises additional, new questions (recall the five WHYs). The manager can rely on four issues to develop realistic parameters for the research plan:

1. *Time.* When are the results needed to develop the final public relations plan by the required deadline? If the organization faces an immediate crisis, lengthy research cannot occur. If the organiza-

tion's focus turns to long-term planning, more time can be devoted to research.

2. *Budget.* How much money and staff time can be devoted to research? Some types of research, such as face-to-face surveys, are expensive. You don't want to spend too much of your program budget on research and have too little left for implementation of the campaign itself. As a result, Broom and Dozier (1990) and Ketchum ("Bottom-line," 1999) both have offered a rule of thumb to guide research spending, suggesting that 8% to 10% of a total program budget should be used for research. Recent data collected from interviews with 110 American companies by PAG/Best Practices ("corporate communication," 1998) suggested that in reality only about 5% of communication budgets go toward research. Most of that research focuses on media exposure and corporate reputation, rather than on more sophisticated, outcome-oriented research.

3. *Levels of expertise available.* Consider who will collect the data and how knowledgeable they are about data collection and analysis procedures. If data collection cannot be farmed out to an independent research firm, make sure the project does not require specialized expertise. As chap.s 10, 11, and 12 discuss, a variety of details related to sampling, question design and analysis can affect the veracity and credibility of research results. Do only what can be done well.

4. *Need for precision and depth (how research will be used).* Sometimes sophisticated research is overkill, but other times more refined information is required. For example, an election on a controversial issue can hinge on the details. Be ready to explain how research will be applied to strategic development and why the level of research proposed is necessary for program success. Public relations managers surveyed in 1996 (Pinkleton et al., 1999) commonly reported that clients wanted research but did not want to pay for it. The program manager needs to provide convincing reasons for performing desired research. This is where it is helpful to include hypotheses, or hunches, regarding what results you expect to find. The ability to explain how the results will direct strategy and how they will affect the likely outcome of the program can help convince the recalcitrant client.

FINAL THOUGHTS

A carefully conceived research plan will lay a strong foundation for program planning. Clear research goals and well-considered research strategies that correspond to the needs and constraints of the situation at hand give the manager the best chance of success in the later stages of program planning. The following chapters provide more background on the strengths and weaknesses of various research methods and sampling techniques. Managers can refer to these as they consider how to make choices that will not cost too much or take too long to implement, but that will guide the effective selection of target publics, program outcomes, communication channels, and message strategies.

SIDEBAR 4.1.
Confessions of a Silver Anvil Judge
by
Larry Chiagouris

The Silver Anvil is the most prestigious award a public relations professional can win. But it doesn't come easy.

This year, I had the privilege of serving as a judge for the PRSA Silver Anvil awards. As a marketing strategist and researcher with more than 25 years in the business, I have judged numerous competitions.

The Silver Anvil award selection process is as good as or better than any other professional awards program. And the winning entries were all worthy of the awards bestowed upon them.

What concerns me, however, is the quality of the entries that did not win Silver Anvils. In some cases, they were so far off in conveying a strong program, that one might conclude that many industry professionals need to revisit what constitutes a successful public relations program.

The entry criteria for the Silver Anvils is very specific, requiring documentation in four major areas—research, planning, execution and results. To win an award, an agency must demonstrate that its entry delivered in all four areas.

WHERE IS RESEARCH?

Many agencies failed to quantify their entry's contribution to each of the four areas. Research was clearly the area with the most room for improvement. Several submissions stretched the definition and in the process devalued the role that research can play in defining the goals and target audience of a public relations program.

For example, many entries seemed to support the notion that research consists of talking to a few editors about their perception of a company and its products. Other submissions relied heavily on what a top executive said was important to the progress of the product or company. While media soundings and senior executive interviews can be important factors in determining the parameters of a public relations effort, they do not begin to go far enough in terms of research.

(Continues)

A strategic public relations program will address the audience that is relevant to the public relations campaign. Many campaigns have multiple audiences, including endusers, employees, members, investors, suppliers, and government officials. Research, when properly utilized, will define the target audience of the campaign and help set priorities.

It will often delineate the existing perceptions, needs and opinions of the program's target audience. Research initiatives should link this understanding to the marketing and brand situation of the product or company. In the process, it should provide a benchmark from which to judge the impact of the public relations program.

WHAT ARE THE GOALS?

Not every research effort has to be extensive or expensive. We have developed a number of quick and relatively inexpensive research tools to use when resources are limited. They include qualitative samples, in-house research panels and sophisticated analysis of existing data.

The planning stage is the second area addressed on the entry form. Here, the most frequent problem was that the choice of goals and objectives was not justified against the clients' business goals. A public relations program should be developed to support the broader needs of the client, with emphasis on corporate reputation and brand building.

The program goals should be articulated in a manner that enables the client to easily evaluate the effectiveness of the program. Many of the entries did not provide any way to quantify progress made towards the program' objectives—making it impossible to evaluate whether of not the program achieved its goals.

The classic example is a statement indicating that a program was designed to "establish the company as a leader." Again, the lack of documentation leads one to question the relevance of a program based upon poorly articulated goals and objectives.

WHERE'S THE SUPPORT?

The third area addressed on the Silver Anvil entry form is the execution of the public relations program. This was where the real fun began.

Copies of press kits, videotapes, audiotapes, and collateral of all kinds filled submissions binders to the brim. The problem for many entries, however, was the lack of information regarding how promotional material supported the program's key messages.

Material generated by the creative team often demonstrated a complete disconnection between the creative and strategic elements of a program. The material looked slick but failed to convey key messages to the target audience. Lavish creative efforts on behalf of a low-budget campaign points to a lack of planning and poor execution on the part of the staff responsible for the program. It many be hard to imagine, but it is possible overspend on production!

The final area on the Silver Anvil entry form is program results. Starting that top management "liked the program" hardly constitutes results befitting a Silver Anvil award winner. To most professionals, letters received from the sales force or customers are also insufficient to be considered for an award.

WHAT IS SUCCESS?

After opening several submissions that included clip reports as proof of a program' impact, I was forced to wonder how some public relations professionals are measuring success? Clips are an indicator of interest on the part of the media, not necessarily of influence on the purchasing behavior or attitudes of the public.

To be considered a successful public relations program, there must be evidence that the goals and objectives of a program have been met. For instance, if the stated goal of a program is to raise brand awareness, the public relations agency needs to provide documentation demonstrating that the goal was achieved. A brand awareness survey conducted before and after the public relations campaign would clearly illustrate whether the brand experienced increased consumer recognition or not.

Some other examples of quantifiable objectives are a 5% increase in sales, 10,000 new hits a month at the company Web site or one million dollars donated to a nonprofit organization.

Not every public relations program is well suited to the Silver Anvil awards. Entries are intended to represent the best a public relations program has to offer in a given year. Submissions that are clearly lacking in one of the four entry criteria devalue not only the awards, but also the public relations industry itself.

Programs that win Silver Anvils almost always demonstrate a tight linkage between the goals of the business and the program results. Failing to do that, other efforts will remain nothing more than submissions.

* * *

Reprinted courtesy of *The Strategist*, a quarterly publication of the Public Relations Society of America.

GATHERING USEFUL DATA
FOR STRATEGIC GUIDANCE

Research Decisions
and Data Collection

Applications of Research
Before Starting the Research Process
Approaches to Public Relations Research
Informal Research Concerns
Research Issues to Consider
Steps to Research Project Design
Final Thoughts

Traditionally, public relations practitioners have relied on strong media relations skills and key media placements to succeed in public relations. Practitioners, executives, and clients generally bought into the myth that public relations works with nuances of public opinion and other intangibles that simply cannot be measured (Cutlip et al., 2000). Public relations campaigns were based on practitioner hunches, knowledge of the market, and simple common sense. Practitioners used savvy media relations skills and well-honed campaign tactics to generate media attention for publicity-seeking organizations. Thick, clip-filled binders were used to demonstrate the value of public relations to promote a company or cause.

Although some practitioners continue to successfully operate this way, several organizational and environmental changes have made this model of public relations nearly obsolete. Fewer financial resources, increasingly competitive markets, and increasing costs, in particular, have resulted in greater organizational attention to public relations programs. The result is that practitioners who enjoyed past success based solely on their practical understanding of local media markets, a well-developed network of contacts, and strong media relations skills increasingly find themselves struggling to gain organizational resources and maintain organizational support in an era of greater program accountability (Pinkleton et al., 1999; "What Trends," 1997).

Even though practitioners' reliance on research has increased, not every successful campaign requires original research. Research can require a substantial investment of resources, and many organizations prefer to plan and evaluate campaigns based on their existing understanding of markets and their assessments of key audience responses. Some situations may require only the tracking of public responses to media placements, for example, or votes on political initiatives. In addition, some public relations efforts are so limited in scope that they simply do not require or receive the resources necessary to conduct even small-scale research. In these situations, both practitioners and the organizations with which they are working may be satisfied with subjective interpretations and the obvious outcomes resulting from public relations programs. Unfortunately, practitioners who lack research are limited to arguing that, perhaps based on their years in the business, they know a situation and can recommend a solution. With no concrete evidence to support these claims, there is little basis for organizational support of such recommendations, and others with different backgrounds or similar levels of experience commonly recommend different options.

Research reveals the perceptions, interests, and opinions of targeted audiences; produces evidence used to select from among competing solutions; and provides a benchmark from which to evaluate campaign success. Research also allows campaign planning and evaluation based on facts rather than on intuition, rule of thumb, or past practices. Practitioners find research particularly useful as the costs and importance of a campaign increase, or as the certainty concerning an issue or public decreases. In practice, each research setting is unique and research decisions often are affected by several constraints, the greatest of which are time and budgetary limitations. The result is that no single "best" research method exists. Instead, the best research method is the one that most completely meets your information needs within the constraints of a given project. Given the often confusing decisions that practitioners must make regarding research projects, the purpose of this chapter is to discuss the practical issues that should be considered before final decisions are made concerning a research project. These issues include questions you should ask and answer before you begin a research project; various constraints that affect research method choices; an overview of formal and informal research techniques; the steps taken in a typical research-planning process; and some issues to consider when dealing with research firms, in-house departments, or consultants.

APPLICATIONS OF RESEARCH

Strategic managers use research throughout the program-planning, implementation, and evaluation process. The ways research applies, however, change as the program evolves. The uses of research also depend on the manager's communication needs. For example, precampaign, or formative, research is used before a campaign is launched to better understand, define, and help segment targeted audiences. Practitioners commonly make use of focus groups or surveys, to examine people's perceptions, opinions, and sources of information regarding a key issue. Practitioners also can use these and other research methods to develop campaign strategies and test messages with target audience members as part of the precampaign or campaign-monitoring process.

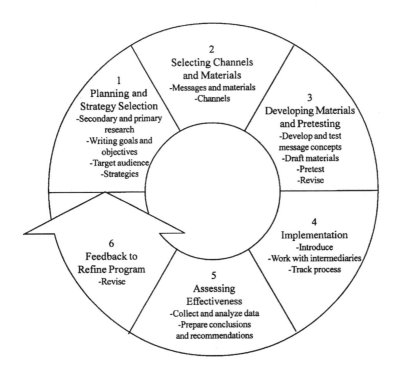

FIG. 5.1. Stages of communication. Strategic planning of communication programs is an ongoing process in which previous experience informs the planning of new programs and the refinement of old programs. Developed by the Center for Substance Abuse Prevention for the planning of alcohol and other drug communication programs.

Practitioners use these research methods to provide benchmark measurements of the awareness, attitudes, and behaviors of targeted audiences. Once practitioners have conducted a campaign, they use benchmark measures to test the effectiveness of a campaign using postcampaign, or evaluative, research. In many cases, postcampaign research really is between-campaign research, because practitioners use it as a platform from which to begin another campaign. Public relations professionals' use of research normally results in fact-based evidence of a campaign's accomplishments (or failures) and may serve as the basis for requesting additional organizational resources or creating new campaign initiatives.

The use of research to measure campaign effectiveness at the end of a communication program helps achieve credibility with organizational management. Organizations are looking for a concrete return on what they perceive as an "investment" of limited resources in public relations. In today's highly competitive markets, practitioner intuition and past experience rarely provide an acceptable basis from which to plan a communications campaign. Practitioner voices are drowned out by competing voices in an organization when their experience and intuition are pitted against research data. Practitioners who have access to such data have a strong credibility advantage over their intuition-reliant peers when it comes to influencing organizational decision making, developing communication strategies, and receiving organizational resources.

Practitioners can use research to help management monitor changes in internal or external environments. It is too easy for organizational management to become insulated from key publics in the busy and often chaotic world of management. The hectic pace and rigorous demands often leave decision makers unaware of the critically important attitudes and opinions of consumers, community members, employees, and other key groups. In this case, public relations research can be used as what Peter Drucker called an organizational "hearing aid" ("Reflections," 1998) to keep management in touch with the attitudes and opinions of those on which organizational success or failure depends.

Practitioners can use research to keep in touch with the competition. The current international marketplace is extremely competitive, as is the struggle for access to limited media space and the contest for the limited attention of target audiences. Savvy public relations practitioners and their clients make it a priority to understand the strategies and tactics of their competition, to increase their own chances for success. Research can provide insight into various interest areas, such as an analysis of the features and appeals in competitors' messages and of audience responses to those message strategies.

Finally, practitioners can use research to generate publicity for organizations and clients. In most cases, organizations produce legitimate research with newsworthy results that benefit the sponsor of a project. In other cases, however, organizations manipulate participants' responses and purposefully misinterpret research results to attract as much media attention as possible. The result is that the media, and ultimately the public, may be mislead by unscrupulous research firms or practitioners who engage in unethical practices in an attempt to make a media splash. Serious research scientists and public relations practitioners should be careful when using research for publicity purposes. There is a strong potential for organizations to misuse research findings, and the media are increasingly skeptical about projects sponsored by organizations with a vested interest in the results. Ultimately, the potential uses of research in public relations are nearly endless; research results can be used to inform nearly every aspect of the public relations process.

BEFORE STARTING THE RESEARCH PROCESS

Before starting a research project there are some basic issues to consider that often are critical to its successful completion. You should start by determining what you want to know from the project with as much specificity as possible. Even exploratory projects should have a clear purpose. Although this may appear obvious, few research projects start with well-defined objectives. Instead, many research projects start with a vague sense of purpose that is so general it is nearly useless. Organizations that want to use research to "better understand the market" or "see what people think of us" probably are wasting their time and money. Keep in mind that research projects are an expensive investment that should provide an anticipated return. The company that engages in a poorly conceived research project and receives a relatively small benefit as a result will pay just as much for its research as the company that uses a well-designed project with specific objectives and benefits accordingly. Although determining informational needs and project objectives can be time consuming and even difficult, it is the first important step in the successful completion of a research project and helps provide the best return on a research investment.

Several questions should be asked when considering a new research project. The first is, "What do we already know about the subject of our research?" Answering this question should help to narrow the scope and focus of a project. Once a project is started, several potential topics and questions typically compete for limited project resources. Unfortunately, specific questions and even whole topics typically must be thrown out of research projects as time and budget-

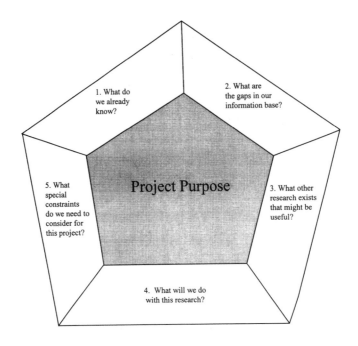

FIG. 5.2. Guiding questions for research decisions. When considering a research project, managers should ask these five questions. All decision making should focus on the purpose of the project to prevent unnecessary or useless research.

ary realities force unrealistic expectations into real-world constraints. When tough decisions must be made about what to keep and what to discard in a research project, an understanding of your current knowledge base is essential.

The next question is, "What are the gaps in our information base?" Although it seems obvious, the answer to this question provides concrete direction to an organization as research topics and potential methods are considered. Avoid approaching a research project as a single study. Think of a project, instead, as part of an ongoing program of research consisting of all the information an organization has collected or is likely to collect concerning a given public or issue. In reality, no single project can answer all the questions an organization has concerning a topic, particularly given the increasingly complex and competitive environment in which many organizations exist. In fact, research studies may raise more questions than they answer. When single studies are viewed as part of a larger, ongoing program of organizational research, their scope and function take on greater focus.

The result is a valuable contribution to an organization's base of knowledge concerning key audiences and issues.

The third question that should be asked is, "What other research currently exists that might be useful?" An organization typically has an array of research available that it can use to inform its decision-making processes. Various syndicated research exists, for example, that provides useful information about target audiences' product and service usage, lifestyle, media usage, and other important characteristics. Similarly, Census Bureau data are available from a university library, and this high-quality, detailed information may be useful for organizations addressing a variety of issues. Professional associations often support research projects that benefit association members. This research, while fairly broad in scope, can provide useful background information from which to begin a new project. Databases may provide useful information concerning a surprisingly diverse array of topics. Finally, trade publications often report research results concerning topics of interest to readers in the field they serve.

Researchers also may be able to reuse previously collected data as part of a new research project. This practice, called *secondary data analysis*, is essentially recycling data. It occurs when researchers use a set of data for a purpose different from its original use. Once researchers collect and analyze data, they often catalog it and set it aside. In other instances, educational institutions, foundations, and other organizations conduct large multipurpose surveys and release the results to the public. In either case, practitioners may reanalyze these data for their own purposes if the data are available for use. If an organization is interested in interpreting changes in public opinion during an election year, for example, it may get access to candidate polling data after the election. In this case, the organization is bound by the methods and questions used in the original study; however, the data still may be useful, and they may cost little or nothing to access. Any of these resources, and various additional ones, may provide information that has a significant bearing on a research project currently in the planning stages.

The fourth question that should be asked is, "What will we do with the results?" Practitioners often initiate research projects as part of a problem-solving process. Research is most useful in this process when organizations know how they will use the results to begin the problem-solving process. Unfortunately, it is not uncommon for organizations to complete major studies and, after a short time, set the results aside and never look at them again. In reality, conducting a study does nothing for an organization. Research findings are only useful when they are put to work by skillful managers who understand how the results will be used as part of the planning and problem-solving process.

The fifth question that should be asked is, "What special constraints do we need to consider for this project?" As discussed in chap. 4, project decisions will depend on the time available to perform the research, budgetary limitations, the expertise available for performance and interpretation of the research, and the extent to which precision and depth are required from the research. In addition, some special situations can arise that may make it advisable to consult a research specialist.

First, practitioners may have trouble collecting information about certain issues and may also have trouble collecting information from hard-to-reach audiences. In some instances, for example, people may be unwilling to discuss their private behavior with intrusive researchers. In other cases, practitioners may find it difficult to locate sample members. How do you find a random sample of pregnant women, for example? What if you want to survey urban residents, 25 to 34 years old who use public transportation? In each of these cases, research methods and sample selection strategies can be customized to provide information concerning specific issues and hard-to-reach populations.

A second special issue that may discourage data collection is a lack of appropriate research facilities. In this case, specialized help is the answer. Research firms, research consultants, statistical analysts or other specialists can provide the facilities to help solve difficult research problems. Practitioners spend their money wisely when they use knowledgeable professionals who have access to appropriate facilities to help them solve difficult data collection issues.

By answering these questions, practitioners will gain a better understanding of the purpose of a research project and the conditions that must be met to make it a success. They also will be able to use research results to give a project the direction necessary to make it a worthwhile investment with an anticipated and valuable return.

APPROACHES TO PUBLIC RELATIONS RESEARCH

At its most basic level, research simply is collecting information, and any number of methods can be used to gather information, each with its own strengths and weaknesses. The most basic designation researchers typically make concerning research methods is formal versus informal or casual approaches to data collection. Rather than fitting research methods neatly into one of these categories, however, research methods range from nonscientific, casual research methods to fully formal, scientific research methods, as discussed in chap. 6. Just because a research method is casual does not mean it has no benefit or practical application. Instead, casual research methods simply fail to meet the standards demanded by formal, scientific research.

A quick look at some casual research methods should make it obvious why researchers consider them nonscientific. One of the most common forms of public relations research, for example, involves using clip files to monitor newspaper and magazine coverage of an organization or issue (similar services can monitor broadcast or web coverage). A practitioner using a clip file can examine the messages targeted audiences receive, gain some understanding of public opinion concerning an organization or issue, and even determine the need for potential responses to media coverage, if necessary.

Using a network of personal contacts is another common form of casual research. When practitioners want to know how members of a targeted audience might respond to an issue or event, for example, they may simply call several acquaintances who generally fit the audience description and ask them for their advice and opinions. Practitioners can use such information as the basis for organizational decision making, even though it is not scientific. Other types of casual research include analyses of letters organizations receive or an analysis of field reports from organizational sources such as agents, representatives, or recruiters. In each instance, information collected by these methods provides an organization with a potentially useful basis from which to make decisions about key issues, events, and targeted audiences.

What is it about this information that makes it casual and nonscientific? For one thing the information may be gathered from a sample that is not representative. When researchers collect data, they usually collect information from a subset, or sample, of the targeted population. When a sample is representative, it has the same distribution of characteristics as the population from which it is drawn. Because of this, the opinions collected from a representative sample should accurately represent the opinions that exist in a population. Although researchers never draw a perfectly representative sample, some samples—based on probability sampling methods (discussed in chap. 10)—have a greater likelihood of being representative than other samples. When practitioners contact a few people to ask their opinions, the opinions expressed cannot possibly represent the range of opinions that exist in a target audience consisting of perhaps millions of people. When practitioners use informal research methods, they typically collect information from a sample that is not representative. Chapter 6 explains this in more detail.

A second characteristic of casual research methods is that practitioners use an informal process when collecting and recording information. When they contact different people, for example, researchers are unlikely to use a standard set of questions with predetermined response categories for each person. Such a questionnaire would defeat the purpose of the research by not allowing practitioners to take advantage of the different areas of expertise and experience of each of their contacts. As with other casual research methods, contacting selected friends or experts does not follow a formal process or set of procedures that practitioners can use to collect information in a precise, reliable manner.

As an additional note, practitioners cannot accurately know or understand public opinion based solely on media portrayals. This practice fails the test of formal research because it is not based on a scientific test of the nature of the relationships among media coverage and the attitudes and opinions of target audience members. There are times, for example, when information and portrayals in the media have an obvious and direct effect on public attitudes or behavior. Tickle-me Elmo, for example, was launched as a 1996 Christmas-season sellout because the toy appeared on the *Rosie O'Donnell* and *Today* shows, arranged by a public relations agency for the toy's manufacturer, Tyco. In this instance, Tyco actually canceled advertising for the toy as stores ran out of the product and skirmishes broke out between parents tying to get their hands on this must-have toy (Fitzgerald, 1996). In other instances, however, media portrayals have little or no effect on attitudes or behavior. In fact, the media are full of persuasive messages warning people not to do some things and encouraging them to do other things. Whereas some people heed these messages, many others simply ignore them. Even when formal research is used, determining causation requires careful attention and planning. Practitioners' observations and assumptions about public opinion based on media placements are risky and necessarily fall into the casual-research category.

In the middle of the casual-formal research continuum are various methods that typically require a more formal process than purely casual methods, but still do not fulfill the requirements of formal, scientific research. The most commonly used research method in this category is focus grouping. Basically, a focus group is a directed group discussion typically consisting of 8 to 12 people. Participants usually are similar with respect to key characteristics such as age, gender, product brand usage, political party affiliation, or any other characteristics deemed important by the project sponsor. The discussion is led by a moderator who asks questions and probes participants' responses. The process is recorded and transcribed, and research professionals and their clients attempt to gain key insights and draw meaning out of the results.

Even after all this effort, researchers still understand that focus group research is only quasiformal because of the size of the sample and the lack of formal research procedures. A study must have an appropriate sample size (discussed in chap. 10) to qualify as formal research. Even the largest focus group normally is too small to meet sample size requirements. In addition, under the best circumstances, scientific research follows a formal set of procedures that researchers apply equally to everyone in a study. When researchers conduct focus groups, the procedures they use generally are not equally applied to everyone. In some cases, for example, a moderator may wish to ask certain participants additional questions based on their unusual opinions. Other participants may be reluctant to speak up or may hesitate to express their true opinions. In these situations, focus groups do not follow a standard procedure closely enough to qualify as formal, scientific research.

Other commonly used quasiformal research methods include surveys that suffer from flaws in the data-collection process, including the use of nonrandom sampling methods. When mall intercept surveys are conducted, for example, members of an interview team typically position themselves at key locations throughout a mall and interview willing shoppers. The shoppers who participate in the survey make up what is called a convenience or incidental sample because they are selected on the basis of accessibility. Researchers use the information collected this way to gain quantitative information concerning the insights, opinions, attitudes, and behaviors of shoppers considered generally representative of a target audience.

Convenience sampling, however, is a nonprobability, nonrandom sampling method. Even though standing in a mall and talking to shoppers as they happen by appears to rely on a random-selection process, this sampling procedure falls short of the requirements of probability sampling. When truly random sampling methods are used, every person in a population has an equal chance of being included in the sample. In this case, even when a carefully constructed questionnaire is used that contains specific response categories, the use of a convenience sample still makes the project's findings unrepresentative and leaves the project short of the standards necessary to qualify as formal, scientific research.

INFORMAL RESEARCH CONCERNS

When researchers label a method casual or quasiformal, it does not mean it is without merit. In reality, casual research methods are among the most commonly used forms of research, and their findings are successfully applied in many settings. At the same time, however, managers should use the results of research based on casual or quasiformal methods carefully. Practitioners who use focus groups, for example, must be careful in their interpretation and application of study results. It is easy to misinterpret focus group results because no matter how many focus groups are conducted, their results provide no numerical measurement and participants' ideas and comments are difficult to analyze statistically. Ultimately, two practitioners who view the same focus group can interpret the results differently.

In addition, the results of focus groups and other informal research methods have little generalizability, or projectability. As already noted, researchers typically collect information from a sample of population members rather than from all population members. When research-ers use formal research methods, they typically select a sample using probability sampling methods. Probability sampling methods have a greater likelihood of accurately reflecting the wide variety of opinions, attitudes, and behaviors that exist in most populations because each member of the population has an equal chance of being included in the sample. The result is that practitioners can generalize or project re-search results from a probability-based sample to all members of a population with relative confidence. Practitioners have no basis for projection when informal research methods are used because the sample may not accurately represent the population from which it was drawn. Occasionally, luck may provide an accurate reflection of popu-lation members by happenstance, but practitioners cannot be sure be-cause they have no way to determine the extent to which a sample represents a population.

Other problems with nonscientific research methods involve selec-tive observations and ego involvement, both of which contribute to re-search results that are subjective instead of objective (Babbie, 1999). When research findings are objective, they unbiasedly reflect the atti-tudes and behaviors of study participants, regardless of the personal views of researchers or project sponsors. On the other hand, selective observation may occur when researchers selectively interpret focus group results so they match the ego needs of a client. When this hap-pens research results are worse than meaningless: they are wrong. These results will misdirect the decisions of organizational managers who are counting on accurate research to inform their decision-mak-ing process. Whereas both formal and informal research methods can suffer from selective observations and the ego involvement of research-ers, these concerns are greater when researchers use informal and quasiformal research methods rather than formal research methods.

When conducted properly, scientific research methods are more likely to result in accurate observations by following a formal process and well-conceived research design to its logical conclusion. As Nachmias and Nachmias (1981) noted, scientific research methods differ from other methods of acquiring knowledge based on their assumptions. At a philosophical level, the assumptions of science include, for example, that nature is orderly and regular, that it is possible to know nature, that nothing is self-evident, and that knowledge is derived from experience. At an applied level, scientific research methods are built on a system of explicit rules and procedures that, when correctly applied, have a high likelihood of producing accurate, reliable results. These research methods are by no means complete and infallible. In fact, social scientists have worked to develop new methods and approaches to observation, inference, and generalization that are consistent with the scientific research approach. The result is that formal research methodology has slowly grown and evolved, as scientists exchange ideas and information. Social scientists have developed standard rules and procedures from this process, resulting in formal research methods and techniques.

These rules and procedures are applied in public relations research to produce valid and reliable information. Various formal scientific research methods are available, including experiments, media content analyses, and surveys. In addition, several commercial databases and syndicated research resources are available that rely on scientific research methods. Survey research is the most commonly used scientific research method in public relations ("Just For Fun," 1994). When researchers use probability sampling procedures and an appropriate formula to determine sample size, they can generalize or project survey results from a sample to a population with a high level of confidence and a known range of error.

Newcomers to research methods should not be intimidated by the lofty goals and sometimes confusing terminology used in scientific research. Just as math expertise is not required to use a calculator, a scientific background is not required to understand formal research methods. Instead, practitioners should learn the strengths, weaknesses, and assumptions of each research method so they clearly understand the advantages and limitations of the information they are using for strategic planning and evaluation. Research methods that may be appropriate for some projects may be inappropriate for other projects. Substantial risks are associated with the misuse of research methods that provide unreliable or misleading information, which results in negative consequences for organizations.

RESEARCH ISSUES TO CONSIDER

Any time researchers collect information, they must consider several issues that affect the quality of the information collected. In some cases, research results should not be trusted as the basis for major decisions because they contain liabilities that may not be well understood. In other cases, researchers understand study limitations and can control them though the use of selected research and sampling methods. Ideally, practitioners' trust in research results should be appropriate to the level of accuracy, precision, reliability, and validity of a research method and the results it produces (Babbie, 1999).

The first of these areas, *accuracy*, concerns whether a research method produces error-free data. Although researchers establish a minimum degree of accuracy for every research method, they do not always require highly accurate research results in applied research settings. In some cases, a general understanding of the attitudes, opinions, and behaviors of targeted audiences is enough, and a research method that provides that kind of information, such as a focus group, is appropriate. When researchers demand a high degree of accuracy, however, they use scientific research methods and probability sampling methods to provide relatively error-free results. In fact, when researchers use probability sampling procedures in survey research, they can calculate the range of error for participants' responses. Although no study is without some degree of error, when research managers use scientific research methods, rely on an appropriate formula to calculate sample size, and use probability-based sampling methods, they are able to evaluate the accuracy of research results with relative confidence.

Research managers also must consider the *precision* of research findings that result from the use of different research methods. When research findings are precise, they are exact. Consider the difference between asking a friend what the weather is like outside and using a thermometer to determine the temperature. In the first instance, our friend may say it looks "warm" or is "hot" outside. In the second instance, a thermometer may indicate it is 98° Fahrenheit. Both answers are informative and useful; however, one answer is more precise than the other.

Although researchers generally desire precise research findings over imprecise research findings, not all research methods produce results with the same degree of precision, and at times precision may be less important. Some research methods produce results that generally lack precision. Because focus groups are essentially a group discussion, for example, it is nearly impossible to measure results exactly within the context of the discussion. A focus group may provide impressions, ideas, or general group agreement or disagreement, but these results will be broad and interpretive to an extent. When researchers require precision, they will more likely turn to a survey questionnaire that contains specific questions and numerical response categories to record the attitudes and opinions of respondents.

This is not to suggest, however, that practitioners find focus groups or other less precise research methods less useful. To the contrary, a high degree of precision often is not necessary in applied research and may even be undesirable. When researchers are exploring people's attitudes and opinions, for example, a highly precise questionnaire is likely to hurt their ability to gather useful information. At this point in the research process, practitioners want to explore people's attitudes and opinions rather than measure them precisely. As an additional note, do not confuse precision with accuracy. It may be more precise to learn it is 98° outside rather than it is "hot," but both answers are inaccurate if snow is on the ground.

Research methods that produce accurate and precise results also should produce reliable results. Strictly speaking, *reliability* is essentially "repeatability." If researchers make repeated measurements of sample members' attitudes, opinions, or behaviors, the results should be similar each time. When researchers use informal research methods, a lack of reliability often is a concern. If I call some of my friends to get their advice on an issue, the results are likely to vary considerably depending on whom I contact. This research method is not reliable. The same reliability concerns are true of quasiformal research methods including mall intercepts and focus groups. When research managers use scientific research methods to collect data, the results generally are highly reliable. As an additional note, research methods that are reliable are not necessarily accurate. As Babbie (1999) noted, a scale that consistently weighs people five pounds lighter than their actual weight (we should all have such a scale) is high in reliability but not accuracy.

Finally, the *validity* of results produced using various research methods should be considered. At a basic level, valid research results are legitimate or genuine. An IQ test is valid measure of intelligence, for example, if it genuinely measures the intelligence of the individual taking the test. Social scientists have divided validity into numerous components in an attempt to reflect all of the nuances of the term and their implications for data collection. Although it is important for research professionals to understand validity concerns in all of their manifestations, we purposefully simplify our discussion and selectively consider applied aspects of validity in keeping with the purposes of this text and the patience of our readers. Kerlinger (1973) suggested two broad categories of validity: external and internal.

External validity refers to the representativeness, or generalizability, of research results. When researchers conduct a study, they draw a sample, or subset, of people from a population as potential participants. When they draw a sample, researchers must be certain it accurately represents the population. In many instances, only a few hundred people will actually complete a survey, and research professionals will use their responses to make inferences about the entire population which may consist of millions of people. When research results are representative, researchers can accurately take sample responses and project them to the entire population. Researchers use probability sampling methods, which require random-selection procedures, to ensure that everyone in a population has an equal chance of being included in a sample. If the sample accurately reflects the population and researchers use a scientific research method, the results of a study will be high in external validity and researchers will be able to generalize study results from a sample to the population with confidence.

In terms of practical implications, informal and quasiformal research methods generally lack external validity. When researchers use focus groups, for example, they do not use probability sampling methods or choose a large enough sample size to make the focus group results high in external validity. In fact, a lack of generalizability is one of the reasons researchers consider these methods informal. Researchers must use fully formal, scientific research methods, including probability-based sampling, to achieve a high degree of external validity.

Kerlinger (1973) illustrated *internal validity* with the simple question, "Are we measuring what we think we're measuring?" If, for example, we want to measure people's voting habits but instead ask for their opinions about how important it is to vote, we have not measured behavior and the measure lacks internal validity. Many methods exist for identifying internal validity.

One of the simplest methods of determining validity is called *face validity*. When researchers check for face validity, they examine a research measure to determine whether it appears to assess, in an obvious way, what it should measure. This form of validity relies on researchers' judgments and generally is nonscientific. This does not mean, however, that face validity is unimportant. For years, market researchers measured brand awareness, for example, when they ultimately wanted to evaluate the effect of an advertising campaign on consumer purchase behavior. It seems obvious that an increased awareness of a brand name should indicate that an advertising campaign has had some effect. Measuring top-of-the-mind awareness and using it as an indicator of consumer behavior, however, raises issues regarding the face validity of the measures.

Content validity refers to the comprehensive nature of research measures. A set of questions high in content validity most fully represents the idea it is supposed to measure. When examining consumers' media-use habits, for example, a questionnaire that asks only about newspaper reading and television viewing lacks content validity. In this case, consumers use a variety of media that are not even part of the questionnaire. A lack of content validity makes a project seriously flawed by compromising its relevance.

A final type of validity, *predictive* or *criterion validity*, concerns the soundness of a research measure when tested against an external standard. In applied research, predictive validity most commonly concerns the ability of a research measure to predict actual performance. Predictive validity is critical when organizations use research to understand and predict the behavior of targeted audiences based on research results. When a driving test has predictive validity, for example, it should be able to predict driving performance. People who perform well on a driving test should actually be able to drive a car safely. If they drive poorly despite performing well on the test, the test may lack predictive, or criterion, validity. In public relations campaigns, awareness and knowledge often are measured with the assumption that they lead to behavior. These measures often lack predictive validity, however, making the research findings an incomplete or incorrect basis from which to develop campaign strategy and predict campaign outcomes.

STEPS TO RESEARCH PROJECT DESIGN

Once managers consider accuracy, precision, reliability, and validity as they relate to the research project at hand, they can turn to the actual design of the project. Despite the uniqueness of every research project, it helps to follow a series of steps in a more-or-less sequential order to guide the design and implementation of a project. The research plan discussed in chap. 4 largely corresponds to the steps followed to implement the project itself. The research-design process briefly discussed here contributes to a logical, orderly decision-making process that maximizes the benefits of a study and the information outcomes it provides. It also minimizes study costs and the risks associated with poor quality data.

1. *Identify or clearly define the research problem.* When research projects lack a well-defined purpose, they produce results that, though interesting, have little usefulness. Clients often ap-

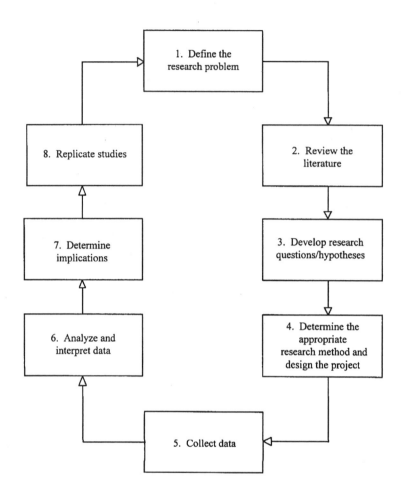

FIG. 5.3. The research process.

proach research firms with a relatively vague understanding of what they need to learn. Their expectation is that the focus of the project will emerge and they will know what they want when they see it. Even exploratory research projects should have clear direction.

2. *Review the literature.* This refers to checking existing sources of knowledge for useful information. At one time, it was difficult to get accurate, reliable market research. As organizations have increased in sophistication, their reliance on research has grown and the supply of existing research available to any organization has

greatly increased. Various syndicated market research, databases, and similar forms of archival research resources can prove useful in developing a project. These resources can help define targeted audiences; provide insight into audience opinions, attitudes, and behavior; answer secondary questions related to the research project; and identify trends that may affect the project.

3. *Develop research questions or hypotheses.* After examining existing sources of research information, managers can develop hypotheses or research questions. In academic research, hypotheses (and research questions to a lesser extent) typically drive the research process and provide expectations about variable relationships and other important research findings. In applied research settings, researchers commonly use research questions instead of hypotheses. Both hypotheses and research questions can be used in applied research settings, however, to help determine the project purpose and to help inform the research-design process. Essentially, hypotheses and research questions concerning key variables help researchers understand their study and the outcomes it is supposed to produce. In this way, they become part of the problem-identification process and give researchers specific outcomes to look for as they engage in a research project.

4. *Determine the appropriate research method and design the project.* Several methods exist for collecting information, and in this book we address the most common methods. Whether practitioners do a research project on their own, or, more likely, deal with an in-house research department or outside research firm, they must understand the strengths and weaknesses of different research methods to make informed decisions and get useful and affordable information. Practitioners who stick to research methods because of familiarity, or who blindly follow the advice of others without understanding the strengths and limitations of different research methods, risk disappointment and can get stuck with inaccurate or useless study outcomes.

5. *Collect data.* Implementation of the study follows research-method selection and study design. Informal research designs require less specific procedures than formal research methods.

6. *Analyze and interpret data.* Analysis and interpretation vary depending on the research method used and the nature of the data. Qualitative data, such as comments provided by focus groups, require broad, more subjective interpretation. Quantitative data, such as answers to surveys, require statistical analysis and more objective interpretation. Meaningful data analysis and interpretation are

the natural outcomes of a well-designed, properly conducted research project.

7. *Determine implications.* Managers should not conduct a meaningful research project and simply set the results on the shelf. Instead, they should examine the results for their practical implications. What do these results suggest in terms of strategy or tactics? How should an issue be positioned in the mind of a critical audience? What public affairs programs are likely to have the greatest audience impact according to study results? What media do these audiences regularly consume and whom in the media do they trust? How do these results help improve understanding or, more important, motivate behavioral change? It is a waste of time and money to conduct a study and simply put the results on a shelf and leave them there.

8. *Replicate studies.* It can take some time for resistant clients to believe the results of research when the results provide bad or surprising news. This makes it critical for managers to make studies replicable, meaning reproducable, so that important findings do not get dismissed.

FINAL THOUGHTS

Public relations programs increasingly rely on research-based planning and evaluation. The benefits of research—to illuminate the perceptions, interests, and opinions of targeted audiences; to produce evidence used to select from among competing solutions; and to provide a benchmark from which to evaluate campaign success—often far outweigh the costs of research. Some managers have the luxury of hiring out research projects to specialists, while others need to implement research projects on their own. Either way, a personal investment in learning about these sometimes-complex topics can lead to increased credibility and autonomy for the communication manager. The following chapters provide a basic grounding in the most important aspects of research.

Making Research Decisions: Informal Research Methods

In a sense, research simply is listening and fact finding, and practitioners most commonly rely on informal methods when engaged in simple fact finding (Cutlip et al., 2000). Such research often is critical to organizations as they monitor their internal and external environments, track public opinion concerning emerging issues, and address potential areas of conflict with target audience members before they become a problem. Informal research methods often provide organizations with quick, inexpensive, and useful ways to listen to critical publics. These include employees, community members, consumer groups, and government regulators. Despite these potential benefits, practitioners take a sizable risk when they use informal research methods as the sole basis for public relations planning and problem solving. Because these methods lack the rigors of scientific research, they have a much greater likelihood of producing inaccurate results.

Recall from chap. 5 that one of the reasons researchers consider a method casual or informal is that it lacks a systematic process. In sci-

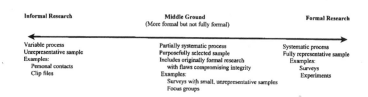

FIG. 6.1. The range of research methods. Research methods fall along a continuum ranging from casual and informal to systematic and formal.

entific research, a formal process ensures that every participant is treated in the same way. In a survey this means, for example, asking participants the same questions in the same order and giving them the same response options except when open-ended questions are being asked. Informal research methods typically do not try to use the same question wording to collect information from every person. This moves the research to the informal side of the continuum shown in Fig. 6.1, but the depth and flexibility gained sometimes can provide advantages over formal fact finding. Sometimes researchers do not, or cannot, use formal research methods. In these cases, the research methods used automatically fall into the informal research category.

The second characteristic that distinguishes informal from formal research has to do with the samples used. As previously noted, researchers rarely conduct a census because of cost and time factors. Instead, they commonly draw a sample from the population and study sample members with the expectation that the responses of the sample accurately represent the opinions, attitudes, and behaviors of all members of that population. When researchers conduct formal research, sample responses generally are representative of the population from which they were drawn, and research staff can calculate the percentage of error that exists in sample responses. When researchers conduct informal research, however, the sample may not represent the population from which it was drawn. In this case, the sample may be too small or may not reflect the views of everyone in the population, and researchers cannot make meaningful error calculations. When a company analyzes the mail it receives from its consumers, for example, the opinions expressed in this small group of letters are not likely to accurately represent the range of opinions among all members of its targeted audience. This does not mean that informal research methods such as a mail analysis are not useful. It is important, however, to understand the limitations of the information collected. Informal research methods generally are useful for exploring problems and for pretesting ideas and strategies. It is not advisable, however, to use them as the sole basis for program planning and evaluation. With this in mind, this chapter will briefly present some of the casual methods most commonly used by public relations practitioners as they engage in the research and planning process.

PERSONAL CONTACTS

The most obvious and common form of casual research involves talking to people. Practitioners can learn a surprising amount simply by asking people—ideally those who are members of a target audience or other important group—for their opinions and ideas. When political candidates or elected officials want to know what voters care about, for example, they may simply get out of their offices and ask people. Personal contacts also might include personal experience in some cases. When practitioners experience the problems and benefits associated with a situation on a first-hand basis, it gives them valuable insights that cannot be gained by sitting in an office reading a report. Practitioners may find personal contacts especially useful when combined with scientific research methods. Contacts may help practitioners gain insight before a formal survey is conducted, for example, or help them understand survey findings that are surprising or counterintuitive. Although talking with people has serious limitations—a few people cannot represent the range of opinions and behaviors that exist in large targeted audiences—practitioners often gain valuable insights and ideas from their personal contacts.

PROFESSIONAL CONTACTS, EXPERTS, AND OPINION LEADERS

Practitioners keep in regular contact with their public relations peers, friends in related fields, superiors, and others who typically possess a wealth of useful experience and knowledge. These contacts may be especially valuable, for example, for practitioners planning or implementing a new program for an organization. If an organization interested in holding a special event never has conducted one, it makes sense to talk to contacts who specialize in events planning and promotion to take advantage of their knowledge and experience. Veteran practitioners are likely to have a wealth of practical advice and their own set of contacts that can benefit the novice. In some cases, it may be advisable to hire consultants or firms who specialize in certain areas of public relations, either for a single project or on a continuing basis.

Public relations professionals also may benefit from talking to key informants or groups, those who are experts in their fields or recognized opinion leaders. This group may include, for example, members of state or local government, editors and reporters, special-interest group leaders, teachers and educational leaders, or union leaders or trade association managers. Normally the procedures used to collect information take the form of an open-ended interview. Practitioners use the discussion to glean information and insights from a select group that is uniquely informed about a topic. The fact that these leaders are experts and opinion leaders, however, raises an important point to consider when using this type of research. These people, because of their position and knowledge, do not reflect the majority of citizens likely to make up a targeted public. In this case, experts' opinions and insights are not necessarily reflective of the broader audiences practitioners normally try to reach.

In addition, their opinions may be shaped by the organizations for which they work. In fact, some organizations such as unions, trade associations, and activist groups typically conduct research that they make available for little or no cost. In many instances, such research provides valuable information and insights to practitioners and their organizations. In other cases, however, organizations may conduct research, not to impartially learn the attitudes and opinions of the public, but to gather support for existing organizational positions and official viewpoints. It is easy to create a research project that looks formal and scientific, but contains untrustworthy results because leading questions or a purposefully selected sample were used. When you use research that has been gathered by a different organization, it is important to learn as much as possible about the research method, including sample-selection procedures and the actual questionnaire or other research instruments used to collect data. This will ensure that you are aware of the potential limitations of the information you are using. Even with its limitations, such information may provide you with unique insights only possible through meeting with experts or opinion leaders, or by examining the information they have at their disposal.

ADVISORY COMMITTEES OR BOARDS

Advisory boards, standing committees, specially appointed panels, and similar bodies provide organizations with specific direction, help them plan and evaluate their programs and events, and help them identify and respond to feedback from the publics they serve. The nature and qualities of such groups differ widely according to their purposes. Public relations professionals may serve on the advisory board of a local nonprofit organization, for example, to help plan and direct its media relations and special events projects. Many local governmental bodies are advised by citizens committees as they address community issues such as urban planning, public transportation, or local safety issues. Other advisory groups may consist of employees, consumers, or students. In fact, any group an organization is serving or anyone who may benefit an organization through expertise or ability generally is qualified to serve in an advisory capacity.

Through their knowledge, experience, and insight, those who serve in an advisory capacity provide organizations with information critical for their successful operation. It is important for organizations to listen to advisory panel members and, when appropriate, work to incorporate their advice into their plans and actions. Members of advisory groups are quick to recognize when they are being used for appearances and their advice has no effect on organizational behavior because it is not given earnest consideration. In these cases, group members are likely to become a source of derision and potential conflict rather than a useful source of information and advice. In addition, the blind usage of advice and information from an advisory group has liabilities. The accuracy and validity of the advice received from such groups provides a limited reference for public opinion and, therefore, cannot represent the range of attitudes and opinions held by all members of a target audience. With this in mind, information gleaned from such groups should be used only as counsel and should not serve as a substitute for scientific approaches to determining the opinions, attitudes, and behaviors of target audience members.

FIELD REPORTS

Many organizations have field representatives including, for example, district agents, regional directors, or sales and service people. These people may have more direct contact with important target audience members than anyone else in an organization as they work their way through a district. The activity reports routinely filed by some field representatives may be a useful source of information to an organization, especially if it contains appropriate questions and has room for additional feedback. Perhaps more important, these people should be encouraged to ask questions, follow up on complaints, and undertake other activities that help them to informally monitor and evaluate an organization and its standing among target audience members.

An organization's desire to learn the truth is one of the most critical aspects of any research, especially with this form of investigation. Field reports—in fact, any formal or informal research method—will not be useful to an organization seeking to justify its actions rather than to learn the truth. The information provided by those in the field only is useful when organizations are willing to hear the truth from their representatives. Having said this, keep in mind that the information provided by field representatives has limitations. These people do not talk to a random sample of targeted audience members and so their observations and suggestions are based on selective information. Input from the field, therefore, should be given appropriate weight, and formal research methods should be used to confirm or disconfirm this information when appropriate.

COMMUNITY FORUMS/GROUP MEETINGS

Public relations practitioners may attend community forums or other formal or informal group meetings to better understand issues of concern to community citizens and to get a sense of community members who are vocal, active, and involved in an issue or topic of importance to an organization (Wilson, 1997). Organizational presence at such meetings should not be concealed, but in most cases also should not be vocal. Organizational members who attend meetings to learn the views of others run the risk of gaining a wrong sense of opinion if they involve themselves in the process because they may temporarily influence or alienate those who might otherwise share their opinions. Instead, those who attend these meetings should report useful information back to an organization so the need for additional, perhaps formal, research can be considered, and a planned and strategic response can be developed to emerging issues or other situations. When conducted properly, this type of informal research helps an organization monitor its internal or external environments, keep abreast of issues and opinions as they develop, and position itself as both positive and negative future developments occur.

TELEPHONE CALLS, MAIL, AND ELECTRONIC MAIL

It is in organizations' best interest to listen carefully when individuals, whether local community members, consumers, members of activists groups, or others, go out of their way to communicate with them. Many people who have questions, concerns, or other grievances never make the effort to communicate with an organization. They may simply sever their ties with the organization, or, depending on their options, complain to their friends and colleagues as they maintain a frustrated relationship with an organization they increasingly dislike. In an era of greater consumer sophistication and public activism, groups are increasingly likely to express their anger in ways that attract public and media attention. Depending on the situation and organizations involved, such expressions may include, for example, public protests, meetings with legislators or government regulators, demonstrations at shareholders' meetings, letter writing campaigns, or other efforts designed to pressure an organization to respond to issues and change its behavior.

Organizations can track phone calls, mail, and e-mail to learn about issues, gauge the level of individual concern, and help determine how to avoid these situations. Toll-free telephone numbers, in particular, are a relatively quick source of information for organizations and can be used to help track the concerns and issues expressed by important publics. Proctor & Gamble, for example, was the target of vicious rumors that it was a proponent of Satanism. At the height of the crisis, the company handled more than 39,000 calls during a 3-month period (Cato, 1982). The calls not only were a valuable source of information for Proctor & Gamble, they gave the company the opportunity to respond individually to consumers' concerns. Similarly, the American Red Cross analyzed more than 1,700 telephone calls in response to concerns about AIDS and the existence of the virus that causes AIDS in the blood supply provided through the Red Cross. Not only were individual questions answered, but the Red Cross determined the informational needs of targeted publics by analyzing a brief form that was completed for each call. This simple analysis provided the organization with invaluable information, even helping it determine specific words to avoid when addressing questions concerning the transmission and prevention of the disease (Davids, 1987).

Organizations routinely use toll-free phone numbers to establish, maintain, and strengthen relationships with consumers. Butterball Turkey, for example, established a Turkey Talk Line in 1982 to answer consumers' questions about all aspects of turkey preparation, ranging from thawing to cooking to carving. Staffed by professionally trained home economists and nutritionists, the line runs 24 hours a day in November and December, and receives 8,000 calls on Thanksgiving Day alone. Butterball also established a web site in conjunction with the Talk Line that received more than 4.4 million hits in 1996 (Harris, 1998). The Talk Line and web site serve as an important reminder to consumers about Butterball's expertise in turkey preparation and provide the company with important information about consumers' questions and interests.

The mail received by an organization, including e-mail for many companies, can be tracked in a manner similar to telephone calls and is a potential source of important information. Once again, tracking mail may be a way for organizations to discover issues of consequence to important audiences and to help them assess the need for formal organizational action concerning an issue or event. Most of the time, those who write or call an organization have problems or complaints. As with many informal methods of research, the sample is not representative of the range of opinions and attitudes that exist among all members of a target public because it is self-selected. At the same time, however, organizations that dismiss negative comments, questions, and criticism as the off-base complaints of a few disgruntled people likely make a serious error in judgment. It is best to take all potential issues seriously, recognizing that the few who speak may represent the opinions and attitudes of a much larger but silent group. In some cases, early warning signs produced through this type of informal research indicate a clear need for formal research to further investigate an issue.

LIBRARY AND INTERNET RESEARCH

Accessing information over the Internet or at the library may constitute formal or informal research depending on the kind of information being sought and, when applicable, the methods used to generate a sample and collect data. Neither the library nor the Internet is a research method, but each provides access to resources that practitioners are likely to find valuable. In fact, Marlow (1996) noted the Internet is transforming the role of the media and libraries because these organizations have large collections of content—or databases—continually open to access from almost anywhere in the world. The resources available over the Internet now include organizational sales, service, and promotional material; informal chat rooms and bulletin boards; media and library systems; and other highly useful databases. In addition to books and other publications, many libraries contain comprehensive media collections that include, for example, years of national, state, and local newspapers and magazines. University libraries also are likely to contain Census Bureau data, an overwhelming array of government documents, and the results of privately and publicly funded studies.

In many cases, practitioners use this information for what is called secondary data analysis, which is the use of data collected by a previous researcher or another research organization for a purpose other than was originally intended (Wimmer & Dominick, 2000). When practitioners use Census Bureau research to learn the demographic characteristics of residents in a specific region, for example, they are engaging in secondary research. In other cases, the reference materials, special collections, online databases, and even some forms of original research conducted over the Internet may be of value to practitioners.

The Internet, which began as a computer network to share information among multiple locations in the 1960s, has proven itself as an irreplaceable tool in the collection and distribution of public relations information. The Internet has become an almost instantaneous source of information for its users, and it allows organizations to communicate directly to potentially interested individuals with no media gatekeeper and few conventional geographic, political, or legal boundaries. As an informal research tool, the Internet allows organizations to conduct competitor research. Organizations increasingly place key documents online to promote themselves, build customer relationships, and sell products and services. Every business with a web site is a potential publisher and may provide a range of promotional literature, product and service manuals, annual reports, position papers, speech texts, and other documents. Communication professionals can easily access these documents to learn about their competition and other organizations (Marlow, 1996).

Organizations also may actively solicit information over the Internet by posting questionnaires or by using bulletin board systems and chat groups that allow people to "talk" online. In fact, this form of communication potentially broadens the range of those who may be contacted for advice or other important information by practitioners. Keep in mind, however, not everyone engaged in online communication is listening or participating in an attempt to be helpful to an organization. In the same way, the advice or other information received from a bulletin board may be from an experienced professional or from a college freshman (Wilson, 1997). In addition, the opinions expressed in a self-selected, or volunteer, sample do not represent all of the opinions and attitudes among members of a target audience. These limitations aside, online communication vehicles provide potentially important sources of communication to practitioners.

More than 5,000 online databases available to practitioners provide access to a previously unimagined amount of information ranging, as one text puts it, from anatomy to zoology, and in business, from advertising to wholesaling (Blankenship, Breen, & Dutka, 1998). Various directories help practitioners find online database resources, including the *Directory of On-Line Information Resources* published by CSG Press in Rockville, Maryland, and *Database Catalog* published by Dialog in Palo Alto, California. One of the most important and quickly growing uses of the Internet for public relations practitioners is to engage in issue tracking and other forms of information retrieval using online subscription databases such as Nexis, Dun and Bradstreet, Dow Jones News/Retrieval, Data Times, and Burrelle's Broadcast Database. Practitioners access these databases to seek information in news and business publications, financial reports, consumer and market research, government records, broadcast transcripts and other useful resources. Online database searches typically provide comprehensive results with speed and accuracy. Although such services can be costly, their use often is relatively cost-effective given the benefits of the information they provide. In addition, the results of research conducted by governments, foundations, and educational organizations may be available online at little or no cost. Such research may provide important information about trends and major developments in fields as diverse as agriculture, education, and labor. In each of these cases, online technology has made it possible for practitioners to cost effectively gather a wealth of information with amazing speed.

Libraries also contain a wealth of information that practitioners are likely to find useful. Almost any public library contains resources of use to practitioners, including Internet access. University libraries, and some state libraries if there is a state capital nearby, contain an almost overwhelming amount of material practitioners will find useful including reference material, special collections, archives, government documents, and similar resources. In fact, large universities typically have one primary library and several smaller, specialty libraries such as a business library or science library. In addition, many metropolitan areas contain special libraries or collections that are privately maintained by a business or association. These libraries contain a depth of material unavailable from other sources on specific topics such as advertising or broadcast history, some of which may be accessible online.

Practitioners looking for specific information or resources but not sure where to begin may find it useful to start with a reference librarian. These experts can locate a surprising number of directories, statistical facts and figures, studies, and other information. If you are looking for specific information, the chances are excellent there is a directory, abstract, book, or other resource that a reference librarian can locate, often in a short amount of time. Although the list of available reference materials would fill volumes, basic indexes include the *Reader's Guide to Periodical Literature*, which contains a listing of articles in 200 major magazines and journals categorized by topic; the *Business Periodicals Index*, which indexes articles in 400 business publications, and the *New York Times Index*, which provides abstracts of news stories chronologically by subject.

Other useful resources vary based on need, but may include the *Statistical Abstract of the United States*, which contains more than 1,000 pages of tables and data about aspects of the United States and provides an overview of the range of additional information that is available; *The Corporate Directory*, which provides information on more than 10,000 firms in the United States including names of their officers, directors and subsidiary firms; *The National Directory of State Agencies*, which, for each state, indicates state agencies by function and provides an alphabetical telephone listing for more than 23,000 state representatives, state government officials, and staff members; the *Thomas Register of American Manufacturers*, which provides information on more than 100,000 product manufacturers including product classifications by city within state; and Simmon's Market Research Bureau data, a series of syndicated market research publications that provide invaluable information including consumers' product and service usage, media consumption, and related information. It is beyond the scope of this text to list and explain the wealth of reference material available at many university libraries; however, this brief discussion should provide some idea of the potential resources available.

One additional library resource that merits special attention because of its potential benefit to public relations practitioners and ease of access is the Census Bureau data contained at many university libraries. The work of the Census Bureau results in one of the most abundant and beneficial set of data available to practitioners, and it is free. The Census Bureau uses different length forms when it conducts the census. Most citizens respond to a basic, short questionnaire that provides a small amount of information. A sizeable portion of citizens, however, fill out in-depth questionnaires that provide additional information of benefit to practitioners. The results indicate where people live and provide additional information, including demographic characteristics such as age, sex, ethnicity, size and disposition of their living unit, type of dwelling, and rental or value of their dwelling unit. This information is available to any individual or organization.

Campbell's Soup, for example, uses Census Bureau data to guide its development of products and refine its marketing strategies for existing products. In one case, marketers for the company surmised that Americans' eating patterns were changing and that breakfast was no longer a traditional group meal. The conclusion was based on data indicating that the number of two-income families was increasing, even though the number of members in a household were declining. The company launched Great Starts, a line of single-serving frozen breakfasts, following additional research to confirm their assumptions. The product line quickly gained a sizable share of a rapidly expanding market. In another instance, the company used Census Bureau data indicating that the population was aging, along with other market research concerning the health interests of older people, to estimate the demand for reduced-salt soups. The result was Special Request, a line of healthier soup products. In each of these cases, Census Bureau data were used in conjunction with other market research to inform the company in its attempt to meet consumer needs and increase company success (Blankenship, Breen, & Dutka, 1998).

Census Bureau research results and a vast array of reference works are just some of the many library materials available. Other useful resources include trade and professional publications, media archives, and other materials. Practitioners generally make the best use of these materials if they have as much information as possible when they begin an information search. When practitioners are seeking specific information, they are likely to find an existing resource that contains the desired information, and both the library and online resources are excellent places to start the research process.

CLIP FILES AND MEDIA TRACKING

Clip files are used by organizations to follow and understand media coverage, to help evaluate public relations campaign outcomes and to get a sense of public opinion based on reporters' stories. In fact, it is safe to say that any organization that is in the news on a regular basis has some way to track media coverage, the results of which typically are organized into some sort of useful file system and analyzed. Although clip files do not serve all purposes well— as the Institute for Public Relations has noted, they measure "outputs" rather than "outcomes" such as gauging public opinion (Lindenmann, 1997)—they allow organizations to track and analyze media coverage. When greater accuracy, precision, and reliability are desirable, a formal content analysis (discussed in chap. 8) should be conducted. Most organizational clip files and other forms of media tracking fall far short of the demands of a formal content analysis, but still serve useful purposes.

Clip Files

A clip file is a collection of media stories that specifically mention an organization, its competition, or other key words, and issues an organization wants to learn about. In terms of print media, for example, a clipping service is likely to clip from virtually all daily and weekly newspapers in any geographic region, including international regions. Other print media that may be covered include business and trade publications and consumer magazines. Once stories are located by a service, they are clipped and tagged with appropriate information typically including the name of the publication, its circulation, and the date and page number of the story. Clients or their agencies then can organize and analyze the clips in whatever format is most beneficial. Services are available to monitor all types of media outlets. Companies such as Burrelle's Press Clipping Service, Bacon's PR and Media Information Systems, Luce Press Clippings, or the Delahaye Group, for example, offer comprehensive services for national and international media. Specialized services can be hired as well, such as same-day clipping to help organizations monitor breaking news or crises, or broadcast monitoring to track video news release use.

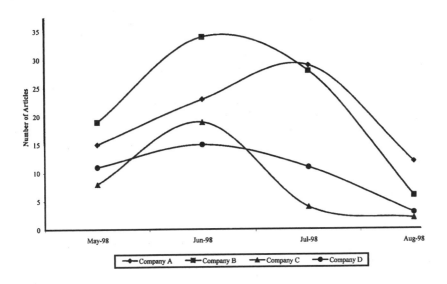

FIG. 6.2. Number of clippings organized by company and publication date. Clipping frequency is one way for organizations to compare their media coverage with competitors' media coverage. Courtesy of KVO Public Relations, Portland, Oregon.

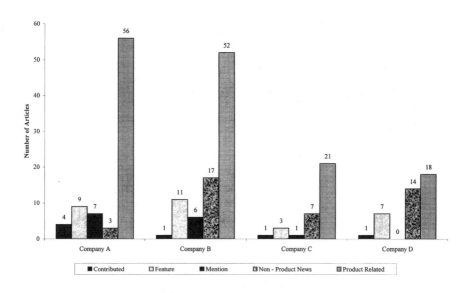

FIG. 6.3. Clippings organized by company and article type. Analysis of content in media coverage can provide organizations with information about types of stories that have attracted media attention. Courtesy of KVO Public Relations, Portland, Oregon.

Although there are differences among each of the services in terms of how they operate, a client generally provides a list of key words, terms, and topics that it wants its service to locate in specific media. The words and terms provided by an organization vary considerably but typically include its own name and the names of its products and services. Other information that may be tracked includes the names of competitors and their products and services, the names of senior management, or other important topics or individuals an organization wants to track. The client also may send its service information about its print or video news releases, public service announcement copy, or other collateral material it expects will generate news coverage.

Practitioners can analyze clip file contents using various techniques. In many cases, practitioners simply count the number of media clips a campaign produces and use their own judgment concerning the purpose of their campaign and the media's treatment of a topic. Such an analysis may be useful for informal campaign reviews and exploratory decision making, but it lacks the quantitative specificity and accuracy necessary to truly determine a campaign's effect on targeted audiences' opinions, attitudes, and behavior.

Advertising Equivalency

In an attempt to quantify the value of media placement, many practitioners compare the results of their publicity efforts with equivalent advertising costs. It is relatively common, for example, to compare the column space and broadcast time generated by a campaign with the "equivalent" cost for advertising placement had the space been purchased. This method of clip evaluation allows practitioners to claim a dollar amount for the media coverage their campaign generates. In some cases, the value of publicity placements are increased or, more commonly, decreased using an agreed-upon formula. This is done because publicity placements are thought to lack some of the benefits of advertising: in particular, a specific message delivered to a specific audience and timed according to planned schedule. The result is that editorial placements typically are given less value than advertising placements because their contents and placement cannot be controlled.

This issue raises a point of contention concerning the benefits of advertising versus the benefits of publicity, and it reveals some of the serious problems associated with claiming dollar amounts for publicity media placements. In reality, it is nearly impossible to compare advertising and publicity placements in terms of their relative value. How do you compare, for example, the value of a full-page print ad that appears in the middle of a publication with a front-page publicity placement? In terms of different publicity placements, how do you determine the value of a story on the front page with a story placed in the middle of a section? Or, how do you compare the value of clips in different media—a narrowly targeted publication that reaches an identified target audience, for example—with general media placement that reaches the public broadly? Also, how do you compare the value of different editorial contexts: a story that is positive, for example, versus a story that is negative or mixed? Each of these issues, and more, presents practitioners with difficult obstacles when determining the relative value of advertising versus publicity, and when determining the value of different publicity clips.

Cost Per Thousand

Another commonly used method of determining publicity-clip value is based on the cost of reaching audience members. Advertisers, for example, commonly determine the most beneficial combination of media, programs, and schedules by evaluating and comparing the costs of different media and different media vehicles, as well as by considering the percentage of an audience that is part of a specific target audience for a campaign. One of the simplest means of comparing media costs is to compare the *cost per thousand* or CPM (M is the Roman numeral for 1,000) of different media. This figure tells media planners the cost of reaching 1,000 people in an audience. If a daily newspaper has 500,000 subscribers and charges $7,000 for running a full-page ad, for example, the cost per thousand is $14 (7,000 ÷ 500,000 × 1,000).

Cost Efficiency

To determine the relative *cost efficiency* of different media, media planners use the same general formula, but reduce the total audience figures to include only those audience members that specifically are targeted as part of a campaign. Using the previous example, if the campaign primarily is directed at males 18 to 34 years old, and 30% of the newspaper's audience fits into that category, the circulation figure can be reduced to 30% of the total audience, or 150,000. The resulting cost efficiency figure is approximately $47 (7,000 ÷ 150,000 × 1,000).

Cost Per Impression

These same formulas can be used in public relations to measure the relative value of publicity clips. The results of publicity clips in public relations are sometimes referred to as *publicity impressions*, so the *cost per impression* (CPI) of publicity clips can be calculated after a campaign has been conducted and compared with advertising campaign costs or other public relations campaign costs. In the same way, cost-efficiency measures of publicity impressions can be calculated. CPM-type measures are difficult to use to compare the value of advertising versus publicity clips, primarily because CPM calculations are performed in the early stages of an advertising campaign and used for planning and forecasting, whereas a campaign must be over before publicity impression costs can be calculated because clips depend on media placement.

More important, neither CPM nor CPI calculations measure message impact; they only measure message exposure. In fact, they are not even a true measure of message exposure, but instead are a measure of the greatest potential message exposure. The exposure numbers they produce are useful in a relative sense, but are "soft" and likely to overestimate audience size.

Limitations of Clip and Tracking Research

Although any of these methods can be used to quantitatively evaluate publicity-clip placements, they are relatively unsophisticated and should not be used as the basis for determining message impact or campaign success. In most cases, formal research methods are necessary to evaluate a range of campaign outcomes from changes in the opinions and attitudes of target audience members to changes in individual behavior. This is not meant to suggest, however, that the use of clip files is not beneficial as a form of casual research.

In fact, there are various potential improvements on the standard clip file and several valuable ways such information can be used. McElreath (1997) described two uses of media tracking and the ways it can benefit an organization. In the first example, Porter Novelli (then known as Doremus Porter Novelli) conducted a substantial issue-tracking project for a pharmaceutical trade association in support of a national public education and lobbying campaign. The project was conducted by the agency as part of what it called its background review service. After meeting with the client to determine and refine the list of topics and issues, the agency conducted computerized database searches to find past media coverage of the issues and topics in newspapers, trade publications, consumer magazines, and wire services; relevant opinion polls and market surveys; and other information including key demographic and economic trends. This information was used to develop a national campaign that included important information on drug liability intended to inform and persuade lobbyists and state legislators about the need for legal reform.

In a second example cited by McElreath (1997), a federal health organization wanted to determine why the airings of its public service announcements (PSAs) concerning the control of high blood pressure were decreasing in some markets. An agency was hired to help solve the problem. As part of its work, the agency brought in a company that specialized in monitoring broadcast media specifically to track electronic media placements. Because the campaign relied on free media placement by editors, reporters, and producers, the agency conducted what it called a gatekeeper audit. Using distribution lists and the results from the broadcast monitoring service, agency executives determined which stations were using the PSAs and their frequency of use. Next, telephone interviews were conducted with representatives from the high-play and low-play stations. Several PSA distribution, scheduling, and formatting changes were made based on the results of the research project. The broadcast monitoring service was used to track use of the improved PSAs. The new results indicated PSA usage greatly increased among all stations, including the previous low-play stations. In both examples, media tracking provided highly beneficial information used to address specific goals and increase the chances for campaign success.

It is important to reiterate a key point in the use and interpretation of media tracking and clip files at this point. As a rule, this research reveals only the media's use of messages. Of course, it provides information concerning a targeted audience's potential exposure to messages, but clip files and tracking studies reveal nothing about message impact. Sometimes the results of media placements are obvious and no additional research is necessary. In fact, in many cases no formal campaign evaluation is conducted because an organization or client believes it easily can identify the impact of a particular campaign. At other times, however, it is desirable to learn more about a message's impact on an audience's level of knowledge, opinions, attitudes, or less obvious behavioral outcomes. When this is the case, clip files and analyses of media-message placements tell practitioners nothing about these outcomes. In addition, public relations campaigns that claim success based on media placement as revealed by clipping services and tracking studies may be overstating the impact of their campaigns. Although clipping services and media tracking may be valuable and important, it is unwise to attempt to determine public opinion and similar information based on media-message placement.

IN-DEPTH INTERVIEWS

In-depth interviewing, sometimes called intensive interviewing or simply depth interviewing, is an open-ended interview technique in which respondents are encouraged to discuss an issue or problem, or answer a question, at length and in great detail. This research method is based on the belief that individuals are in the best position to observe and understand their own attitudes and behavior (Broom & Dozier, 1990). This interview process provides a wealth of detailed information and is particularly useful for exploring attitudes and behaviors in an engaged and extended format.

Initially, an interview participant is given a question or asked to discuss a problem or topic. The remainder of the interview generally is dictated by the participant's responses or statements. Participants typically are free to explore the issue or question in any manner they desire, though an interviewer may have additional questions or topics to address as the interview progresses. Normally, the entire process allows an unstructured interview to unfold in which participants explore and elaborate about their attitudes and opinions, motivations, values, experiences, feelings, emotions, and related information. The researcher encourages this probing-interview process through active listening techniques, providing feedback as necessary or desired, and occasionally questioning participants regarding their responses to encourage deeper exploration. As rapport is established between an interviewer and a participant, the interview may produce deeper, more meaningful findings, even on topics that may be considered too sensitive to address through other research methods.

Most intensive interviews are customized for each participant. Although the level of structure varies based on the purpose of the project and, sometimes, the ability of a participant to direct the interview, it is critical that researchers not influence participants' thought processes. Interviewees must explore and elaborate on their thoughts and feelings as they naturally occur, rather than attempting to condition their responses to what they perceive the researcher wants to learn. As Broom and Dozier (1990) noted, the strength of this research technique is that participants, not the researcher, drive the interview process. When participants structure the interview, it increases the chances the interview will produce unanticipated responses, reveal latent issues, or other unusual, but potentially useful, information. Once collected, such information typically is confirmed or disconfirmed through the use of a research method possessing greater reliability and validity before it is used as the basis for a public relations campaign or program.

In-depth interviews typically last from about an hour up to several hours. A particularly long interview is likely to fatigue both the interviewer and the interviewee, and it may be necessary to schedule more than one session in some instances. Because of the time required to conduct an in-depth interview, it is particularly difficult to schedule interviews, especially with professionals. In addition, participants typically are paid a good sum for their work. Payments, which range from $50 to $1,000 or more, are normally higher than payments provided to focus group participants (Wimmer & Dominick, 2000).

In-depth interviews offer several benefits as a research method. Perhaps the most important advantages are the wealth of detailed information they typically provide and the occasional surprise discovery of unanticipated but potentially beneficial information. Wimmer and Dominick (2000) suggested that intensive interviews provide more accurate information concerning sensitive issues than traditional survey techniques because of the rapport that develops between an interviewer and an interviewee.

In terms of disadvantages, sampling issues are a particular concern for researchers conducting in-depth interviews. The time and intensity required to conduct an interview commonly results in the use of small, nonprobability-based samples. The result is that it is difficult to generalize the findings of such interviews from a sample to a population with a high degree of confidence. For this reason, potentially important findings discovered in-depth interviews should be confirmed or disconfirmed using a research method and accompanying sample that provide high degrees of validity and reliability. Difficulty scheduling interviews also contributes to study length. Whereas telephone surveys may conclude data collection within a week, in-depth interviews may stretch over several weeks or even months (Wimmer & Dominick, 2000). The usefulness of in-depth interviews is greatly limited by sample-selection issues.

In addition to sample concerns, the unstructured nature of in-depth interviews leads to nonstandard interview procedures and questions. This makes analysis and interpretation of study results challenging, and it raises additional concerns regarding the reliability and validity of study findings. Nonstandard interviews also may add to study length because of problems researchers encounter when attempting to analyze and interpret study results. As a final note, the unstructured interview process and length of time it takes to complete an interview result in a high potential for interviewer bias to corrupt results. As rapport develops between an interviewer and an interviewee and a basic level of comfort is realized, the researcher may inadvertently communicate information that biases participants' responses. Interviewers require a great deal of training to avoid this problem, which also can contribute to study cost and length.

Despite these limitations, in-depth interviews can be successfully used to gather information not readily available using other research methods.

Q METHODOLOGY

Q methodology is a general term used by Stephenson (1953) to describe a research method and related ideas used to understand individuals' attitudes. This method of research combines an intensive, individual method of data collection with quantitative data analysis. Q methodology requires research participants to sort large numbers of opinion statements (called Q-sorting) and to place them in groups along a continuum. The continuum contains anchors such as "most like me" to "most unlike me." Numerical values are then assigned to the statements based on their location within the continuum, and the results are statistically analyzed.

For the most part, Q-sorting is a sophisticated way of rank-ordering statements—although other objects also can be Q-sorted—and assigning numbers to the rankings for statistical analysis (Kerlinger, 1973). In public relations, a Q-sort might work like this: A set of verbal statements concerning the image of an organization is printed on cards and given to research participants. Participants are asked to sort the cards into separate piles based on the extent of their agreement or disagreement with each statement. The result is a rank order of piles of cards placed on a continuum from "most approve" to "least approve," with varying degrees of approval and disapproval between each extreme. Researchers assign the cards in each pile a number based on their location. The cards in the highest, "most approve" category, for example, might be assigned a 10. The cards in the next highest "most approve" category might be assigned a 9, and so on. The cards placed in the lowest, "least approve" category would receive a 0. The resulting Q-sort would contain a rank ordering of statements that reveal the participant's beliefs about the organization.

The number of cards used in a Q distribution ranges from less than 50 to 140. For statistical reliability, a good range for most projects is from 60 to 90 statements (Kerlinger, 1973).

The sorting instructions provide a guide for sorting Q-sample statements or other items and are specified according to the purpose of the research (McKeown & Thomas, 1988). Researchers may ask participants to sort opinion or personality statements on a "most approve" to "least approve" continuum, or to describe the characteristics of an ideal political candidate or organization on a "most important" to "least important" continuum. Q-sort instructions also can concern fictional or hypothetical circumstances.

Finally, participants may sort statements according to their perceptions. In a political study, for example, participants may sort statements using "what you believe is most like a liberal" and "what you believe is most unlike a liberal" for continuum anchors (McKeown &

Thomas, 1988). There are many additional anchors and instructions that can be used in Q-sorts, and the flexibility of the method in this regard provides a wealth of opportunities for researchers.

Sample-selection procedures are a particular challenge in Q-method research. It is difficult to draw a large, representative sample, particularly given the time requirements and intensive nature of the data-collection process (Kerlinger, 1973). The result is that researchers typically draw small, convenience samples (McKeown & Thomas, 1988). The use of small, nonprobability-based samples makes it difficult to generalize study results from a sample to a population with confidence. Although some might suggest the use of nonrandom samples is a limitation of minor consequence, the reality is that both theoretical and descriptive research require testing on samples of sufficient size—ideally drawn using a probability-based procedure—to produce trustworthy results.

Q methodology is potentially useful, but also controversial. The research technique is flexible and may be particularly useful when researchers are exploring the opinions and attitudes of important target audience members. In fact, many participants seem to enjoy participating in Q studies (Kerlinger, 1973). In addition, study results can be statistically analyzed, and Q methodology provides an objective way to identify and intensively study individuals' opinions and attitudes.

Nevertheless, the use of small, convenience samples greatly hinders the external validity of study results. There simply is no way to confidently generalize results from the sample of study participants to the population they supposedly represent. In addition, there may be complex statistical concerns about the assumptions of statistical tests applied to Q-sort results. In particular, Q-sorts may violate a key assumption concerning the independence of participant responses. When this assumption is violated, many forms of statistical analysis are no longer acceptable for use in analyzing study results. These two limitations, in fact, are the primary reasons Q methodology is presented in this text as an informal research method. In addition to these concerns, some critics complain that the sheer magnitude of sorting 60 to 100 statements or more is beyond the ability of most participants and a high number of categories requires participants to make too fine distinctions among items (Kerlinger, 1973). It is clear that, although Q-sorts provide a potentially rich and useful method of exploring the opinions and attitudes of key target audience members in great depth, they have limitations that should be considered carefully when interpreting study results. It is particularly important to consider the use of follow-up research, such as a survey that uses a large, probability-based sample, to understand the results of a Q-sort as they relate to a larger population (Broom & Dozier, 1990).

FINAL THOUGHTS

It is important to keep in mind that informal research methods may suffer from several significant limitations that make them difficult to use with complete confidence. This, in fact, is the reason they are considered informal and casual. This does not mean informal research methods never should be used. Informal research methods generally are the most common research methods used by practitioners. But, practitioners should interpret the results of informal research carefully and understand the limitations of the methods they are using. Considering the advice of selected members of a target audience, for example, makes sense in most situations and such input can be an invaluable help in the research and planning processes. At the same time, however, the prudent practitioner will consider this information for what it is—the opinions of a few people—instead of giving it the full weight of a scientifically conducted, formal opinion poll.

What does this mean for public relations practitioners? When possible, informal research methods should be used to supplement formal research methods rather than to replace them. This provides practitioners with information they can use as primary and secondary planning resources. Unfortunately, many practitioners engage primarily in informal research because of limited budgets, time, and other constraints. In these situations, it is wise to take every precaution in interpreting and using research results correctly. It is better to have no research than to base a campaign on incorrect research results. No research method is infallible, but special care should be used in interpreting research results produced through informal methods.

7

Making Research Decisions: The Focus Group

The focus group long has been a mainstay of public relations and marketing research, but it remains a controversial method for research and message testing. Practitioners often tell horror stories about focus groups that provided misleading information for a campaign that later failed. Nevertheless, the method recently has begun to gain more respect as a valid research tool, rather than a "cheap and dirty" alternative to "real" research.

A recent proliferation of scholarly and how-to books and articles has made it possible for more practitioners to use the tool more effectively and wisely. Although focus groups still have limitations, careful application of the method can provide indispensable guidance available from no other tool. As John Palshaw of Palshaw Measurement Inc., cautioned (1990), focus groups are designed to generate ideas, not evaluate them.

CHARACTERISTICS OF FOCUS GROUPS

A focus group is a semistructured, group interview analyzed using qualitative methods. Focus groups explore the attitudes, opinions, behaviors, beliefs, and recommendations of carefully selected groups. Focused discussions, led by a moderator, usually include 6 to 12 participants and take place over 1 to 3 hours. Sessions attempt to define problems, gather reaction to proposed solutions to problems, and explore feelings and reasons behind differences that exist within the group or between the group and the organization. Organizations typically use focus groups to get feedback during product or service development, to test messages for product or service introductions, to guide decisions about packaging design and promotional messages, to determine appropriate types of outlets and target publics for products or messages, to gauge public reaction to issue positions, and to explore opinions concerning company performance and community citizenship. Message testing explores participants' perceptions of the accuracy, clarity, and relevance of a message, as well as the credibility of the source.

More specialized uses of focus groups also exist. Focus groups can be used to gain a better understanding of groups whose perspectives are poorly understood by an organization. This can help an organization respond more effectively to the group's concerns. Focus groups also can help an organization explore its strengths and weaknesses relative to other organizations. In addition, focus groups can be used for brainstorming purposes, to develop strategies for solving a problem instead of simply testing strategies already under development. Focus groups can help an organization gain insight into complex behaviors and conditional opinions, for which survey questionnaires could provide conflicting or seemingly definite information. As a result, focus groups often are used as a supplement to survey research.

Group dynamics in a focus group can be used to reach consensus on an idea, such as the most credible source for a message or the best location for an event. Finally, focus groups can be used to pretest and refine survey instruments, particularly when likely responses to a question are unknown, such as the biggest barriers to a customer's use of a proposed product or service.

Instead of questionnaires, focus groups use protocols to guide discussion. Protocols range from rough outlines to carefully constructed moderators' guides. Presession questionnaires can be used for screening. In addition, focus groups often use visual aids such as story boards, mockups, or other sample materials for pretesting. Whereas surveys try to take a dispassionate, outsider's perspective to obtain the most objective information about a targeted population from a repre-

TABLE 7.1
Comparative Features of Focus Groups and Surveys

	Survey	Focus Group
Sample size	Large (hundreds)	Small (6–12)
Time required from participants	5–45 minutes	1–3 hours
Data-collection device	Standardized instrument	Rough to formal "protocols" or outlines
Sample characteristics	Heterogeneous (varied)	Homogeneous (similar)
Format of communication	Structured and individualized	Socially oriented
Characteristics of data	Standardized and reliable	Can probe answers in depth; group dynamics can bias responses
Convenience	Can be expensive particularly if timing is tight	Inexpensive and quick to implement
Reach	Requires telephones and people who answer them	Can use variety of techniques to recruit select individuals, can take place virtually anywhere, but individuals often forget to come
Analysis	Can be quick, especially with computer-aided data collection	Initial reactions quick but in-depth analyses time consuming and costly

sentative group, focus groups try to work more from inside the target group, exploring individuals' perspectives in depth to gain a deeper understanding of their decision-making processes. Surveys, in other words, try to avoid bias; focus groups try to explore and understand it.

ADVANTAGES AND DISADVANTAGES OF FOCUS GROUPS

Focus groups should not be viewed as alternatives to survey research, as the two methods have different strengths and weaknesses. The focus group offers characteristics that give it a uniquely useful role in problem definition and message testing. Because focus groups are socially oriented, for example, they make it possible to uncover information about an issue that would not come out in individual interviews or in surveys. People initially may not recall using a product or service but may be reminded of a relevant situation as a result of another participant's observations during the focused discussion. In addition, the focused discussion makes it possible to probe positive or negative responses in depth. Because people can explain what they mean and moderators can probe for clarification, focus groups provide good face validity. In other words, managers can be confident they are interpreting what people said in ways consistent with what they meant. This can be more difficult in a survey, for which individuals must check a box even if the question seems vague or the possible response categories do not reflect their views perfectly.

Focus groups also provide quick, relatively inexpensive results to guide a program that requires fast implementation. Although overnight survey services are available, they can be expensive and make it difficult to develop a tailored survey instrument that maximizes the relevance of findings obtained. Political campaigns, meanwhile, can use focus groups to try out possible responses to a competitor's political advertisement in time to air a response within a day or two.

Another advantage of focus groups is their flexibility. Literacy, for example, is not needed for a focus group whereas it is required for a written questionnaire. People without telephones or with caller ID may never respond to a telephone survey but may participate in a focus group if recruited properly. In addition, focus groups can be held in different locations, even in a park. This makes it easier to recruit from populations that may be unable or unwilling to travel to a research facility.

Focus groups have drawbacks that limit their usefulness and increase the risk of obtaining misleading information that can compromise public relations program effectiveness. For example, although the group dynamics of a focus group make it possible for information to come out that might not be uncovered through individual interviews, group dynamics also make it more difficult to control the direction and tenor of discussions. A carefully trained moderator is essential to draw the full range of opinions out of focus group participants and to prevent individuals from dominating the group. Groups vary depending on the characteristics of the participants, the timing, and the environment, which makes their reliability questionable. They also can be difficult to assemble because individuals from targeted populations may be busy, resistant, or forgetful.

Because of these limitations, focus groups should never be used in confrontational situations, for statistical projections, if the unique dynamics of social interaction are unnecessary for information gathering, if confidentiality cannot be assured, or if procedures such as sampling or questioning are driven by client bias rather than by researcher design.

The usefulness of a focused discussion depends on the willingness of participants to share their perspectives freely and honestly. As a result, focus groups must take place in a comfortable, nonthreatening environment. The composition of an appropriate setting requires attention to the makeup of the group itself, as well as the surroundings in which the discussion takes place. A poorly constructed environment can hamper discussion or make it difficult to ascertain true opinions. A focus group of parents, for example, may mask differences in perspective between mothers and fathers. Misleading information obtained from a restricted discussion can doom a campaign.

SELECTING AND RECRUITING PARTICIPANTS

People tend to feel most comfortable when they are with others like themselves. As a result, focus group participants usually are selected to be "homogeneous," which means similar in certain characteristics. These characteristics depend on the issue explored by the group. For example, a discussion of a college's responsiveness to student financial aid issues could mix male and female students, because they are likely to share similar problems regarding funding their education. On the other hand, a discussion of date rape is less productive if the group includes both men and women. Because women often are the victims of date rape, this may make both the men and the women uncomfortable talking about it in front of each other. As a result, separate focus groups can take place to explore the beliefs and feelings of men and women about date rape. Similarly, a discussion of workplace issues may need to probe the views of managerial personnel and secretarial personnel separately because employees may not feel comfortable speaking freely in front of their supervisors.

The most productive focus groups recruit participants who are similar but who do not already know each other. If they know each other, interpersonal dynamics such as power roles already have been established and can make open discussion and discovery more difficult. This becomes important in focused discussions that must mix participants with different perspectives, such as employees and supervisors, to explore the dynamics between them. This type of situation can work only if the participants feel they can be open with one another and only if the discussion can take place in a constructive, civil way. In other words, if participants need to include employees and supervisors, they should not include employees and their own supervisors.

Focus group participants often are recruited with respect to homogeneity in demographic characteristics such as age, income, educational level, product usage patterns, or group membership. Screening tests ascertain these characteristics to ensure that participants qualify for inclusion in the study. Such tests can be performed via telephone during recruitment or in the outer lobby on arrival. Several separate focus groups may be required to obtain reactions from different target publics.

Because the focus group method is qualitative not quantitative, it is not necessary to hold a certain number of focus groups to ensure a corresponding degree of reliability. Whereas a survey uses probability sampling to provide reliable results within a 95% level of confidence, focus groups are inherently biased by design. As a result, organizations typically rely on a combination of intuition, budgetary restrictions, and time constraints to determine the number of focus groups that will be held. If time and budget allow, focus groups should continue until all vital target publics have been represented or until the information obtained seems redundant; that is, little new information emerges from additional focus groups. In reality, however, organizations rarely have the time or budget to hold more than two to four focus groups.

Cost varies widely for focus groups. Hiring a professional firm to run a focus group can require $3,000 to $5,000, but organizations can run their own focus groups if they prepare carefully. The cost using existing staff and volunteer participants can be as low as the cost of popcorn or pizza and soft drinks. According to Morgan and Krueger (1998), fees for professional moderators range from about $75 to $300 per hour, or $750 to $1,500 and upward on a per diem or per group basis.

Focus group participants usually get paid for their time. The going rate depends on the type of sample recruited. Focus groups of children may provide prizes or free products as compensation. Focus groups of adults usually pay around $35 to $50 apiece. Recruitment of expert participants such as executives, physicians or other professionals may require significantly greater payment, perhaps $300 apiece.

It is necessary to recruit more participants than are actually needed for the group. In fact, researchers usually recruit twice the number needed to allow for no-shows and individuals who for some reason become ineligible. When recruiting from special populations, in particular, unforseen circumstances can prevent attendance. People also tend to forget, so preparation requires a multistep process of recruitment, acknowledgment, and mail and telephone reminders.

When time is tight, recruitment of focus group participants can take place in a shopping mall that has a market-research facility on the premises. Usually, however, focus group recruitment takes place 1 to 2 weeks before the session. Respondents can be recruited using different methods, but often are contacted by telephone. Following the initial contact, recruits should receive a written confirmation of the invitation to participate that also serves as a reminder. Reminder phone calls the day or two before the session also helps to boost attendance. Attendees should provide contact numbers upon recruitment so they can be reached at home or at work.

The location of focus group facilities can help or hurt recruitment. The facility should be easy to find, such as in a shopping mall, relatively close to participants' home or work places, and should have plenty of safe parking available. When recruiting parents, it also may be necessary to provide child care. Proper facilities and staffing must be provided to gain the confidence of parents.

Timing can make a difference for focus group success. Most focus groups take place in the evening and avoid weekends or holidays. Other times, such as the lunch hour, may be appropriate for special cases. If two groups are planned for a single evening, the first typically begins at 6 p.m. and the second at 8:15 p.m.

FOCUS GROUP SETTINGS

Participants tend to speak more freely in an informal setting. Conference rooms are better than classrooms; circular seating is better than lecture-style seating; coffee tables are better than conference tables; comfortable chairs or sofas are better than office or classroom chairs. Some organizations rent hotel suites for focus group discussions, whereas others use rooms specifically built for focus group research. Focus group facilities typically include a two-way mirror, behind which clients can sit to observe the discussion as it unfolds, without disturbing the participants. They also include a buffet table or another area for refreshments, because snacks and beverages tend to promote informality. Snacks need to be simple, however, so that the participants pay more attention to the discussion than to their food. They can range from a complete meal such as sandwiches to a small snack such as popcorn.

To aid analysis and for later review by the client, discussions should be recorded unobtrusively on audiotape or videotape, or on both. Participants should be advised of all data-collection and observation procedures. Taping and observation should never be done in secret or without the participants' consent. They also must be informed if their anonymity may not be assured, such as by their appearance on videotape. Often, for the discussion, participants wear name tags but provide only their first names. Sometimes they go by pseudonyms for additional privacy protection. At no time should participants be identified by name in focus group transcripts or reports.

STAFFING

Focus groups generally require a team effort. Besides staff for the planning and recruitment phases of the focus group, the interview itself usually requires several staff members. Besides the moderator, who leads the discussion, the event requires at least one other staff member to serve as coordinator. The coordinators (or coordinator) welcome and screen participants; handle honoraria; guide them to the refreshments and make sure refreshments are available; check and run equipment; bring extra batteries, duct tape, and other supplies; and interact with the client. In addition, the coordinator or another staff member takes prolific notes during the session. This is necessary because: (a) transcription equipment can and does break down, or someone pushes "play" instead of "record" on the tape recorder; (b) some people may speak too softly for their comments to register on an audiotape; (c) it may be difficult to identify the source of a comment, particularly if several participants speak at once; and (d) the note taker can provide an initial real-time analysis of themes emerging from the discussion. The note taker may develop the final report in collaboration with the moderator.

CHARACTERISTICS OF THE MODERATOR

The focus group moderator is the key to an effective discussion. The moderator must be able to lead discussion, providing both structure and flexibility to keep discussion on track but allowing participants to pursue issues in depth. Because the moderator must be skilled in group dynamics, some people specialize in focus group leadership and can command an expert's salary to do so.

The moderator must display an air of authority while establishing an atmosphere of warmth and trust so that participants feel free to speak their minds. The moderator strives to keep the structure of the questioning strategy from becoming too obvious, because that could detract from the informality that increases the likelihood of open discussion. In addition, the moderator must treat all participants with equal respect, staying neutral while encouraging all points of view. Moderators never offer their own personal opinions. Moderators also avoid using phrases such as "excellent," "great," "wonderful," or "right," which signal approval or a particular point of view. The moderator also must be able to prevent any member of the group from dominating and must be able to draw out hesitant members.

Effective moderators memorize their topic outlines or protocols so they can pay full attention to the unfolding dynamics of the group. An abbreviated checklist can help them keep on track. The best focus groups direct the discussion themselves to a great extent, instead of having their discussion directed by a highly structured questionnaire. As a result, moderators must be ready to make adjustments, including the sudden addition or deletion of questions by the client, who can get messages to the moderator during the focus group by way of an ear microphone or notes. The moderator may need to modify a questioning strategy that fails with a particular group, or pursue an unexpected discovery that, while unplanned, can provide useful information. Morgan and Krueger (1998) recommended the use of 5-*second pause* and *probe* strategies to elicit more information from respondents (see also Krueger, 1994). The 5-second pause can prompt others to add their comments to one just made. The probe responds to an information-poor comment such as "I agree" with a rejoinder such as "would you explain further" or "can you give an example of what you mean?"

Moderators have a sharp but subtle awareness of their own body language so they can provide nonverbal encouragement without biasing responses. For example, leaning forward toward a participant can encourage the individual to go more deeply into a point, but too much head nodding gives the appearance of endorsement that can make another participant hesitant to express disagreement. Similarly, eye contact can provide encouragement to a member who seems withdrawn, whereas a lack of eye contact can help prevent another individual from dominating discussion by denying that individual the attention desired. Eye contact can seem aggressive to individuals who are shy or who come from cultural backgrounds that consider direct eye contact confrontational, so the moderator needs to understand and act sensitively toward cultural differences.

Even the moderator's dress can make a difference. Although a blue suit, white shirt, and tie can provide an air of authority, for example, it also can give the impression of formality and leadership that some may find offensive or threatening. The moderator needs to both lead the group and fit in with group. As a result, there may be times when the ethnic background, gender, and age of the moderator emerge as important characteristics. Participants often assume the moderator is an employee of the organization under discussion, which can hinder or bias responses. The moderator needs to do everything possible to communicate neutrality.

DEALING WITH DIFFICULT GROUP MEMBERS

Moderators must anticipate the possibility of losing control of a group. Usually, dominant or disruptive participants can be managed using body language and occasional comments. For example, a moderator can hold up a hand as a stop sign to one participant and signal to another, "let's hear from you now." A moderator also can suggest that participants answer a question one by one, going around the room, rather than allowing the most assertive respondents to speak out first every time. Seating charts, along with place cards on the table, can help moderators refer to people by name. If a group becomes too wild or conflictual, or individuals too antagonistic or disrespectful, a 5-minute break can help calm everyone down. In extreme cases, a particularly disruptive individual can be asked to leave during the break. The individual is thanked for participating and told that he or she was needed for the first part of the discussion but that the second part of the discussion will be different and not everyone will be needed. It is important to be firm but polite.

PROTOCOL DESIGN

The focus group protocol, or outline, is designed to provide a subtle structure to the discussion. Unlike surveys, which rely primarily on closed-ended questions, focus group questions should be open ended. They include a combination of uncued questions and more specific, cued questions (probes) that can help spark responses if discussion lags. Uncued questions are ideal ("What impressions do you have of the XYZ organization currently?") because they give participants the most freedom to introduce new ideas. Cued questions provide more context or probe for more depth ("What about the news coverage of the incident bothered you the most?"). The protocol provides just enough structure to help the moderator stay on track. It also progresses from general questions to more focused questions, so that participants have a chance to get comfortable before confronting the most difficult issues.

Closed-ended questions also can be useful if the focus group is being used to explore reasons for answers that might appear on a survey. Analysts, however, should be careful not to extrapolate from focus group participants' answers to closed-ended questions. Clients often appreciate both types of information but can be tempted to make more out of focus group "surveys" than is appropriate.

The subtleties of question construction can have a great effect on the type of discussion that takes place and the value of the information shared. Question phrasings should avoid using "why" because that term can seem confrontational and can stifle open responses. Instead, questions should rely on "how" and "what" phrasing. For example, instead of asking respondents, "Why do you dislike this poster?" ask, "What did you dislike about this poster?" Questions also should avoid dichotomous phrasing ("Did you enjoy the event?") because participants may answer the question literally or ambiguously ("Yes," or

"Pretty much") without providing any context ("What do you remember about the event?"). Sometimes, however, a yes/no question can prod a reticent group into a simple answer that can be explored in depth through follow-up probes. Krueger (1994) also recommended opening with more positive questions and saving negative questions for later so that the overall tone of the group remains constructive, acknowledging both sides of an issue.

Two especially useful question strategies recommended by Krueger include *sentence completion* and *conceptual mapping*. Sentence completion questions can be introduced verbally by the moderator or handed out in writing. Participants are asked to complete sentences that request information on their motivations or feelings ("When I first heard about the change in policy I thought ..."), often in writing using notepads and pencils provided for the purpose. This enables the moderator to obtain the initial views of every member even if they change their minds during discussion or feel hesitant to speak out. Conceptual mapping asks participants to consider how an organization or product relates to other, similar organizations or products. For example, participants could be asked to "map" political candidates such that the most similar are closest together. The discussion then focuses on what characteristics each participants used to establish similarity, such as trustworthiness, conservatism, or experience. Conceptual mapping requires that participants have some prior impressions or knowledge on which to base their judgments.

According to Krueger (1994), the focus group protocol has five general sections of main questions, to which cued probes can be added to ensure discussion flows smoothly.

1. *The opening question.* This question functions as a warm-up or ice breaker and is intended to demonstrate to participants that they have characteristics in common with one another. It should be answered quickly by the participants, requiring only 10 to 20 seconds from each. Krueger advised that these questions should be factual ("How any children do you have, and how old are they?") rather than attitude- or opinion-based ("What is your favorite flavor of ice cream?"). Questions should avoid requiring disclosures of occupational status because that can create power differentials that hinder group dynamics.

2. *Introduction questions.* These questions set the agenda for the discussion by addressing the topic of interest in a general way ("What was your first impression of ..." or "What comes to mind when you think about ..."). These questions are designed to get participants talking about their experiences relevant to the issue but are not intended to provide much information for later analysis.

During this period, participants should begin to feel comfortable talking about the topic with each other.

3. *Transition questions.* These questions begin to take participants into the topic more deeply so they become aware of how others view the topic ("What events have you attended at the Coliseum this year?"). They provide a link between the introductory questions and the key questions that follow.

4. *Key questions.* These two to five questions form the heart of the focus group inquiry and directly address the issues of concern to the client. They can focus on message testing, conceptual mapping, idea generation, or whatever information is of interest to the client. These questions usually are written first, with the remaining questions built around them.

5. *Ending questions.* These questions bring closure to the discussion to make sure all viewpoints have been represented and to confirm the moderator's interpretation of overall themes expressed. These can take the form of suggestions or recommendations for the client. Respondents are asked to reflect on the comments made throughout the session. These questions take the form of a final reaction ("All things considered ..."), which often is asked of each member one by one; a summary confirmation, in which the moderator gives a 2 to 3 minute overview of the discussion followed by a request for verification ("Is this an adequate summary?"); and a final, standardized question ending the discussion following another overview of the study ("Have we missed anything?"). Krueger (1994) recommended leaving 10 minutes for responses to this question, especially if the focus group is early in a series. The answers to this question can give direction to future focused discussions.

MESSAGE AND IDEA TESTING

When using focus groups to try out campaign strategies, it is important to investigate a full range of possibilities and not just the one or two favorites of the client or agency. The manager does not want to limit the ability of the focus group to produce surprises or disconfirm assumptions. Given the crowded marketplace of ideas that exists in the media and everyday environment, breaking through the morass presents public relations programs with a challenging task. This challenge can tempt message producers to "push the envelope," going for the most shocking message or the most colorful message or the funniest message. As chap. 14 explains, however, messages need to accomplish more than getting the target audience's attention. They also need to be perceived as relevant, memorable, motivating, accurate, and credible.

Extremes may or may not be necessary to break through the clutter, and extremes may help or may backfire once people begin to pay attention to the message. As a result, it is useful to test strategies ranging from the tame to the outrageous. The messages tested for the Talk to Your Kids campaign, shown in Fig. 7.1–7.3, provide such a range.

Managers should keep in mind that the target publics for messages may include gatekeepers as well as the ultimate audience. The Washington State Department of Alcohol and Substance Abuse, for example, wanted to run a media campaign exhorting parents of children between 3 and 10 years of age to talk with their children about alcohol. Because funds for paid placements were limited, they needed the cooperation of the Washington State Association of Broadcasters. As a result, they tested messages with parents and with broadcasters, who had different concerns. Because many broadcasters accept advertising for beer, they shied away from messages that seemed especially strident. They were supportive of the campaign, however, and ended up providing nearly $100,000 of free exposure for the final announcements during prime viewing hours.

Make sure the most important messages about alcohol come from you.

FIG. 7.1. Rough of "Boy and TV" alcohol campaign advertisement. This image of a boy in front of a television was changed to a girl in print advertisements after feedback from focus group participants suggested that the image was too stereotypical. The image of the boy was still used for a television ad. Image courtesy of the Division of Alcohol and Substance Abuse, Department of Social and Health Services, Washington State.

Make sure the most important message about alcohol comes from you.

Whether you know it or not, your children are already receiving powerful messages about alcohol.

Just by watching TV, they repeatedly see adults drinking to have fun. Drinking to relax. Even drinking to look attractive and be popular.

Parents can't control all the information young children receive about this drug. However, you can prepare them for the peer pressure and onslaught of pro-alcohol messages to come.

Call **1-800-662-9111**, or write for our free guide, "Talking To Your Kids About Alcohol."

And do it soon. Because they've already started listening.

Washington State Substance Abuse Coalition
Talking to Your Kids About Alcohol Brochure
12729 N.E. 20th, Suite 18, Bellevue, WA 98005

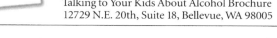

FIG. 7.2. Final version of boy and television advertisement. This image of a girl in front of a television was created in response to focus group comments. Image courtesy of the Division of Alcohol and Substance Abuse, Department of Social and Health Services, Washington State.

This wouldn't look so innocent if
you had heard Lisa offer Mr. Bear
another scotch and soda.

FIG. 7.3. Rough of "Tea Party" alcohol campaign advertisement. The words "scotch and soda"
in the headline accompanying this image of a girl having a tea party with her teddy bear
were changed to "glass of wine" after focus group respondents suggested that the hard-liquor
phrase was too extreme. A second focus group reacted positively to the "glass of wine" version,
and the revised image was accepted for use in television ads for the campaign.
Image courtesy of the Division of Alcohol and Substance Abuse, Department of Social and
Health Services, Washington State.

RUNNING THE GROUP

The moderator begins by welcoming the participants, introducing the
topic of discussion and purpose of the meeting very generally, and lay-
ing out the ground rules for discussion. The explanation of the study
should be truthful but vague, to avoid leading participants. The strategy of the focus group method, after all, is to let the group steer discussion to the extent possible. Ground rules usually cover the following
points:

1. Participants should speak up so everyone can hear what they
   have to say.
2. Only one person should speak at a time to make sure comments
   are not missed.
3. Each person should say what they think, and not what they think
   others want to hear. Honest responses are important, and re-

spondents have been asked to participate because their true opinions are valued.

4. Negative comments are at least as useful as positive ones. ("If we thought we were doing a perfect job already, we wouldn't be holding this focus group. We need to know how we can do things better.")
5. No right or wrong answers exist to the questions asked.

Moderators sometimes find it helpful to have participants jot down their answers to questions before opening a discussion. Participants also can be asked to deposit note cards into labeled boxes on the table, so that the raw responses can be analyzed later and compared with opinions shared only during the discussion. This technique effectively reveals minority opinions.

ANALYZING RESULTS

Analysis of qualitative data can range from an intuitive overview to rigorous scrutiny using methods accepted by scholars. Computer programs for content analysis of qualitative data exist, such as VBPro (Miller, 2000). Time pressure usually prevents the most detailed analysis, but some scientific principles apply even to the most succinct report of results. Krueger (1994) and others recommended the following principles:

1. *Be systematic.* Establish a procedure ahead of time that makes it possible to disconfirm assumptions and hypotheses. The procedure can be as simple as searching for themes and using at least two direct quotes to illustrate each point. Every interpretation should consider whether alternative explanations might provide an equally valid analysis.
2. *Be verifiable.* Another person should arrive at similar conclusions using similar methods. Keep in mind that focus groups can provide information that a client will find threatening or disheartening. To convince a determined or defensive client that a change in policy or strategy is necessary, the evidence must be compelling.
3. *Be focused.* Keep in mind the original reasons for holding the focus group and look for information that relates to those points. Focus groups that go on for three hours can produce transcripts well over 50 pages. Researchers must have a strategy ready to reduce the voluminous mass of data into meaningful chunks of information.

4. *Be practical.* Perform only the level of analysis that makes sense for the client and the situation. A complete transcript, for example, may not be necessary if the issues explored were fairly simple, and it may take time away from other planning activities during a tight implementation deadline.

5. *Be immediate.* During delays, the focus group observers' impressions may fade, compromising their ability to analyze the data. All observers should make notes during the focus group and immediately afterward to identify themes and direct quotes that seem important. These observations can be confirmed, fleshed out, and supplemented during later analysis but often provide the most valid and vivid conclusions.

FINAL THOUGHTS

The focus group is probably the method most often employed by public relations professionals. It also is probably the method most often misused, which likely contributes to client and managerial skepticism of its value. The focus group offers tremendous benefits to the practitioner aiming to pretest strategies or understand communication processes in some depth. As long as the communication manager respects the limitations of the focus group, it can be an indispensable tool for responsive and effective communication program planning.

Making Research Decisions: Formal Research Methods

Characteristics of Formal, Scientific
  Research Methods
Survey Research Overview
Experiments
Content Analysis
Final Thoughts

Public relations practitioners need more sophisticated research methods as their informational needs evolve from simple fact finding and casual analysis to a more sophisticated understanding of the opinions, attitudes, and motivations of target audience members. In a perfect world, researchers follow a formal, scientific process; use a representative sample of participants that produces results that can be generalized from the sample to population with confidence; and produce objective results instead of subjective results that reflect the opinions or desires of the researcher or other interested parties. Rarely is the world of scientific research perfect, but carefully planned and conducted projects have a greater likelihood than informal research of serving as a reliable basis for campaign planning or evaluation.

Formal research in public relations examines the attitudes, opinions, behaviors, and other important characteristics of target audience members; measures and describes important media characteristics; learns about and explains audience motivations and behaviors; and explains and evaluates media messages and campaign effects. Ultimately, the results of such research help public relations practitioners and their organizations or clients successfully understand target audience opinions, attitudes, and behaviors; predict and measure program outcomes; and increase the likelihood of program success.

130

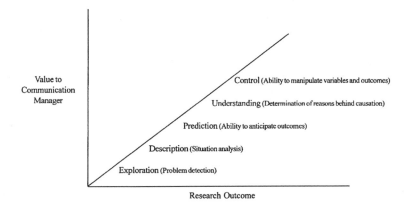

FIG. 8.1.   The goals of science. Maximum control of a situation requires the ability to predict what will happen, understand why things happen, and control what will happen. At a lesser level, explorations of a problem and descriptions of constraints and opportunities also are useful outcomes of research, and are prerequisites for strategic planning.

Even though all formal research methods could apply to some aspect of public relations, practitioners do not use all scientific research methods regularly. In addition, communication managers more commonly use informal research methods than formal research methods, despite the increase in sophistication, generalizability, known accuracy, and reliability that formal research methods can provide. For this reason, this chapter introduces readers to a range of formal research methods including surveys, experiments, and in content analyses. Detailed discussions of survey research methods and related topics will follow in later chapters, because surveys are the most commonly used formal research method in public relations.

CHRACTERISTICS OF FORMAL,
SCIENTIFIC RESEARCH METHODS

Understanding research methods increases our knowledge of how to learn about the social world (Adler & Clark, 1999), including the world of our target audiences. The ways we learn about the world of our targeted audiences have benefits and limitations.

Understanding these benefits and limitations in methods used to learn about the world affects how much we can trust the data we use to inform our decision making as we plan, execute, and evaluate public relations campaigns. Data-collection methods greatly influence the degree of trust we can place in different kinds of information.

Although public relations research can greatly increase the likelihood of program success, poorly conducted research that misinforms campaign planners can have a strong, negative effect on program performance. In the same way, research conducted properly but misapplied to a public relations problem or campaign can have a negative effect on campaign effectiveness. This might be the case, for example, when a focus group (informal research) is used to gauge audience attitudes and opinions in the design phase of a campaign. If the results of the focus group are inaccurate, the campaign will fail to inform and motivate its target audience members. Most practitioners do not need to be formal research experts, but they must know and understand basic research issues to use research effectively.

In general, formal, scientific research is *empirical* in nature (derived from the Greek word for "experience"), or concerned with the world that can be experienced and measured in a precise manner (Wimmer & Dominick, 2000). One way to learn about people, for example, is to read their horoscope. This may provide interesting information, but is such information trustworthy? Although some would argue it is accurate, others would prefer to use a more dependable research method to gather information, a method with proven reliability. This is where formal and informal research methods can differ significantly. Research collected using informal methods may be interesting but not completely trustworthy because we are not sure about the accuracy of the results. Although the information produced by informal research methods may be highly accurate, researchers have no way to gauge its accuracy because there is no way to evaluate it scientifically. With formal research methods, however, researchers use several procedures to ensure that the information collected is trustworthy beyond a reasonable doubt, or at least that they understand the potential limitations and liabilities of such information. Because of this, researchers carefully monitor the level of trust they can place in data collected using formal research methods.

Sometimes informal research methods produce the same information as formal research methods, but often they do not. When practitioners talk to a small group of close friends who live in a specific school district, for example, they may discover the same general attitudes and opinions that would be expressed if they conducted a survey of randomly selected persons who live in the same district. Due to selection biases, however, the results practitioners obtain through informal conversations are likely to differ greatly from the results they would obtain through a formal survey. Formal research methods allow us to understand more about the limitations and risks associated with the information we collect. This is why it is unwise to engage in campaign planning or risk a large public relations budget on information collected solely through informal research methods.

No single feature makes a research project formal and scientific, but several study attributes contribute to a high degree of accuracy and scientific reliability when combined. We examine some of the most important features of formal research in this book, recognizing that not all formal research methods are the same, and each method has its own strengths and weaknesses.

First, research that is formal and scientific produces results that are *objective*. This means the research results do not unduly reflect the biases of researchers or the attitudes and opinions of a few selected individuals, but instead reflect events, facts, and behaviors as they exist or naturally occur in a population or group studied. When researchers conduct focus group research, for example, the results of the research depend on the participants in the group. With different focus group participants, the results will probably differ. The opinions of one or two domineering members of a focus group may sway group opinions despite the attempts of the moderator to counterbalance such influences. In addition, researchers must interpret the results of the discussion without a definitive method of objective evaluation. Focus group findings, as a result, are subjective interpretations by the researcher and client.

A formal survey, however, provides objective results. Even if different samples from the same population are selected for surveys, the results are demonstrably similar most of the time (normally 95%) when similar questions are asked, and appropriate probability sampling methods are used. This occurs because scientific methods help ensure the attitudes and behaviors measured in the survey are represented in approximately the same proportion as they naturally occur in a population. In fact, the use of probability sampling methods ensures researchers can calculate the *range of error*—the degree of skepticism we need to apply to the results—for descriptive results. This makes it easy to understand how trustworthy the data are. In addition, numerical results require little or no subjective interpretation. The result is that, although both research methods may produce useful information, the information produced by a focus group is less trustworthy than the information produced by a survey.

Second, scientific research follows a systematic set of procedures to provide for the uniform collection of data. This process helps ensure that each participant in a study gets treated the same way and that all participant responses get measured the same way. When focus groups are conducted, responses to questions are recorded verbatim and interpreted within the larger context of the group discussion. There is no formal, systematic method for measuring participant responses. In fact, this is a strength of focus groups in that it allows each participant to express individual opinions, lets participants respond to each other, and allows the moderator to ask follow-up questions. It also is a weakness of focus groups, however, because measurement of participant responses is inexact and subjective. When a formal survey is conducted, systematic measurement methods typically include the use of numerical, or numerically based, scales. The use of such scales ensures that, to the extent possible, each participant's responses get measured and recorded in the same way. As a result, the use of systematic measures and an established process or set of procedures helps make a research method formal or scientific.

Third, scientific research results use a representative sample to the greatest extent possible, and the limitations of samples that are not completely representative are well understood. Researchers draw a sample and project research results to a population because it is uncommon (and usually impractical and unnecessary) for researchers to collect information from every member of a population. Instead, information typically is gathered from a selected subset, or sample, of population members. Statisticians have shown that a census is not necessary to gather accurate, reliable data in most instances. When probability-based sampling methods and a sample of appropriate size are used (discussed in chap. 10), they help ensure that the behaviors and attitudes of sample members reliably depict the range of behaviors and attitudes found in a population. The result is a sample that is representative, or has the same distribution of characteristics as the population from which it was drawn. In reality, no sample is perfectly representative; however, samples collected using probability methods have more trustworthiness than other samples.

This type of trustworthiness is called *external validity* or projectability. That is, survey results can be projected from a sample to a population with a certain level of confidence (which we can calculate mathematically). In practical terms, focus group results generally lack external validity, or projectability, because participants normally are selected using a nonprobability sampling method and the number of participants is small—too small to represent all members of a target audience with any degree of reliability. Scientific research, however, uses a probability-based sampling method and has a sample size sufficient to represent the target audience members from which it is drawn.

Fourth, researchers should be able to reproduce the results of formal research projects. This is known as *replication*. If the results of a project were unique to a single study, we would conclude they may be biased, perhaps because of faulty sampling procedures or problems with the data-collection process. When study results are replicable, they provide accurate information for the population under study.

Returning to the focus group example, the results of focus groups are largely unique to a single study. Differences among groups arise because of differences in participants' experiences, opinions, observations, and the like. More important, researchers cannot know with certainty how accurate focus group results are because their findings lack external validity. Researchers commonly conduct multiple focus groups with similar audiences hoping to avoid highly unusual results that do not represent the characteristics of the population under study. When a formal survey is conducted using probability-based sampling methods, however, researchers can have a high level of confidence that the results of their project are not unique to their study, but reflect the characteristics of the population from which the sample was drawn. The ability of other researchers to replicate research findings is an essential characteristic of formal, scientific research.

A research project generally is considered formal to the extent that it incorporates the characteristics of objectivity, systematic collection of data, representative samples, and replicable results into its design. The following discussion of scientific research methods is designed to introduce you to the range of possibilities available for research projects. We begin with a review of survey research, followed by a discussion of experimental research designs, and media content analyses. Because of the wide application of survey research to public relations, more specific aspects of survey research design are discussed in chap. 9.

SURVEY RESEARCH OVERVIEW

Survey research is used extensively by organizations in different fields including all levels of government, political organizations, mass media corporations, educational institutions, entertainment conglomerates, financial institutions, and other product manufacturers and service providers. In public relations, the purpose of survey research is to collect accurate measurements of people's attitudes, beliefs, and behavior by asking them questions. Organizations commonly turn to survey research when they want to understand their target audiences' awareness, opinions, attitudes, knowledge, behavioral motivations, media use, and other information necessary for successful campaign implementation or evaluation.

As shown in Fig. 8.2, research is useful at all stages of the program-planning, implementation, and evaluation process. Survey research, more specifically, often is used in the planning and evaluation phases of a campaign. In the campaign planning phase, *precampaign* surveys help practitioners establish target audience benchmarks so campaign goals can be set. If one of the purposes of a campaign is to in-

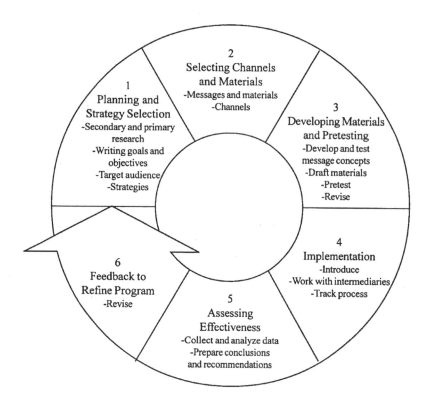

FIG. 8.2. Stages of communication. Strategic planning of communication programs is an ongoing process in which previous experience informs the planning of new programs and the refinement of old programs. Developed by the Center for Substance Abuse Prevention for the planning of alcohol and other drug communication programs.

crease target audience awareness of a client's product, for example, current audience awareness levels must be established so appropriate goals and objectives can be determined. In this way, precampaign research findings provide a point of reference for the campaign.

Postcampaign surveys are used as a part of campaign evaluation to help determine whether goals and objectives have been accomplished. If a program aims to increase target audience awareness of a client's product by 20%, a postcampaign survey is one of the ways practitioners can determine the campaign has met its goals. Simply put, campaign outcomes are determined by comparing postcampaign research results with precampaign benchmarks. Postcampaign research also may serve as "between-campaign" research. That is, many organizations simply transition from one or more existing campaigns to new campaigns without stopping to conduct new research at every point between campaigns. In these cases, postcampaign research may serve some precampaign research purposes when additional programs are in the planning or early implementation stages.

Sometimes surveys and other forms of research are conducted during a campaign to provide intermediate campaign evaluations. This monitoring helps determine whether a campaign is on course. In such a case, research results are used to monitor campaign progress and to make corrections in campaign strategies and tactics.

In addition, surveys generally fall into one of two broad categories. *Descriptive surveys* document current circumstances and conditions, and generally describe what exists in a population. The federal government, for example, uses its Current Population Survey to determine the total number of adults who are unemployed in the United States. Voters are regularly surveyed by political candidates, special interest groups, and the media to determine the level of support for a particular candidate or policy initiative, or to understand and predict election outcomes. Most applied public relations research projects are descriptive in nature.

Analytical surveys, on the other hand, attempt to explain why certain circumstances, attitudes and behaviors exist among members of a specific population. This type of survey research is likely to rely on advanced forms of statistical analysis to test hypotheses concerning the relationship among a group of variables under study. Academic researchers, for example, commonly study the relationship between exposure to negative political advertising and attitudes about politics and political participation. In many cases, surveys serve both descriptive and analytical purposes. In each instance, practitioners, or a PR research outfit, follow formal procedures and use a systematic process to ensure the data collected are objective, reliable, and accurate. Regardless of the use of a survey, most survey research projects generally follow the same planning process. Initially, researchers determine the objectives of the research project. Next, researchers design the study. During this phase of a survey they determine the population and sampling procedures used in the project, select a specific interview method, and design and pretest the survey instrument or questionnaire. Then, the research team collects, edits, and codes data. Finally, researchers analyze and interpret results.

Survey Planning

Initially, the most important aspect of survey research planning involves identification of the goals and objectives of the research project. This normally involves identifying a research problem and the potential hypothe-

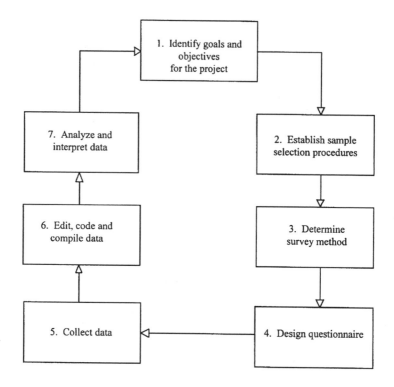

FIG. 8.3. The survey planning process. To help ensure project success, researchers generally follow these steps in a systematic manner when planning and implementing surveys.

ses and research questions a project will address. Campaign practitioners often give this aspect of a research project relatively brief attention because they are busy, and purposes of many projects appear obvious. As discussed in chapter 3, however, the most successful research projects are those that have a high degree of direction. Surveys that lack direction often fail to live up to their potential as a planning or evaluation tool. For this reason, although applied research projects typically use research questions, practitioners may find it useful to think about expected research outcomes as a way to formalize their expectations concerning the results of a research project.

Survey Sampling

Sample selection procedures depend on survey objectives. As discussed in chap. 10, sampling procedures range from convenient to complex. They also vary in terms of their trustworthiness. A scientific technique called probability sampling, explained in chap. 10, usually provides an accurate and reliable understanding of the characteristics of a population when sampling methods are used correctly. For this reason, the use of proper sampling methods is one of the most critical aspects of any research project and an especially important characteristic of scientific survey research.

Determining the Data-Collection Method

The three primary means of collecting survey data are personal interviews, mail surveys, and telephone surveys. Computer-assisted data collection, through online bulletin boards for example, also is growing in usage as informational needs and technology resources make its use practical. Selecting a proper data-collection method is critical to the success of a research project, and each method of data collection has its own strengths and weaknesses. There is no single best survey research method, but there is almost always a best survey research method to use given the limitations and requirements of a research project.

The choices at first may seem overwhelming. If the purpose of a project is to interview business professionals working in telecommunications industries, for example, telephone and interpersonal interviewing probably are poor choices because participants will be too busy to respond to a researcher's request for information. Respondents can fill out mail surveys at their convenience, however, so this method shows more promise with this group of respondents. In addition, mail surveys tend to cost less. If time is a major concern, however, regular mail surveys might not be the best research method because it takes longer to complete a project. Completion times for mail surveys typically range from a few weeks to several weeks or more if multiple mailings are necessary. Given time concerns, an electronic-mail survey may be a viable option for data collection. There may be significant sampling limitations in the use of such a survey, however, making it less appealing. There also may be other research methods to consider.

Research professionals must address various important issues when considering data-collection methods. Selecting an appropriate survey method is crucial to the successful completion of a research project. This topic is addressed in greater detail in chap. 9.

Questionnaire Design

Proper questionnaire design contributes significantly to the trustworthiness of survey results. Good survey questions, when combined with appropriate data-collection methods, produce accurate responses.

Poor survey questions, or inappropriate data-collection methods, produce untrustworthy results that can misinform public relations managers.

Poorly designed questionnaires often bias participants' responses. In this case, researchers are no longer measuring respondents' true attitudes, opinions, and behaviors, but instead are measuring manufactured participant "responses" they have created through a poorly designed questionnaire. These responses are not useful because they simply do not represent the true responses of research participants or the target publics they represent. A public relations campaign or other program based on such erroneous information is likely to fail. Erroneous information may worsen situations in which practitioners use research as the basis for problem solving.

Several questionnaire characteristics that seem relatively unimportant can bias participant responses, including question wording, question response categories, and question order. In addition, when interviews are administered by another person either face to face or over the telephone, interviewers can bias survey results as they interact with participants. This topic is an important part of almost all research methods, and chap. 11 addresses questionnaire design issues in greater detail.

Data Collection

Data collection typically is the next step in the survey research process, and in many respects it is the beginning of the final phase of a research project. By this point, the researcher has made many of the most difficult decisions, and, although there may be surprises, research projects that are well designed tend to run relatively smoothly (Robinson, 1969). Practitioners' levels of involvement in data collection range from managing all aspects of data collection to leaving all aspects of data collection to a research project manager or field service provider. Although practitioners may leave projects in the hands of capable managers with relative confidence, it generally is in their best interest to monitor data collection at least to some extent. Occasionally, practitioners need to make critical decisions concerning data collection. When survey response rates appear unusually low or respondents do not understand a question, for example, practitioners should be involved in determining the best solution. A minimum level of practitioner involvement is warranted during data collection to help ensure the knowledge gathered will best serve the purposes of the research project. As a result, chap. 12 presents information to aid in the data-collection and analysis process.

Editing and Coding

Editing and coding are the processes used to translate the information collected in questionnaires into a form suitable for statistical analysis (Warwick & Lininger, 1975). When a computer-assisted telephone interviewing (CATI) system is used, editing may not be necessary. When interviewers record participant responses using paper and pencil, however, some editing is usually necessary. Editing questionnaires typically involves checking responses to eliminate or correct incomplete or unintelligible answers. Questionnaires should be edited by a supervisor during data collection to detect errors and provide rapid feedback to their source (often an interviewer who is not paying careful attention). Particular attention should be given to missing answers and inconsistencies or a lack of uniformity among interviewers, because interviewer differences in wording questions or recording participant responses introduces error.

Editing may be necessary when a questionnaire has open-ended responses or other data that need categorization. Editing is best conducted by a few trained supervisors working with a fixed set of rules. Using these rules, editors typically place responses into mutually exclusive and exhaustive categories to facilitate data analysis. Often unseen intricacies are involved in this type of editing, requiring a high degree of consistency among editors to generate reliable results.

Coding is the process of preparing the data for computer analysis. The essential task in coding is to translate survey data into quantified form so it can be easily accessed and analyzed. Each survey project should have a code book, which is a column-by-column explanation of the responses and their corresponding code numbers. Coding questionnaires consists of reading each question, referring to the code book, and assigning the appropriate code for the respondent's answers. These data are then put into a computer for analysis. Chapter 12 provides additional information concerning editing and coding participant responses.

Analysis and Interpretation

Statistical analysis and interpretation is the next step in survey research. Although a thorough discussion of statistical procedures is beyond the scope of this text, a brief review of commonly used analytical techniques appears in chap. 12.

Survey Critique

Survey research can be an interesting and effective means of studying public relations issues and publics. A primary advantage of survey research is that a project can be conducted relatively quickly. As noted in chapter 5, not all research methods are quick, but telephone surveys and some forms of personal interviews may be conducted in a relatively short time. Cost may be an advantage, as well. The cost of most survey research is reasonable considering the amount of information gathered. In addition, different methods of data collection provide for cost control through the selection and implementation of more or less expensive survey methods. The relatively low cost and ease of implementation make survey research attractive to communication managers.

Nevertheless, no research method is foolproof, and survey research has its limitations. First, survey research cannot provide direct evidence of causation. When evaluating campaign outcomes, for example, survey research cannot prove with certainty that a campaign has had a particular effect on target audience opinions, attitudes, and behaviors. In addition, researchers occasionally attempt to specify causes when research results do not support such conclusions. For example, if survey research indicates boating accidents increase as ice cream sales increase, we might be tempted to conclude ice cream is a culprit in boating accidents. Of course, nothing could be further from the truth. Both ice cream sales and boating accidents simply increase as the weather warms up, and they clearly are not related in terms of a cause-and-effect outcome. Although this example is absurd, researchers need to beware of making conclusions that are equally, if perhaps more subtly, absurd using research data that do not support their "findings."

Other weaknesses of survey research are specific to the data-collection method used in a project. Large personal interview surveys may be costly, for example, requiring researchers to train field supervisors and interviewers, as well as covering travel expenses and other costs associated with interviews. Similarly, mail surveys typically take longer than other survey research methods to complete because of the time associated with mailing the questionnaires to a sample and receiving responses back from participants. It is important to know the specific strengths and weaknesses associated with each method of data collection, and these are discussed in detail in chap. 9.

Other concerns associated with survey research apply in some way to all survey data-collection methods. Sometimes respondents are inaccurate in the answers they provide, for example, whether in a direct interview or on a mailed questionnaire. These responses introduce error into survey results. The reasons for this problem are variable. Sometimes, respondents simply do not remember information about themselves or their activities. Rather than admit they do not know the answer, they may simply make up a response. This also is a problem when respondents lack knowledge regarding the subject of a question, but answer the question rather than admit they do not know.

Respondents may also provide incorrect answers in an attempt to find favor with interviewers. Some survey questions include responses that are more socially desirable than alternative choices. In other instances, participants may simply choose to deceive researchers by providing incorrect answers to questions. At times, respondents may attempt to determine the purpose of a survey and provide the responses they think researchers are looking for. Survey results concerning complex subjects are further complicated by respondents who find it difficult to identify and explain their true feelings. As a result, practitioners should consider the potential drawbacks to the successful completion of a survey before a research project is started.

Despite the weaknesses of survey research, its benefits outweigh its drawbacks for many research projects. Survey research is particularly useful for description and association, a necessity given the largely exploratory and descriptive nature of many applied projects. A carefully prepared questionnaire contributes to results that are reliable and accurate. Telephone surveys, in particular, enable collection of a large amount of data within a short time at a reasonable cost. Given the needs of data collection, and the time and budget constraints placed on many research projects, survey research often is an excellent research method choice. This is why it is the method of formal research used most often by communication managers.

EXPERIMENTS

In the most basic sense, an *experiment* involves taking action and observing the consequences of that action (Babbie, 1999). In a sense, experiments are a natural part of public relations because in most cases, practitioners take action of one sort or another and then gauge the effect of that action (in experimental language called a "treatment") on target audience opinions, attitudes, or behavior. Although various study designs exist, generally an experiment requires at least one group of participants to receive a *treatment* (such as exposure to part of a public relations campaign). The effect of that treatment can be determined by comparing participants' before-treatment responses with their after-treatment responses on a series of questions designed to measure their opinions or attitudes, for example (Broom & Dozier, 1990).

Experimental research designs can provide important contributions to public relations program planning and evaluation because they allow practitioners to isolate campaign variables and control them. This high degree of control allows researchers to use experimental designs to systematically examine variables that may or may not influence target audience members. If campaign planners want to determine voter responses to potential campaign advertisements, for example, they might measure the attitudes and projected voting behaviors of a relatively small sets of voters (perhaps 40 or 50), expose them to the advertising, and measure their attitudes and projected voting behavior again. If no other variables were introduced in the process, the changes that took place from the first measurement to the second measurement would be due to the advertising.

In an applied setting, the use of true experiments is relatively rare. Given the previous political advertising example, campaign managers are more likely to conduct a focus group and get participant feedback on different advertising executions (called *copytesting* in advertising) than to conduct an experiment. As a rule, informal research methods such as focus groups produce results that are low in external validity and reliability, and there is no scientific basis for understanding the potential inaccuracies that exist in informal research. The result is that incorrect findings could be used as the basis for making important campaign decisions.

Controlled experiments, on the other hand, are the most powerful means of determining campaign effects because they can be used to determine causation. This is the primary benefit of experiments. From a scientific perspective, three conditions are necessary to determine causation. First, the cause (variable A) must precede the effect (variable B) in time. Second, a change in the first variable (A) must produce a change in the second variable (B). This is called *concomitant variation*, and the idea is that a change in one variable depends on a change in another variable, such as summer "causing" popsicle sales and boating accidents. Third, all other possible causes of an effect must be eliminated or controlled in the experiment. This ensures that the relationship between the variables is not caused by a third variable. By using experiments, researchers can examine and understand variable relationships under uncontaminated conditions. This allows them to develop greater insight into variable relationships, such as the effects of political advertisements on voters.

Researchers use systematic procedures when they conduct experiments. Initially, they select the setting for the experiment. Next, they design or plan the project. In this phase researchers decide how to measure and manipulate variables, select a specific study design, and develop and pretest the materials used in the experiment. Finally, researchers collect, analyze, and interpret data.

Settings

The two main settings in which researchers conduct experiments are in a research laboratory or similar facility used for research purposes and in the field. A laboratory setting is advantageous because it provides researchers with the ability to control almost all aspects of an experiment. By controlling outside influences, researchers can make exact determinations regarding the nature of the relationships between variables. Generally, the more controlled and precise an experiment is, the less error that is present. By controlling the conditions under which an experiment occurs, researchers can reduce the risk of contamination from unwanted, unplanned sources.

The artificial nature of research laboratories or similar facilities have disadvantages. Isolated research environments that are highly controlled to exclude potential interference are different from most real-life circumstances. In measuring voters' responses to televised political advertisements, for example, it would probably be better to test voters at home where they normally watch television. This environment is a natural setting that is likely to contain all the distractions and other influences people encounter when they watch television. It is in this environment that we would most likely get participants' most natural responses. Unfortunately, these distractions and other influences also are likely to change research results. This contamination makes the determination of causation nearly impossible. Practitioners have to balance these advantages and disadvantages when choosing a design. When researchers pull people out of their natural settings and place them in controlled environments such as laboratories, they may react differently to the materials used in the experiment (televised political ads in this example) because this is not their normal viewing environment. Ultimately, the controlled artificiality of research settings tends to produce results high in internal validity (when a measure precisely reflects the concept that it is intended to measure) but low in external validity (the generalizability of results from a sample to a population).

Field experiments are conducted in the environment in which behaviors concerning the subject under study naturally occur. In other words, the "field" is the environment in which participants live, work, or relax. The dynamics and interactions of small groups, for example, may be studied at places where small groups of people naturally congregate such as common meeting areas in college dormitories. Field experiments tend to have a higher degree of external validity because the real-life settings used in field research are normal environments. The control available in field experiments, however, is rarely as tight as that available in laboratory experiments, because of the uncontrollable factors that exist in any natural environment.

Terms and Concepts

Before we discuss specific designs, we should briefly examine (or reexamine in some cases) some important terms so you have a better understanding of the research designs to be discussed. The basic purpose of an experiment is to determine causation. In an applied public relations setting, practitioners might be interested in determining the effect of a public relations campaign or program on the opinions, attitudes, and behaviors of target audience members. Each of these represent *variables* we are examining. In its simplest sense, a variable is a phenomenon or event that can be measured or manipulated (Wimmer & Dominick, 2000). In this case, the public relations program being tested is the *independent variable*. The independent variable is the variable that is manipulated in an experiment to see if it produces change in the *dependent variable*. Changes in the dependent variable depend on, or are caused by, the independent variable. If we wanted to examine the effects of potential campaign messages on target audience members, the messages are the independent variables. As independent variables, the campaign messages affect the dependent variables in the experiment, the opinions or attitudes of target audience members toward our organization.

In addition, we might manipulate the independent variable (the content of a campaign message) to determine how to make it more effective. We might consider a humorous message versus a serious message, for example. In this case, variable manipulation is a critical aspect of study design. We must make sure our humorous and serious messages are equal in terms of key points and features, so the only difference between the messages is the existence of humor or the lack of humor. If all other message characteristics are equal, any differences in participants' responses to the messages likely will be due to humor. This controlled experiment allows us to test the effect of humor on participants' responses to our message and gives us the scientific basis for determining cause and effect.

Initially, you may notice that in experimental research designs, subjects are assigned to a *condition*. A condition consists of all the people in an experiment who are treated the same way. In a source credibility experiment, for example, some participants are exposed to a message delivered by a high-credibility spokesperson, while other participants are exposed to a message delivered by a low-credibility spokesperson. Each group exposed to the same spokesperson in our example is part of the same condition.

Participants in the same condition are exposed to the same *treatment*. A treatment occurs when the participants in a condition are exposed to the same material, or *stimulus*, which typically contains the independent variable. Although it sounds confusing, it is really very simple. In the credibility experiment, for example, the message from a high-credibility source is one stimulus, and each participant who receives that stimulus receives the high-credibility treatment (these participants are in the same condition). In the same way, the message from a low-credibility source is a different stimulus. Participants exposed to the message from the low-credibility source receive the low-credibility treatment and are in the same condition.

Some participants may be placed in a condition in which they receive no treatment, or at least a meaningless treatment. These participants are in the *control group* or *control condition*. The control group contains people who are not exposed to any meaningful stimuli. Members of the control group can be used for comparison in an experiment because they receive no treatment; they are not exposed to an independent variable in any form. By using a control group, researchers can understand and control the effects of simply conducting the experiment on participants (Babbie, 1999). In medical research, for example, one group of participants may receive an actual drug, whereas the control group members are given a placebo (sugar pills are commonly used). This allows researchers to determine the amount of patient improvement due to the new drug versus the amount of patient improvement due to other factors, including participants' improved mental outlook perhaps caused by the special medical attention they are receiving.

Finally, participants should be assigned to either a treatment condition or a control condition in a *random* manner. When random assignment is used, each participant has an equal chance of being included in a condition. Random assignment helps to eliminate the potential influence of outside variables that may hinder the determination of causation (Wimmer & Dominick, 2000). If participant assignment is not random, researchers cannot be sure the participants in each condition are equal before exposure to experimental stimuli. When the participants in each condition are not equal, this is called *selectivity bias*. Random assignment helps ensure the differences detected in an experiment are caused by exposure to the stimuli and are not caused by differences among participants.

Research Designs

There are several potential ways to design an experiment, and, as long as an experiment allows for the determination of causation and addresses the need for internal and external validity, no single design is best. Instead, the best experimental design typically depends on the hypothesis or research questions, the nature of the independent and dependent variables, the availability of subjects, and the resources available for the project. The three experimental designs with the widest acceptance among social scientists are the *pretest-posttest design with a control group*, the *posttest-only design with a control group*,

TABLE 8.1
Pretest-Posttest Design with Control

Group	Random Assignment	Pretest	Treatment	Posttest
1	Yes	X	X	X
2	Yes	X		X

and the pretest-posttest design with additional control groups, commonly referred to as the *Solomon four-group design*.

The pretest-posttest design with a control group is a fundamental design of experimental research. It is widely used and applicable to a variety of different settings. When researchers use the pretest-posttest with control group design, they randomly assign subjects to two groups, or conditions, and initially measure the dependent variable (this is the pretest) for each group. An independent variable manipulation is then applied to one of the groups, followed by further testing to determine independent variable effects. The order of the research procedures, random assignment of subjects to conditions, and use of a control group helps eliminate or avoid many of the potential problems that threaten to ruin the internal validity of the experiment. Although a detailed discussion of these problems (called *threats to validity*) is beyond the scope of this book, readers may be interested in reading a short but important book by Campbell and Stanley (1963). Because each condition is the same and only one condition receives an experimental treatment, any significant differences that exist between participants in the conditions after the experimental manipulation have been caused by the treatment.

A second design that is commonly used in experimental research is the posttest-only design with a control group. In this research design, there is no pretest. Instead, subjects are randomly assigned to separate conditions. One group is exposed to the experimental manipulation (treatment). The treatment is followed by a posttest of both groups, and participants' dependent variable scores are compared. Pretesting, though an important part of experimental research, is not required to conduct a true experiment (Campbell & Stanley, 1963). Instead, the random assignment of participants to conditions allows researchers to assume participants in each condition are equal at the beginning of the experiment. The random assignment of subjects controls for selectivity biases. This design is especially useful to researchers when pretesting is unavailable or inconvenient, or may somehow interfere with the experiment (Campbell & Stanley, 1963).

TABLE 8.2
Posttest Only Design with Control

Group	Random Assignment	Pretest	Treatment	Posttest
1	Yes		X	X
2	Yes			X

TABLE 8.3
Solomon Four-Group Design

Group	Random Assignment	Pretest	Treatment	Posttest
1	Yes	X	X	X
2	Yes	X		X
3	Yes		X	X
4	Yes			X

The Solomon four-group design is a combination of the first two designs. The Solomon design uses four conditions, in conjunction with random assignment, to help control threats to validity and to allow researchers to determine unwanted effects of pretesting. Participants in the first condition receive a pretest, a treatment, and a posttest. Participants in the second condition receive a pretest and a posttest with no treatment. Those in the third condition receive no pretest, a treatment, and a posttest. Those in the final condition receive only a single measurement, the equivalent of a posttest. The Solomon four-group design is the most rigorous of the experiment designs, allowing researchers to separate and identify treatment effects independently of the effects of pretesting. In other words, researchers can figure out whether posttest scores changed because people learned how to answer the questions better from taking a pretest, as opposed to whether the experimental treatment explains the difference in posttest scores. The biggest drawbacks to the use of the four-group design are practical. Four groups are required to properly execute the design, requiring a high number of subjects and increased costs.

Various other designs may be used that are considered something other than fully experimental. These designs are most commonly considered preexperimental or quasiexperimental and include case studies and the one-group pretest-posttest design, among other design

TABLE 8.4
One-Group Quasiexperimental Pretest-Postest Design

Group	Random Assignment	Pretest	Treatment	Posttest
1	No	X	X	X

TABLE 8.5
Two-Group Quasiexperimental Pretest-Posttest Design (Common Variation)

Group	Random Assignment	Pretest	Treatment	Posttest
1	No	X	X	X
2	No	X		X

possibilities. Quasiexperimental studies suffer from design flaws because they lack control conditions and/or researchers use nonrandom procedures to assign participants to different conditions in an experiment. Quasiexperimental designs may be used for various purposes including exploration, but their methods cannot be considered scientific and their results, therefore, are not trustworthy.

It is often impossible or impractical to use probability sampling methods when recruiting research participants for studies. Instead, researchers commonly select participants using incidental, or convenience, samples in research experiments (see chap. 10). Because research participants may not be completely representative of a target audience or other population, the results of an experiment may lack external validity, or generalizability from the sample to the population. In general, this is not as detrimental for explanatory research such as experiments as it is for descriptive research such as surveys. Social processes and patterns of causal relationships are generally stable across populations and, because of this, are more generalizable than individual characteristics (Babbie, 1999). In reality, the samples used in experiments are so small they would not be highly representative even if probability sampling were used. With this in mind, convenience sampling normally suffices in experiments when probability sampling is impossible or impractical. Even though probability sampling may be impossible, researchers use random assignment to ensure participants are equal in each condition in an experiment.

As with any other research or communication project, pretesting variable manipulations, measurements, and the procedures used in an experiment is necessary before data collection begins. Pretesting allows researchers to correct any deficiencies in the procedures used for data collection, as well as providing a check of independent variable manipulations. A *manipulation check* is particularly important in helping ensure the success of a study. A manipulation check is a procedure that ascertains whether something that was supposed to happen actually did happen. For example, if one community was supposed to see a scary type of public service announcement and another community was supposed to see a humorous type of announcement, a manipulation check would determine whether the people in the communities thought the scary message was actually scary and that the humorous message was actually funny.

Finally, researchers must develop a procedure for telling participants what the purpose of the study is and how the study's results will be used. Participants' questions are answered at this time, in a process called *debriefing*. Debriefing allows researchers to eliminate the potential harms, however small, that may result from research participation. Debriefing should be comprehensive enough to remove any effects on participants that may have been created during a research project.

Bias in Data Collection, Analysis, and Interpretation

It is essential for researchers to collect, analyze, and interpret data in a careful manner. Practitioners should pay particular attention to the introduction of bias during data collection. Bias may be introduced in several ways, including through the behavior of researchers. Any changes in participant behavior due to the actions of researchers introduce bias into the experiment, unless the behavior of the experimenter is intended to be part of the study. Researchers may inadvertently encourage a behavior they are looking for through demonstrations of tension or relief, for example. One way researchers control unintended experimenter influences is through the use of automated procedures and equipment such as VCRs and videotapes. Experimenter bias may also be minimized by using researchers who are unaware of the purpose of a study, or researchers who have differing expectations regarding experimental outcomes.

Experiment Critique

When conducted properly, formal experiments allow researchers to isolate variables and establish causation. This is a powerful benefit that is provided only by properly designed and executed experiments. In laboratory experiments, researchers have a high degree of control over the research environment, independent and dependent variables, and the selection and assignment of subjects. This high degree of control and isolation of research environments provides conditions that are free from the competing influences of normal activity and ideal for examining independent and dependent variable relationships (Wimmer & Dominick, 2000). Although field experiments do not allow as high a degree of control as laboratory experiments, they generally provide enough control for researchers to make determinations of causation when properly conducted.

Another benefit of experiments to practitioners is their ease of replication. Since the variables and manipulations used in experiments are typically made available to other researchers, it is common for social scientists to replicate research findings. Replication may take the form of an identical experiment or one that provides replication under slightly different conditions. The successful replication of research findings contributes to increased confidence in the validity and generalizability of research findings (Babbie, 1999).

Finally, the cost of experimental research can be low when compared with other research methods. Laboratory research, in particular, tends to be limited in scope requiring relatively little time and relatively few subjects. These requirements often combine to provide a high degree of power at a relatively low cost.

There are two primary disadvantages to using experiments: the artificial situation and the introduction of bias. Although isolation and control are necessary in the determination of causation, research environments may be so isolated and so controlled that they do not represent environments found in natural social settings. Here, the external validity, or generalizability, of research findings may be hindered. The artificiality of laboratory research settings presents a particular problem in applied campaign studies because it does not reflect the busy, competitive environment in which most communication campaigns are conducted. In this instance, the generalizability of research findings from laboratory experiments to public relations campaign settings may be limited.

A second disadvantage of experimental research is the potential for introducing bias. Bias may be introduced through various sources during an experiment. The result is that research outcomes are inaccurate and provide a poor basis for campaign planning and execution.

Finally, experiments can be challenging to conduct. It can be difficult, for example, to measure complex human processes using a series of simple questions. It may be that participants have never considered the reasons for some of their attitudes and behaviors, and they may find it difficult to identify their responses. Sometimes, participants simply are unable to express their feelings, even if it only involves answering a few questions. It also can be difficult to manipulate the stimuli used in experiments or execute procedures with the care necessary to determine causation. In fact, it is possible to plan an experiment that is virtually impossible to conduct. Experiments, like all research methods, are useful only for specific situations, and their limitations should be considered carefully.

CONTENT ANALYSIS

Content analysis is a scientific research method used for describing communication content such as message characteristics in a quantitative, or numerical, form. Many public relations practitioners work to place messages in the media on a regular basis and continually monitor and track media coverage concerning issues, events, and clients. Right or wrong, public relations clip files have long served as the basis for evaluating public relations campaign success and often are seen as a critical measure of practitioners' achievements (Broom & Dozier, 1990). Evaluating the contents of a clip file or other important media messages—including the messages of competing organizations—often is difficult. The sheer volume of material can make even a basic description and analysis a daunting task. When additional information is desired concerning specific content attributes of different stories, the tone of media coverage, or the balance of media portrayals, for example, the task becomes seemingly impossible.

Content analysis is a research technique used for the objective, systematic, and quantitative description of specific aspects of communication (Berelson, 1952). Content analyses are objective because their results are not based on the informal observations and biases of those conducting the study, but instead rely on an objective classification system. They are systematic because a set of procedures is established and a formal process is followed when media content is analyzed. Content analyses are quantitative because the results of the classification process produce numerical classifications of content that are subjected to appropriate statistical analyses. The result is a scientific (that is, trustworthy) description of communication content in terms of specific themes, styles, and techniques.

If an organization wanted to better understand the ways it was portrayed in the media, for example, it might decide to have an employee comb through a collection of media to determine frequency of coverage, evaluate the general tone of the stories, and note recurring themes and major issues. Alternatively, the organization could conduct a formal content analysis. In this case, researchers would determine the aspects of media coverage most important to the company, and the media content would then be categorized and analyzed quantitatively based on the critical components of media coverage. The results and conclusions from such a study would be both sophisticated and accurate, and would provide an unbiased assessment of the media coverage concerning the organization. Study findings could serve as the basis for future media relations efforts or might be part of an analysis of the messages of competing organizations. The results also might serve as a benchmark if the company decided to undertake an effort to improve its media coverage.

Content analyses typically require several steps similar to those used in survey research. In fact, a content analysis is a lot like a survey, except that researchers collect samples of messages rather than of people. Initially, investigators identify a research problem and develop research questions or hypotheses. Next, they choose an appropriate media sample. Then, they determine procedures and categories for coding the content. Researchers must train those who code the data, and they usually conduct a small pilot study (the equivalent of a pretest) to ensure the study is well designed. Content coding takes place once the pilot study proves successful, followed by the data analysis and interpretation.

Research Problem and Questions/Hypothesis Development

As with any other research project, investigators should clearly map out the purpose of the study, including any problems that they must address, in the first phase of a content analysis. This helps researchers design a useful study with realistic procedures. A good research design clearly integrates the procedures for selecting the sample, the content categories and other aspects of the analysis, and study design into a comprehensive plan, as discussed in chap. 4. By implication, an investigator must determine the reason for the study, specify the evidence needed to test ideas or relationships, and know the methods of analysis that will be used once the data are gathered and coded.

Content analysis can apply to almost any form of communication. Researchers most often use it to address research questions or hypotheses concerning specific message attributes. This may include an analysis of messages over time (such as to see whether media coverage has become more positive), an analysis of messages occurring in different situations (including different or competing campaigns), or an analysis of messages directed to different audiences (such as trade publications versus general interest magazines). Often, analysts examine the relationship between two or more variables, such as the mention of a campaign theme along with the tenor of a message.

Researchers sometimes go beyond description to make inferences about the origins of messages based on the results of a content analysis. Such analyses generally focus on the author of a message to associate authorship with meanings and values inherent in the messages analyzed, such as to determine whether certain reporters or media outlets favor particular types of story themes. Finally, too often researchers erroneously use content analyses to make inferences about the effects of messages on receivers, such as effects of violent content on children's behavior. Content analyses conducted for this purpose are fatally flawed because they make several untenable assumptions. As chap. 14 explains, people interpret similar messages differently. Exposure to a message does not lead to uniform message effects. Simply put, content analyses do not allow researchers to determine causation.

Sample Selection

Researchers must select the messages to analyze after they have determined research questions, hypotheses, or both. First, they determine the body of messages, or population, from which the sample will be drawn, just as the survey designer chooses a population of people to study. In this process, also known as defining the "universe" or "sampling frame," investigators choose the body of content from which they will draw their sample, such as popular magazines published during the past six months. Just as with survey research, content analysts usually do not try to analyze all relevant messages (this would be a census). The sheer volume of potentially relevant messages almost always makes some form of sampling necessary, especially given the time and monetary limitations that accompany most research projects. Researchers should make sure the message population is comprehensive and logically consistent with the purposes and goals of the study.

It is important to distinguish between all the content potentially relevant to a study and a subset, or sample, of content needed to answer research questions or test hypotheses. Various techniques lend themselves to the selection of materials for analysis. Sampling techniques are discussed in chap. 10.

Content analyses may require some type of multistage sampling involving sample selection procedures at two or more levels. At the initial stage of sample selection researchers might select specific media sources—daily newspapers during an election cycle, for example—from among all possible sources. At a second stage of sampling, researchers might select specific stories from each selected newspaper. Additional stages may be necessary, as well. Researchers may find it advantageous to first select specific pages, for example, and then select specific stories as an additional sampling stage.

Units of Analysis

Researchers must determine the unit of analysis and content categories used in a study before data collection begins because content can
be analyzed in different forms. Each form of content analyzed is reduced to a *unit* for measurement and evaluation. A unit of analysis is
an individually distinct portion of content (Riffe, Lacy, & Fico, 1998),
meaning the element researchers actually count. Units of analysis can
include stories or articles, words or terms, themes, paragraphs, char-
acters, and more. In a study designed to examine the media's portrayal
of an organization, for example, the units of analysis may include positive, negative, or mixed stories about the corporation, specific aspects
of the corporation's image in stories, the mention of specific corporate
programs in stories, the names of competing organizations mentioned, and other relevant information. Specification of the units of
analysis can present challenges and generally requires pretesting
through trial and error. Often researchers begin with a rough-draft definition of a unit. Then they analyze a sample of representative content
to determine problems in identification. Such a procedure typically results in the modification and further refinement of unit descriptions.

Categories of Analysis

Researchers code and classify units of analysis, placing them into categories created for a study. For example, each article may be labeled as
favorable or unfavorable. Well-constructed categories are essential,
forming the substance of an investigation. Researchers who develop
content categories that are vaguely drawn or poorly articulated will
produce a study with inferior quality and limited usefulness. To be effective, category systems should be *mutually exclusive, exhaustive,*
and *reliable.*

Categories are mutually exclusive when a unit of analysis can be
placed into only one category. If a unit simultaneously falls into more
than one category, revisions are necessary for either or both categories. One means of avoiding problems related to exclusivity is to have
category definitions that possess a high degree of specificity. When category units are well defined, fewer questions are likely regarding unit
placement among categories.

Categories must be exhaustive, in addition to being mutually exclusive. Categories that are exhaustive provide space for every existing
unit of analysis. It is necessary to expand content categories when
units are discovered that are not covered by existing categories. When
only a few miscellaneous units are not covered by existing category systems, researchers may use an "other" category.

Finally, the category system must be reliable. To be considered reliable, different coders should agree on the placement of units of analyses within categories most of the time. This is called *intercoder reliability*. Content categories that are poorly defined and lack specificity generally suffer from low intercoder reliability. Conversely, well-defined category systems increase intercoder reliability. The extensive pretesting of sample data for unit placement will helps researchers develop and refine categories until they are mutually exclusive, exhaustive, and reliable.

Coding Content

Coding content involves the placement of units of analysis into content categories. This process is generally the most time-consuming aspect of content analysis, requiring researchers to train coders, develop a pilot study, and code the data. Reliability is critical in content analysis because content analyses are supposed to produce objective results. Researchers must use reliable measures to produce study results that are objective (Wimmer & Dominick, 2000). The measures used in a study are reliable when repeated measurement of the same material produces the same results. Normally, the same set of data is coded by two coders working independently. Analysts can compare the results of each coder's work using a sample of data to determine the level of accuracy between the coders. This produces a test of intercoder reliability. Intercoder reliability can be calculated using one of several methods. Holsti (1969) reported a simple formula commonly used for calculating intercoder reliability:

$$\text{reliability} = \frac{M}{n1 + n2}$$

In this formula, M represents the number of coding decisions agreed on by coders, and each n refers to the total number of coding decisions made by the first and second coder, respectively. This formula has some limitations, but it is simple and easy to use. Readers may be interested in using other formulas depending on their need for a more sophisticated measure of reliability, but Holsti's method is generally acceptable in most content analyses.

The thorough training of coders generally results in a more reliable analysis. It is helpful to have several training sessions in which coders work on sample data. The results are compared between coders and differences are discussed and possibly recoded. Detailed instruction sheets should also be provided to coders. Rigorous training efforts result in higher intercoder reliability. After a thorough training period, a pilot study may be conducted to check intercoder reliability. As a result of the pilot study, researchers may need to revise definitions and category boundaries, and coding sheets may need to be altered. This process should continue until coders are comfortable with the materials and procedures, and a high degree of reliability is maintained.

Finally, the content is coded. The use of standardized score sheets developed during training aids in the quick and accurate collection of data. Templates may also be used to measure media space. Broadcast media used for analysis is often taped allowing coders to start and stop the tape at their convenience. As a final note, researchers can enhance data collection with the use of computers, which they also can use to tabulate results.

Content Analysis Critique

The objective and systematic nature of this research method often helps researchers produce content descriptions and analyses that are high in validity and reliability, and avoid the subjective interpretations of less rigorous methods of analyzing content. In addition, many content analyses are inexpensive to conduct and can be used to examine content as it evolves over long periods. This gives researchers an important perspective not easily available in other scientific methods of research. Further, although most research methods typically pose little risk to participants, content analyses involve even less risk because human participants are not part of the population under investigation (Babbie, 1999). Together, these benefits make content analysis an attractive and useful research method.

Content analysis should be used carefully despite its potential usefulness. Kerlinger (1973) suggested that content analysis is not an easy method to use correctly. The primary concerns include problems of reliability, validity, and inference. The concept of reliability is of maximum importance in content analysis. A high degree of reliability may be particularly difficult to achieve when analyzing content such as negative political advertising. Determining whether a negative advertisement contains a direct attack on an opponent, for example, may involve making several slight distinctions between ads. Does an ad in which a candidate is referred to, but not named, contain a direct reference? Do ads that refer to a candidate's political party and/or position without mentioning the candidate by name contain a direct reference? Do ads that contain negative testimonials without naming a candidate contain direct references? Even determining whether an ad is negative or positive often involves making judgment calls. These types of difficulties are common in content analyses. They typically create problems for coders and contribute to low levels of reliability in content studies.

Validity in content studies is typically determined by the degree to which an instrument actually measures what it is supposed to measure. Validity is directly connected to the procedures used in content analysis. When sampling designs are incorrect, if categories are not mutually exclusive and exhaustive, or if reliability is low, the results of a content analysis possess a low degree of validity.

The final concern regarding the use of content analysis involves problems associated with inference. The strength of most content analyses depends on their ability to provide a precise description of communication content. Content studies often purport, however, to present conclusions and interpretations of wider application than the content itself. Such interpretations are untrustworthy. Practitioners purchasing content analytic services from an agency should carefully evaluate the claims made. Several reputable firms, such as Ketchum Public Relations's Publicity Tracking System, offer specialized and sophisticated content analysis techniques. The problem comes when a company equates content analysis with public opinion analysis. Remember that public opinion resides in the public, not in the content of media messages.

FINAL THOUGHTS

Formal research methods provide essential information for the public relations manager. Because formal methods offer objectivity, systematic data collection, representative samples, and replicable designs, they provide trustworthy information. Only dependable information can help practitioners accurately describe situations and publics, predict the outcome of an election, understand the reasons why public opinion seems to have turned against an organization, and exert some control over what happens in the future. Each formal method has its strengths and weaknesses, which means that each method can be used well or misused badly. As a result, a good understanding of the benefits and limitations of each method can help the managers do independent, in-house research. It also enables managers to knowledgeably weigh the promises and strategies of research firms, and to purchase reputable services that provide useful information at a reasonable cost.

❧ 9 ❧
Making Research Decisions: Survey Research

Mail Surveys
Telephone Surveys
Personal Interviews
Final Thoughts

A survey is a method of collecting information directly from members of a population. It usually involves interviews and questionnaires that participants fill out alone or with the assistance of an interviewer. This method of research has experienced an enormous surge in usage over the past several years and today is a regular part of many organizations' public relations programs. Survey research is an indispensable part of organizations' attempts to monitor their internal and external environments; solve complex problems; understand the opinions, attitudes, and behaviors of key target audience members; track public opinion; engage in sophisticated public relations campaign planning and evaluation; and, in some cases, seek media attention for an organization or client.

What is responsible for the rapid increase in the use of survey research? Organizations have increasingly felt the need to understand the opinions, attitudes, and behavioral motivations of their key target audience members, including legislators and government regulators, community members, consumers, employees, and other important groups. The environments in which organizations operate are more competitive; target audiences are more sophisticated and, in some cases, given to greater activism. Single-issue activist groups, employees, and others are more likely to use the media to engage organizations in public "debates" using publicity and promotion techniques to gain the attention and support of the media, community watchdog groups, government regulators and key target audiences. Practitioners want to ensure a high level of performance for their programs and campaigns, particularly as the costs of a campaign or program increase, or as organizational certainty about a campaign or program decreases. In this case, survey research serves as a kind of insurance, providing critical information to practitioners as they plan and implement public relations programs and campaigns. Valid, reliable information replaces practitioners' reliance on past practices, hunches, industry standards, as previously noted. In these circumstances, survey research is an invaluable part of public relations planning and problem solving.

Finally, organizational management wants to know how resources are being used and the return on investment they provide to an organization. Practitioners commonly have used favorable media coverage, key story placement, media clip counts, and similar methods to communicate the value of their publicity and promotions work to organizational management and clients (Pinkleton et al., 1999). Clients and managers are initially impressed when practitioners bring in large clip-filled binders and low cost-per-impression numbers. They grow skeptical, however, when larger, more important questions are asked about the effect of public relations activities on the attitudes and behaviors of key target audience members ("PR Needs," 1993; "PR Pulse," 1994; Robinson, 1969). In this instance, survey research provides a more sophisticated means of tracking changes in the opinions, attitudes, and behaviors of target audience members, and it is an indispensable tool for practitioners communicating the benefits of public relations activities to organizations and clients.

These are among the most critical issues practitioners face and are a large part of the reason practitioners' use of survey research has increased so rapidly over the past several years. As noted in chap. 8, surveys generally are descriptive or analytical in nature. Descriptive surveys characterize conditions and circumstances as they exist in a population, and analytical surveys attempt to explain why current conditions exist. In fact, many surveys serve both purposes, and this often meets practitioners' and organizations' needs for information. As a group, survey research methods also possess several advantages in the collection, analysis, and interpretation of information.

Researchers primarily use mail, telephone and personal interviews to conduct surveys, and are increasingly using electronic surveys in different forms. Researchers can use each method in a relatively straightforward approach or adapt a method to reach new audiences or to meet the demands of a particular research situation. In addition, technology such as the Internet is contributing to the development of new survey research methods. In a typical survey, researchers initially set objectives for a research project, and then design the study. When researchers design a study, they normally select a population and establish sampling procedures, select a survey method, and design and pretest a questionnaire. Next, members of a research team typically collect, edit, and code data. Finally, researchers analyze and interpret the results.

Because chap. 8 presents the survey-research-planning process, this chapter focuses on understanding some of the key advantages and disadvantages of each survey method. This discussion raises an important issue. Clients and organizations, often looking to make quick decisions, frequently want to identify the single "best" survey research method. The reality is there is no best method of survey research, and it is a risky oversimplification to sort methods based on a scale of "goodness" or strengths and weaknesses (Frey, 1989). The method that is best for a project depends on various factors. Beyond the informational requirements of a project, researchers must consider the target audience, the survey topic or topics, and the importance of reliability and validity. In addition, a project's budget and time frame often have a disproportionately large effect on survey-method selection (Pinkleton et al., 1999). As Dillman (1978) pointed out, the question of which method is best cannot be answered in abstract terms. The potential advantages and disadvantages of each method do not apply equally, or even at all, to every survey situation. Choosing the most appropriate research method is critical, and, for this reason, the use of a survey method must be considered in relation to the needs and constraints of each situation.

With this in mind, it is beneficial for practitioners to understand each survey research method. The flexibility and adaptability of different survey methods inevitably leads to conflicting suggestions from researchers or others concerning the "best" survey method to use for a project. Practitioners serve their own interest by understanding at least some of the key issues associated with the use of one survey method over another in a research situation, as well as other critical aspects of survey implementation such as issues associated with the use of probability versus nonprobability sampling. This understanding allows them to make an informed decision and makes them sophisticated consumers of the research products they, in effect, purchase. The remainder of this chapter presents each of the primary survey research methods broadly and includes information about the potential benefits and limitations of these methods.

MAIL SURVEYS

Mail surveys are conducted by mailing a questionnaire to a sample of individuals. Participants fill out the questionnaires on their own and mail the surveys back to the researcher. A cover letter is mailed with the questionnaire to explain the purpose of the survey and encourage sample members to respond. Stamped, addressed reply envelopes typically are enclosed to encourage respondents to complete the surveys and mail them back to researchers. Researchers often use mail surveys because of their low cost and ease of administration. If a mailing list is available (and it often is), it is relatively easy to use it as the source of a probability-based sample. Several challenges face researchers using survey research including the length of time it takes to complete a project and the relatively low response rates. Despite these concerns, the low cost and ease of administration of mail surveys are among the advantages that make them an attractive choice.

Mail Survey Considerations

There are many nuanes of successful survey research, and this is especially true of mail surveys (see Table 9.1). A mail survey is a self-administered questionnaire. This requires that the cover letter and questionnaire be carefully constructed and written to optimize the participation rate of sample members. Unfortunately, no matter how well a questionnaire and cover letter are written, this is not enough to ensure the success of a mail survey (Dillman, 1978). The result is that mail surveys often suffer from the lowest rates of response among the

TABLE 9.1
Characteristics of Mail Surveys

Selected Benefits	Selected Limitations
Inexpensive (lowest cost per respondent).	Frequently suffer from low response rates (often requires inducements and multiple mailings).
Reaches widely dispersed sample members easily.	Data collection may take a long time.
Mailing lists make it easy to generate probability-based sample.	No questionnaire flexibility; short, self-explanatory questionnaire needed.
May provide high degree of anonymity (useful for sensitive topics).	Survey respondent may not be selected sample member.
No interviewer bias.	Members of certain groups less likely to complete questionnaire

primary survey research methods, despite researchers' best efforts to encourage participation. Although there are many keys to a successful mail survey project, practitioners should pay special attention to the cover letter and questionnaire, and the sampling method and response rate to ensure the success of mail survey.

A well-written cover letter is critical to the success of a survey because it must introduce a survey to potential respondents who are busy and uninterested, and motivate them to fill out the survey and return it immediately. A cover letter usually is the only opportunity a researcher has to pique the interest of sample members, establish a minimal level of rapport, and anticipate and answer key questions. The difficulty of writing a good cover letter is increased because a long, dense letter that satisfactorily answers everyone's questions will discourage careful reading, or worse, will cause potential respondents to simply throw the questionnaire in the trash with the day's junk mail. The first two paragraphs of a cover letter usually explain who is sponsoring the study and what the study is about, and convince the reader the study is useful. Later paragraphs are used to convince readers that their response is critical and assure them of confidentially. All of this must be accomplished without biasing participants' responses (Czaja & Blair, 1996; Dillman, 1978). Writing an effective cover letter can be difficult and perplexing. Given the importance of the cover letter to the success of a mail survey, researchers should draft and pretest different letters to ensure they have written a compelling letter (see chap. 11).

Mail surveys also require the use of carefully written and pretested questionnaires. The mail questionnaire requires more careful writing and construction than any other type of questionnaire, because it must be completely self-explanatory. An attractive questionnaire of reasonable length with plenty of white space and clear, simple instructions is a good start. The absence of an interviewer means no opportunity for interviewers to encourage survey response, gloss over poorly written questions or instructions, or answer even basic participant questions (Dillman, 1978). Although a telephone number or E-mail address can be provided for such purposes, participants rarely use them. In fact, participants should not need to contact researchers to understand questions and instructions. Instead, the instructions and questions used in mail surveys must be written so they are uniformly understood by as many potential respondents as possible (Czaja & Blair, 1996). Poorly written questions decrease the reliability and validity of survey results, and sample members who do not understand questions or instructions are unlikely to participate, resulting in low response rates.

Pretesting a questionnaire is essential to ensure that readers understand survey instructions, questions, and response categories. When a questionnaire is pretested, individuals who are similar to sample members in terms of key sample characteristics—such as age, education level, work experience, or other relevant qualities—actually complete the survey, making note of confusing or unclear questions and instructions. Other aspects of the questionnaire also are noted and discussed at length with researchers such as length of time needed to complete the survey and various features of questionnaire design. There are many ways to pretest a questionnaire, and no single method is particularly advantageous. The key is to pretest all written material potential respondents will receive, preferably several times. Experience shows that problems can sneak into even the most comprehensively tested questionnaires. Most survey problems, however, are caught and corrected through multiple pretests.

Even when mail surveys are well written and comprehensively pretested, they often suffer from low response rates, typically the lowest response rates of the primary survey research methods. Although there are different formulas for determining survey response rates, the response rate generally is the percentage of sample members who, once contacted, actually participate in the survey (see chap. 12). A low response rate raises concerns of *nonresponse bias*. Nonresponse bias is the potential distortion of survey findings that results from differences between those who participate in a survey and those who do not (Adler & Clark, 1999). Simply put, when enough sample members choose not to participate in a survey, their lack of participation ruins the external validity, or generalizability, of a study's results, and accurate generalization from the sample to the population is not possible.

Surveys that are well designed help increase participant response rate. Although each project is different, there are several elements to a successful project and a number of ways researchers work to increase mail survey response rates. Dillman (1978) noted that integration and consistency among the individual elements of a mail survey are keys to increasing mail survey participation. These most commonly include the use of prenotification and reminder cards or letters, as well as sending new cover letters and an additional copy of the questionnaire to nonrespondents. Initially, a prenotification card or letter can be an effective way to prepare respondents for survey participation. Typically, sample members receive this mailing one or two weeks before the questionnaire and cover letter are sent, and it is used to create understanding and even a small degree of anticipation among sample respondents. The cover letter and questionnaire are mailed next. The cover letter and questionnaire typically are followed by a reminder card or letter, or even better, a new letter and questionnaire, two or three weeks later. This process often is repeated more than once to offer potential respondents as many opportunities as possible to participate in the survey. Chapter 11 has more on design issues.

Research suggests that follow-up mailings are an effective way to increase mail survey participation. In general, the longer sample members delay responding, the lower the likelihood that they will participate. Properly timed follow-up mailings provide additional encouragement to respond. Various other ways help increase mail survey response rates, as well. Research suggests that other techniques generally produce higher response rates such as sponsorship by a university or other respected institution; questionnaires mailed in envelopes with stamps rather than metered or bulk rate markings; the enclosure of a stamped, self-addressed return envelope with the survey; and the use of monetary incentives such as $1 or other small inducements (sometimes small gifts are used such as a pencil or pen).

There are other ways to increase response rate as well, but some attempts to increase response rates are not successful and even may reduce participation in some cases. Using personalized envelopes or questionnaires, for example, when respondent anonymity is important or the topic of a survey is sensitive is ineffective. It is critical for researchers to understand as much as possible about the topic and sample members, and to pretest all aspects of a survey to increase their ability to obtain valid, reliable results from sample members.

The representativeness of mail survey results is increased through probability sampling methods, as discussed in chap. 10. One benefit to mail surveys is that the names and addresses of randomly selected members of a population can be purchased from vendors who sell samples, often at a reasonable price. In addition, these same companies typically can provide highly specialized samples at a higher price. Such samples often are invaluable because they allow researchers to complete a survey using a probability-based sample, helping to increase the reliability and validity of survey results. Some organizations and associations use their own mailing lists as the basis for a probability sample. The mailing list serves as the *sampling frame* (a list of population members from which a sample is drawn), and researchers can randomly draw names and addresses from the list to form the sample. In this way, it is a relatively simple process for researchers to generate a probability-based sample to use when conducting a mail survey.

Practitioners should take care in the interpretation of research results, however, when mailing lists serve as the basis for a sample. Even though the sample is probability based, the results are only directly generalizable to members of the mailing list. Ideally, a mailing list contains all of the members of a population. In this case, the results of the survey are likely to represent the true opinions and attitudes of all population members (given a certain range of error at a specific level of confidence; see chap. 10 for these calculations). In other instances, however, a mailing list is not a complete list of all members of a population. This might be the case, for example, if you were trying to survey members of a professional association using the association's mailing list. Any sample generated using such a mailing list would produce results that were directly generalizable only to members of the association, and not to all members of the profession. This matter may seem small and technical, but it is significant. Research results are only as trustworthy as the sample on which they are based. Researchers should use mailing lists with care and consider the ramifications of sampling decisions before plunging into data collection. There is no way to increase the generalizability of a survey's results once a study is complete.

Finally, one of the newest approaches to survey research is to use computerized self-administered questionnaires (CSAQ). When CSAQ interviews are conducted, a respondent receives the questionnaire by way of a floppy disk, bulletin board, or other means, and runs the data-collection software, which asks questions and records answers (Babbie, 1999). Researchers may E-mail a questionnaire to sample members directly, for example, or notify them they have been selected to participate in a survey via E-mail and ask them to access a questionnaire on a bulletin board. Such surveys generally have all the benefits of regular mail surveys with some additional advantages. In particular, electronic surveys commonly cost even less than regular mail surveys because of the lack of postage and production costs, and immediate delivery shortens the time it takes to complete a project.

CSAQ interviews also have some significant disadvantages. Perhaps most important, a sample is limited to persons with computers and/or on-line access. Although the use of technology is rapidly expanding, much of the population does not have computers and/or online access. In addition, when surveys are posted on bulletin boards, it may be difficult to control who actually completes a questionnaire. Ultimately, the reliability and external validity of a survey's results may be extremely low as a result of these limitations. In addition, online communication is far from problem free. Documents and attachments sent via electronic mail commonly suffer a host of problems. They may end up reformatted to such an extent that they are difficult or impossible to read, or sample members may be unable to open them at all. Electronic survey research still is being developed. Although this kind of research has much potential, practitioners should be careful before undertaking an important project using largely untested research methods.

Mail Survey Critique

Mail surveys are generally the least expensive survey research method. This benefit alone contributes greatly to their popularity as a research method. Although there are situations in which other survey methods may cost less, in most instances, mail surveys provide the ability to cover a large geographical area at the lowest cost per respondent (Dillman, 1978). For many surveys, the costs of developing and producing a questionnaire, securing a sample, and analyzing and interpreting the results are similar. Two methodological benefits significantly reduce the cost of mail surveys relative to other research methods. The first is postage; sample members can be reached for the same cost whether they are across town or across the nation. Although telephone surveys can also be inexpensive, mail surveys consistently enjoy a cost savings because of mail distribution. The second cost-savings benefit results from lower administrative costs. The data are not collected by interviewers, and mail surveys generally require fewer people to manage the data-collection process. Although a knowledgeable staff is needed to assemble materials, track responses, mail follow-ups, and edit and code returned questionnaires, mail surveys almost always require fewer administrative resources than other survey methods.

Mail surveys also are useful for reaching widely dispersed sample members. Although other methods can be adapted to reach dispersed sample members, often at increased costs, mail surveys easily address this issue. In addition, mail surveys allow for selective probability sampling through specialized mailing lists. Although researchers must be concerned about the limited generalizability of survey results when lists are used as the sampling frame, mailing lists can make excellent sampling frames in appropriate research settings. Researchers may use a selected list, for example, when they need to sample a highly specialized professional population. Mail surveys also may be used to collect information from sample members who are busy and unlikely to participate in a telephone or personal interview.

Researchers may use mail surveys when a high degree of respondent anonymity is desired (Mangione, 1995). Respondents are more likely to provide candid answers to questions concerning sensitive subjects because they are not speaking directly to an interviewer. Research suggests, for example, that respondents can more easily answer questions about highly personal issues such as drunk driving convictions or personal bankruptcy using self-administered questionnaires (Aday, 1989; Locander, Sudman, & Bradburn, 1976). In addition, researchers generally are less concerned over the introduction of interviewer bias into study results when mail surveys are used. Respondents typically are sensitive to both verbal and nonverbal cues during the interview process, and sometimes interpret these cues as supportive or unsupportive of their opinions, attitudes, and behaviors. They may change their responses as a result. Survey results concerning racial prejudice, for example, would be ruined if participants changed answers because they sensed interviewer disapproval for their prejudicial opinions and attitudes. Instead of an accurate measure of racial prejudice, study results would be skewed by participants who provide socially desirable responses because of apparent interviewer influence. Researchers who are studying sensitive subjects or who have concerns regarding the potential for interviewer bias can use mail surveys to eliminate such problems.

Perhaps the greatest concern in the use of mail surveys is their low response rates. It is not uncommon for mail surveys to have response rates ranging from 10% to 40% (Wimmer & Dominick, 2000). A low return rate casts doubt on the validity and reliability of a survey's findings by introducing nonresponse bias. Mail surveys with enough follow-up to obtain a high response rate typically require at least 8 weeks to conduct regardless of a sample's size or its geographic location (Czaja & Blair, 1996; Schutt, 1996). In many instances, 8 weeks is too long to wait given the time constraints that typically accompany research projects, particularly when telephone surveys can be conducted in less than half that time. In addition, the need for incentives and multiple mailings increase survey costs (see chap. 11).

Another significant problem with mail surveys is that questionnaires must be self-explanatory and relatively short to encourage survey participation. Because no one is available to explain questions or provide additional information, survey instructions, question wording, and question skip patterns—necessary when certain questions apply to some but not all participants—must be extremely simple and clear. Even when questions and instructions are clear, some respondents skip questions or even entire sections of a questionnaire for any number of reasons. Additionally, researchers can never be sure who has actually filled out a survey. Despite the fact that surveys usually are directed to specific individuals, individuals other than selected sample members may be asked or allowed to fill out questionnaires. Finally, returned surveys are less likely to be received from respondents who are of low education, who do not like to read or write, and who are not interested in the survey subject (Czaja & Blair, 1996; Wimmer & Dominick, 2000). Any of these concerns, working individually or togther, may introduce bias and threaten the reliability and validity of study results.

TELEPHONE SURVEYS

Telephone interviewing involves contacting respondents and conducting personal interviews by telephone. This method of data collection represents a middle ground between personal interviews and mail surveys (Wimmer & Dominick, 2000). Telephone surveys offer many of the advantages of personal interviews at a cost that is often competitive with that of mail surveys. Although not offering the degree of flexibility present in personal interviews, telephone surveys offer more control and generally higher response rates than most mail surveys, and they often can be completed in less than half the time it takes to complete a mail survey. In many research situations, telephone surveys can provide substantially the same information as a face-to-face interview at about half the cost (Groves, 1989). These benefits have contributed to a rapid increase in researchers' use of telephone survey research.

Telephone Survey Considerations

Telephone surveys (see Table 9.2) require interviewers to introduce the survey to sample members; obtain cooperation; present instructions, questions, answer categories, and other relevant information; motivate participants to answer questions, answer any questions participants have; and administer the survey and record answers (Saris, 1991). Throughout this process, an interviewer ideally operates as a neutral vehicle through which a respondent's answers are communicated to researchers (Wimmer & Dominick, 2000). It is a complex process that requires carefully trained interviewers. Telephone surveys require well-written questionnaires and instructions because they rely solely on verbal communication. Because of this, survey design and construction are based on utility rather than on aesthetics. The interviewers' job is made more difficult, and quality of the data collected is

TABLE 9.2
Characteristics of Telephone Surveys

Selected Benefits	Selected Limitations
Relatively inexpensive (reasonable cost per respondent).	Interviewer bias may occur.
Data collection can be completed quickly.	Not every household has a telephone (potential source of bias).
Reaches widely dispersed sample members relatively easily.	Product and service innovations make it difficult to reach sample members.
Lists or random digit dialing make it easy to generate probability-based sample.	Short, largely self-explanatory questionnaire required.
Response rates relatively high.	Limited interview flexibility.
Rapport established with respondent can help gain compliance.	Respondents may not answer thoughtfully.

lowered, if instructions, questions, and response categories are unclear. Problems also are likely if question order does not proceed in an obvious manner with the aid of transitional statements, if question placement is irregular or lacking apparent topical organization, or if the survey lacks easily understood instructions (Frey, 1989). Interview questions and survey design issues often revolve around the needs of an interviewer to attract and keep a potential respondent's attention. Questionnaires typically flow from "warm-up" questions designed to maximize respondent interest; to issue-oriented questions that provide critical information about respondents' opinions, attitudes, and behavioral motivations; and conclude with routine demographic questions. Open-ended questions, which require interviewers to record a respondent's answer verbatim are used sparingly because they take time, interrupt questionnaire flow, and require additional coding during data analysis. Given the importance of a well-designed survey instrument, questionnaire pretesting and comprehensive interviewer training are a pivotal part of telephone survey success.

Although each survey is different and typically requires specialized interviewer training, there are common threads to successful training of telephone interviewers. First, researchers want interviewers to pay particular attention to the survey introduction because this is the first point of caller contact. Then, interviewers need to learn to read questions exactly as they are written; practice answering respondents' questions; practice selecting survey participants after initial phone contact has been made, if necessary; and learn how to help certain respondents use appropriate response categories. All of this must be accomplished while providing neutral feedback and probes so participant responses will not be influenced. Interviewers also must be prepared for difficult skip patterns or survey questions that, though necessary, are unusual or potentially bothersome to respondents, such as questions concerning their age or income. Finally, interviewers must complete a call record. This is a record of the result of each call attempt, and it provides researchers with information they need to determine sample members who receive additional call attempts and the response rate for a survey. The number and complexity of these and other issues necessitate thorough interviewer training before ever calling sample members (tips for training interviewers are contained in chap. 12).

In addition, precontact in the form of letters or cards effectively increases response rates in a manner similar to mail survey research. Prenotification letters or cards also can help legitimize a study by providing information about why sample members will be contacted, what kind of information will be requested, and what the benefits are of participation. Providing general information concerning the timing of survey phone calls helps to reduce the surprise associated with receiving an unanticipated phone call from an unknown source. Depending on the sample, many survey calls are placed on weeknight evenings (excluding Friday) from 6 p.m. to 9 p.m. Finally, callback attempts help increase participant contact and response. Callbacks typically are made to sample members who were not contacted during an initial call attempt. Although the number of callbacks differ according to survey characteristics, Wimmer and Dominick (2000) reported that three callbacks produce contact about 75% of the time.

As with all research methods, the external validity, or generalizability, of telephone survey results depends on the use of probability-based sampling methods, which are explained in chap. 10. One benefit of telephone survey research is that, similar to mail surveys, names and phone numbers of randomly selected members of a population can be purchased from commercial sample vendors, allowing researchers to complete a survey using a probability-based sample relatively easily. These same companies typically can provide specialized samples at a higher price.

When researchers choose not to purchase a sample, they often can use telephone directories, typically available for free or low cost, as the basis for sampling. Of course, no telephone directory is entirely representative of a population because of the households with unlisted telephone numbers. In some communities, the proportion of households with unlisted telephone numbers exceeds 50% (Survey Sampling, Inc., 1994), leaving a large portion of the population unavailable for sampling from a telephone directory, particularly in urban areas (Frey, 1989; Lavrakas, 1993). Researchers typically use a random digit dialing (RDD) technique to overcome problems with unlisted telephone numbers. The importance of randomization is explained in chap. 10.

RDD theoretically provides an equal probability of reaching a household with a telephone access line regardless of whether its telephone number is listed or unlisted, and it replicates what would occur if a complete sampling frame existed (Lavrakas, 1993). There are several RDD techniques including some that are computer based. Most RDD techniques rely on standard area codes and telephone number prefixes that correspond geographically to a desired population, and they use a randomization technique to produce a telephone number suffix.

In some of the more common but cumbersome RDD techniques, research staff members draw telephone numbers out of an appropriate telephone directory by hand and randomly change the last four digits to create a new number. They may add a number between 1 and 9, for example, to the last digit of a phone number. The added digit can be a constant or can be assigned randomly to each new number. In the "plus-one" method, 1 is added to the last digit of a telephone number suffix to produce a new telephone number. So, if staff members draw the telephone number 441-7165, they dial 441-7166. In a common variation of this technique, researchers use a table of random numbers (typically found in the back of statistics textbooks) to generate numbers used to replace one or more telephone number suffix digits (Frey, 1989; Lavrakas, 1993). Although such techniques produce unusable telephone numbers such as businesses or government offices, which adds to survey costs, they also produce a probability-based sample that provides coverage of unlisted telephone numbers.

Once initial telephone contact is made, some studies require randomization within each household contacted. If the household itself is the unit of analysis, any adult member can provide the information needed and within-household selection procedures are not necessary. When researchers seek results that are generalizable to an entire population of adults rather than households, however, interviewers must use a systematic process for selecting the member of the household to interview. If staff members do not use selection procedures, the resulting sample may include disproportionately high numbers of women and older adults, who are most likely to be home when interviewers call (Lavrakas, 1993; Salmon & Nichols, 1983).

Scholars and research practitioners have developed various selection procedures to avoid possible bias resulting from interviewing the person who answers the telephone. Unfortunately, they can be complex and unwieldy to use (Kish, 1965). When such selection procedures are used, they typically increase survey costs because of the extra time required to identify and select respondents and the need to make additional callbacks when selected respondents are unavailable. In addition, interviewers may experience additional refusals because interviewees are confused or frustrated by complex procedures that must be followed before an interview begins. One method that has gained widespread acceptance for randomizing respondent selection is to ask for the eligible person in the household whose birthday was most recent or who will have the next birthday (Salmon & Nichols, 1983). Although there are concerns that these methods do not always produce a completely randomized sample, the birthday-selection methods have been widely embraced by both scholars and research practitioners because they are generally effective, easy to use, not time consuming, and not intrusive (Lavrakas, 1993).

Finally, computer-assisted telephone interviewing (CATI) has become common among universities and commercial research firms and is perhaps the most significant technological advancement to telephone interviewing. When CATI systems are used, computers are used by interviewers to facilitate nearly every aspect of the interview process. The computer dials the telephone number and the interviewer reads the introduction, respondent-selection procedures, and questionnaire off the screen. Interviewers use the computer to record and code responses, and to help with statistical analysis at the end of the day. A CATI system is particularly useful if a questionnaire has complicated skip patterns or if the randomization of questions within a survey is desirable. The development of computer technology in connection with data collection is growing rapidly, and when a research organization properly implements a CATI system, it has the ability to improve the quality of telephone survey research.

Telephone Survey Critique

The benefits of telephone survey research have contributed to an increase in the popularity of this type of data collection. In particular, telephone surveys are relatively cost effective. Although they are generally more expensive than mail surveys, they often are less expensive than personal interview surveys. In addition, the short time in which researchers can complete a telephone survey is highly advantageous. Given the importance of cost and time factors in many research project decisions (Pinkleton et al., 1999), these factors make telephone surveys the frequent choice of research professionals and public relations practitioners.

In addition, telephone survey data-collection methods have improved over the past several years to the point that telephone survey research compares favorably with other methods of data collection in terms of data quality. Research staff can collect data from a widely dispersed sample and ensure the representativeness of the data relatively easily. If a list suitable as a sampling frame is available, research staff can draw a probability-based sample. If a suitable list is not available, staff members often can use random digit dialing to produce a probability-based sample. Either way, researchers use telephone surveys to produce data with a high degree of reliability and external validity.

Telephone surveys also tend to have strong response rates, often much higher than mail survey response rates. Although there is concern that response has been falling, telephone survey response rates commonly range from 60% to 90% (Czaja & Blair, 1996). Telephone surveys are especially likely to enjoy strong respondent participation when research staff members write and pretest survey introductions and questionnaires carefully; send prenotification cards or letters; use callbacks as needed; and when the project is sponsored by a university or respected institution. Interviewers who are well trained and experienced also help increase response rates and increase the quality of the data collected.

Interviewers help provide some degree of question flexibility in telephone surveys. Although telephone surveys are not as flexible as personal interviews, interviewers are available to clarify terms, explain questions to reduce respondent confusion, negotiate complex skip patterns, and help the data-collection process move forward in a smooth and orderly fashion. In addition, interviewers may be able to establish rapport with respondents that helps them obtain complete and accurate information, and sometimes convince respondents to complete an interview. At the same time, the use of interviewers raises concerns about the potential for introducing bias into survey results. Interviewers should have no influence on respondents' answers, but instead serve simply as a means of data collection. Interviewers require thorough training to learn how to provide neutral feedback and answer respondents' questions in a nonbiasing manner. In addition, interviewers should have a high level of experience when there is concern about the potential for bias.

Survey results also can be biased through sampling limitations. According to Czaja and Blair (1996), in 1990 approximately 5% of the households still were without telephones. Although a relatively small number, rural areas, some areas in the southern United States, and areas that are economically depressed have higher percentages of houses without telephone access. Residents who do not have telephone access are unavailable for survey purposes, and telephone survey results cannot accurately represent their opinions, attitudes, and behaviors. In addition, answering machines, call waiting, call forwarding, caller identification, and other technological marvels hinder telephone interviewing. They often require multiple call attempts and make it harder to reach potential respondents. Even after initial contact is made, respondents may suspect they are the target of a sales attempt, or simply resent an interruption, and terminate an interview before it is completed. Ultimately, these obstacles reduce the external validity and reliability of telephone survey research findings.

Finally, telephone interviews are limited in some respects. Perhaps most obvious, researchers' use of visuals and similar interview aids is severely hampered. In addition, instructions, questions, and response categories must be easy to understand because they are being read over the telephone to a respondent. Participants must be able to remember the question and the appropriate response categories; they also typically have no time to examine personal records or other information before responding to a question. Open-ended questions are difficult to use in a telephone survey because they require the interviewer to record a response verbatim and often result in short answers that are difficult to interpret without some discussion. In addition, researchers have no control over the survey environment. Incoming calls, the doorbell, children, or a loud television commercial commonly interrupt an interview, sometimes requiring interviewers to schedule a callback that may result in an incomplete interview.

Interviews also must be kept relatively short. Most respondents are unwilling to spend a great amount of time on the phone answering questions from a stranger. Although 30 minutes or less is an acceptable interview length, many market researchers try to keep an average interview under 10 minutes. It can be difficult or impossible to collect a large amount of high-quality data in such a short interview. Despite these difficulties, telephone survey research is a proven research method that is used frequently by scholars and market research practitioners.

PERSONAL INTERVIEWS

When personal interviews are conducted, interviewers typically collect information in a respondent's home, office, or other convenient location. Research staff members administer questionnaires in a face-to-face interview, recording respondent's answers and possibly collecting other information. There generally are two types of personal interviews: unstructured and structured. In an unstructured, in-depth interview, interviewers ask broad questions and respondents are given freedom to respond as they wish. The results of these interviews typically lack a high degree of validity and reliability because of the unstructured nature of the interview and sample limitations. The result is that in-depth interviews are largely an informal research method (discussed in chap. 6).

In a structured interview, questions are asked in a predetermined order and interviewers have less freedom to deviate from the questionnaire, also called a survey schedule. The result is a flexible interview process that often produces high-quality data, has a strong response rate, and lends itself well to various topics and question types. For these reasons, many scholars and market-research professionals have historically favored personal interviewing as a survey research method. Several issues, however, have reduced personal interviewing for survey research purposes. Factors such as a high cost per completed interview, the length of time needed for completion of a research project, and the need for a high degree of administration and coordination have contributed to a decline in the large-scale use of personal interviews. Nevertheless, personal interviewing is a flexible and effective survey method that serves many survey research projects settings.

Personal Interview Considerations

In many research situations, several important benefits result from having an interviewer collect data in a one-on-one meeting with a sur-

TABLE 9.3
Characteristics of Personal Interviews

Selected Benefits	Selected Limitations
Higher response rates.	Often expensive; typically highest cost per respondent.
Interviewers establish rapport with participants.	Requires high degree of administration and interviewer training.
Often results in high quality data.	Data collection may take a relatively long time.
Bias from sampling frame often is low.	Strong potential for interviewer bias.
High degree of interview/questionnaire flexibility.	Some sample members difficult to reach.

vey participant (see Table 9.3). A face-to-face meeting allows interview staff to interact and build rapport with potential participants, helping to increase survey response rates. In addition, after an unsuccessful contact attempt at the household of a sample member, an interviewer may visit with neighbors or generally observe the characteristics of a household or neighborhood to determine a better time to return for an interview (Groves & Lyberg, 1988). As a result, personal interview surveys historically have the highest response rates of any of the primary research methods, typically ranging from 65% to 95% (Czaja & Blair, 1996). A high level of personal interaction also increases the likelihood that interviewers will get complete and accurate information by creating a comfortable interview atmosphere. This factor is important when interviews are long or questionnaires contain complex questions and/or skip patterns. In this instance, the interviewer has a great deal of influence over the administration of the questionnaire and other aspects of the data-collection process. Personal interviews also are highly flexible, much more so than other survey methods. Research staff can answer respondents' questions; seek additional information to clarify ambiguous responses; show charts, pictures, or graphs; and even estimate respondent information such as general appearance or general living conditions. Finally, personal interviews do not depend on the literacy or education level of respondents, nor are they limited to persons with telephones, computers, or online access. Although this does not eliminate sampling bias concerns in personal interviews, it does address some sampling bias concerns. Ultimately, the use of face-to-face interviews can significantly improve the reliability and external validity of survey results.

Personal interviews, however, are susceptible to bias. Interviewer-related bias, or error, occurs in face-to-face interviews when participants vary their answers because of the person conducting the interview (Fowler & Mangione, 1990). Participants who sense that interviewers agree or disagree as they respond to certain questions, for example, may wittingly or unwittingly alter their answers to survey questions. Respondents also may hesitate to report sensitive information and are more likely to provide socially desirable responses in personal interviews (Czaja & Blair, 1996). In research concerning racial attitudes, for example, participants are more likely to give socially desirable responses when the interviewer and interviewee are of different races (Campbell, 1981).

The need for extensive interviewer training and standardized interview techniques is important in personal interview surveys, given the importance of the interviewer in the data-collection process. Although it is difficult to accomplish, a standardized interview process in which all interviewers conduct their work in a consistent manner reduces interview-related error (Fowler & Mangione, 1990).

Two aspects of personal survey administration merit special attention. The first is the need for thorough interviewer training, explained in chap. 12. A well-trained research staff is critical to the success of personal interview surveys. Well-trained staff members help encourage survey participation among sample members; draw thoughtful, relevant information to survey questions; and produce data that are high in accuracy, reliability, and external validity. Poorly trained staff members, on the other hand, are more likely to collect poor quality data and even bias survey results through their actions and statements. Problems may occur when poorly trained interviewers fail to probe inadequate answers, record respondents' answers incorrectly, ad lib questions rather than reading them as written, and behave in a way that could bias respondents' answers. There is no standard training program because there is no standard survey. The type and intensity of training depends on the goals of the study, the number of interviewers, their previous experience, the study's time frame, and the complexity of the questionnaire, among other things. Most training sessions attempt to communicate the goals of the study, develop basic interviewing skills, familiarize interviewers with the questionnaire and objectives for each question, and help interviewers learn to manage difficult interview situations (Warwick & Lininger, 1975).

The second aspect of personal survey administration that merits special attention is appropriate supervision. Proper training must be combined with effective supervision to contribute to a highly successful personal interview project. Field supervision takes place where training leaves off and occurs during actual data collection. The importance of field supervision is heightened in personal interview studies because data collection is decentralized. That is, interviewers are necessarily spread over a relatively broad geographic area. Some of the most critical aspects of field supervision include organizing work groups for neighborhoods or other geographic locations, arranging work assignments for research staff members, establishing production quotas for interviewers, reviewing completed work, serving as a liaison with the research office, and helping maintain a high level of commitment to the study among interviewers (Warwick & Lininger, 1975). Accomplishing these tasks requires strong organizational skills. Fowler and Mangione (1990) suggested that organizations pay attention to five critical aspects of each interviewers' work: the number of interviews each interviewer conducts during a period; the number of hours each interviewer works; the response rate of each interviewer; the quality of each interviewer's completed interviews; and the overall ability of each interviewer, including interactions with survey participants. Given the key role of interviewers in the data-collection process and the decentralized nature of personal surveys, interviewer training and effective field supervision contribute greatly to the success of these projects.

Personal Interview Variations

Group-Administered Surveys

Group-administered surveys combine some of the features of personal interviews and some of the features of mail surveys. The survey is given to members of a group who complete the survey individually, usually with minimal input from a survey administrator. Research staff members typically give group-administered surveys to existing groups of people who are part of a selected sample. Groups such as students, employees, or members of the armed forces typically are used for samples. Sometimes, participants are recruited at shopping malls and taken to a vacant store location or in-mall research facility where they are given a survey. In this case, participants typically are thanked for their participation with a small inducement, similar to mail surveys. In each case, research staff members administer the survey in a group setting.

Group-administered surveys also may be given at conventions or meetings. In fact, technology has made it possible to measure participants' responses immediately, providing the basis for group discussion and feedback. Elway Research in Seattle, for example, uses what it calls a "group interaction system" to collect and monitor participants' responses to questions. Questions are asked of the group and participants can respond using a handset that transmits their opinions to a computer. The data are saved and analyzed instantly. Survey results can be projected for viewing by all participants to see and discuss, or displayed to meeting organizers on a monitor in a separate room. This system makes it possible to determine and discuss participants' opinions immediately, and sample members can participate equally in an anonymous fashion.

This raises some of the concerns of group-administered surveys, however. In some cases, group members may feel coerced to participate. If participants' anonymity is compromised, they may not answer questions honestly. In addition, most group-administered surveys require the permission of organizational management since they typically take place on organizational property. If the survey is an instrument of organizational management and not independently sponsored, or if participants suspect this is the case, they may be less likely to answer question honestly (Schutt, 1996). In addition, many preexisting groups do not lend themselves to probability-based sampling procedures. Although it is possible to use probability sampling for group-administered surveys—in particular, cluster sampling—such sampling may be difficult to execute. When probability-based sampling is not used, survey results generally suffer from limited reliability and external validity. Group-administered surveys have useful applications, but like all research methods, researchers should use them carefully to produce data that are accurate and reliable.

Mall Intercept Surveys

Mall intercept surveys, or simply mall intercepts, are a common method of collecting data in a personal interview format. Well-dressed interviewers, typically wearing matching-colored blazers and carrying clipboards, are a common sight in most malls today. Researchers also use other locations for intercept studies, including downtown areas, college campuses and other areas that attract large numbers of people. When mall intercepts are conducted, interviewers stand at strategic locations throughout a mall and orally administer a survey to shoppers. Shoppers may be asked to fill out a survey in a manner similar to group-administered surveys. An inducement may be used, depending on various considerations, including the topic and length of the survey, the need for a quick completion time, whether shoppers or others typically will complete a questionnaire without an inducement, and the study's budget.

Mall intercepts offer several benefits that have made them relatively popular, particularly among market researchers. Perhaps most important to many market researchers, the method can be used quickly if necessary and is inexpensive relative to other research methods. Combined, these two benefits make mall intercepts an attractive research method given the time and budgetary constraints that hinder many research projects. In addition, the method is relatively uncomplicated and provides some flexibility in data collection.

Mall intercepts have some key limitations that researchers should consider before undertaking a project. Perhaps most important, although a probability-based sampling method is possible in an intercept study, it is difficult as a practical matter. Even if researchers used a probability-based sampling method, the results would only be directly generalizable to shoppers at a single location. For these reasons, nonprobability sampling methods are commonly used that, although convenient, limit the external validity and reliability of the study's findings. In addition, many shoppers avoid mall interviews raising further concerns about the validity and reliability of study results. Interviews typically suffer from poor interview conditions because of noise, foot traffic, and other distractions, and researchers must keep questionnaires short and to the point. Although intercept studies are useful in certain circumstances and popular among research practitioners, researchers should use them carefully and remember their results suffer from limited reliability and generalizability concerns.

Personal Interview Critique

Researchers use personal interview surveys for several reasons, many of which concern data quality. Researchers conducting face-to-face surveys can achieve high response rates, often 65% or higher (Czaja & Blair, 1996). These response rates, which are enhanced by the use of prenotification letters and the ability of interviewers to interact with sample members, help reduce bias due to nonresponse. In addition, interviewers usually can establish a strong rapport with survey participants. This provides them with an opportunity to probe respondents' answers when they are inadequate or unclear. Personal interviews typically take place in sample members' homes. This allows them to consult personal records or locate other information. The home also is a comfortable interview environment and tends to make respondents less sensitive to questionnaire length. In addition, sampling frame bias is low when Census Bureau data are used as a basis for the sampling frame because all individuals in a population have a chance, at least in theory, of being included in the sample. As a result of these characteristics, researchers can use personal interview surveys to produce high-quality data.

Personal interview surveys also offer interviewers a high degree of flexibility in obtaining research information. One-on-one interviews lend themselves to questions requiring high degrees of depth or detail, and the interviewer can use visual aids or other interview devices if necessary. Interviewers can also explain questionnaire items that are confusing to respondents, particularly if the respondent misunderstands the intent of a question or is confused by a response category. Researchers can even estimate some information, although this should be done sparingly because of the potential to introduce error into survey results. The flexibility of one-on-one interviews also allows researchers to use complex questionnaires with difficult skip patterns. The flexibility and quality of data produced through personal interview surveys have historically made this research method highly desirable to researchers.

Unfortunately, personal interview surveys suffer from significant drawbacks that have limited the use of this survey method. Probably the greatest drawback to personal interview surveys is cost. Personal interviews generally are the most expensive survey research method. Although cost comparisons are not always available, Czaja and Blair (1996) estimated that a national personal interview survey would cost more than twice as much as a similar telephone interview survey, often at least $250 per hour-long interview. These costs result from the need for field supervisors and extensive interviewer training, as well as travel expenses and other costs. In addition, personal interviews generally take longer than telephone interviewing because of logistical complexities. The administration of a personal interview survey can be costly and complex when sample members are geographically dispersed. These are significant limitations given the importance of time and cost factors in many research decisions.

Another significant disadvantage in the use of personal interviews is the possibility of interviewer bias. The physical appearance, age, dress, race, sex, and verbal and nonverbal communication skills of the interviewer may influence respondents to provide answers that do not accurately reflect their feelings. In addition, participants may be hesitant to report highly personal behavior. The resulting bias ruins the reliability and generalizability of research results. A high degree of careful interviewer training and field supervision is required to avoid interviewer bias, which also contributes to survey cost and length. Finally, some samples are difficult, or even dangerous, to access for a personal interview. Busy work schedules make it difficult to schedule interviews with many adults. In other cases, sample members live in areas with high crime rates. Each of these sample members is important as potential respondents and must be interviewed if possible, but reaching them presents a special challenge when personal interview surveys are conducted.

FINAL THOUGHTS

Survey research is an indispensable part of organizations' attempts to monitor their internal and external environments, solve complex problems, and plan and evaluate public relations campaigns. Despite suggestions to the contrary, there is no best method of survey research, and the potential advantages and disadvantages of each method do not apply equally, or even at all, to every research situation. The best method for a project depends on various situation-specific factors, and, because of this, the use of a survey research method must be considered in relation to the needs and constraints of each situation.

It is important for practitioners to understand each survey research method because of this. Practitioners serve their own interest by understanding the key issues associated with the use of one survey method over another in a research situation, as well as other critical aspects of survey implementation such as issues associated with the use of probability versus nonprobability sampling. This knowledge allows them to make informed research decisions and engage in sophisticated problem-solving and campaign-management activities.

❧ 10 ❧
Making Research Decisions: Sampling

Sampling is a powerful tool and a critical part of public relations research. Practitioners use sampling in partnership with the research methods they select to help them solve complex problems, monitor their internal and external environments, and engage in sophisticated campaign planning and evaluation. Sampling helps practitioners get accurate information quickly at a relatively low cost. It provides practitioners with a way to collect information from a limited number of target audience members, called a sample, and draw conclusions about the entire target audience. These processes are based on principles of statistical sampling and inference.

Although it sounds complex, it really is simple. If we want to know whether our spaghetti sauce needs more garlic, we usually take a small sample and taste it. It is not necessary to eat all of the sauce to determine whether more garlic is needed (and by the way, more garlic is almost always needed). Researchers sample people in the same way. It is not necessary to contact all members of a target audience to understand their

184

opinions, attitudes, and behaviors. Instead, practitioners can learn this information from a properly selected sample of target audience members with a high degree of confidence that they are accurate. The purpose of this chapter is to explain basic aspects of sampling including both probability and nonprobability sampling methods and sample size calculations, in a simple, easy-to-understand manner. Math phobes should note that only a relatively small amount of math will be used. The emphasis is on developing a conceptual understanding of the principles of sampling and statistical inference.

SAMPLING BASICS

Even though sampling methods are relatively easy to understand and use, explanation of a few basic terms and concepts makes it easier to understand sampling practices. Although these definitions are not terribly interesting, they make it a lot easier to incorporate principles of sampling and inference. At a basic level, readers should know about the difference between a population and a sample. A *population* or *universe* consists of all the members of a group or an entire collection of objects. In public relations, a population most commonly refers to all the people in a target audience or public. When researchers conduct a *census*, they collect information from all members of a population to measure their attitudes, opinions, behaviors, and other characteristics. These measurements, called *parameters*, are the true values of a population's members. A parameter is a characteristic or property of a population. Parameters contain no error, because they are the result of information collected from every population member. Often, parameters are expressed in summary form. If our research reveals that 59% of voters in King County, Washington, support a tax initiative, for example, this characteristic is a parameter of the population of all voters in King County.

It is often difficult or impossible for research professionals and social scientists to conduct a census that tends to be expensive and time consuming. More important, a census is unnecessary in most situations. By collecting information from a carefully selected subset, or *sample*, of population members, researchers can draw conclusions about the entire population, often with a high degree of accuracy. This is why sampling is such a powerful part of public relations planning and problem solving.

A sample is simply a subset of a population or universe (Sudman, 1976). When researchers conduct a survey using a sample, they use the resulting data to produce *sample statistics*. Sample statistics describe the characteristics of the sample in the same way that population parameters describe the characteristics of a population. Statistics result from the *observed scores* of sample members instead of from the true scores of all population members, and they necessarily contain some error because of this. The amount of error contained in sample statistics, however, usually is small enough that researchers can estimate, or infer, the opinions, attitudes, behaviors, and other characteristics of a population from sample statistics, often with a high degree of confidence.

If you find all of this confusing, read this section again slowly and it will become more clear, although no more exciting (we suggest taking two aspirin first). This topic and chapter improve in terms of their ease of understanding, but it is important to have a basic understanding of sampling terminology and concepts before we discuss other aspects of sampling. It also becomes more clear as we move into discussions of sample representation, sampling techniques, and sample size calculations.

GENERALIZING FROM A SAMPLE TO A POPULATION

Researchers normally collect data to make generalizations. During a state gubernatorial election in Michigan, for example, a political campaign manager may survey a sample of registered voters to determine the opinions of all registered voters in the state. In this case, the campaign manager wants to generalize the results of the survey from a relatively small sample (perhaps consisting of no more than several hundred people) to all registered voters in the state. This process of generalization, when researchers draw conclusions about a population based on information collected from a sample, is called *inference*. Researchers generalize findings from samples to populations on a regular basis. How can researchers generalize in this way and be confident they are right? A sample must accurately represent the population from which it is drawn to allow investigators to make valid inferences about the population based on sample statistics.

An often-used example from the annals of survey research helps make the point. In 1920, editors of the *Literary Digest* conducted a poll to see whether they could predict the winner of the presidential election between Warren Harding and James Cox. Editors gathered names and addresses from telephone directories and automobile registration lists and sent postcards to people in six states. Based on the postcards they received, the *Literacy Digest* correctly predicted that Harding would win the election. *Literacy Digest* editors repeated this same general process over the next several elections and correctly predicted presidential election winners in 1920, 1924, 1928, and 1932.

Literacy Digest editors again conducted a poll to predict the winner of the 1936 election. This project was their most ambitious yet. This time, they sent ballots to 10 million people whose names they drew from telephone directories and automobile registration lists, as before. More than 2 million ballots were returned. Based on the results of its survey, the editors predicted that Republican challenger Alfred Landon would receive 57% of the popular vote in a stunning upset over Democratic incumbent Franklin Roosevelt. Roosevelt was reelected, however, by the largest margin in history to date. He received approximately 61% of the popular vote and captured 523 electoral votes to Landon's 8. What went wrong?

Simply put, the sample was unrepresentative. The sample was drawn from telephone directories and automobile registration lists, both of which were biased to upper income groups. At that time, less than 40% of American households had telephones and only 55% of Americans owned automobiles. The omission of the poor from the sample was particularly significant because they voted overwhelmingly for Roosevelt, whereas the wealthy voted primarily for Landon (Freedman, Pisani, & Purves, 1978). Not only was the sample unrepresentative, but the survey method and low response rate (24%) contributed to biased results.

This often-told story illustrates a key point about the importance of sample representativeness. The results of research based on samples that are not representative do not allow researchers to validly generalize research results. It is unsafe for investigators to make inferences about a population based on information gathered from a sample when the sample does not represent the population from which it was drawn. It is a simple, but important, concept to understand.

In fact, George Gallup (of Gallup poll notoriety) understood the concept well. In July 1936, he predicted in print that the *Literary Digest* poll would project Landon as the landslide winner and that the poll would be incorrect. These predictions were made months before the *Literacy Digest* poll was conducted. He also predicted that Roosevelt would win reelection and perhaps receive as much as 54% of the popular vote. Gallup's predictions were correct, even though his numbers concerning the election were off. How could Gallup be sure of his predictions? The primary basis of his explanation was that the *Literary Digest* reached only middle- and upper-class individuals who were much more likely to vote Republican. In other words, he understood that the *Literacy Digest* sample was not representative (Converse, 1987).

As an additional note, for those who believe that a larger sample is always better, here is evidence to the contrary. When *nonprobability* sampling methods are used, sample size has no scientifically verifiable effect on the representativeness of a sample. Sample size makes no difference because the sample simply is not representative of the population. A large, unrepresentative sample is as unrepresentative as a small, unrepresentative sample. In fact, had a probability sampling method been used in accordance with an appropriate survey method, a sample size of less than 1% of the more than 2 million voters who responded to the *Digest* poll almost certainly would have produced a highly accurate prediction for both the *Literary Digest* editors and George Gallup.

SAMPLING METHODS

Sampling is the means by which researchers select people or elements in a population to represent the entire population. Researchers use a *sampling frame*—a list of the members of a population—to produce a sample, using one of several methods to determine who will be included in the sample. Each person or object in the sample is a *sampling element* or *unit*. When practitioners study target audience members, the sampling frame typically consists of a list of members of a target audience, whereas the sampling unit is an individual person. All the sampling units together compose the sample. If a nonprofit organization wants to examine the perceptions and opinions of its donors, for example, the sampling frame might be a mailing list of donors' names and addresses, whereas the sampling unit would be the individual names and addresses selected from the list as part of the sample. When researchers generate a sample, they select sampling units from the sampling frame.

A researcher's goal when drawing a sample is to accurately represent the population from which the sample was drawn. This allows them to make inferences about the population based on information collected from the sample. There are two types of samples: *probability* and *nonprobability*. Researchers select probability samples in a *random* way so that each member of a population has an equal chance, or probability, of being included in a sample. When researchers draw a nonprobability sample, an individual's chance of being included in a sample is not known. There is no way to determine the probability that any population member will be included in the sample because a *nonrandom* selection process is used. Some population members may have no chance of being included in a sample, whereas other population members may have multiple chances of being included in a sample.

When probability, or random, samples are chosen, scholars normally can make accurate inferences about the population under study based on information from the sample. That is, probability samples tend to produce results that are highly generalizable from a sample to a population. When researchers select samples in any way other than probability-based/random sampling, they cannot be sure that a sample accurately represents the population from which it was drawn. In this case, they have no basis for validly making inferences about a population from the sample. Even though a nonprobability sample may perfectly represent a population, investigators cannot scientifically demonstrate its level of representativeness. For this reason, the results of research that use nonprobability samples are low in generalizability (external validity).

Why use nonprobability sampling if the research results it produces are not representative? In some cases, a nonprobability sample may be used because it is quick and easy to generate. At other times, the cost of generating a probability-based sample may be too high, so researchers use a nonprobability sample instead. The use of a nonprobability sample is not automatically a problem or even necessarily a concern. It is a significant limitation, however, in practitioners' application of research results to public relations planning and problem solving. Nonprobability samples are often used in exploratory research or other small-scale studies, perhaps as a precursor to a major study. In addition, some commonly used research methods, such as focus groups or mall intercept surveys, use nonprobability sampling almost exclusively.

The lack of generalizability should serve as a warning to public relations practitioners. Do not assume research results based on nonprobability samples are accurate. When practitioners want to explore a problem or potential solution in an informal fashion, get input on an idea, or obtain limited feedback from members of a target audience, a nonprobability sample normally is an acceptable choice. As editors of the *Literary Digest* discovered, however, nonprobability samples have limitations and should not serve as the sole basis for a practitioner's decision making about a major problem or solution, or serve as the primary means by which practitioners collect information about target audiences and develop program initiatives.

NONPROBABILITY SAMPLING METHODS

There are several methods of generating nonprobability samples. No matter how random the selection process appears in each of these sampling methods, researchers do not select sample members in a random manner. This means that population members have an unequal chance of being selected as part of a sample when investigators use these sampling methods. Some population members will have no chance of being included in the sample, whereas other population members will have multiple chances. The most common types of nonprobability samples are incidental (convenience) sampling, quota sampling, dimensional sampling, purposive (judgmental) sampling, volunteer sampling, and snowball sampling.

Incidental, or Convenience, Sampling

Researchers form incidental, or convenience, samples by using whomever is convenient as a sample element. A public opinion survey in which interviewers stop and survey those who walk by and are willing to participate constitutes such a sample. Most mall intercepts use convenience samples because their sample consists of shoppers who happen to walk by and are willing to complete a questionnaire. Like all nonprobability samples, incidental samples do not generally provide accurate estimates of the attributes of target population. There is simply no way to determine the degree to which research results from a convenience sample are representative. Like all nonprobability sampling methods, incidental samples are most appropriate when research is exploratory, precise statistics concerning a population are not required, or the target population is impossible to accurately define or locate (Johnson & Joslyn, 1986).

Quota Sampling

In this method, researchers interested in the subgroups that exist in a population draw their sample so it contains the same proportion of subgroups. Investigators fill the quotas nonrandomly, typically using sample members who are convenient. In practice, research staff members typically base quotas on a small number of population characteristics such as respondents' age, sex, educational level, type of employment, or race or ethnicity. An interviewer conducting a survey on a college campus, for example, might be assigned to interview a certain number of freshmen, sophomores, juniors, and seniors. The interviewer might select the sample nonrandomly by standing in front of the university library and asking people to complete a survey. The interviewer would stop surveying members of individual population subgroups as each quota was filled.

Dimensional Sampling

This method is similar to quota sampling in that researchers select study participants nonrandomly according to predetermined quota, but sample quotas are extended to include various population attributes. Generally, interviewers ensure that a minimum number of individuals are included for various combinations of criteria. Extending the college survey example, interviewers might nonrandomly select participants to meet additional criteria, or dimensions. Interviewers might have to interview a minimum number of males and females, traditional and nontraditional students, or married and unmarried students, for example, in addition to the class quota. Interviewers might use a seemingly endless number of potential attributes to broaden a sample.

No matter how many attributes interviewers use to determine samples, both quota and dimensional sampling rely on nonprobability selection methods. The result is that researchers cannot determine whether their participants fully represent the similarities and differences that exist among subgroups in the population. Ultimately, there is no scientific way to determine whether a nonprobability sample is representative and no scientific evidence to suggest quota sampling is more representative than other nonprobability sampling methods. Researchers correct the nonprobability selection weakness of quota sampling and dimensional sampling when they use *stratified* sampling, which we address shortly.

Purposive Sampling

In purposive, or *judgmental*, sampling, interviewers select sample members because they meet the special needs of the study based on the interviewer's judgment. A researcher's goal when using purposive sampling typically is to examine a specially selected population that is unusually diverse or particularly limited in some way, rather than to study a larger, more uniform population (Johnson & Joslyn, 1986). If a product manufacturer wants to open a new plant in another country, for example, company management needs to learn the concerns of local business, government, and labor leaders. In this case, the sample is relatively small and diverse, and interviewers may simply select sample members using their own discretion to determine which respondents fit into the sample and are "typical" or "representative." This creates situations in which sample-selection decisions may vary widely among interviewers. Even if the definition of the population is reasonably clear, the procedures used in drawing a sample may vary greatly among interviewers, limiting the comparability of sample members (Warwick & Lininger, 1975). These nonrandom selection procedures limit the generalizability of research results based on purposive samples, as is the case with all nonprobability sampling methods.

Volunteer Sampling

When media organizations ask viewers to write or E-mail their opinions, they are using a volunteer, or self-selected, sample. Instant, phone-in polls have become a common way for the media to determine and report "public opinion," for example, to attract and keep the interests of viewers and listeners. There are numerous potential sources of bias when research is based on a volunteer sample. First, sample representation is hindered because only the people who are exposed to the survey have an opportunity to participate. All other potential respondents are unaware of the poll. Second, those who feel strongly about the topic of a poll may view the survey as an opportunity to "vote" for their viewpoint. Such individuals may respond more than once and/or encourage other like-minded individuals to respond in the same way. The result is that volunteer samples are not representative, and research results based on volunteer samples are highly untrustworthy. Organizations that use volunteer samples should use them for their entertainment value, not their scientific value.

Snowball Sampling

When researchers use snowball sampling, they collect data from a limited number of population members, and ask these individuals to identify other members of the population who might be willing to participate in the survey. The sample continues to grow as new research participants direct interviewers to additional sample prospects. The sample snowballs, starting from a small number of people and growing larger as each new participant suggests other potential participants.

Researchers may have no choice but have to rely on snowball sampling when they can locate only a few members of a population. If a social welfare organization wanted to learn about the particular difficulties of migrant workers, for example, it might start by interviewing those few migrant workers it could locate. After each interview was concluded, interviewers could ask participants to identify other migratory workers who might be willing to participate in the study. Interviewers hope the sample would grow to a desirable size through this process. Research results based on such a sample, however, have little or no generalizability, no matter how large the sample grows. A snowball sample uses nonrandom methods of selection, and because of this, there is no way to scientifically determine the degree to which it represents the population from which it is drawn. As with other nonprobability-based research results, research findings based on snowball samples should be interpreted and generalized carefully.

PROBABILITY SAMPLING METHODS

In probability sampling each element in a population has an equal probability of being selected as part of the sample. Researchers generate probability samples using a random selection process so each member of a population has an equal chance, or probability, of being included in a sample. The use of probability sampling normally allows investigators to make accurate inferences about a population based on information collected from a sample. Investigators' inferences, or conclusions, about the population are not perfectly accurate even when probability sampling is used. Researchers calculate estimates of this error within a given level of probability. The result of this process is that research findings based on probability samples normally are highly representative. That is, they possess a high degree of generalizability, or external validity. The most common type of probability sample is simple random sampling. Common variations of simple random sampling include systematic sampling, stratified sampling, and cluster sampling.

Simple Random Sampling

Researchers must ensure that each member of a population has an equal chance of being included in a sample and select each sample element independently to produce a random sample. This is the most basic method of random sampling, and investigators use it to ensure that the sample they produce is representative of the population. Although true representation is never guaranteed unless a census is taken, the use of a random-selection process significantly reduces the chances of subgroup overrepresentation or underrepresentation, which helps eliminate sample bias. Researchers then can estimate, or infer, population parameters based on sample statistics. Although these inferences are not perfect—they have some error—investigators use statistical procedures to generate estimates of this error within a given level of probability.

From a practical standpoint, the primary requirement for simple random sampling is that each element in the population be clearly and unambiguously identified through the use of a comprehensive sampling frame. This allows the direct, independent and random selection of sample elements, typically through a list in which each element is identified (Warwick & Lininger, 1975). The most common methods of simple random sampling use a list of population members for a sample frame. Research staff members might number each element in the list sequentially, for example, and select the sample by drawing numbers from a table of random numbers. The numbers pulled from the table correspond to the numbered elements in the sampling frame. The result is a random sample that normally is highly representative of the population from which it was drawn.

If the Public Relations Society of America (PRSA) wanted to survey its members to determine their level of satisfaction with its programs and services, a project manager could take a membership list and assign a number to each PRSA member sequentially. The manager would create the sample by randomly drawing numbers assigned to PRSA members. Research staff typically use a table of random numbers for this purpose. A staff member would draw each number until an appropriate sample size was generated. If properly conducted, this random process would produce a probability sample of PRSA members who have a high likelihood of accurately representing the attitudes and opinions of all PRSA membership.

Systematic Random Sampling

Researchers use an unbiased system to select sample members from a list when they use systematic random sampling. This system allows them to generate a probability-based sample that normally is highly representative of the population from which it was drawn, without some of the inconveniences associated with simple random sampling. Those who use simple random sampling often find the process long and tedious, especially with a large sample and/or population and of manual selection procedures. Researchers who must assign numbers to individual sample elements and draw random numbers from a table to create the sample find the process wearisome. When researchers use systematic random sampling, they develop an uncomplicated system using the total sample size and the size of the population to help them draw a probability-based sample relatively easily.

First, research team members determine the final sample size they need for a study. This is the number of people who will actually complete interviews. Researchers often need to generate a total original sample that is several times larger than is required for their final sample, because of the number of sample elements that cannot be contacted or refuse to participate in a survey. Once researchers determine the total sample size, they determine a *sampling interval* by dividing the size of the sampling frame (this is the total population) by the desired total sample size. The result is a number (n) which researchers use to generate a sample by selecting every n^{th} element from a sampling frame. Researchers must select the first sample element randomly from the frame to produce a probability sample so they randomly select the first element from within the sampling interval. They complete the sample-selection process by selecting every n^{th} element from the sampling frame. The result is a systematic random sample.

An example helps make systematic random sampling more clear. If corporate personnel managers wanted to survey their classified staff as part of a program to improve employee relations, their first step is to determine the final sample size they want for the study. Sample size calculations are discussed later in this chapter, but for this example, let's say that after some careful thinking and a little fun with math, ad-

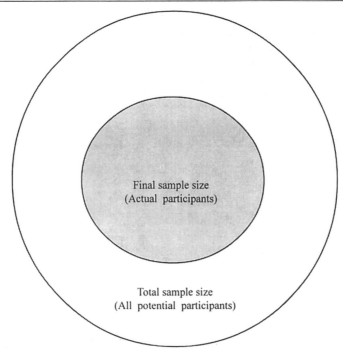

FIG. 10.1. The relationship of final sample size to total sample size. Communication managers need to generate a total original sample that is several times larger than required for their final sample because of the number of people who cannot be contacted or refuse to participate in a survey.

ministrators determine they want a final sample size of approximately 400 from the approximately 6,000 employees who work as full- or part-time classified staff. After some additional calculations (explained in chap. 12), researchers determine that an original total sample size of 850 classified staff members would produce about 400 completed surveys from participants. The projects' directors decide to use a mailing list of classified staff members as a sampling frame because it contains the names and addresses of all classified staff members and has no duplicate listings. They divide the sampling frame (6,000) by the original sample size (850) to determine the sampling interval (approximately 7). The first sample element must be selected randomly, so project managers put the first seven names in the directory on individual pieces of paper, put them in a box and shake it up, and draw a name. If project managers drew the 5th name on the list, they would proceed to draw the sample by starting at Name 5 and selecting every 7th name. Thus, researchers would draw Name 5, Name 12, Name 19, Name 26, and so on. By using the sampling interval (7 in this example), researchers produce a systematic random sample.

Systematic random samples and simple random samples are not exactly the same; however, systematic samples closely approximate simple random samples to produce a probability sample that normally is highly representative. In terms of bias, the greatest danger researchers face when they use systematic sampling is *periodicity.* Periodicity refers to bias that occurs when a sampling list has a cyclical repetition of some population characteristic that coincides with a sampling interval. If this occurs, the sample elements selected are not generalizable to the population from which they were drawn. Researchers should be careful to inspect population lists before sampling to make sure there are no obvious signs of periodicity. When researchers are careful, the potential for bias in systematic sampling normally is small. Ultimately, researchers use systematic random sampling more than simple random sampling because of its simplicity and usefulness in complex sampling situations (Sudman, 1976).

Stratified Sampling

Researchers divide a population into different subgroups, or strata, when they engage in stratified sampling, similar to quota sampling. The key difference between the methods is that investigators use a random, probability-based method to select sample elements when they engage in stratified sampling, whereas they use a nonrandom, nonprobability-based method to select sample elements when they engage in quota sampling. Researchers have two primary reasons for stratification: to control the representativeness of the sample and to use different probability-based selection procedures in different strata (Warwick & Lininger, 1975). Researchers also may use stratified sampling when they are primarily interested in the key similarities and differences among the strata, when the prior information they have for individual strata is different, or to improve sampling efficiency when research costs differ by strata (Sudman, 1976).

Researchers use two types of stratified sampling: proportional and disproportional. When they use *proportional* sampling, project managers draw sample members from each stratum in proportion to their existence in the population. The resulting sample proportionally represents individual strata as they exist in a population. Researchers use *disproportionate* sampling to help ensure the overall sample accurately represents the opinions, attitudes, and behaviors of a significant stratum within the population. Project managers may use disproportionate sampling when strata are too small to be accurately represented in a sample selected through other means. In this case, research staff may find it necessary to weight the data to obtain unbiased estimates of the total population. This may be necessary, for example, when researchers' use of other probability sampling methods would underrepresent the opinions, attitudes, and behaviors of minority members of a population. When researchers use either proportional or disproportional stratified sampling to their advantage, they can produce highly representative, probability-based samples.

Cluster Sampling

Researchers select sample elements in groups rather than by individuals when they use cluster sampling. The sample frame consists of clusters rather than individuals, and each cluster serves as a sample element. The clusters researchers use for sampling commonly are preexisting natural groups or administrative groups of the population. These may include geographical designations such as neighborhoods, cities, counties, or zip code areas, for example, or other common groupings such as universities, hospitals, factories, or schools.

Researchers often use cluster sampling to make data collection more efficient (Sudman, 1976). If a metropolitan school district wanted to learn about the attitudes and experiences of its students, it could send interviewers to meet one on one with individually selected student sample members. This process, however, would be expensive and increase the time needed to complete the project. If researchers used schools as sample clusters and randomly selected from among them, less time and travel would be required, and the efficiency of data collection would be increased.

Cluster sampling also is used when a comprehensive list of sample elements is not available. If an organization wanted to sample city residents as part of a community relations program, project managers would likely have trouble locating a complete list of all community residents, and the process would be costly and time consuming. If researchers wanted to use cluster sampling, they could create a sampling frame by using city blocks as clusters. After research staff identified and labeled each block, they could randomly select an appropriate number of blocks. Next, researchers would randomly sample dwelling units within each block. Finally, interviewers would randomly sample people living in each dwelling unit and collect data. This sampling process is known as *multistage sampling* because sampling takes place in different stages. Researchers sample city blocks in the first stage, followed by dwelling units and individual people.

Researchers' primary concern when using cluster sampling is the potential for increased error relative to other probability-based sampling methods. When investigators use cluster sampling, standard error may increase if sample members' attitudes, behaviors and other characteristics are largely the same, or homogeneous, within each cluster. In this instance, samples selected from within homogeneous clusters will not reflect the diversity of attitudes and behaviors that exists in the larger population. This problem can be countered, in part, by selecting a high number of small clusters and selecting a relatively low number of sample elements from within each cluster (Johnson & Joslyn, 1986).

Cluster samples, along with systematic and stratified samples, are acceptable alternatives to simple random sampling. In each case, sample elements have an equal chance for selection. Ultimately, researchers' choice of a sampling method often depends on the time and money available for a project, the population being sampled, the subject under investigation, and the availability of a comprehensive list of target population members.

HOW BIG SHOULD A SAMPLE BE?

One of the first questions clients, managers, and others involved in a research project typically ask is what is the "best" sample size for a project. Unfortunately, as is the case so often in life and particularly in survey research, the answer typically is a firm "it depends." In fact, the methods researchers use to determine the appropriate sample size for a study can be relatively complicated and even controversial. Research professionals often use different formulas to calculate sample size—in some cases based on different assumptions about population characteristics—and may suggest conflicting sample sizes, as a result. Not surprising, several common misperceptions exist concerning sample size calculations including the following:

Myth 1: Bigger samples are always better. The *Literary Digest* case demonstrates the fallacy concerning bigger sample sizes. When researchers use probability sampling methods, a mathematically calculated sample size based on an appropriate formula nearly always produces trustworthy results with known ranges of error. Researchers can use simple math to verify this information. When researchers use nonprobability sampling methods, there is no scientific way to determine how well a sample represents a population, or how much error survey results contain. Remember, a large, unrepresentative sample is no more representative than a small, unrepresentative sample. In addition, a representative sample that is unnecessarily large is a waste of resources. A sample's size should be the result of a researcher's purposeful decision-making process, not a number researchers stumble upon as they try to generate the largest sample possible.

Myth 2: As a rule of thumb, researchers should sample a fixed percentage of a population to produce an acceptable sample size. It is not uncommon for those uninitiated in survey research methods to suggest using a fixed percentage of the population to determine sample size. If researchers sampled 10% of a 50,000-person population, for example, they would generate a sample of 5,000 participants. Once again, probability-based sampling methods allow the use of mathematical formulas to calculate sample sizes that normally produce highly trustworthy results with known ranges of error. Arbitrarily sampling a certain percentage of the population is unnecessary and results in an arbitrary sample size. Such a practice is as illogical as if you ate a certain percentage of the food in your refrigerator because you were hungry. Just as the amount of food you eat should be based on your body's needs (with notable exceptions for mocha almond fudge ice cream and chocolate in any form), so should a study's sample size be based on the requirements of a research project instead of on an arbitrary percentage of a population.

Myth 3: Researchers should base sample sizes on industry standards or "typical" sample sizes used in other research projects. In reality, there is little that is standard about a research project. Although researchers may use familiar formulas to determine the sample size for a study, they should not use these formulas without careful consideration. A project's unique needs, the individual characteristics of a population and sample, and other issues greatly affect sampling decisions. Researchers serve the needs of clients and organizations best when they make thoughtful sample-size decisions, based on the unique requirements of individual research projects.

Having said all of this, we must engage in a small amount of backpedaling. Many public relations students (and some practitioners for that matter) have varying degrees of math phobia and short attention spans when it comes to highly technical or theoretical information. It is necessary to understand a little theory and use a small amount of basic algebra to calculate sample sizes. With this in mind, in this text we use simple sample-size calculations and avoid math when possible. We also try to provide a basic conceptual understanding of these formulas and the concepts they use. In short, we take some shortcuts to make these topics as accessible as possible. The result is that we do not follow our own advice in some instances. Please keep in mind there is more to this sometimes complicated topic than we discuss in this text. If you find these basic concepts and formulas easy to understand, or if you will be involved in research on a regular basis, you should read more on additional aspects of sample-size calculations so you are fully informed.

For the math-challenged among us, we offer our encouragement. Read the next section slowly, draw pictures of the concepts if it helps you understand them, and try the math out yourself. Put in a little effort and you should emerge with a clear understanding of the topic. To explain sample-size calculations, first we provide a conceptual understanding of sample-calculation concepts and processes. Then, we do some basic sample-size calculations, based on the concepts we have explained. Finally, we calculate the amount of error that exists in survey data once researchers have completed a survey.

CALCULATING THE APPROPRIATE SAMPLE SIZE

Anyone can determine the optimal size for a sample with precision, provided they understand a few key concepts based on probability theory and a bell-shaped curve. These concepts include sample distribution and standard deviation, confidence level, confidence interval, and variance. Once you grasp these concepts, it is easy to understand the basis for sample-size calculations; the rest is simply a matter of applying the formulas.

Sample Distribution and Standard Deviation

Sample distribution and standard deviation are the first and, in some ways, most complex concepts to understand. A *sample distribution* is a grouping or arrangement of a characteristic that is measured for each sample member, and it reflects the frequency with which sample characteristics are assigned to each point on a measurement scale (Williams, 1992). Almost any characteristic that researchers can measure has a sampling distribution, but in survey research investigators typically study sample members' opinions, attitudes, behaviors, and related characteristics. If we were to chart a sampling distribution, the result would be shaped like a bell provided the sampling distribution was normal. It would be tall in the middle where the average of the sampling distribution is located because most people would be near the average. There would be fewer people toward either edge, or tail, of the bell because fewer people would have characteristics or behaviors so far above or below the average.

If we were practitioners at university health facility, for example, we might conduct a survey to better understand smoking behavior among students. We could ask a randomly selected student sample to fill out a questionnaire that contained attitudinal and behavioral questions, including a question about the number of cigarettes participants had smoked in the past 7 days. Participants' responses would likely vary greatly. Many students would have smoked no cigarettes in the past 7 days, while other students would have smoked a high number of cigarettes. When we computed students' response to our smoking question, we could use the information to generate a sample distribution. If our research revealed the average number of cigarettes smoked in the past week by participants was 3.5, this number would be placed under the middle of the curve at its tallest point and most participants would be near the average, or mean, in the large part of the bell-shaped distribution. Our sample's smoking distribution would get smaller at its tails because fewer participants would smoke in numbers that were far above or below average. Figure 10.2 contains a normally distributed, bell-shaped curve for the smoking example.

As we planned our campaign, we would make inferences about the population (all students at our university) based on the responses of our sample. Error occurs when researchers take measurements from a sample and use them to make inferences about a population because there are differences between a sample distribution and a population distribution. We could not determine the exact average number of cigarettes smoked weekly by students at our university, for example, unless we conducted a census by interviewing every student. We have not conducted a census, and, because of this, the responses of our sample will not exactly represent the true responses of the population. In our smoking survey, our sample mean for cigarettes smoked in the last 7

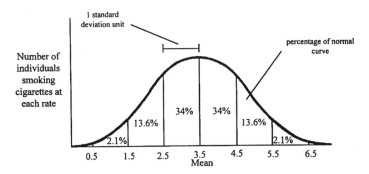

FIG. 10.2. Smoking distribution example. The number in each portion of the curve shows the percentage of the sample that corresponds to each segment. For example, 34% of this sample smokes between 2.5 and 3.5 cigarettes per week. The percentages added together equal over 99% of a normal distribution. The segments of the curve are divided according to standard deviations from the mean.

days might be 3.5, whereas the true value for the population might be 3.8. The difference between the opinions and behaviors of the sample, and the opinions and behaviors of the population, is error.

As researchers, we must understand this error, so we use a tool to measure it called *standard deviation*. Standard deviation is a standardized measure of dispersion (or variation) around a mean. Standard deviation is, essentially, a standardized unit of measurement that researchers use to measure distances from a sampling distribution's midpoint to its outer limits (don't get lost here). Think of standard deviation as a simple unit of measurement. Researchers use standard deviation to measure distance from the mean in a bell-shaped curve in the same way a carpenter uses inches to measure the length of a board.

Researchers use standard deviation for various purposes. If the publishers of a book survey 10 people and ask them to read and rate it using a scale of 0 to 10, for example, the text might receive an average rating of 5. If all 10 people who read the book actually rated the text as a 5, the average rating is highly accurate and there is no standard deviation. If 5 people rate the text as a 10, however, and 5 people rate the text as a 0, the mean rating still is 5. This time the average rating is not very accurate. No one, in fact, actually gave the text a 5 rating. The standard deviation would be relatively large because there is a lot of dispersion around the mean. Although the means are the same in each case, they actually are different and standard deviation helps us measure and understand this. Using our smoking survey example, if every participant in our smoking survey said they smoked 3.5 cigarettes in the last 7 days, our mean would be highly accurate and we would have no deviation from the mean. When we ask sample members about their smoking habits, however, we will undoubtedly receive different responses and we can use the mean and standard deviation to understand these responses.

How do standard deviation and sample distribution help us when we calculate sample size? Standard deviation gives researchers a basis for estimating the probability of correspondence between the normally distributed, bell-shaped curve of a perfect population distribution, and a probability-based sample distribution that always contains some error. Researchers call standard deviation measurements "standard" because they associate with, or measure, specific areas under a normal curve. One standard deviation measures about 68% of a normally distributed curve; two standard deviations measure a little over 95% of a normally distributed curve; and three standard deviations measure over 99% of a normally distributed curve. Research professionals use standard deviations to calculate sample sizes because of their instrumental role in measuring the area under a normally distributed curve. In particular, researchers use standard deviations to determine a sample's confidence level, as we will demonstrate.

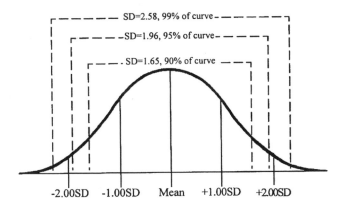

FIG. 10.3. Normally distributed bell-shaped curve. Along the normal distribution, 1.65 standard deviations (SD) measure 90% of the curve; 1.96 standard deviations measure 95% of the curve; 2.58 standard deviations measure 99% of the curve.

Confidence Level

A *confidence level* is the degree of certainty researchers can have when they draw a inferences about a population based on data from a sample. Basically, it is the level of probability researchers have that a characteristic they find in a sample can be accurately generalized to the population. In essence, the confidence level answers the question, "How confident are we that our sample is representative of the population?" A confidence level of 90% means researchers are 90% confident the sample accurately represents the population. In the same way, a confidence level of 95% means researchers are 95% confident the inferences they draw about the population from the sample are accurate.

This raises an important question: Are researchers really 90% or 95% confident about the representativeness of the sample, or are they simply guessing, perhaps based on their experience? In fact, researchers' claims of a confidence level are accurate because the confidence level is based on standard deviation. Remember, a standard deviation allows researchers to estimate probability between a normally distributed population curve and a less than perfect sampling distribution because standard deviation measurements associate with specific areas under the curve. A standard deviation of 1.65 measures 90% of a normally distributed curve, a standard deviation of 1.96 measures 95% of a normally distributed curve, and a standard deviation of 2.58 measures 99% of a normally distributed curve. Remember these numbers because we will use them again shortly.

This means that when researchers calculate sample size, they select standard deviations associated with specific areas under a normally distributed curve to provide the desired confidence level. When investigators use 1.65 in the sample-size formula, they calculate a sample size that provides a 90% confidence level; when they use 1.96 in the formula, they calculate a sample size that provides a 95% confidence level; when they use 2.58 in the formula, they calculate a sample size that provides a 99% confidence level.

Most often, researchers use 1.96 standard deviations to calculate sample size, resulting in a 95% confidence level. A confidence level of 95% means our sample statistics will accurately represent the true parameter of a population 95% of the time. Here is another way to think about this: If we conducted a survey of the same population 100 times, our sample responses would be accurate in 95 of the 100 surveys we conducted. The 95% confidence level is a standard convention of social science, but researchers can use other confidence levels. In particular, if researchers desire a high degree of confidence when making inferences about a population based on data from a sample, they may choose a higher confidence level. Rarely do researchers use a lower confidence level.

Confidence Interval

A *confidence interval* is a range or margin of error that researchers permit when making inferences from a sample to a population. As noted, the inferences researchers make about a population based on sample data are not completely accurate. Unless investigators conduct a census, the observed values they collect from a sample (statistics) will not provide completely accurate information concerning a population's true values (parameters).

The population parameter falls somewhere within the range of the confidence interval, although researchers are never exactly sure where the parameter is located unless they conduct a census. The confidence interval usually is stated as a positive-to-negative range, such as +/–3% error or +/–5% error. A confidence interval of +/–3% has a total error margin of 6%, whereas a confidence interval of +/–5% has a total error margin of 10%. If 57% of registered voters in California express support for a citizens' initiative in a survey with a +/–5% confidence interval, for example, the true population value may be as high as 62% (+5%) or as low as 52% (–5%).

What is an acceptable confidence interval in a survey? As is often the case in survey research, the answer depends on various factors. Many applied public relations and market research surveys have a +/–5% confidence interval, but there is nothing critical about this range of error. Researchers commonly choose smaller confidence levels when they want to reduce the margin of error and increase the precision of the inferences they draw concerning a population. When media organizations poll the public to predict election outcomes, for example, they often use a smaller confidence interval, such as +/–3%. Ultimately, researchers should make confidence interval decisions based on the necessities and challenges of individual research projects.

It may surprise you to know that the confidence level and the confidence interval do not have to add to 100. Those new to research often assume the confidence level and confidence interval must add to 100 because researchers often conduct surveys with a +/–5% error at a 95% confidence level. It is incidental that these numbers add to 100. It is legitimate to conduct a survey with a +/–3% margin of error at a 95% confidence level, for example, or a survey with a +/–2.5% margin of error at a 99% confidence level. In addition, many researchers use a 95% confidence level as a standard and only make adjustments to the confidence interval when calculating sample size. Researchers should make decisions concerning confidence levels and confidence intervals based on the requirements of individual research projects.

Variance

Variance is simply dispersion. When researchers calculate sample size, it helps them to understand how the characteristic or variable they are examining is dispersed throughout a population. If we want to understand the use of public transportation in our community as a way to reduce traffic and pollution, for example, it would be useful to know the percentage of community members who actually use public transportation. In short, we want to know how public transportation use is dispersed throughout our community as a characteristic of the population.

For research purposes, it is useful to consider variance as a simple percentage. Community members who use public transportation, for example, fit into one category that makes up a certain percentage of the population. Community members who do not use public transportation do not belong in the category and make up the remaining percentage of the population. The percentages add up to 100%. Researchers can examine the dispersion of most variables this way because a population can be divided into two categories on the basis of almost any characteristic. This includes, for example, students who smoke cigarettes and students who do not smoke cigarettes; community residents who live in a certain neighborhood and residents who live in other neighborhoods; workers who are employed and workers who are unemployed; people who think coffee is a major food group and people who do not.

Any time researchers examine a variable or characteristic, they want to know its dispersion within a population because they can use this information to help them calculate sample size. Population members who have a characteristic or variable fit into a single category, and researchers use this to distinguish them from the rest of the population. In the formula we examine shortly, the percentage of a population that belongs to a category is expressed as a decimal. The remaining percentage of the population (that does not belong to the category) also is expressed as a decimal and is subtracted from 1. Together, these two numbers add to 1.0 or 100% of the population.

Despite the importance of variance, researchers often have to set aside variance percentages when they calculate sample size because percentages only reflect the dispersion of a single characteristic or variable in a population. Researchers commonly examine multiple variables in a single survey, each with a different percentage of dispersion. Each variable would require a different sample size, which is impractical and unnecessary. Researchers address this problem by using the largest measure of variance available to calculate sample size because, at a minimum, it provides an acceptable measure of dispersion for all variables. To use the largest measure of variance, researchers use .5 (or 50%) as the percentage of a population that belongs to a category. Researchers also use .5 as the percentage for the rest of the population because $1 - .5 = .5$ and these percentages add up to 1.0, or 100% of the population. Although it is not necessary for researchers to use .5 and $1 - .5$ in every sample-size calculation, this practice is almost always required by the necessities of a multifaceted research project, and so we use it in all of our sample-size calculations.

SAMPLE SIZE CALCULATIONS

Now that you understand standard deviation, confidence level, confidence interval, and variance, you are ready to calculate sample size. Researchers commonly use the following formula, or variations of it, to calculate sample size:

$$n = \left(\frac{cl}{ci}\right)^2 (v)(1-v)$$

Where:

n (number) = final sample size or number of completed interviews;

cl (confidence level) = the standard deviation associated with a specific area under a normal curve and corresponding to the desired confidence level (by definition, 90% confidence level = 1.65; 95% confidence level = 1.96; and 99% confidence level = 2.58);

ci (confidence interval) = the margin of error expressed as a decimal (+/–3% error would be expressed as .03; +/–5% error would be expressed as .05; +/–10% error would be expressed as .10);

v (variance) = the variance or distribution of a variable in a population, expressed as a percentage in decimal form. For our purposes, variance is always .5. Note also that 1 – *v* is the percentage of a population that has no variable distribution; 1 – *v* always is .5 when *v* is .5, as we have recommended.

Here is a basic sample-size calculation using this formula. The sample size is calculated at a 95% confidence level and a +/–5% margin of error (confidence interval):

$$n = \left(\frac{1.96}{.05}\right)^2 (.5)(.5) = 384$$

Based on this formula, we need a final sample size of 384 people to participate in our survey to produce findings with a +/–5% margin of error at a 95% confidence level.

What if we want less error (a smaller confidence interval), meaning more confidence in the precision of our survey results? It is easy to adjust the formula to fit the demands of any research situation. In the following calculations, for example, we determine sample sizes based on different confidence levels. We calculate each sample size with a +/–5% confidence interval, but with different confidence levels to show how different confidence levels affect sample size. To change confidence levels, we use standard deviations that correspond to different areas under a normally distributed, bell-shaped curve. Recall that the standard deviation for a 90% confidence level is 1.65; the standard deviation for a 95% confidence level is 1.96, and the standard deviation for a 99% confidence level is 2.58. Notice that we increase sample size each time we increase the confidence level. The only difference in each calculation is the level of confidence researchers have when they make inferences from a sample to a population. Here is the sample size for a survey with a 90% confidence level and a +/–5% margin of error:

$$n = \left(\frac{1.65}{.05}\right)^2 (.5)(.5) = 272$$

Here is the sample size for a survey with a 95% confidence level and a +/–5% margin of error:

$$n = \left(\frac{1.96}{.05}\right)^2 (.5)(.5) = 384$$

Finally, here is the sample size for a survey with a 99% confidence level with a +/–5% margin of error:

$$n = \left(\frac{2.58}{.05}\right)^2 (.5)(.5) = 666$$

How do changes in the margin of error (confidence interval) affect sample size? In the following calculations, we determine sample sizes with the same level of confidence but differing margins of error. Each sample size is calculated at a 95% confidence level. Here is the sample size for a survey with a +/–10% margin of error at a 95% confidence level:

$$n = \left(\frac{1.96}{.10}\right)^2 (.5)(.5) = 96$$

Here is the sample size for a survey with a +/–5% margin of error at a 95% confidence level:

$$n = \left(\frac{1.96}{.05}\right)^2 (.5)(.5) = 384$$

Finally, here is the sample size for a survey with a +/–3% margin of error at a 95% confidence level:

$$n = \left(\frac{1.96}{.03}\right)^2 (.5)(.5) = 1,067$$

In each sample size, we reduced the margin of error while maintaining a consistent level of confidence.

ERROR CALCULATIONS

The same information you learned to calculate sample size also helps you calculate the margin of error for a survey, once you have collected data. In most cases, final sample size is not 384 or 1,060 completed interviews, even if this is researchers' targeted sample size. Researchers aiming for a specific sample size typically collect additional interviews for various reasons. Research staff may have to throw out some interviews, for example, because of problems with data collection, such as a survey that is only partially complete. At other times, researchers may collect a larger sample size so they have a stronger basis from which to make sample subgroup comparisons. Regardless of the reason, researchers can use standard deviation, confidence level, and variance to calculate the margin of error that exists in a survey's results based on their sample size. Here is the formula:

$$e = cl\sqrt{\frac{(v)(1-v)}{n}}(100)$$

Where:

e (error) = the final margin of error for the completed survey based on sample size;

cl (confidence level) = the standard deviation associated with a specific area under a normal curve and corresponding to the desired confidence level (by definition, 90% confidence level = 1.65; 95% confidence level = 1.96; and 99% confidence level = 2.58);

v (variance) = the variance or distribution of a variable in a population, expressed as a percentage in decimal form. As before, variance is always .5. $1 - v$ is the percentage of a population that has no variable distribution; $1 - v$ always is .5, when v is .5 as we have recommended;

n (number) = final sample size of completed interviews.

Here is the margin of error for a survey in which the final sample size is 485. The calculation is made based on a 95% confidence level:

$$1.96\sqrt{\frac{(.5)(.5)}{485}}(100) = 4.45$$

In this example, the margin of error for this survey is +/–4.45% based on 485 completed interviews.

How do changes in the confidence level affect the margin of error for a sample? In the following calculations, we determine margins of error for surveys with the same sample sizes at different levels of confidence.

Each margin of error is calculated using a sample size of 575. Here is the margin of error at a 90% confidence level:

$$1.65\sqrt{\frac{(.5)(.5)}{575}}(100) = 3.44$$

Here is the margin of error at a 95% confidence level:

$$1.96\sqrt{\frac{(.5)(.5)}{575}}(100) = 4.09$$

Here is the margin of error at a 99% confidence level:

$$2.58\sqrt{\frac{(.5)(.5)}{575}}(100) = 5.38$$

These calculations reveal the trade-off between confidence level and the margin of error, or confidence interval, for a survey. If researchers want to increase their level of confidence or certainty as they make inferences from sample data to a population, they must be willing to accept a larger range of error in their survey's results. If researchers desire a smaller range of error, they must be willing to accept a lower confidence level when they make inferences.

ISSUES AND ASSUMPTIONS

The formulas presented here require various assumptions and raise some important issues. We have addressed many of these issues and assumptions in the preceding sections, but readers may need to alter the formula or disregard it completely as the assumptions on which the formula is based change. One of the primary assumptions of all sample size formulas, for example, concerns researchers' use of probability sampling methods. When researchers use nonprobability sampling methods, no sample-size formula will produce an accurate sample size because it is impossible to determine the representativeness of the sample.

One issue we have not addressed concerns the need to correct the formula according to a population's size. Researchers sometimes use sample-size formulas that contain something called finite population correction. *Finite population correction* is an adjustment factor that is part of a sample-size formula. Table 10.1 contains population-corrected sample sizes for probability-based survey results with a +/–5%

TABLE 10.1
Population-Corrected Sample Sizes

Population Size (N)	Sample Size (n)	Population Size (N)	Sample Size (n)	Population Size (N)	Sample Size (n)
5	5	650	242	2,500	333
10	10	700	248	3,000	341
15	15	750	254	3,500	346
20	19	800	260	4,000	351
25	24	850	265	4,500	354
50	44	900	269	5,000	357
75	63	950	274	6,000	361
100	80	1,000	278	7,000	364
150	108	1,100	285	8,000	367
200	132	1,200	291	9,000	368
250	152	1,300	297	10,000	370
300	169	1,400	302	15,000	375
350	183	1,500	306	20,000	377
400	196	1,600	310	25,000	378
450	207	1,700	313	50,000	381
500	217	1,800	317	75,000	382
550	226	1,900	320	100,000	383
600	234	2,000	322	275,000+	384

Note. Figures reported are for probability-based survey results with a +/–5% margin of error at a 95% confidence level. Calculations are based on Cochran's (1977) formula for finite population correction. Further information is available in Kish (1965). According to this formula, even populations over 1 million require a sample size of 384.

margin of error at a 95% confidence level. The appropriate sample size for a population of 1 million people is 384, the same sample size we calculated for a survey with a 95% confidence level and a +/–5% margin of error.

Is it necessary for researchers to correct for population size? Generally, researchers have no need for population correction unless the size of the population is small and the sample is more than 5% of the total population (Czaja & Blair, 1996). In most sample surveys, population correction makes little difference in sample-size calculations and researchers simply exclude a population correction factor because it is unnecessary. In fact, researchers would generally use the same sample size for a survey of registered voters in Chicago, a survey of registered voters in Illinois, or a survey of all registered voters in the entire United States! Although there are important exceptions, once a population reaches a certain size, sample sizes generally remain consistent. For this reason, and to keep our sample calculations simple, the sample size formula we have presented does not include population correction.

FINAL THOUGHTS

Sampling is a powerful tool that helps practitioners obtain accurate information at a reasonable cost. Researchers' selection of a proper sampling method is as important as their selection of a proper research method to the success of a study. Even the most carefully planned and executed study will produce untrustworthy results if you use an improper sampling method. Although sampling can be complex, it is in your own best interest to learn all you can about the sample-selection procedures used in a study. Few people would buy an automobile without first inspecting the vehicle they are purchasing. Still, a surprising number of practitioners make research "purchases" without ever inspecting one of the most critical elements of their research project, the sampling procedures used in a study.

As demonstrated in this chapter, it is not necessary for practitioners to become sampling experts to understand many important issues related to sampling selection. It is necessary, however, for practitioners to understand basic distinctions in sampling methods and to work with researchers to ensure that the sample used in a study has the greatest chance of accurately representing the attitudes, opinions, and behaviors of the population from which it is drawn.

🎜 11 🎜

Making Research Decisions: Questionnaire Design

Writing a questionnaire seems simple. As a famous survey researcher named G. W. Allport once said, "If we want to know how people feel: what they experience and what they remember, what their emotions and motives are like, and the reasons for acting as they do–why not ask them?" (Selltiz, Jahoda, Deutsch, & Cook, 1959, p. 236).

Unfortunately, just asking them is not as easy as it sounds. To avoid getting misleading results, questions must be clear, must elicit honest and reliable answers, and must keep the respondent interested in providing answers. The construction of questions must differ according to whether they are being read or heard, and the researchers can ask only as many questions as respondents have the time and energy to answer. It is easy to write bad questions, and difficult to write good ones. Guidelines for questionnaire design typically focus on the importance of clarity, simplicity, and objectivity. Other important considerations include making questions interesting and the questionnaire logical, so that respondents feel motivated to answer carefully.

Given the myriad of details that can make or break a questionnaire, the best questionnaires often turn out to be those you would have written once it is too late and you have the answers to the one you already used. To avoid having postsurvey regrets, questionnaires should be pretested with attention to every detail and specifically with members of the intended sample of respondents. Important issues to consider when writing questionnaires include: validity and reliability concerns as they relate to the sample, the topic, and the client; levels of measurement and why they matter; ways to ensure clarity and avoid bias; types of questions and how the information each type provides differs; and questionnaire layout and design to ensure logical flow and visual clarity.

UNDERSTANDING RELIABILITY AND VALIDITY

What is a "fast" city? If you are the communication manager for the local chamber of commerce, would you want your city rated as "fast" or as "slow"? National and regional rankings of cities, universities, corporations, and other organizations get published all the time. Depending on your interpretation, "fast" could mean exciting or it could mean stressful. Meanwhile, "slow" could mean boring or it could mean mellow and comfortable. When *Psychology Today* published its feature on fast cities (see Sidebar 11.1), the things that made a city fast included the length of time it took to get waited on in a bank, the speed at which people walked down the street, the number of people who wore watches, the speed with which people talked, and the rates of coronary heart disease in the city population. A ranking of 1 on this list probably would not make city leaders happy. But how can ratings based on objective data be refuted effectively?

The answer is that measures need to be valid and reliable. A valid measure is one that has the intended meaning. If people generally can agree that the things used to measure something such as a fast city are appropriate, the measures are considered valid. A reliable measure has consistency. If virtually anyone can replicate the study using the same measures and come out with similar answers, the measures are considered reliable. The fast city measures could be attacked as invalid by arguing that coronary heart disease has no relationship to bank teller speed, except perhaps for the bank teller.

For measures to be valid, the *concept* or idea they represent must be clear and the *operationalizations*, the actual measures themselves, must seem appropriate. To a great extent, determining validity is an exercise in persuasion. Reliability is easier to verify objectively.

Threats to validity and reliability sometimes are subtle, making it important to think carefully about the context in which surveys will be answered and interpreted. The measure itself should seem appropriate, and the scale used to measure it must seem appropriate. For example, operationalizing a concept such as a "livable" city might seem

SIDEBAR 11.1.
Measuring a City's Pace

To see if there is any relationship between a city's characteristic pace and its rate of CHD, we looked at four indicators.

Walking speed: We clocked how long it took pedestrians to move 60 feet along relatively uncrowded streets. To eliminate the effects of socializing, we timed only people walking alone. We also excluded children, pedestrians with large packages or obvious physical handicaps, and window shoppers.

Working speed: We timed how long bank clerks took either to give change, in set denominations, for two $20 bills or to give us two $20 in return for change.

Talking speed: In each city we tape-recorded how long it took postal clerks to explain the difference between regular mail, certified mail, and insured mail. We then calculated their actual "articulation" rates by dividing the number of syllables in the response by the total time it took.

The watch factor: As a simple measure of concern with clock time, we counted the percentage of men and women who were wearing wrist watches.

Individually, each of these measures has its weaknesses: They all tap into special groups, not the city's general population; the second two are confounded by skill and efficiency; and the last is affected by fashion as well as concern with time.

Finally, we created an index of the overall pace of life in each city by giving the four scores equal weight and adding them together. The chart below shows how the cities ranked, from 1st to 36th, in each category.

Fast Cities, Slow Cities, How They Rank

City	Overall Pace	Walking Speed	Bank Speed	Talking Speed	Watches Worn	CHD*
Boston, MA	1	2	6	6	2	10
Buffalo, NY	2	5	7	15	4	2
New York, NY	3	5	7	15	1	1
Salt Lake City, UT	4	4	16	12	11	31
Columbus, OH	5	22	17	1	19	26
Worcester, MA	6	9	22	6	6	4
Providence, RI	7	7	9	9	19	3
Springfield, MA	8	1	15	20	22	7
Rochester, NY	9	20	2	26	7	14
Kansas City, MO	10	6	3	15	32	21

(Continues)

SIDEBAR 11.1. (Continued)

City	Overall Pace	Walking Speed	Bank Speed	Talking Speed	Watches Worn	CHD*
St. Louis, MO	11	15	20	9	15	8
Houston, TX	12	10	8	21	19	36
Paterson, NJ	13	17	4	11	31	4
Bakersfield, CA	14	28	13	5	17	20
Atlanta, GA	15	3	27	2	36	33
Detroit, MI	16	21	12	34	2	11
Youngstown, OH	17	13	18	3	30	6
Indianapolis, IN	18	18	23	8	24	22
Chicago, IL	19	12	31	3	27	13
Philadelphia, PA	20	30	5	22	11	16
Louisville, KY	21	16	21	29	15	18
Canton, OH	22	23	14	26	15	9
Knoxville, TN	23	25	24	30	11	17
San Francisco, CA	24	19	35	26	5	27
Chattanooga, TN	25	35	1	32	24	12
Dallas, TX	26	26	28	15	28	32
Oxnard, CA	27	30	30	23	7	34
Nashville, TN	28	8	26	24	33	14
San Diego, CA	29	27	34	18	9	24
East Lansing, MI	30	14	33	12	34	29
Fresno, CA	31	36	25	17	19	25
Memphis, TN	32	34	10	19	34	30
San Jose, CA	33	29	29	30	22	35
Shreveport, LA	34	32	19	33	28	19
Sacramento, CA	35	33	32	36	26	23
Los Angeles, CA	36	24	36	35	13	28

*Lower numbers indicate faster speeds, more watches worn, higher CHD rates. CHD indicates rates of coronary heart disease, adjusted for the median age in each city. From "Type A Cities and Your Heart," by Robert Levine. Reprinted with permission from *Psychology Today* magazine, copyright © 1989, Sussex Publishers, Inc.

fairly straightforward. *U.S. News and World Report* publishes a feature on this issue every year focusing on characteristics such as crime rates, housing costs and employment rates. Most people would agree that a more livable city would feature a lower crime rate, lower housing costs, and higher employment rates. But wait: rising housing costs make a city more attractive, not less attractive, to those investing in real estate. So a high score on housing costs could mean less livable to some people and more livable to others. Meanwhile, some might argue that the most appropriate measure of livability would be people's perceptions of safety and satisfaction, rather than more objective measures of crime rates, numbers of parks and so on.

Moreover, the measures chosen to operationalize livability might be criticized as insufficient to measure the concept appropriately. Perhaps factors such as average commute times, numbers of cultural events, and the quality of public schools (as indicated by standardized tests?) also need to be included to provide a valid measure. The three-quarters of the population who do not have children of school age, however, may not consider public school quality a primary determinant of a city's livability. In addition, some people might consider other factors, such as nearby access to parkland, as critical to quality of life, whereas others might consider a booming nightlife a higher priority. And what about weather? Is a warm temperature an advantage or a disadvantage? It depends on whether you prefer to snow ski or water ski. Thus, to measure a fairly simple idea such as a livable city, the measures chosen must be sufficient in number to represent enough about the concept, they must seem appropriate as indicators of the concept, and the measurement scales used must be unambiguous, such that a high score on a measure clearly represents a high level of the concept.

Statistics from the Federal Airline Administration (FAA) and the National Transportation Safety Board (NTSB) in the *Wall Street Journal* (Dahl & Miller, 1996) focusing on airline safety illustrated the difficulty of measuring concepts that seem important to measure in a way observers will accept as valid. As shown in Table 11.1, when airline safety was measured according to the rate of all accidents, with an accident defined as an situation in which an aircraft sustains serious damage or persons are seriously hurt or killed, United Airlines had the worst record among the seven airlines rated and USAir had the best record. Under this definition, a coffee cup spill resulting in a burn or a broken leg resulting from tripping while disembarking would count against a company as much as a crash that killed someone. When measured according to the rate of all accidents and incidents, with an incident defined as a situation less severe than an accident but that affects the safety of operations, United Airlines rose one spot in the rankings and

TABLE 11.1
Validity and Reliability of Airline Safety Rankings

Airlines' Records for Safety 1992–1995			
Rating / Ranking	By All Accidents	By All Accidents and Incidents	By Accidents With Fatalities or Serious Injuries
Best	USAir (0.17)	American (0.42)	Northwest (0.00)
	Northwest (0.18)	Northwest (0.46)	Delta (0.00)
	American (0.22)	USAir (0.58)	Continental (0.00)
	Delta (0.36)	Delta (0.64)	United (0.03)
	Continental (0.36)	TWA (0.73)	American (0.14)
	TWA (0.36)	United (0.90)	USAir (0.14)
Worst	United (0.43)	Continental (1.12)	TWA (0.18)

As this table shows, an airline's safety record can appear better or worse depending on the way ratings are computed. Some airline rankings remain consistent across rating types but others change dramatically. Ratings are based on frequency per 100,000 departures. An accident is defined as a situation in which an aircraft sustains serious damage or people are seriously hurt or killed. An incident is less severe but affects the safety of operations. Data reported by Dahl & Miller (1996) using Federal Aviation Administration/National Transportation Safety Board data.

USAir sank two. The definition of what counted as an incident, however, was criticized as vague according to the *Wall Street Journal* (Dahl & Miller, 1996). Then, when measured according to the rate of accidents with fatalities or serious injuries, United Airlines rose another two spots and USAir sank to sixth place. "This is the whole reason this sort of ranking is misleading to the public," the *Wall Street Journal* quoted a spokesperson from the Air Transport Association as saying, "There just isn't a good yardstick." In other words, no perfectly valid measure exists.

Reliability, too, is an important characteristic for measures, with two primary components. First, the indicator of a concept must be replicable, or reusable with a similar result. In the airline example, measuring safety according to accidents with fatalities or serious injuries could be criticized as unreliable if reported annually because such accidents (fortunately) occur rarely. Trans World Airlines jumped from a zero accident rating in 1993 to the worst ranking in 1994 because it had two accidents that year.

The second component of reliability is how consistently the various operationalizations of a concept measure it. The operationalizations are the ways the researcher measures an idea, such as by counting fatal accidents, injury-producing accidents, or incidents that posed potential danger but caused no injuries. Consistency of the measures is important because observers tend to find a group of measures more convincing than any single measure. For example, if a city that rates highly on employment rates and cultural events also rates highly on individuals' reports of perceived safety and happiness with the town, these measures as a group can be called reliable. Some people may think employment rates are more important than personal reports of happiness, and others may consider personal reports more important, but they all may accept the others' measures if they are convinced they "hang together" consistently. This type of reliability can be measured statistically.

When constructing a questionnaire, it is important to scatter questions that measure a concept instead of clustering them together. The reason for this is that people's answers can suffer from *response set*, which means they answer a set of questions similarly because they are answering too quickly or not thoughtfully enough rather than because they think similarly about each question in the set. Response set can make measures look statistically reliable but can render them meaningless or invalid.

LEVELS OF MEASUREMENT AND WHY THEY MATTER

Survey questions fall into four general levels, shown in Table 11.2, that dictate how the questions can and should be analyzed. It is important to know your level of measurement because the level dictates the types of statistical tests you can perform on the data. Usually clients hope to determine how certain beliefs or behaviors relate to other beliefs and behaviors. If measures have been collected at a low level of measurement, this will seriously limit the analyst's ability to investigate relationships of interest.

To choose the appropriate level, questionnaire designers need to consider how they will use the information gathered. Sometimes, for example, a client may wish to know whether people first heard about an organization from the newspaper or from a friend. Other times, however, the organization may need to know how often newspapers and friends are sources of information, or how credible the informa-

TABLE II.2
Levels of Measurement for Credibility

Nominal Level	Which of the following companies do you find credible?
Ordinal Level	Rank the following companies from most credible to least credible, with the most credible company receiving a 5 and the least credible company receiving a 1.
Interval Level	How credible are the following companies?

<table>
<tr><td></td><td colspan="2">Not at
all credible</td><td colspan="2">Very
credible</td></tr>
<tr><td>1</td><td>2</td><td>3</td><td>4</td><td>5</td></tr>
</table>

Ratio Level	How many times in the last year have you wondered whether the following companies were telling you the truth?

0	1	2	3	4	5 or more

tion received from these sources seems. Each of these needs requires a different level of measurement.

The first level of measurement is called the *nominal* level, meaning names or categories of things. This level of measurement is useful when an organization needs to know how many people fit into particular categories. The possible answers for a nominal variable are mutually exclusive and exhaustive. In other words, they have no overlap and include all possible responses. For example, a question assessing gender would include "male" and "female." A question assessing information sources could include "mass media" and "interpersonal sources." Including "mass media" and "newspapers" would be redundant instead of mutually exclusive because the newspaper is a form of mass media. Eliminating "interpersonal sources" or including "friends" but not "coworkers" or "family" would not be exhaustive. Nominal variables can be useful, but little statistical analysis can be performed using this type of variable. They have little explanatory power, as people either fit a category or do not fit. They cannot fit a little bit or a lot.

The second level of measurement is called the *ordinal* level, indicating some meaningful order to the attributes. These questions have answers that are mutually exclusive, exhaustive, and ordered in some way. A popular type of ordinal question is the ranking question, as in "Please rate the following five publications according to how much you like them, with the best one rated 1 and the worst one rated 5." It would be possible to know which publications do best and worst, but it would not be possible to know whether Publication 2 is liked a lot better than Publication 3 or just a little bit better.

The ranking question often creates problems and generally should be avoided. Not only does it provide information of limited use it also frequently confuses or frustrates respondents. Ranking is difficult to do and tends to discourage respondents from completing a questionnaire. Sometimes respondents may consider two items or more items to be ranked in a tie, and other times they may not understand the basis on which they are supposed to determine differences. For example, when asked to rank the corporate citizenship of a group of companies, respondents may not feel they have enough information on some companies to distinguish them from others. Respondents often rate several things as the same number, rendering their responses to the entire question useless to the analyst. If two or more items are tied, they no longer are ranked. The answers no longer are mutually exclusive, which makes the question of less use than even a nominal variable would be.

Organizations that want to rank may find it better to let rankings emerge from the data rather than trying to get respondents to do the ranking themselves. They can do this by creating a question or a group of questions that can be compared with one another, such as, "Please rate each of the following information sources according to how much you like them, with a 4 indicating 'a lot,' a 3 indicating 'some,' 2 indicating 'not much,' and a 1 indicating 'not at all.'" The mean score for each information source then can be used to create a ranking.

The third level of measurement is the *interval* level. This is the most flexible type of measure to use, because it holds a lot of meaning, giving it a great deal of explanatory power and lending itself to sensitive statistical tests. As with the previous levels of measurement, the interval measure's responses must be mutually exclusive, exhaustive, and ordered. The order, however, now includes equal intervals between each possible response. For example, a survey could ask people to indicate how much they like a publication on a 10-point scale, on which 10 represents liking it the most and 1 represents liking it the least. It can be assumed the respondent will think of the distances separating 2 and 3 as the same as the distances separating 3 from 4, and 9 from 10. Most applied research—and some scholarly research—assumes perceptual scales such as strongly agree–strongly disagree or very important–not important at all can be considered interval-level scales. Purists disagree, saying they are ordinal because respondents might not place an equal distance between items on a scale such as *not at all ... a little ... some ... a lot* in their own minds. Fortunately, statisticians have found that this usually does not present a major problem. Nevertheless, this is a controversial issue (Sarle, 1994). Researchers should construct such measures carefully and should pretest them to ensure they adhere to the equal-distance assumption as much as possible.

The fourth level of measurement is the *ratio* scale, which is simply an interval scale that has a true zero. This means the numbers assigned to responses are real numbers, not symbols representing an idea such as "very much." Ratio scales include things such as the number of days respondents report reading the newspaper during the past week (0–7), the number of minutes spent reading the business section, or the level of confidence they have that they will vote in the next presidential election (0%–100% likelihood of voting). This type of scale is considered the most powerful because it embodies the most meaning.

TYPES OF QUESTIONS AND THE INFORMATION EACH PROVIDES

Various strategies exist for eliciting responses at each level of analysis. Keep in mind that respondents will find complex questions more difficult and time consuming to answer. As a result, the survey designer has to make trade-offs between getting the most meaningful information versus getting any information at all. For example, a lengthy and complex mail survey may end up in the trash can more often than in the return mail. Even if the questions are terrific, the few responses that come back may not compensate for the loss of information resulting from the number of nonresponses.

Likewise, people answering a telephone survey will find complicated questions frustrating because they tend to comprehend and remember less when hearing a question than when reading a question. This is the reason telephone surveys often use generic response categories such as the Likert-scale type of response, in which answers range from strongly agree, to agree, to neutral, to disagree, to strongly disagree. People on the telephone often have distractions in the background and other things they would rather be doing, making them less involved in the survey. This makes it easier for them to forget what a question was, what the response options were, or how they answered a previous question on the survey.

For ease of response and analysis, questions on surveys usually are closed ended, meaning respondents choose their favorite answer from a list of possibilities. Open-ended questions, which ask a query but provide space for individual answers instead of a response list, invite more information but often get skipped by respondents and are time consuming to analyze afterward. As a result, surveys typically limit the number of open-ended questions to 2 or 3 of 50. The primary types of closed-ended questions are the checklist, ranking scale, quantity/intensity scale, Likert-type scale, frequency scale, and semantic differential scale.

Checklists

The checklist is a nominal variable, providing categories from which respondents can choose. They can be asked to choose only one response, or all that apply.

Checklist example:

Please indicate whether you are male or female:

    [ ] Male   [ ] Female

Please indicate which of the following publications you have read this week (check all that apply):

    [ ] Newspapers [ ] News Magazines [ ] Other Magazines [ ] Newsletters

Ranking Scales

Ranking scales are ordinal variables, in which respondents are asked to put items in the order they think is most appropriate. Ranking scales are problematic because they incorporate a series of questions into a single item, requiring respondents to perform a complex and often confusing task. They must decide which choice should come first, which should come last, which comes next, and so on until the whole series of comparisons is completed.

Ranking example:

Please rank the following issues according to how important they are to your decision about a congressional candidate this year. Put a 1 by the issue most important to you and a 5 by the issue least important to you:

[ ] Taxes
[ ] Economy
[ ] Environment
[ ] Education
[ ] Crime

Questionnaire designers can help respondents answer a ranking question by breaking it into a series of questions, so the respondents do not have to do this in their heads. Although this method makes it easier for respondents to answer ranking questions, it uses a lot of valuable questionnaire space.

Among the following issues, which is the *most* important to your decision about a congressional candidate this year?

[ ] Taxes
[ ] Economy
[ ] Environment
[ ] Education
[ ] Crime

Among the following issues, which is the *next most* important to your decision about a congressional candidate this year?

[ ] Taxes
[ ] Economy
[ ] Environment
[ ] Education
[ ] Crime

Among the following issues, which is the *least* important to your decision about a congressional candidate this year?

[ ] Taxes
[ ] Economy
[ ] Environment
[ ] Education
[ ] Crime

Quantity/Intensity Scales

The quantity/intensity scale is an ordinal- or interval-level variable, in which respondents choose a location that best fits their opinion on a list of options that forms a continuum.

Quantity/intensity example:

How much education have you completed?

[ ] Less than high school degree
[ ] HS degree or GED
[ ] Some college (no degree; may be currently enrolled)
[ ] Vocational certificate or AA degree
[ ] College graduate (Bachelor's)
[ ] Some graduate work (no degree)
[ ] Master's or other graduate professional degree
[ ] Doctoral degree

Likert-Type Scale

The most frequently used scale is known as the Likert scale.

Likert scale example:

Please indicate whether you strongly agree, agree, disagree, or strongly disagree with the following statement:

The Bestever Corporation is responsive to public concerns

[ ] Strongly agree
[ ] Agree
[ ] Disagree
[ ] Strongly disagree

Other variations on the Likert scale appear frequently on questionnaires. Some popular response ranges include:

Very satisfied/Somewhat satisfied/Somewhat dissatisfied/Very dissatisfied
Strongly oppose/Oppose/Support/Strongly support
Very familiar/Somewhat familiar/Somewhat unfamiliar/Very unfamiliar
A lot/Somewhat/Not much/Not at all
A lot/Some/A little/None
Always/Frequently/Seldom/Never
Often/Sometimes/Rarely/Never
Excellent/Good/Fair/Poor

Quantity/intensity example:

Please indicate if the following reasons have been *very important, somewhat important, not very important, or not at all important* to your decision whether to give to the Mostimportant Association in the past.

The tax benefits resulting from giving	VI SI NVI NAI
Because you like being involved with the MA	VI SI NVI NAI

Another variation of the Likert scale is known as the feeling thermometer, which can be modified to measure levels of confidence, degrees of involvement, and other characteristics. The feeling thermometer as presented by Andrews and Withey (1976) who use 10- or 15-point increments ranging from 0 to 100 to indicate respondents' warmth toward a person, organization, or idea.

Feeling thermometer example:

100	Very warm or favorable feeling
85	Good warm or favorable feeling
70	Fairly warm or favorable feeling
60	A bit more warm or favorable than cold feeling
50	No feeling at all
40	A bit more cold or unfavorable feeling
30	Fairly cold or unfavorable feeling
15	Quite cold or unfavorable feeling
0	Very cold or unfavorable feeling

Yet another variation of the Likert scale uses pictorial scales, which can be useful for special populations such as children, individuals lacking literacy, or populations with whom language is a difficulty. Often, the scales range from a big smiley face (very happy or positive) to big frowny face (very unhappy or negative), or from a big box (a lot) to a little box (very little).

Frequency Scales

The frequency scale is an interval or ratio scale. Instead of assessing how much a respondent embraces an idea or opinion, the frequency question ascertains how often the respondent does or thinks something.

Frequency example:

How many days during the past week have you watched a local television news program?

[ ] 7 days
[ ] 6 days
[ ] 5 days
[ ] 4 days
[ ] 3 days
[ ] 2 days
[ ] 1 day
[ ] 0 days

About how many times have you visited a shopping mall during the past month?

[ ] 16 times or more
[ ] 11–15 times
[ ] 6–10 times
[ ] 1–5 times
[ ] 0 times

Sometimes frequency scales are constructed in ways that make it unclear whether equal distances exist between each response category, which makes the meaning of the measure less clear and the assumption of interval-level statistical power questionable.

Frequency example:

In the past 6 months, how many times have you done the following things?

	Never	1–2 times total	3–4 times total	1–3 times a month	1 time a week	Over once a week
Been offered an alcoholic beverage						
Attended a party where alcohol was served						
Drank an alcoholic beverage						
Had four or more drinks in a row						
Rode with a driver who had been drinking alcohol						
Got sick from drinking alcohol						

Semantic Differential Scales

The semantic differential scale is an interval-level variable, where respondents locate themselves on a scale that has labeled end points. The number of response categories between the end points is up to the questionnaire's designer, but it is useful to have at least four response options. More options make it possible for respondents to indicate nuances of opinion; beyond a certain point, which depends on the context, a proliferation of categories becomes meaningless or even confusing. An even number of response categories forces respondents to choose a position on the issue or refuse to answer the question, whereas an odd number of response categories enables respondents to choose the neutral (midpoint) response.

Semantic differential example:

Please rate your most recent experience with the Allgetwell Hospital staff:

Incompetent — — — — — — Competent
Impolite — — — — — — Polite
Helpful — — — — — — Unhelpful

Semantic differential questions are useful because they can provide a lot of information in a concise format. Written questionnaires especially can include a list of semantic differential items to assess the performance of an organization and its communication activities. Because this type of question includes information as part of the answer categories themselves, some consider these items more valid than Likert-scale items. For example, a Likert-scale question asking if the staff seemed competent could bias respondents who do not want to disagree with the statement, whereas a semantic differential question that gives equal emphasis to "competent" and "incompetent" as end points may elicit more honest answers. Psychologists have demonstrated that agree/disagree question batteries can suffer from acquiescence (Warwick & Lininger, 1975), which occurs when people hesitate to express disagreement.

Measuring Knowledge

Often an organization wants to determine what people know about a topic. One option is to give a true/false or multiple-choice test. The advantage of the multiple-choice test is that, if carefully written, it can uncover misperceptions as well as determine the number of people who know the correct answers. The wrong answers, however, must be plausible. A second option is to ask open-ended questions where people must fill in the blank. This requires a lot of work from the respondent but potentially provides the most valid answers. A third option is to ask people how much they feel they know, rather than testing them on what they actually know. This technique seems less intimidating to respondents. Finally, follow-up questions can ask people how sure they are of a particular answer.

ENSURING CLARITY AND AVOIDING BIAS

Wording can affect the way people respond to survey questions. As a result, it is important to pretest for clarity, simplicity, and objectivity. Using standardized questions that have been pretested and used successfully can help prevent problems. Of course, because every public relations issue has unique characteristics, standardized batteries of questions suffer from lacking specific context. Often a combination of standard and unique items serve the purpose well. When designing questions, keep the following principles in mind:

1. *Use words that are simple, familiar to all respondents, and relevant to the context.* Technical jargon and colloquialisms usually should be avoided. At times, however, the use of slang may en-

hance the relevance of a questionnaire to a resistant target public. For example, asking college students how often they "prefunk" could elicit more honest responses than asking them how often they "use substances such as alcohol before going out to a social function," which is both wordy and could have a more negative connotation to the students than their own terminology. When using specialized terms, it is important to pretest them to ensure the respondents understand them and interpret them as intended. Try to choose words that will not seem patronizing, class specific, or region specific. Choosing to ask about "pasta" instead of "noodles" when assessing audience responses to messages about an Italian restaurant could alienate some respondents who think "pasta" seems pretentious.

2. *Aim for precision to make sure the meaning of answers will be clear.* Avoid vague terms. For example, the word "often" may mean once a week to some people and twice a day to others. "Recently" could mean "this past week" or "this past year." Terms such as "here" and "there" do not set clear geographic parameters.

Do not leave room for interpretation. People responding to a question about how often in the past year they have donated to a charitable organization may consider each monthly contribution to a church a separate donation. The sponsor of the survey, however, may have intended for respondents to indicate how many different organizations they have made donations to during the past year. Avoid hypothetical questions because people often are not very good at, or may have trouble being honest about, predicting their own behavior. Direct questions about cause or solutions also may be difficult for respondents to answer validly (Fowler, 1995). It is better to let the reasons for things emerge from the data analysis by looking at the associations between attitudes and behaviors instead of asking respondents to make those associations for the researcher.

Finally, because the use of negatives in a question can result in confusion, use positive or neutral statements, providing respondents the opportunity to disagree. For example, instead of asking, "Do you think the Neverong Corporation should not change its partner-benefits policy?" a survey can ask, "Do you think the Neverong Corporation's partner-benefits policy should change or stay the same?"

3. *Check for double-barreled questions.* Each question must cover only one issue. Asking if respondents rate staff as "polite and efficient," for example, makes it impossible for respondents to choose "polite but inefficient" or "impolite but efficient" as their an-

swer. Sometimes a double-barreled question is subtle and the problem occurs because a phrase requires respondents to embrace an assumption they may not hold. For example, asking "How likely are you to use this service on your next visit to Funpark?" assumes there will be a next visit.

4. *Check for leading or loaded questions.* A leading question prompts the respondent in one direction instead of treating each possible response equally. Asking the question, "How much did you enjoy your visit?" leads respondents in the direction of a positive answer, whereas the question, "How would you rate your visit?" allows enjoyment and disappointment to be equivalent answer categories making it easier for respondents to choose the negative answer.

A loaded question biases the answer through the use of emotionally charged words, stereotypes, or other words that give a subtle charge to a phrase. Loading can occur in the question or in the answer. For example, the question given earlier asking respondents to indicate which issues are most important to them in an upcoming election mentions only some of the possible alternatives about which voters may care. Health care, abortion, social security, welfare, agricultural issues, and race/gender equality are among the many issues not even mentioned. In addition, loading can occur by using words that have positive or negative connotations, such as "unwed moms" versus "single mothers." Loading also can occur in frequency scales. Asking people whether they had 0, 1, 2, 3, 4, 5, 6, 7 or more alcoholic drinks during the past week, for example, gets more people to acknowledge having 3 or 4 drinks than asking people whether they had 0, 1, 2, 3 or more alcoholic drinks during the past week (Fowler, 1995). People often feel marginalized by picking what seems like an extreme response.

5. *Check for social desirability effects.* Some people find it difficult to express an opinion or report a behavior they think is inconsistent with what most other people think or do. Some also find it difficult to give a response they think the surveyor disagrees with or disapproves of. It is well documented, for example, that a higher percentage of people claim to have voted in an election than actually turn out at the polls. Try to write questions so that people find it easy to give a negative response.

One technique for reducing social-desirability bias is to include an introduction to a sensitive question that makes any response seem normal and acceptable. For example, Fowler (1995) noted that asking people if they own a library card can seem threatening because a "no" response could be perceived as a lack of interest in reading, which might seem socially unacceptable. As a result, Fowler suggested the following introduction: "Many people get books from libraries. Others buy their books, subscribe to magazines, or get their reading material in some other way. Do you have a library card now, or not?" (p. 36).

6. *Provide enough context to enable people to respond realistically or remember accurately.* On the whole, questions should be as brief as possible so they can be digested with the least effort. Nevertheless, the goal of questionnaire design is to construct questions such that answers will provide the most meaningful information possible. As a result, adding some context can be useful. It helps, for example, to ask people to recall behaviors over a limited time or from a recent time, such as during the past week.

In general, questionnaire designers should avoid yes/no items. Besides providing information of limited usefulness for statistical analysis (dichotomous questions are nominal variables), this type of question leaves no room for a respondent to answer "maybe" or "well, it depends." Answers to dichotomous questions, as a result, can be misleading. Similarly, questions usually should avoid "always" and "never" as categories. "Almost always" and "almost never" give people the opportunity to be more context specific.

QUESTIONNAIRE LAYOUT AND DESIGN

Most discussions of survey design focus on how to construct the questions themselves, but other aspects of design, such as how items appear on a page or the order in which questions appear, also can make a difference to respondents.

Ease of Reading

It helps to give respondents "chunks" of questions at a time. A series of questions without a break can become boring and confusing. People may get lost in a written questionnaire that has 10 items in a row, for example, checking off their responses to Question 6 on the line for Question 5. The following items, assessing respondents' interest in different types of university-related news, for example, are difficult to follow in a continuous format.

The following are topics that might be covered in a publication from Central State University. For each one, please tell me whether you are *very interested, somewhat interested, not very interested, or not at all interested* in receiving information about each topic:[1]

12. The university's branch campuses	VI	SI	NVI	NAI	RF/DK
13. Student accomplishments	VI	SI	NVI	NAI	RF/DK
14. The financial needs of the university	VI	SI	NVI	NAI	RF/DK
15. The work of the administration	VI	SI	NVI	NAI	RF/DK
16. How donations are being used	VI	SI	NVI	NAI	RF/DK
17. News about teaching	VI	SI	NVI	NAI	RF/DK
18. Athletic accomplishments	VI	SI	NVI	NAI	RF/DK
19. News about university research	VI	SI	NVI	NAI	RF/DK
20. University nostalgia and history	VI	SI	NVI	NAI	RF/DK
21. News about alumni	VI	SI	NVI	NAI	RF/DK
22. News about campus life	VI	SI	NVI	NAI	RF/DK

These questions are easier to answer in chunks. Generally, chunks of three or four items at a time work well.

The following are topics that might be covered in a publication from Central State University. For each one, please tell me whether you are *very interested, somewhat interested, not very interested, or not at all interested* in receiving information about each topic:

12. The university's branch campuses	VI	SI	NVI	NAI	RF/DK
13. Student accomplishments	VI	SI	NVI	NAI	RF/DK
14. The financial needs of the university	VI	SI	NVI	NAI	RF/DK
15. The work of the administration	VI	SI	NVI	NAI	RF/DK
16. How donations are being used	VI	SI	NVI	NAI	RF/DK
17. News about teaching	VI	SI	NVI	NAI	RF/DK
18. Athletic accomplishments	VI	SI	NVI	NAI	RF/DK
19. News about university research	VI	SI	NVI	NAI	RF/DK
20. University nostalgia and history	VI	SI	NVI	NAI	RF/DK
21. News about alumni	VI	SI	NVI	NAI	RF/DK
22. News about campus life	VI	SI	NVI	NAI	RF/DK

[1]VI = very interested, SI = somewhat interested, NVI = not very interested, NAI = not at all interested, RF/DK = refused or don't know.

Respondents on a telephone survey also can get fatigued by a long list of items and will benefit from a break during which the surveyor gives a new introduction, even if the questions in the next section do not focus on anything new.

Example from a phone survey:

OK, now I need to know if you **[READ SLOWLY] strongly agree (SA), agree (A), disagree (D), or strongly disagree (SD)** with each of the following statements about politics and the media. [REPEAT CATEGORIES AS NECESSARY.]

	(5)	(4)	(3)	(2)	(1)	(9)
19. The media rarely have anything new to say.	SA	A	n	D	SD	RF/DK
20. I'm interested in campaigns and election information.	SA	A	n	D	SD	RF/DK
21. The news media only pay attention to bad news about political issues and candidates.	SA	A	n	D	SD	RF/DK
22. Candidates for office are interested only in people's votes, not in their opinions.	SA	A	n	D	SD	RF/DK
23. My vote makes a difference.	SA	A	n	D	SD	RF/DK

This won't take much longer and we really appreciate your help. These next few questions also are about politicians and the media. Do you **strongly agree (SA), agree (A), disagree (D), or strongly disagree (SD)** that:

	(5)	(4)	(3)	(2)	(1)	(9)
24. Politicians are out of touch with life in the real world.	SA	A	n	D	SD	RF/DK
25. I pay attention to campaign and election information.	SA	A	n	D	SD	RF/DK
26. There's often more to the story than you hear in the news.	SA	A	n	D	SD	RF/DK
27. Political campaigns are too mean spirited.	SA	A	n	D	SD	RF/DK
28. I actively seek out information concerning the government and politics.	SA	A	n	D	SD	RF/DK
29. I have a say in what the government does.	SA	A	n	D	SD	RF/DK

It also is important to remember how easily people answering telephone surveys can get lost. Because they do not see the questions, they can forget what a series of questions is about or what the response options are. In addition, changing response options frequently will slow them down and may make it difficult for them to keep track of what they are supposed to be doing. Forcing them to slow down can help improve the validity of answers by making sure they think carefully about their answers, but it also can hurt validity by causing utter confusion. Pretesting, over the phone, is essential.

Directionality and Response Set

Another issue that can affect validity is known as *directionality* and it refers to the order in which response categories are presented. It helps both respondents and analysts to associate negative opinions with lower numbers and positive opinions with larger numbers. Some questionnaires, for example, ask respondents to choose a numbered response instead of checking a box. This can make a questionnaire easier to read—it makes the middle of a scale more obvious—and it also makes data entry easier because the computer usually has to receive numbers.

Example of numbered responses on a written survey:

How important are the following for helping you choose your preferred candidates or issues?

	Not at all important						Very important
Newspapers	I	2	3	4	5	6	7
Radio	I	2	3	4	5	6	7
Television	I	2	3	4	5	6	7
Magazines	I	2	3	4	5	6	7
Friends	I	2	3	4	5	6	7
Family	I	2	3	4	5	6	7

Questionnaire designers also should pretest for response set, which is a form of response bias. If response categories always have the negative response first (on the left if on a written questionnaire) and the positive response last (on the right), people may begin to answer questions too quickly, without thinking them through. Response set can make a group of questions seem related simply because they appear near each other on the questionnaire. In other words, people may have marked similar answers on the questions out of convenience or habit, instead of because they thought deeply about each question and agreed that a similar answer applied to each.

Using "Skip Patterns" Effectively

Sometimes a question will not apply to all respondents. In this case a screening question, or a series of screening questions, is used. This series of questions is known as a *skip pattern*. On a written questionnaire, it is important to make it clear when and which questions should be skipped. Often instructions such as, "GO TO Q. 6," appear next to the appropriate response to the screening question. Sometimes, questionnaires include graphic elements such as boxes or arrows to guide respondents. Such devices can make a questionnaire look cluttered and confusing, however, so skip patterns should be pretested carefully.

HANDLING "DON'T KNOW" RESPONSES

One subtle but major issue in the use of surveys is how to handle people who do not have an opinion on a particular question. One of the problems with survey research is that most people do try to offer an opinion for the researchers, even if they must manufacture an opinion on the spot. For example, the average respondent queried about the economic situation in Mozambique probably knows little about Mozambique's economy, unless it has been in the news. Few people knew much about Kosovo until Slobodan Milosevic decided to "ethnically cleanse" the province. Nevertheless, if asked for an opinion many people offer one, even though some may decline to answer the question. Such opinions, based on little or no information, mean little because they are unstable. They are pseudodata, not real data.

Researchers must be ready to handle respondents' potential lack of opinion. The most common way is to include a "don't know" response among the answer categories. The drawback of making it easily available is that respondents may be tempted to use it. Making it subtly available is easy to do on a telephone survey, because the interviewer can be instructed not to read that option. On a written survey, the respondents will see the option if it is available. Respondents will use the "don't know" option for one of two reasons: either they truly don't know, or they don't feel like answering the question. To prod people who are not motivated to think about an issue to report an opinion, even if it is top of the mind, surveyors eliminate the "don't know" option, forcing respondents to leave the question entirely blank if they do not want to answer it.

It is important to consider two issues here. The first is that "don't know" can be a meaningful response, of great usefulness to the communication manager. For example, if a large proportion of participants respond "don't know" to a question about corporate reputation, the organization can conclude that it does not have a bad reputation even if it does not have a good reputation. In other words, it may learn that instead of running a persuasion campaign, it needs to launch an awareness campaign. This frequently is the case, but organizations must be skilled at collecting and interpreting "don't know" responses to make the appropriate diagnosis.

Another important issue about "don't know" responses is that "don't know" should not be interpreted the same way as "neutral." Likert scales, for example, often feature a neutral category, which can tempt people to avoid taking a position on an issue. Nevertheless, "neutral" does not necessarily mean the respondent has no information on which to base an opinion. A neutral opinion is an opinion. Responding "neutral" to a question about providing child care in the workplace, for instance, may mean "I don't care, this doesn't affect me," or "I am satisfied either way," rather than "I have no information on which to base an opinion." Both options can be made available to respondents to avoid misinterpreting the findings.

Another way to handle the possibility of "don't know" responses is to provide information in the introduction to a question that gives the respondent background on which to base an opinion. This has important advantages and disadvantages. For example, three members of the state legislature in Washington state included the following questions on a 1997 survey of their constituents:

About 9 in 10 Washington voters in a recent nonpartisan survey said education was their number one issue this year. About two in three people surveyed said education was underfunded and worse than it was 4 years ago. How would you address this?

Divert funding from other areas of state government and put it into higher education?	YES	NO
Increase enrollment on-campus opportunities at our state's colleges and universities?	YES	NO
Increase enrollment opportunities at branch campuses?	YES	NO
Increase the number of courses available to students at off-campus sites via television, e-mail and the Internet?	YES	NO
Build more classrooms, laboratories and other facilities for off-campus instruction?	YES	NO

The value of this strategy is that it gives a client the opportunity to see how respondents will react to an issue of emerging importance, which they may not yet know much about. This can help the client respond to the issue effectively.

The risk associated with this strategy is that it can bias the question in the direction of the information selected for inclusion. Some organizations do this intentionally on bogus questionnaires sent out as fund-raising appeals, or to attract media attention through "created" opinion. This is a blatantly unethical practice, denounced by the American Association of Public Opinion Researchers, and it violates the principles of the PRSA code of professional ethics (see Sidebar 11.2).

Some organizations do this in hopes of educating the public; the problem is that only a small sample of the public is answering the survey. Surveys are opportunities to gather unbiased information to guide a campaign. Still others use them to see if providing certain information on a survey can change people's responses. This type of survey is known as a "push poll" and often is used by political campaigns. Not only is the information provided on such "surveys" biased in favor of the sponsoring candidate, but the survey often ends with a fund-raising appeal. Turning surveys into vehicles for persuasion and fund raising defeats the purpose of collecting objective data and compromises the reputation of surveyors trying to do authentic research. It is no wonder, with such unethical practices going on, that fewer people agree to answer market research (or any other) surveys.

DESIGN FEATURES THAT AFFECT RESPONSE RATE

Every survey requires an introduction so that respondents are informed of the study's purpose. The introduction also represents an opportunity to motivate respondents to cooperate. Mail surveys and telephone surveys have different introductions, specially suited to the context. Nevertheless, the primary information to include in an introduction remains the same and includes what the study is about, who the sponsor is, how the results will be used, why respondents should be a part of the study (how they were chosen and why they should care about this), and the extent to which their responses will be confidential or anonymous. Anonymous means that no one, including the researchers, will know respondents' identities. Confidential means the researchers will have identifying information for some purpose, such as matching respondents from the same household or calling back to gather more information later, but their identities will be kept secret from everyone else. Some organizations have "human subjects committees" or "institutional review boards" that must approve of study materials and may require additional elements as well.

SIDEBAR 11.2.
Statement Condemning Push Polls

The following statement was adopted by the AAPOR Council at its January 1996 meeting:

AAPOR joins the National Council on Public Polls (and other professional survey organizations) in condemning a political campaign tactic, commonly called "push polls," which masquerades as legitimate political polling. These are not polls at all. They are a form of political telemarketing.

A "push poll" is a telemarketing technique in which telephone calls are used to canvass potential voters, feeding them false or misleading "information" about a candidate under the pretense of taking a poll to see how this "information" affects voter preferences. In fact, the intent is not to measure public opinion but to manipulate it—to "push" voters away from one candidate and toward the opposing candidate. Such polls defame selected candidates by spreading false or misleading information about them. The intent is to disseminate campaign propaganda under the guise of conducting a legitimate public opinion poll.

Push polls violate the AAPOR Code of Ethics by intentionally lying to or misleading respondents. They corrupt the electoral process by disseminating false and misleading attacks on candidates. And because so-called "push polls" can easily be confused with real polls, they damage the reputation of legitimate polling, thereby discouraging the public from participating in legitimate survey research.

In order to reduce the impact of "push polls," it is important that the survey research community respond promptly when this technique is used. To do so, we need to know about "push polls" when they happen. If you are a "respondent" in a "push poll" or otherwise become aware of one, please collect as much information about the situation as possible and call the President of AAPOR, Michael Kagay (212/556-3888), or the Chair of the Standards Committee, Kathleen Frankovic (212/976-6615 or 415/864-3259), Associate Chair, Warren Mitofsky (202/980-3031) or send e-mail to Kagay: kagay@nytimes.com); Frankovic: kaf@cbsnews.com, Mitofsky: mitofsky@mindspring.com. With your help, we can reduce the influence of this unethical campaign practice, which also damages legitimate survey research.
Eleanor Singer
Standards Committee, 1996
American Association for Public Opinion Research

***

Reprinted with permission from the American Association for Public Opinion Research.

The Mail Survey Introduction

Mail surveys should have a cover letter introducing the study. It should be brief (never longer than one page), on letterhead (to identify the sponsoring institution and lend credibility to the study), include a contact person for questions or concerns, indicate how long the survey will take to fill out (be honest), and make it clear how to return the questionnaire (providing a self-addressed, stamped, return envelope is essential). The respondents should be thanked for cooperating and told how important their participation is. It also helps to give respondents a deadline for returning the questionnaire, of no more than a week, so they don't forget about it. Finally, the letter may include information about an incentive provided for cooperating with the study.

The Telephone Survey Introduction

Introductions by telephone need to be even shorter than those by letter. If possible, keep the introduction to two sentences. In those two sentences, identify the sponsor and purpose of the study, the way respondents have been selected, the length of time required for answering the survey, and the importance of the respondent's part in the study. It also helps to have the callers identify themselves by name so respondents do not think the caller has anything to hide. At the end of the introduction, proceed directly to the first question on the survey. Do not ask permission to begin explicitly, because this invites participants to tell you that you have called at an inconvenient time. Instead, you solicit their permission to begin through the explanation of the survey and the assurance that their answers are important. This introduction makes it obvious that you plan to ask questions and that you hope they will answer. Because they probably will be skeptical of your motives and more interested in whatever they were doing before you called, you want to get right to the first question on the survey to gain their confidence and capture their interest. You want to make the first question nonthreatening, general, and interesting so the respondents will think the questionnaire is easy and worth their time (see Sidebar 11.3).

Nuances can make a difference. For example, identifying the organization at the outset gives the project more credibility and can make it clear this is not a sales call. In addition, calling the project a "study" instead of a "survey" makes it sound less threatening and makes it clear this will be not be one of those sales calls masquerading as a survey. In addition, saying you have called them long distance (if you really are) or that your study is being sponsored by a university or respected institution can make their selection and the study itself seem more special (Dillman, 1978).

SIDEBAR 11.3.
A Standard Telephone Introduction with a Screening Question

Hello, my name is _____. I'm calling long distance
from _____. We're conducting a study of _____ and
I have a few questions for a registered voter 18 years of age or older.

Are you registered to vote?

[IF YES: BEGIN SURVEY. **DO *NOT* STOP TO ASK PERMISSION TO BEGIN**]

[IF NO: Is someone else in your household registered to vote? May I speak with that person please? BEGIN AGAIN WITH NEW RESPONDENT.]

IF NO: Thank for your time. Good-bye.

Prenotification Cards or Letters

The use of prenotification cards to tell respondents that a survey will be happening soon helps boost response rates. If they understand the purpose of the study ahead of time, they will be less likely to throw away an envelope that looks like a direct-mail solicitation or to hang up on a call from an individual who sounds like a telephone solicitor. Letters or postcards both suffice, but postcards offer the advantage of being readable at a glance and less costly to mail. Envelopes may go unopened into the trash.

Follow-up Mailings

Most mail surveys only achieve a 30% to 40% response rate with a single mailing. Research has found, however, that reminders can boost response rates to 75% or better. It may take four reminders to achieve a 75% return, with each reminder netting fewer responses. As a result, the research manager needs to decide the extent to which the cost of reminders is worth the additional responses. Generally, each reminder garners half the number of responses the previous mailing achieved. As a result, a single reminder can increase a 30% response rate to a 45% response rate, or a 40% response rate to a 60% response rate.

Incentives

It is difficult to give telephone respondents a concrete reward for their participation, although credit card companies have tried promising a

General Manager

THE WALL STREET JOURNAL.

200 Liberty Street
New York, NY 10281
Subscriber Services 1-800-JOURNAL
Product/Service Information 1-800-832-1234

September 20, 1999

DOWJONES

Dear Wall Street Journal Subscriber,

We would like to better understand your business news and financial information needs. Would you please complete this brief survey about your use of THE WALL STREET JOURNAL and your professional and personal interests? Your answers will help us do a better job of developing products and services that meet your needs.

For your convenience, we have provided a postage-paid envelope in which to return this survey. As a token of our appreciation we have enclosed a dollar bill, which may brighten the day of a child you know. We appreciate your willingness to participate in this survey and thank you in advance for your cooperation.

Sincerely,

General Manager

P.S. Occasionally, a select group of Wall Street Journal advertisers wish to make special offers (such as discounted services or previews of new products) specifically to subscribers who respond to this survey. Please check this box if you *do not* wish to receive any of these offers: ☐

FIG. 11.1. Sample cover letter with incentive.
Used with permission from *The Wall Street Journal.* Copyright © *The Wall Street Journal.*

bonus credited to the respondent's account in return for answering a survey. Mail surveys, however, frequently include incentives. Usually the incentive is provided ahead of time to motivate the person to respond, instead of afterward as a reward. Monetary incentives ranging from $1 to $5 are especially popular, with amounts over $1 rare. Other incentives can include a gift certificate or product samples. Organizations sometimes promise donations to a charity, in hopes of appealing to respondents' sense of altruism, as illustrated in Fig. 11.1. Questionnaires returned in person can include a raffle ticket that can be deposited in a separate container alongside the questionnaire container to preserve the anonymity of the questionnaire.

Sensitive Questions

Sensitive questions should never appear at the beginning of a survey. Instead, the most sensitive questions come at the end so that respondents who may quit the study because of a particularly offensive question will already have answered most of the questionnaire. This is why demographic questions almost always appear at the end of a survey. Many people especially dislike identifying their income levels, ethnic background, and age.

Encouragement

Because respondents to telephone surveys cannot see the questionnaire, they will be worrying about how long the interruption will take. If the questionnaire seems to go on too long, they will lose interest. As a result, it helps to thank them every so often for continuing, as well as to assure them the end will come soon. For example, one phone survey about the media and politics includes the phrase, around Question 23, "This won't take much longer and we really appreciate your help. These next few questions ..." Then, anticipating increasing impatience from the respondent, the survey includes more encouragement at Question 30, "I have just a few more questions about your use of the media ..." before beginning the introduction for the next set of questions. Before the demographic questions at the end of the survey, a last bit of encouragement ensures respondents that these are the final set of queries.

Length

No perfect length exists for a questionnaire, although a good bit of research focuses on the topic. For example, people seem more likely to participate in a mall-intercept survey limited to a 5" × 8" card. It is difficult to keep people on the phone longer than 5 to 8 minutes, which means a telephone survey over 40 to 50 questions will suffer from attrition as people begin to hang up. Questions appearing at the end of the survey will end up with a smaller sample of responses than questions appearing at the beginning of the survey. In mail surveys, a longer mail survey will get less cooperation than a shorter survey, but the number of pages is not always the deciding factor. For example, respondents may prefer the ease of reading and feeling of accomplishment that comes from having fewer questions and more white space, even if that necessitates using more pages. Some survey designers find a two-column format makes questionnaires more reader friendly. Disagreement exists about the use of single-sided versus double-sided printing. Double-sided printing cuts the number of pages but can confuse respondents, who may end up skipping pages by accident. As with everything else, it helps to pretest surveys using different formats to see which works the best.

Interviewer Directions

Untrained or confused interviewers can ruin a survey. Interviewers must sound enthusiastic, polite, and confident. They also need to present questions clearly, which means they need to enunciate carefully and speak slowly. To prevent interviewer bias from affecting the validity of the responses, they need to present the surveys in a consistent way. As a result, interviewer directions must be clear. Chapter 12 discusses interviewer training in some detail.

Generally, instructions to the interviewer appear in all caps or in brackets to set off the information from the parts that get read aloud. Words that require special emphasis can be italicized or put in boldface. Information read by an interviewer should sound conversational in tone rather than formal.

Sample interviewer instruction:

As I read the following list of information sources, please tell me whether the source is **[READ SLOWLY] very important, important, unimportant, or very unimportant** to you: [REPEAT CATEGORIES AS NECESSARY.]

Cultural/Language Sensitivity

Knowing the target public well can aid design and secure a better response. For example, question wording may need to change depending on the age of the participants. Translators may be needed if a phone survey aims to interview people who do not speak English. Mail surveys, too, can benefit from making translations available. As shown in Fig. 11.2, Washington state made a big effort to reach recent immigrants with its surveys and information intended to help ensure good health care for babies and toddlers.

FINAL THOUGHTS

Clearly, a myriad of design issues contribute to the effectiveness of a questionnaire. Research managers need to write questions in a way that will provide the most meaningful and unbiased information. The order of questions must seem logical and interesting to the respondent, and the directions to respondents and interviewers must prevent confusion. Pretesting should check for the existence of subtle bias in word choice.

CHILD PROFILE

English

IF YOU HAVE TROUBLE UNDERSTANDING THE MATERIALS, OR IF YOU NEED HELP FINDING HEALTH CARE, YOU CAN CALL HEALTHY MOTHERS, HEALTHY BABIES AT 1-800-322-2588. WHEN YOU CALL, TELL THE PERSON THE NAME OF YOUR LANGUAGE AND STAY ON THE LINE UNTIL YOU ARE CONNECTED WITH AN INTERPRETER.

Amharic

ከዚህ ጽሑፍ ውስጥ ያልገባችሁ ሃሳብ ካለ ወይም የህክምና አገልግሎት ካስፈልጋችሁ፣ ጤናማ እናቶች፣ ጤናማ ህፃናት (ሄልዚ ማዘርስ፣ ሄልዚ ቤቢስ) በመባል የሚታወቀውን የህክምና ክፍል በ 1-800-322-2588 በመደወል መጠየቅ ትችላላችሁ። በምትደውሉበት ጊዜ ለምታነጋግሩት ሰው የቋንቋችሁን ስም ብትገልጹ፣ አስተርጓሚ ሊያዘጋጅላችሁ ስለሚችል የስልኩን መስመር በመያዝ ጠብቁ።

Cambodian

បើលោកអ្នកមានការពិបាកយល់នូវសម្ភារៈទាំងឡាយ ឬក៏ត្រូវការជំនួយក្នុងការស្វែងរកមន្ទីរព្យាបាលជម្ងឺ លោកអ្នកអាចទូរស័ព្ទទៅផ្នែក Healthy Mothers និង Healthy Babies តាមរយៈលេខ 1-800-322-2588 ។ នៅពេលលោកអ្នកទូរស័ព្ទមក សូមប្រាប់អ្នក លើកទូរស័ព្ទនូវភាសាដែលលោកអ្នកនិយាយហើយរង់ចាំទាល់ដែលគេបន្តទូរស័ព្ទទៅអ្នកបកប្រែ។

Chinese

如果您無法完全理解這些資料，或者您需要幫助尋找醫療保健服務，請打電話至“健康母親、健康寶寶”熱線 (Healthy Mothers, Healthy Babies)，號碼是 1-800-322-2588。當您打電話時，請告訴接線員您說什麼語言，並請耐心等候直到接線員將您與一位翻譯接通。

Korean

만약 귀하께서 자료를 이해하시는데 문제가 있거나 건강관리자를 찾는데 도움이 필요하시면 무료 전화인 1-800-322-2588 건강한 엄마, 건강한 아기(Healthy Mothers, Healthy Babies)로 전화를 하십시요. 전화를 하실 때 전화 받는 분에게 귀하가 사용하시는 언어를 말씀하시고 통역원과 연결이 될 때 까지 전화를 들고 계십시요.

Laotian

ຖ້າຫາກວ່າທ່ານມີບັນຫາບໍ່ເຂົ້າໃຈຄຳອະທິບາຍ ຫລືທ່ານຕ້ອງການຄວາມຊ່ວຍເຫລືອຫາບ່ອນຮັບການປິ່ນປົວ ທ່ານອາດຈະໂທໄປຫາ ໂຄງການແມ່ສົມບູນເດັກສົມບູນ (Healthy Mothers, Healthy Babies) ຢູ່ທີ່ເລກໂທ 1-800-322-2588 ເມື່ອທ່ານໄດ້ໂທໄປຫາແລ້ວ ຈົ່ງບອກຜູ້ຮັບສາຍວ່າທ່ານປາກພາສາຫຍັງແລ້ວລໍຖ້າຈົນເຖິງມີນາຍພາສາມາຮັບສາຍ.

Russian

ЕСЛИ У ВАС ТРУДНОСТИ В ПОНИМАНИИ МАТЕРИАЛА, ИЛИ ВАМ ТРЕБУЕТСЯ ПОМОЩЬ В ПОИСКЕ МЕДИЦИНСКОГО ОБЕСПЕЧЕНИЯ, ТО ВЫ МОЖЕТЕ ПОЗВОНИТЬ «ХЕЛСИ МАЗЕРС, ХЕЛСИ БЭЙБИС» ПО ТЕЛ. 1-800-322-2588. КОГДА ВЫ ЗВОНИТЕ, НАЗОВИТЕ ГОВОРЯЩЕМУ С ВАМИ ЯЗЫК, НА КОТОРОМ ВЫ ГОВОРИТЕ, И ЖДИТЕ ПОКА ВАС СОЕДИНЯТ С ПЕРЕВОДЧИКОМ.

Somali

HADII AY DHIBATO KA'HAYSATO DAAWOOYINKA IYO QALABKA DARYEELKA CAAFIMAADKA AMA AAD U BAAHANTAHAY CAAFIMAADKA JOOGTADA ALI IYO WIXII LA MID AH WAXAAD U YEERTAA TELEFOONKA 1-800-322-2588 MARKA CIDDI KULA HADASHO U SHEEG LUUQADDADA KUNA SII JIR LAYNKA TELEFONKA SI LAGUUGU XIRO TURJUBAAN.

Spanish

SI TIENE USTED CUALQUIER PROBLEMA PARA ENTENDER ESTOS MATERIALES, O SI NECESITA AYUDA PARA ENCONTRAR CUIDADO PARA LA SALUD, PUEDE LLAMAR A HEALTHY MOTHERS, HEALTHY BABIES AL 1-800-322-2588. CUANDO LLAME, DIGALE A LA PERSONA EL NOMBRE DE SU IDIOMA Y QUEDESE EN LA LINEA HASTA QUE SEA CONECTADO CON UN INTERPRETE.

Tigrigna

ብዚኦም ዝስዕሉ ዘለዉ. ጸሑፋት ዘይትረኣኽም ነገር እንተሉ ወይ ድማ ናይ ሕክምና ኣገልግሎት ትደልዩ እንድኣር ዖይንኽም ኣብ ናይ ጥዕነት እደታኣን ቀዳወን (ሄልዲ ግዛርስ ፡ ሄልዲ ቢሊስ)ዛዒዓ ሕክምና ግኽስኣ ብ 1-800-322-2588 ብፍድኣ በትሕት ትኸኣሉ ኣኸም ፡ ኣብ ትድወሉሉ ግዜ ንቲ. ተዛርቦም በዓ ኣናይ ጽገ ትዛረቡ ኸምዘለኹም ፓስ ንገርኩም ጽገኣኸም ዝዛረብ በዓ (ትርጓም እነገኣኮት)በፕኣለኮም ስለዝኸኣለ ኣብ መስመር ዖይንኽም ሐለዉ =

Ukrainian

ЯКЩО ВИ ІСПИТУЄТЕ ТРУДНОШІ В РОЗУМІННІ МАТЕРІАЛУ, АБО ВАМ НЕОБХІДНА ДОПОМОГА В ОТРИМАННІ МЕДИЧНОГО ЗАБЕЗПЕЧЕННЯ, ТО ВИ МОЖЕТЕ ПОДЗВОНИТИ „ХЕЛСІ МАЗЕРС, ХЕЛСІ БЭЙБИС" (HEALTHY MOTHERS, HEALTHY BABIES) ПО ТЕЛЕФОНУ 1-800-322-2588. КОЛИ ВИ ДЗОНИТЕ, НАЗОВІТЬ РОЗМОВЛЯЮЩЕМУ З ВАМИ МОВУ, НА ЯКІЙ ВИ РОЗМОВЛЯЄТЕ, ТА ЧЕКАЙТЕ ПОКИ ВАС СОЄДИНЯТЬ З ПЕРЕКЛАДЧИКОМ.

Vietnamese

NẾU BẠN GẶP KHÓ KHĂN TRONG VẤN ĐỀ THÔNG HIỂU CÁC TÀI LIỆU, HOẶC NẾU BẠN CẦN GIÚP ĐỠ TRONG VIỆC TÌM DỊCH VỤ Y TẾ, BẠN CÓ THỂ GỌI CHO HỘI HEALTHY MOTHERS, HEALTHY BABIES TẠI SỐ ĐIỆN THOẠI 1-800-322-2588. KHI BẠN GỌI, BẠN HÃY NÓI CHO NGƯỜI NGHE ĐIỆN THOẠI BIẾT BẠN NÓI NGÔN NGỮ GÌ, RỒI CẦM ĐIỆN THOẠI CHỜ ĐỢI, VÀ HỌ SẼ KIẾM NGƯỜI THÔNG DỊCH ĐỂ NÓI ĐIỆN THOẠI VỚI BẠN.

FIG. 11.2. Healthy Mothers introduction translation. Developed by the University of Washington and the Center on Human Development and Disability, and funded by the Washington State Department of Health.

No perfect survey exists, but various strategies can boost response rates and increase the validity of responses. The details can make the simple task of asking questions seem overwhelmingly complicated, but the use of preexisting instruments or batteries of questions can provide useful models to follow. For the manager working within a tight budget, the principles laid out in this chapter should make it possible to run a reliable, valid and useful survey. In addition, various books, and even software such as PUBLICS (Cameron, 1997), specifically designed for public relations research, can guide managers through the process. Meanwhile, for managers able to hire experts to do the job, the principles presented here can make it easier to monitor a survey research firm to ensure top-quality results.

❧ 12 ❧
Collecting, Analyzing, and Reporting Quantitative Data

The best survey is one that is easy to answer, easy to analyze, and easy to report. Although most of the work goes into the writing of questions themselves, research managers also need to think ahead to analysis and reporting strategies. Designing surveys and training interviewers with data entry in mind can improve the speed and reliability of results. Planning what results need to be reported can aid analysis and ensure data are collected in a way that makes it possible to create necessary tables and figures. Once the results become available, the manager can think about how to share good, bad, or surprising news with the client.

DESIGNING SURVEYS FOR EASY DATA ENTRY

Several formats can be used to create easily analyzed questionnaires. Many survey research centers, for example, use CATI (Computer Assisted Telephone Interviewing) systems, in which telephone or personal interviewers enter data directly into the computer as they talk with respondents. Managers also can use do-it-yourself systems such as PUBLICS (Cameron, 1997), which provide question templates for survey

246

designers that can be customized. Statistical packages such as SPSS provide more sophistication, supplying software for questionnaire design, data entry, and powerful analyses. The cost for these systems ranges from several hundred dollars to tens of thousands of dollars.

CATI or computer-assisted data collection (CADAC) can eliminate the need for cumbersome data-entry procedures. Interviewers using a CATI system typically wear a headset and ask questions prompted by the computer. As they type in the answers from each participant, the computer automatically updates the database to incorporate the new information. This type of system also is growing more popular for personal interviews, particularly for sensitive issues. Survey participants can enter their responses into the computer anonymously, without the interviewer knowing their opinions or behaviors. According to Shanks and Tortora (1985), computer-aided data entry can reduce data-entry errors by 77%. In addition, it can reduce confusion on complicated questionnaires that include conditional, or branching, questions. Conditional questions separate participants into groups depending on their response. For example, consumers who answer yes to a question about having previously purchased a company's product can go on to answer questions about the product's quality and the company's responsiveness. Consumers who answer no answer a different set of questions that may focus on their potential interest in the company's or their competitors' products. CADAC or CATI systems now are common among professional research firms.

Nevertheless, survey questionnaires often must be entered manually. In this case, several design issues can make data entry more efficient.

Directionality

As mentioned in chap. 11, attention to directionality can make results more intuitive to report. Directionality refers to the match between the numbers that represent answers to questions in the computer and the idea they symbolize. For example, on a Likert scale, a 5 is used to represent "strongly agree" and a 1 is used to represent "strongly disagree" so that a high score means more agreement instead of less agreement. Always use a high number to indicate a positive response, even if the question is negatively worded. For example, a higher number should represent "very often" on a scale measuring "how often have you had difficulty receiving your order on time?"

Coding and Code Books

Some questionnaire designers include the numbers for data entry purposes on the questionnaires themselves, whereas others rely on a separate code book. The code book is a copy of the questionnaire with annotations that direct data-entry personnel. The annotations include short variable names—abbreviations for the questions—along with information on where in a computer data set the answers appear and what numbers represent each answer. We address each of these issues separately.

The advantage to including numbers on the questionnaire is that data-entry personnel see a constant reminder of the codes they must enter, making memory lapses less likely. This can help considerably on complicated questionnaires. Numbers also can help the respondents follow along when answers include a lot of response options. In the example below, note how much easier it is to find the center of the scale when it includes numbers instead of blanks:

Which of the following best describes
our customer service representatives?

Incompetent	1	2	3	4	5	6	7	8	9	Competent
Impolite	1	2	3	4	5	6	7	8	9	Polite
Unhelpful	1	2	3	4	5	6	7	8	9	Helpful

Which of the following best describes
our customer service representatives?

Incompetent	_	_	_	_	_	_	_	_	_	Competent
Impolite	_	_	_	_	_	_	_	_	_	Polite
Unhelpful	_	_	_	_	_	_	_	_	_	Helpful

Questionnaire designers should be careful, however, to ensure the questionnaire does not become so cluttered with numbers that it becomes difficult to read or seemingly impersonal. Usually some codes appear only in the code book. Telephone questionnaires can include more codes, as long as the instrument remains easy for interviewers to read. It helps both interviewers and data-entry personnel to have sets of answers clustered in small groups, such as in the following example:

OK, thinking again about some election issues, please think now about the public schools where you live, and tell me how good a job your schools are doing educating students in each of the following areas. Use a scale from 1 to 5, with 1 meaning *very poor* and 5 meaning *very good*:

	VP				VG	
26) The first area is basic subjects such as reading, writing, and math	1	2	3	4	5	DK/RF
27) training students for a specific job?	1	2	3	4	5	DK/RF
28) preparing students for college?	1	2	3	4	5	DK/RF
29) teaching moral values?	1	2	3	4	5	DK/RF

Note that the example includes abbreviations for the interviewers (such as DK/RF for "don't know or refused to answer") that respondents will not need to hear or see.

Edge Coding

Usually, variable names and locator information for the data set in the computer appear only in the code book and in the margins. The use of margins for coding information is known as edge coding. These codes include the following:

1. Tracking information. Often survey supervisors want to keep a record of which interviewer completed each questionnaire, on which day the survey took place if data collection occurs over several days or weeks, and any other information of background importance. Each set of answers gets an identification number, which makes it easier to check for and correct mistakes in data entry. This information usually appears in the top margin of a questionnaire, as shown below:

Caller:_____   Date:_____   Phone No._____   ID #_____

College:_____   Year:_____   Last Gift to:_____

Phase III Questions for University Foundation
Fall 1998

First, I am going to read a short list of ways you might hear about Superior University. For each one, please tell me if you have heard about SU through this source *often, sometimes, rarely, or never* during the past year.

2. Question information. Most information regarding where answers to each question will appear in the computer go in the left
margin next to the questions, as shown below:

We're already halfway through our survey, and we really appreciate your help.
Now, if you have declined to give money to SU at any time in the past, please tell
me if each of the following issues have been *very important, somewhat important, not very important, or not at all important* reasons for your decision.

			__(8)__		(N/A, Have never refused to give)	
		4	3	2	1	8	9
(32) GETTO	27. You just didn't get around to it	VI	SI	NVI	NAI	N/A	RF/DK
(33) AFFORD	28. You felt you couldn't afford it	VI	SI	NVI	NAI	N/A	RF/DK
(34) DISSAT	29. You are dissatis-fied with the quality of education at SU	VI	SI	NVI	NAI	N/A	RF/DK
(35) NODIFF	30. You feel your gift would not make a difference to students at the university	VI	SI	NVI	NAI	N/A	RF/DK

Note that the abbreviations for each question appear in all caps and
require no more than eight letters. Many computer programs cannot
accommodate variable names longer than eight letters. The information in parentheses refers to the location of the question responses in
the data set. This number points either to the cell in a spreadsheet or
the space (or, in computer language, the "column") on a line in an
ASCII data set, which may look like this:

1 0118 124442412442 444444242442**4242**12 2222121021012 131110010023

1 0117 124443323442 44424324424**2234**22 2233333101012 121110010023

1 0116 124442524442 25524445444**4323**21 3333222020612 141110610011

1 0115 124541542434 24424442444**4444**33 1133322080611 331110010022

1 0114 125323243521 55514532432**2254**43 3334332100632 131199999999

3. Answer codes. The highlighted numbers, in columns 32 to 35,
provide the answers to the questions regarding barriers to giving.

The 2 indicates "not very important," the 4 indicates "very important," and so on.

Note that the lines of numbers have some empty spaces. Saving a space at the end of a long group of items or at the bottom of each page of the questionnaire makes it easier for data-entry personnel to know if they have skipped a number somewhere. For example, if two lines of data look like this:

1 0118 124442412442 4444442424424**2422**12 2222121021012 131110010023

1 0117 14443323442 44424324424**2234**22 2233333101012 121110010023

the person entering data will know immediately that something was skipped in the third group of numbers.

Notice also that the second group of numbers in each line is consecutive. This number is the questionnaire's identification number and makes it possible to find a problematic questionnaire quickly. If, for example, the problem in the line of numbers above was not noticed immediately, the identification number makes it possible to isolate the questionnaire that needs to be re-entered. Without an identification number on each questionnaire (usually in the top right-hand corner, where the example says "ID #"), corrections can become an enormous headache. Keep in mind that some corrections always will be needed; this is called "data cleaning."

Data Entry Conventions

You can assign any number to any answer, but many people are accustomed to seeing things a certain way. For example, it is common to assign a 1 to a yes answer and a 0 to a no answer. In a series of items for which respondents "check all that apply," each checked response would get a 1, and each blank response would get a 0.

Most questions do not need more than seven or eight response categories. As a result, another conventional number code is 8, which indicates "don't know." For refusals, some people use a 9, whereas others use a blank. Although the blank works well, the 9 is more useful for "eyeballing" lines of data. Compare the two sets of data that follow:

1 0121 113399354312 24533324222**4514**32 2233121306453 243321546023

1 0122 341562439963 99942364512**3331**99 3321234523461 442235943211

1 0123 523451543435 55345999123**352**144 4443643211199 346899993339

1 0121 1133 354312 24533324222**451**432 2233121306453 243321546023

1 0122 34156243 63   423645123**331** 3321234523461 442235 43211

1 0123 523451543435 55345 123**352**144 44436432111 3468 333

It is difficult to know if a question has been skipped in the second group. The first group, on the other hand, can be "eyeballed" for typos.

Very long questionnaires may require more than one line of type for each questionnaire. Most computer programs refer to each line as a record and need to know that each questionnaire requires two records. A data set with two lines per case may look like this:

1 0118 124442412442 44444424244**2422**12 2222121021012 131110010023

7700001011001

1 0117 124443323442 44424324424**223**422 2233333101012 121110010023

6400001000001

1 0116 124442524442 25524445444**4323**21 3333222020612 141110610011

6600001001001

1 0115 124541542434 24424442444**4444**33 1133322080611 331110010022

6900001001001

1 0114 125323243521 55514532432**225**443 3334332100632 131199999999

999999999991

Remember the code book must allow enough space for each answer. Some answers, such as age, may require space for two digits. In addition, some questions will have multiple answers ("check all that apply"), each of which will need to be coded as a separate item, as shown below:

50. What is your race or ethnicity? (MARK ALL THAT APPLY)

____ 1) AFRICAN AMERICAN   4) NATIVE AMERICAN____

____ 2) ASIAN   5) WHITE____

____ 3) HISPANIC   6) OTHER_____

              [CODE AS 1/0]   9) RF

Open-Ended Questions

Most computer programs do not lend themselves to qualitative analysis, so data entry of open-ended data usually requires a special program. Open-ended questions usually are skipped during data entry of closed-ended questions. A separate word processing file can be used to keep track of identification numbers and open-ended comments for each question. A file or notebook also should be kept for interviewers and data-entry personnel to log problems or anomalies that will require decisions from the research manager, such as what to do with a respondent who has checked between two responses instead of checking one response clearly.

TRAINING INTERVIEWERS

Interviewers must act polite even if respondents do not, read slowly and clearly, avoid lengthy conversations, and read each question in a consistent way. Interviewer training is an essential part of reliable data collection. Interviewer instructions vary slightly depending on the organization, the project and the facilities, but some general guidelines apply to most situations. In their classic survey research text, Warwick and Lininger (1975) suggested several keys to standardized personal interviewing, which apply equally well to telephone interviews.

1. *Use the questionnaire carefully, but informally.* The questionnaire is a tool for data collection. Interviewers must be familiar with the purposes of the study and the questionnaire, including question order, question wording, skip patterns, and the like. Interviewers who are well prepared can take a relaxed, informal approach to their work. This helps maximize interviewers' ability to collect high-quality data and avoid carelessness in the interview process.
2. *Know the specific purpose of each question.* Interviewers should understand what constitutes an adequate response to each question to satisfy the purposes of the research project and to improve their use of the questionnaire. This information should be discussed as a part of interviewer training and reviewed before data collection begins.
3. *Ask the questions exactly as they are written.* Even small changes in question wording can alter the meaning of a question and a participant's response. Researchers must assume each participant has answered the exact same question. The consistent, unbiased wording of each question provides a strong foun-

dation for the accuracy and reliability of study results. Neutral comments such as, "There are no right or wrong answers, we just want to know your opinion," should be used sparingly and only when interviewer feedback is required.

4. *Follow the order indicated in the questionnaire.* The order of questions in a survey instrument has been purposefully determined and carefully pretested. Interviewers who make arbitrary changes made in question order reduce the comparability of interviews and potentially introduce bias into questions that are sensitive to question order.

5. *Ask every question.* Interviewers should ask every question, even when participants have answered a previous question or make comments that seem to answer a later question. Respondents' answers to questions often change as a result of small changes in question wording. In addition, the intent of questions that seem similar often are different. Researchers develop and pretest question wording carefully and with a specific purpose in mind. Unless respondents terminate an interview early, each question must be asked of each respondent.

6. *Do not suggest answers.* Interviewers should never assume to know a respondents' answer to a question, even after a respondent has answered seemingly similar questions in a consistent manner. All answers should be provided by the respondent.

7. *Provide transitions when needed.* A well-written questionnaire should contain transitional phrases that help the respondent understand changes in topics, question types, or question response categories. Interviewers should use these transitional phrases to help guide a respondent through a questionnaire.

8. *Do not leave any question blank.* Interviewers should make every effort to have participants answer every question, except those intentionally left blank because of skip patterns. Although researchers may choose to use a questionnaire even if questions are left blank, omitted questions reduce the reliability and external validity of survey results. It is best if each respondent answers every applicable question.

CALL SHEETS

Telephone surveys typically use call sheets that have lists of numbers and places to record the outcome of each call attempt (see Fig. 12.1). Sometimes special information is included on a call sheet, such as giving history for donors or providing an individual's code number if an organization is calling another individual—such as a spouse or a par-

Telephone Call Sheet
UNIVERSITY FOUNDATION, FALL 1998

CALLER'S NAME: _____ DATE: _____

1ˢᵗ CALLBACK CALLER'S NAME: _____ DATE: _____

2ⁿᵈ CALLBACK CALLER'S NAME: _____ DATE: _____

Phone #	Name				When?
		Coll: ___	Year: ___	Last Gift To: ___	CM RF NA BZ DIS CB: OTH:

Colleges: 1) CAHE 2) Bus & Econ 3) Educ 4) El Eng 5) Eng & Arch 6) Lib Arts 7) Phar 8) Sci 9) Vet Sc 0) Other/None
Last Gift Categories: 1) Athletics 2) Academics/Colleges 3) Students/Residence/Scholarships 4) Other 5) Alumni Assn

FIG. 12.1. Sample telephone call sheet for a survey of university donors. A call sheet provides researchers with a detailed record of every call attempt. In this survey, specific individuals are being called, and records exist regarding the individuals' giving history to the university. The codes are as follows: Coll indicates college, with numbered options provided at the bottom of the calling sheet; year indicates year of graduation from the university; Last gift to indicates the designation applied to the donors' most recent gift, with codes provided at the bottom of the calling sheet; CM indicates completed interview: RF indicates refused interview; NA indicates no answer; BZ indicates busy signal; DIS indicates disconnected number; CB indicates call-back appointment has been made; OTH provides an opportunity for callers to jot down other observations or difficulties associated with the call attempt.

255

ent—to obtain more complete information from a household. The basic information appearing on most call sheets includes the following:

CM = completed interview,
RF = refused,
NA = no answer (sometimes AM appears separately to indicate answering machine),
BUS = business/beeper/fax/modem,
BZ = busy signal,
TM = terminated,
DIS = disconnected/out of service,
LB = language barrier,
NE = no eligible respondents at this number.
CB = call back appointment (interviewers fill in the details, and
OTH = other (interviewers fill in the details).

TIMING OF TELEPHONE SURVEYS

The optimum times of day and days of the week for doing telephone surveys vary depending on geographic region and time of the year. Although calling on Sunday evenings usually works well, for example, a manager will not want to plan a survey for Super Bowl Sunday. Generally, however, weeknights between 6 p.m. and 9 p.m. are considered reasonable hours for calling.

REPORTING RESPONSE RATES

Research reports must include information regarding how many people approached for the survey actually completed it (see Sidebar 12.1). Because probability sampling and inferential statistics assume 100% of eligible respondents will participate, people evaluate the validity of conclusions based partly on the response rate obtained. Several pieces of information need to be reported:

The total sample size. This is the total number of people (or phone numbers or addresses) used in the study. For example, for an RDD survey, a manager might draw a sample of 2,500 random phone numbers to achieve a final *n* of 800. Chapter 10 addresses how to draw the right size of total sample to achieve the desired valid sample.

The valid sample size. This is the number of sample elements (individuals, households, companies, etc.) in the total sample that remain after removing invalid phone numbers or addresses. These include nonworking phone numbers, respondents who do not fit the profile necessary to be included in the sample (such as not regis-

---

SIDEBAR 12.1.
American Association for Public Opinion Research

III. Standards for Minimal Disclosure

Good professional practice imposes the obligation upon all public opinion researchers to include, in any report of research results, or to make available when that report is released, certain essential information about how the research was conducted. At a minimum, the following items should be disclosed:

1. Who sponsored the survey, and who conducted it.
2. The exact wording of questions asked, including the text of any preceding instruction or explanation to the interviewer or respondents that might reasonably be expected to affect the response.
3. A definition of the population under study, and a description of the sampling frame used to identify this population.
4. A description of the sample selection procedure, giving a clear indication of the method by which the respondents were selected by the researcher, or whether the respondents were entirely self-selected.
5. Size of samples and, if applicable, completion rates and information on eligibility criteria and screening procedures.
6. A discussion of the precision of the findings, including, if appropriate, estimates of sampling error, and a description of any weighting or estimating procedures used.
7. Which results are based on parts of the sample, rather than on the total sample.
8. Method, location, and dates of data collection.

March 1986

***

Reprinted with permission from the American Association for Public Opinion Research

---

tered to vote), and respondents who do not speak English when surveyors do not speak other languages. In addition, research managers typically remove phone numbers and addresses from a sample if interviewers have made three to five attempts to reach someone at that location. The eliminated numbers are considered unreachable. Some market research firms only make one or two attempts, called *call-backs* in phone-survey lingo, but this practice is questionable scientifically. If an insufficient number of attempts has been made before the completion of the study, the location is considered a noncontact location (see below) and must remain in the valid sample. It is in the research manager's interest to minimize the number of noncontacts, because they lower the response rate and can raise questions about the study's quality.

Valid Sample Size = Total Sample Size – Ineligibles – Unreachables

The completion rate. This is the number of people who complete a survey out of the *total* sample size. If the researcher can anticipate the completion rate, this will determine how big a sample must be drawn to achieve the desired number of completed surveys. For example, if the completion rate is 31% and a sample of 384 is needed, the manager determines, by dividing 384 by .31, that 1249 numbers will be required to end up with 384 completed surveys.

$$\text{Total Sample Size} = \frac{\text{Target } n \text{ Completed Surveys}}{\text{Completion Rate in Decimal Form}}$$

$$\text{TSS} = \frac{384}{.31} = 1{,}249$$

The response rate. This is the number of people who completed a survey out of the *valid* sample size. This is the number most people want to see. Because the valid sample size is smaller than the total sample size, this number shows that a survey's quality is better than the completion rate makes it seem. Research managers strive to keep this number as high as possible. Unfortunately, phone surveys these days often have response rates as low as 45% to 55%, although some achieve rates as high as 80%. Mail surveys with a single mailing (no reminders) usually garner only about a 30% response rate.

$$\text{Response Rate} = \frac{\text{Completed Questionnaires}}{\text{Valid Sample Size}}$$

The refusal rate. This is the number of people who declined to answer the survey out of the valid sample size. Research managers strive to keep this number low.

$$\text{Refusal Rate} = \frac{\text{Refusals}}{\text{Valid Sample Size}}$$

The noncontact rate. This is the number of people who could not be reached out of the total sample and, therefore, never had the opportunity to complete the survey or refuse to do so.

$$\text{Noncontact Rate} = \frac{\text{Noncontacts}}{\text{Total Sample Size}}$$

REPORTING UNIVARIATE RELATIONSHIPS

The minimum information usually required for a research report is frequencies; percentages; means; and, for some clients, standard deviations. The frequencies tell the client how many people answered each question using each response. Frequency tables usually include percentages as well, so the reader can make informed comparisons across questions. These can be presented using tables, bar charts, histograms, or pie charts. Charts and figures should include both simple frequency information and percentages, as in Table 12.1.

The table includes both the number of people who answered the question and the number who did not (called "missing"). The valid percentage is based on the number of people who answered the question (338), whereas the unadjusted percentage refers to the total sample size (400). In this example, the numbers used on the survey appear along with the descriptions of the responses, but most research reports include only the descriptions.

TABLE 12.1
Sample Frequency Table: Purpose of Most Recent
Visit to Convention Center

		Frequency	Percent	Valid Percent
Valid	1.00 Attend a sporting event	121	30.3	35.8
	2.00 Attend a musical or theater performance	54	13.5	16.0
	3.00 Attend a fair or exhibit	51	12.8	15.1
	4.00 Attend a rally or workshop	30	7.5	8.9
	5.00 Attend a graduation ceremony	17	4.3	5.0
	6.00 Attend a private social function	13	3.3	3.8
	7.00 Get information	10	2.5	3.0
	9.00 Other	42	10.5	12.4
	Total	338	84.5	100.0
Missing	Total	62	15.5	
Total		400	100.0	

TABLE 12.2
Interest Levels Among Age Groups

| | | Actively Look for Information on This Issue | | | | | |
| | | 1.00 low | | 2.00 neutral | | 3.00 high | |
		Count	Row %	Count	Row %	Count	Row %
Age group	1.00 LT 35	7	8.0%	0	.0%	80	92.0%
	2.00 35 to 49	13	10.3%	0	.0%	113	89.7%
	3.00 50 or older	18	15.8%	1	.9%	95	83.3%

TABLE 12.3
Characteristics of Low, Neutral, and Highly Interested Publics

| | | Age Group | | | | | |
| | | 1.00 LT 35 | | 2.00 35 to 49 | | 3.00 50 or older | |
		Count	Row %	Count	Row %	Count	Row %
Actively look for information on this issue	1.00 Low	7	18.4%	13	34.2%	18	47.4%
	2.00 Neutral	0	.0%	0	.0%	1	100.0%
	3.00 High	80	27.%	113	39.2%	95	33.0%

REPORTING RELATIONSHIPS AMONG VARIABLES

Often a client wants to compare results for several groups, such as education levels, gender, ethnicity, or membership. The most intuitive presentation format is the crosstab table, shown in the following example. Crosstab tables usually present frequencies and column or row percentages. Note that in the first example, the table is arranged so that the row percentages display how many participants of each age group actively look for information. In the second example, the row percentages display how many participants of each interest level come from each age group. The first table can help the public relations manager understand the age groups better. The example shown in Table 12.3 can help the manager determine which age groups best reflect low-, neutral-, or high-interest groups. The research manager needs to determine which presentation of the information will be most helpful to the program planner.

It is possible to include both types of information in the same table, by displaying both row and column percentages, or even total percentages. As shown in this third example (Table 12.4), however, too much information can create confusion. Evaluate the public relations programming needs carefully before creating the tables.

Crosstab tables only lend themselves to breakdowns across a limited number of categories. For a variable such as age, which can range from 18 to 100 or more, the variable needs to be condensed into decades or market-oriented categories (such as 18–34) for the crosstab table to be interpretable. Strive to make tables readable at a glance.

Statistics such as the *chi-square* can be used to discover especially notable differences across groups. Many clients, however, do not want to see the statistics themselves and may find too much statistical information intimidating. Keep the presentation interpretable while ensur-

TABLE 12.4
Crosstab Table With Too Much Detail

			Age Group			
			1.00 LT 35	2.00 35 to 49	3.00 50 or older	Total
Actively look for information	1.00 low	Count	7	13	18	38
		% Within actively look for information	18.4%	34.2%	47.4%	100.0%
		% Within age group	8.0%	10.3%	15.8%	11.6%
	2.00 neutral	Count			1	1
		% Within actively look for information			100.0%	100.0%
		% Within age group			.9%	.3%
	3.00 high	Count	80	113	95	288
		% Within actively look for information	27.8%	39.2%	33.0%	100.0%
		% Within age group	92.0%	89.7%	83.3%	88.1%
Total		Count	87	126	114	327
		% Within actively look for information	26.6%	38.5%	34.9%	100.0%
		% Within age group	100.0%	100.0%	100.0%	100.0%

ing statistical rigor behind the scenes. Meanwhile, always be prepared for the client who appreciates statistical depth.

Another way to present relationships is through a correlation coefficient. Correlations are useful for examining the strength and direction of relationships between two interval-level (such as "very interested" to "not at all interested") or ratio-level (such as "0 times to 7 times") variables. They are less intuitive for a client without a statistical background, however. It can be useful, therefore, to run correlations as background while presenting condensed versions of the scales in a crosstab table. Condensing the data may mask subtle relationships, so check the tables to make sure they do not seem to tell a different story from the original statistics.

A correlation coefficient ranges between –1 and +1. A –1 indicates the two variables are exact opposites: for example, if younger people always like an event featuring Barney the Dinosaur more, with people always disliking Barney more as they get older. A +1 indicates the two variables are perfect matches: for example, if the price people will pay for a product increases exactly in proportion to how valuable they think the product is. Of course, such perfect relationships do not exist. The statistician, therefore, looks to see whether the coefficient is "significantly" different from 0, which would indicate that two variables change with no relevance to each other. The closer the coefficient is to +1 or –1, the stronger the relationship is between the two variables. In the information seeking example, examining the relationship between age and interest level, the correlation between the two original variables is about –.17, indicating a small and negative association between age and interest. Older people, in other words, have slightly less interest than younger people have, but the difference is not dramatic.

The research manager may encounter times when complex relationships need to be considered using sophisticated multivariate statistics. For the most part, this sort of analysis still needs to be translated into results interpretable by a statistical novice or math phobe. Keep in mind that even the most sophisticated analysis is useful only if it is understandable, and the most prescient research is helpful only if it gets used. Keep the presentation as simple and compelling as possible.

FINAL THOUGHTS

In the blur of program-planning deadlines, the public relations manager can be tempted to plunge into a research project without thinking through the details of data entry or later presentation. The more public relations managers think ahead, however, the more useful the final report is likely to be. The research plan can serve as an invaluable tool for determining what a research report should look like. Managers often map out the final report before doing the research, demonstrating—without the numbers, of course—what the answers to the questions raised in a situation analysis should look like. Planning to this level of detail can help ensure that the questions asked on a survey are designed to make it possible to create the tables desired. In addition, planning ahead for data entry and analysis helps focus the research manager's work and can save both time and money. Just as effective public relations program plans focus on the final outcomes—the goals and objectives—from the start, the most effective research projects envision the final report well before the first survey responses are collected.

USING THEORY
FOR PRACTICAL GUIDANCE

⚜ 13 ⚜
What Theory Is
and Why It Is Useful

What Is a Theory
Finding a Good Theory
A Theoretical Framework for "Symmetrical"
  Public Relations
A Theoretical Framework for "Asymmetrical"
  Campaigns
Final Thoughts

Despite the admonition of a famous social scientist named Kurt Lewin that "nothing is as practical as a good theory" (Marrow, 1969), practitioners and students of public relations often seem skeptical. After all, the term *theory* sounds academic not applied, and theories usually emanate from academics in ivory tower institutions, seemingly insulated from real-world complications. But Lewin was right: A good understanding of a few "good theories" enhances the strategic manager's success. Theories—essentially generalizations about how people think and behave—help determine appropriate goals and objectives for a public relations program. Scientifically tested theories also help public relations programmers develop effective strategies to achieve those goals and objectives.

Because applying theory makes public relations planning more scientific and less haphazard, it helps ensure effectiveness. The value of being scientific does not diminish the need for creativity, but science makes it possible to *predict* what will happen, such as anticipating the results from a mailing versus a radio ad campaign; *understand* why something has happened, such as why attendance was poor at a special event; and *control* what will happen (to the extent this is possible). To achieve success, the manager wants as much control as feasible, and applied theory provides the most control possible in a field notorious for its uncertainty.

WHAT IS A THEORY?

Theories explain why people behave in certain ways and how people are likely to respond to something. This gives the strategic manager the ability to make predictions based on an understanding of communication processes and effects. This is especially important to communication managers because much public relations communication takes place through gatekeepers such as reporters and opinion leaders instead of through paid advertising, increasing the opportunities for plans to go awry. In addition, many public relations results seem difficult to quantify. These difficulties force managers to choose: Accept the inability to control process and outcome along with its consequence, a lack of credibility, or find a way to exert more control, which requires developing the best understanding of likely explanations and predictions of communication processes and effects.

In truth, we all operate on the basis of theories every day. Many predictions come from personal experience. Savvy practitioners know that pitching a story to a reporter on deadline breeds failure. Localizing a story makes it more attractive. Media relations experience teaches practitioners what sorts of things to say (and not say) when pitching a story to an editor, and what types of publications will find a story about a pastry chef interesting. All of these predictions illustrate theories. For example, the need to avoid the reporter's deadline pressure illustrates the larger point, or theory, that "timing affects receptivity." The need to localize a story exemplifies the theory that "relevance affects acceptance." Finally, the appropriateness of specialized publications, such as culinary magazines, to the pastry chef story demonstrates the theory that "proximity increases relevance." To the extent the manager can control the variables of timing, relevance and proximity, the better the manager can control the result of media relations activities. To the extent the manager learns from others' experiences instead of from personal trial and error, the manager will endure fewer opportunities to learn from mistakes.

FINDING A GOOD THEORY

Theories cannot offer guarantees; instead, they improve the probability of success. Because of the way the scientific method works, theories never get proven beyond any doubt. They gain "support," and they can be disproved. A scientific test of a theory sets up a situation in which

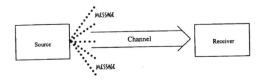

FIG. 13.1. The linear model of communication. The linear model is popular and easy to understand but does not accurately reflect the way communication really works.

the theory has to either succeed or fail. To gain support (never "proof") a theory must demonstrate success at least 95% of the time in a given statistical test. The more times a theory gets tested, and the more methods and contexts used to test it, the more confidence a practitioner can place in the theory's predictions. As a result of testing, theories often evolve; for example, testing may show that a theory applies better in some contexts than in others. This makes it important to keep up to date on what's new in communication, organization, and persuasion theory to know the nuances that give theories the most relevance to situations encountered by professionals. This becomes particularly important when a theory creates controversy or fails too many tests.

One of the most popular theories used by practitioners, also the most criticized, is called the *linear model* of communication or the *bullet theory* of communication. Although the model originally was developed to illustrate the constraints messages encounter when sent electronically through wires, too many people have embraced the illustrative model as an explanatory device, a theory of how communication works. Much research has shown the bullet theory is too simplistic. Nevertheless, many publicity-based communication programs essentially operate on that outdated theory, assuming that just "getting the message out" will have desirable effects.

Gaining exposure via the media can serve a valuable purpose. But a reliance on publicity greatly limits the practitioner's ability to achieve and measure success for important persuasive goals such as behavior change or important relational goals such as trust and commitment. Just because a message gets a lot of exposure doesn't mean anyone will pay attention to it, understand it, believe it, or act differently because of it. As a result, clip counts can be meaningless to a program focused on attitude change, behavior change, or even knowledge change. Because activities that do not contribute demonstrably to goal achievement waste time and resources, programs should include publicity only to the extent that reasons exist to predict and explain how publicity will help achieve stated goals. These reasons are theories.

Theories often use fancy social science terms that have special meaning to scholars looking for nuances, but good theories usually can be boiled down into sensible language that is fairly simple to apply. Some theories especially relevant to public relations practitioners focus on how relationships work, and others focus on persuasion. Theories focused on relationships correspond to what Grunig and Hunt (1984) called the "symmetrical model" of public relations, and theories focused on persuasion correspond to Grunig's (1989) "asymmetrical model" of public relations. According to Grunig, strategic managers often operate on the basis on both models, instead of on one exclusively. Two remaining models of public relations management—the publicity model and the public information model—operate on the basis of the outdated bullet theory, focusing solely on distributing messages. These two models cannot be considered strategic management.

A THEORETICAL FRAMEWORK FOR "SYMMETRICAL" PUBLIC RELATIONS

Several useful theories explain how the symmetrical model of public relations works, as well as what makes it work so well. These theories explain why public relations is relevant and useful for an organization. They also guide problem identification and goal setting because they help the manager understand when and why issues should be considered problems or achievements. Four theories are especially important for the public relations manager, whose ultimate focus rests on long-term relationship building.

Systems Theory—Adaptation and Adjustment

According to systems theory, organizations are most effective when they acknowledge they interact with, affect, and are affected by their environment. They need to bring in resources that enhance their success and deflect threats that can compromise their survival. Organizations in *open systems*, which means in real life, exchange information, energy, and material with their environments. Organizations operating in *closed systems* exist in a vacuum without interacting with or exchanging things with any other organization or person. In an open system, the organization sometimes implements changes (such as flextime hours) to adjust to changes in the environment (such as increasingly difficult commute traffic). The organization also tries to obtain accommodations from the environment (such as having the county pay for access road maintenance) that help it operate effectively. According to the open systems model (Broom & Dozier, 1990; Cutlip et al., 2000;

TABLE 13.1
Necessary Activities According to Systems Theory

Surveillance	Interpretation	Advising Management
Gather information about environment	Prioritize issues	Suggest concrete actions
Gather information about opportunities and challenges	Prioritize publics	Suggest measurable objectives
	Anticipate changes	
	Develop recommendations	

Grunig & Hunt, 1984), organizations that close themselves off from this exchange process become inert, or disintegrate. In other words, they become irrelevant or ineffective.

Activities necessary to succeed, according to systems theory, include surveillance, interpretation, and advising management. Surveillance—also called scanning—means gathering information about the environment and possible challenges or opportunities (data collection). Interpretation means having the ability to make sense of the information gathered to be able to prioritize issues and publics, anticipate how the situation may change in ways that may help or hurt the organization, and develop recommendations for action (theorize). Advising management means making credible suggestions for concrete actions that will achieve measurable objectives consistent with organizational goals. To sum up systems theory, organizations do not exist in a vacuum. They need to perform ongoing research to understand changing environmental constraints and possibilities.

Co-Orientation Theory

This theory helps to delineate what makes communication productive. According to co-orientation theory (McLeod & Chaffee, 1972; Newcomb, 1953), people and organizations relate to one another successfully to the extent they think similarly about ideas. The co-orientation model shows the ways two parties may relate to the same idea. Each party will have impressions both about the idea and about what the other party thinks about the idea. The two parties can agree and know that they agree, but they also can think they disagree. On the other hand, they may disagree but think they agree. Even more confusing, they may think they are discussing the same idea, such as improving customer service responsiveness, when in fact they are thinking about different ideas, such as a need for new procedures versus a need for

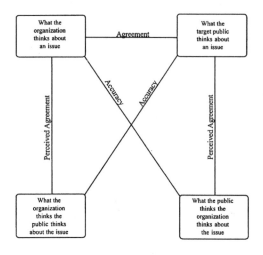

FIG. 13.2. The co-orientation model. The co-orientation model focuses the manager's attention on relationships, consistent with the overall mission of public relations.

additional training. According to co-orientation theory, the most effective communication takes place when both parties agree and when they know they agree, which means they have achieved consensus.

Grunig and Huang (in press) wrote that the application of co-orientation theory promotes long-term success but its usefulness may not seem obvious when examining only short-term outcomes. Clients and CEOs may not understand how measures such as agreement, accuracy, and understanding relate to the achievement of organizational goals such as increased sales, increased membership renewals, or passage of an important bill in Congress. As a result, managers trying to demonstrate long-term communication effectiveness should focus on outcomes such as trust, control mutuality, relational commitment, and relational satisfaction. *Trust* is defined as the belief the other party will not exploit one's goodwill. *Control mutuality* refers to the degree to which the parties believe they have enough control over the relationship and the other party's goals and activities. *Relational commitment* means the desire to maintain the relationship, including level of interest in maintaining membership, level of acceptance of the organiza-

TABLE 13.2
Measurable Outcomes of a Mutually Beneficial Relationship

Trust

Control mutuality

Relational commitment

Relational satisfaction

tion's goals, willingness to exert effort on behalf of the organization, and extent to which the party believes the benefits of maintaining the relationship outweigh the costs of discontinuing it. Finally, *relational satisfaction* is defined as the degree to which a relationship seems fulfilling. Stafford and Canary (1991) suggested that relational satisfaction may be the most important measure of an effective relationship, but measures such as trust and commitment seem especially well suited to the demonstration of communication's contributions to organizational goals.

According to co-orientation theory, organizations should try to maximize levels of agreement, understanding, and accuracy among the organization's communicators and stakeholders. These indicators of successful communication contribute to long-term success measured by outcomes such as trust and commitment. Co-orientation theory demonstrates the importance of taking a long- term view of the organization's relationship with its stakeholders despite the temptation to focus on short-term goals such as the success of the next product promotion.

Situational Theory of Strategic Constituencies

This approach responds to the truism that "you cannot please all of the people all of the time." An organization must prioritize its efforts, and that includes the publics on which it focuses. Higher priority goes to publics whose opposition or support can either help or hinder the organization's ability to achieve its goals and mission. Publics can be internal to the organization (e.g., union employees), external to the organization (such as environmental groups), or both (such as employees who are members of environmental groups). According to Grunig and Repper (1992), strategic constituencies can be segmented into categories of active, potentially active (latent) and passive publics.

An active public is made up of individuals who perceive that what an organization does matters to them (called level of involvement), that the consequences of what an organization does affects them (called *problem recognition*), and that they have the ability to do something to affect the organization's actions or the consequences of those actions (called *constraint recognition*). Actions can be positive, such as purchasing stock or maintaining memberships, or negative, such as engaging in boycotts and lawsuits.

A latent public is one that has the potential to become active. These are people who should care about an issue because it could affect them but who may not be interested, may not know about the issue, or may not have the ability to take action.

Active publics can be divided into three types:

1. the long haul: those interested in all aspects of the issue;
2. special interests: those interested only in certain aspects of the topic;
3. hot button: those who get interested only if an emotional debate ensues.

A fourth category—apathetic publics—don't care about any aspect of the issue and have no relevance to the organization.

Excellence Theory

According to excellence theory, building mutually beneficial relationships with strategic constituencies saves money by preventing problems such as lawsuits, boycotts, and strikes, and by increasing employees' satisfaction, which enhances productivity and quality. According to Dozier, Grunig, and Grunig (1995), excellence theory integrates systems theory and the situational theory of strategic constituencies explained in the previous section. It proposes that managed communication helps achieve organizational goals because it helps reconcile organizational goals with the expectations of its relevant publics (Grunig, Grunig, & Ehling, 1992). Excellence theory proposes that public relations is most *effective* when the senior public relations manager helps shape organizational goals and helps determine which external publics are most important strategically. Public relations management will be most *successful* when it operates strategically, by identifying (segmenting) active publics and developing symmetrical communication programs whose success can be measured (Grunig & Huang, in press; Grunig & Repper, 1992).

Summarizing the Symmetrical Perspective

The combination of theories integrated into excellence theory takes a holistic view of public relations and organizational success. According to this viewpoint, organizations must operate with an understanding of and respect for others who coexist in their social system. Because the system constantly evolves, the environment can change in ways that can affect the organization in beneficial or detrimental ways. Publics operating in the environment also evolve, which means their relevance to the organization—the degree to which their support makes a difference to organizational success—also will change. Organizations' success depends on their ability to integrate the needs and desires of relevant publics into organizational goals and activities to gain and maintain their trust and commitment.

This view can be summarized as an "us and us" (us-us) philosophy. It also can be summarized as the practice of social responsibility. According to this philosophy, the mission of public relations is to develop and maintain "win-win" situations for the organization and the publics on whose goodwill its success depends. This can be contrasted with an "us and them" (us-them) philosophy, which often devolves into an "us versus them" situation. The reason for this is the us-them philosophy fails to integrate strategic publics' values into organizational goals. Instead, it views organizational values and goals distinct from publics' values and goals. According to systems theory, the us-them approach is likely to fail because it discounts the organization's interdependence with its environment. According to co-orientation theory, the us-them approach is likely to fail because communication will lack shared understanding and will be less likely to achieve consensus. According to situational theory, the us-them approach does not recognize that active and latent publics can take action damaging to the organization's ability to succeed and will do so if they feel the need and find the opportunity. According to excellence theory, the us-them approach fails to appreciate that responsiveness is less expensive and more effective than indifference.

TABLE 13.3

Comparison of the Us-Us and Us-Them Operating Styles

	Us/Us	Us/Them
View of strategic publics	Publics are stakeholders or partners	Publics are adversaries
Character of communication	Integrates publics' values into organizational goals	Communication lacks shared understanding
Focus of goals	Win–win situations (consensus)	Self-preservation (consensus unlikely)
Communication style	Focus on responsiveness (accommodation and advocacy)	Indifference or counteraction (advocacy only)

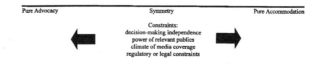

FIG. 13.3. Cameron's continuum of symmetrical contingencies.

According to the us-us philosophy, symmetrical public relations benefits the organization because strategic communication programs are essential to existence in an interdependent social system. The public relations manager's ability to understand strategic publics, communicate successfully with them, and advise management on the implications of evolving relationships can have long-term, measurable effects on the bottom line.

What Makes the Symmetrical Ideal "Practical"

Grunig (1989) noted that few organizations put the symmetrical philosophy into practice, although the idea is not new. These organizations may not believe sufficient evidence supports the symmetrical imperative, or they may view the approach as impractical or difficult to apply. Cameron (1998) suggested that practitioners' ability to practice symmetrical public relations depends on various contingencies, such as independence in decision making, the power of relevant publics, the climate of media coverage, and regulatory or legal constraints. According to Cameron, companies operate on a continuum that ranges from pure advocacy to pure accommodation. Pure advocacy refers to developing and delivering messages in support of a position without seeking feedback for compromise. Depending on the situation, companies' location on the continuum will vary. Although perfect symmetry may not exist between an organization and its publics, striving for symmetry demonstrates the willingness to meet another viewpoint part way and to at least seriously consider alternative perspectives on an issue. To attempt this is to practice social responsibility.

Plenty of evidence supports the view that public relations management as the practice of social responsibility reaps measurable success. Although managers with a social conscience may embrace socially responsible management for its intuitive appeal, even the most hard-core pragmatist can seize on its bottom-line benefits, summarized by Feldstein (1992) and demonstrated by many others. The benefits include the following:

1. *Consumer loyalty.* Increasingly, studies have demonstrated that consumer loyalty has value to an organization that translates

into measurable profits. For example, a study by the Walker Group ("In Focused," 1996) showed that consumers are 90% more likely to buy products or services from a socially responsible company. In addition, the *Harvard Business Review* ("Building Customer," 1996) reported that even small reductions in consumer defection rates had remarkable effects on profits. For example, reducing defections by 5% increased profitability of a client to an auto service chain by more than 20%, to insurances brokerages by over 40%, to software by about 30%, and to credit cards by over 80%.

2. *Employee morale.* Businesses have discovered that employee morale is not a nicety, but an important factor affecting recruitment, retention, quality and profitability. For example, fear of job loss can hurt morale, which can contribute to accidents, mistakes, and decreased productivity. Helping morale, on the other hand, can increase productivity and loyalty. For example, Johnson and Johnson's Balancing Work and Family Program ("A Look," 1997) demonstrated that 71% of employees who used the company's flexible time and leave policies cited the policy as a "very important" reason for staying with the company. Two years into the program, employees maintained that their jobs were interfering less with their family lives even while the number of hours worked on average had increased. Meanwhile, companies such as Xerox and IBM have found that potential employees like the idea of working for a company that promotes volunteerism among employees. The Families and Work Institute has found, however, that nearly 40% of companies do not actively communicate policies such as their work-family programs to employees. Companies such as Allstate, on the other hand, provide managers with training—in Allstate's case, 3 days' worth—on how to foster a supportive work environment. Good employee relations can help recruitment as well as retention, with several magazines now ranking companies on issues such as family friendliness (Jackson, 1998).

3. *Shareholder value.* Retaining efficient and creative employees increases profits because quality and productivity increases, and less money needs to be spent on recruitment and on problems related to quality control or employee grievances. Retaining loyal customers reduces the need for attracting new customers and can sharply increase profits.

4. *Community goodwill.* Another apparent nicety that should be viewed as essential, community goodwill, or support, can make or break a company in times of crisis. For example, when Los Angeles erupted in rioting following the Rodney King beating by police officers in 1991, McDonald's found its restaurants standing unscathed

in neighborhoods that had been essentially razed and looted. McDonald's attributed its survival to the fact they had long been involved in activities intended to benefit the communities in which they operated and the employees who worked for the company in those communities.

5. *Community well being.* Because employees, customers, and potential employees all live in the community, the well being of the community affects the well being of the company. Although many of the effects are indirect, good schools, safe streets, thriving arts, and health promotion all benefit the company by improving the environment in which the organization exists. As Feldstein (1992) wrote, 90% of the $144 billion given to charity in 1990 came from individuals, and only 5% came from businesses. He reported estimates that 87% of Americans give to charities and 78% volunteer their time. Many companies, as a result, have been divesting themselves of a major opportunity to help their communities and thereby help themselves. Both large- and small-scale projects make a difference. For example, companies such as Helene Curtis Industries, Inc. in Chicago and Columbia Sportswear in Portland "adopt" families and buy holiday gifts and household necessities for them. The consumer goods company, Tom's of Maine, meanwhile, runs a 5%-for-volunteering program, which allows employees to spend 5% of their work time helping nonprofit organizations. Starbucks encourages customers to join in their embrace of issues by providing their own grants and promotes the purchase of personalized bookmarks to go with donated children's books and the purchase of a coffee sampler that benefits an international social assistance group.

Keys to Making the Symmetrical Ideal Sensible

Managers need not worry that acting socially responsible can lead to giving away the store, because that would be asymmetrical and counterproductive. As Richmond (1990) wrote, stakeholders will understand the organization must ensure its own success. Indeed, as McDonald's learned so dramatically, stakeholders who see their values incorporated into the organization's values and goals have a vested interest in helping ensure the organization's survival. The manager can operate on several principles drawn from Richmond's sensible approach to corporate responsibility, what he has called "putting the public in public relations":

1. *Be honest.* There is no shame in being straightforward that your organization needs to profit from its relationship with its publics.

2. *Be creative.* There is no need to give away huge amounts of resources to promote mutually beneficial relationships. A hotel, for example, can offer special services such as a tour of an award-winning kitchen and a meal as a door prize for a nonprofit group holding a special event at the hotel. Or the hotel can provide the room for free provided the organization agrees to include a no-host bar.

3. *Do your research.* The manager must know the public to find common ground on which to build understanding that leads to mutually beneficial goals. Richmond, for example, knew that a major southwest association was determining where to hold its next Seattle-based conference. Richmond learned that one of the two major charities supported by the organization also was supported by his client, the Seattle Sheraton. The charity was happy to encourage the organization to support the business of another benefactor, and the organization was pleased to give its business to organization that shared its philanthropic priorities.

4. *Find the right fit.* Philanthropic efforts should be strategic, but this means they should reflect genuine concerns of the sponsoring organization and should not seem insincere or mercenary. Boston's IDPR Group ("In Focused," 1996) advised that programs should reflect the organization's business interests and offer opportunities for its expertise to make a difference. It also should be relevant to the values and interests of active and latent publics. Philanthropic programs should reflect an organization's core beliefs, actively involve individuals at all levels of employment within the company, and correspond to the organization's behavior. Focusing efforts in a small number of areas can magnify the organization's impact.

5. *Always monitor and evaluate the relationship.* Never assume that plans will carry through as expected or that the health of a relationship is assured indefinitely. This often requires simple actions instead of sophisticated research techniques. Richmond, for example, advised the Sheraton to buy some tables at events hosted in the hotel both to show support for the organization and to ensure quality control during the event.

6. *Remember that little things can count big.* Small donations can come back to an organization many times over. Richmond's Seattle Sheraton, for example, saw a company's function moved from another hotel to its hotel because the Sheraton unknowingly had donated a room to a key decision maker's son's elementary school for a raffle in a town located 20 miles away. Likewise, small insults can cost big business. It's a good idea to remember that, in a social system always in flux, every relationship has the potential to affect other relationships.

A THEORETICAL FRAMEWORK
FOR "ASYMMETRICAL" CAMPAIGNS

Another set of theories can help guide the manager developing a campaign. These theories, from communication, psychology, sociology, and marketing, take a more short-term, "asymmetrical" view and emphasize persuasion. Although theories focused on campaign issues emphasize the asymmetrical approach, managers should use them with long-term relational goals in mind. For example, although campaigns focus on changing people's minds or behaviors, such as approving zoning changes that allow a company to move into a neighborhood, the manager must recognize organizations need to respond to the public as well, such as by helping develop a solution to neighborhood concerns about traffic. Theories of public relations strongly suggest that an organization's long-term success depends on its ability to develop and maintain good relationships with key stakeholders. Even organizations taking the long view, however, need to engage in persuasion.

Persuasion (O'Keefe, 1990) is a "successful, intentional effort at influencing another's mental state through communication in a circumstance in which the persuadee has some measure of freedom" (p. 17). This aspect of freedom distinguishes persuasion from coercion, which is an attempt to force compliance by taking away the target's freedom to disagree. The definition of persuasion includes other important elements to consider:

Success. Persuasion does not occur unless the effort to influence another succeeds.

Intent. Persuasion occurs on purpose. Change can occur accidentally, but that is not persuasion.

Mental state. Persuasion often focuses on changing a behavior, such as increasing sales or the number of votes in favor of a particular issue, but changing behavior is not enough if attitudes do not correspond to the behavior. If attitudes and behavior conflict, coercion may have taken place instead of persuasion. On the other hand, sometimes attitude change, such as increased trust, is enough to satisfy organizational goals, without an associated specific behavior.

Through communication. Persuasion uses communication instead of force to achieve goals.

Persuasion and Ethics

After a long discussion of the importance of symmetrical practices and social responsibility, students of public relations often worry that engaging in persuasion somehow is unethical. Indeed, the asymmetrical approach to communication management often gives public relations a bad reputation because of its us/them embrace of persuasion as unidirectional change. The media and other publics notice the lack of reciprocity on the part of the organization and resent what can seem like efforts to take advantage of others. Nevertheless, just as every individual operates according to personal theories, everyone engages in efforts to persuade. Even babies quickly learn they must communicate their needs and desires to others in the hope of getting those needs and desires fulfilled. As grown-ups and public relations professionals, we often need to persuade others to help us achieve our goals. But just as we learn to give as well as receive in our personal relationships, organizations at times must permit themselves to be persuaded by others, to be responsive to strategic publics' needs and desires. In other words, persuasion on behalf of an organization should occur in the context of the symmetrical approach to public relations. The PRSA Code of Professional Ethics (see Sidebar 13.1) provides a useful yardstick for evaluating whether persuasive efforts remain within ethical bounds.

SIDEBAR 13.1.
Code of Professional Standards for the Practice of Public Relations

1. A member shall conduct his or her professional life in accord with the public interest.
2. A member shall exemplify high standards of honesty and integrity while carrying out dual obligations to a client or employer and to the democratic process.
3. A member shall deal fairly with the public, with past or present clients or employers, and with fellow practitioners, giving due respect to the ideal of free inquiry and to the opinions of others.
4. A member shall adhere to the highest standards of accuracy and truth, avoiding extravagant claims or unfair comparisons and giving credit for ideas and words borrowed from others.
5. A member shall not knowingly disseminate false or misleading information and shall act promptly to correct erroneous communications for which he or she is responsible.
6. A member shall not engage in any practice which has the purpose of corrupting the integrity of channels of communications or the processes of government.
7. A member shall be prepared to identify publicly the name of the client or employer on whose behalf any public communication is made.
8. A member shall not use any individual or organization professing to serve or represent an announced cause, or professing to be independent or unbiased, but actually serving another or undisclosed interest.

(Continues)

SIDEBAR 13.1. (Continued)

9. A member shall not guarantee the achievement of specified results beyond the member's direct control.
10. A member shall not represent conflicting or competing interests without the express consent of those concerned, given after a full disclosure of the facts.
11. A member shall not place himself or herself in a position where the member's personal interest is or may be in conflict with an obligation to an employer or client, or others, without full disclosure of such interests to all involved.
12. A member shall not accept fees, commissions, gifts or any other consideration from anyone except clients or employers for whom services are performed without their express consent, given after full disclosure of the facts.
13. A member shall scrupulously safeguard the confidences and privacy rights of present, former, and prospective clients or employers.
14. A member shall not intentionally damage the professional reputation or practice of another practitioner.
15. If a member has evidence that another member has been guilty of unethical, illegal, or unfair practices, including those in violation of this Code, the member is obligated to present the information promptly to the proper authorities of the Society for action in accordance with the procedure set forth in Article XII of the Bylaws.
16. A member called as a witness in a proceeding for enforcement of this Code is obligated to appear, unless excused for sufficient reason by the judicial panel.
17. A member shall, as soon as possible, sever relations with any organization or individual if such relationship requires conduct contrary to the articles of this Code.

* * *

The complete code with interpretations for specific contexts of practice appears in the appendix.

Article 1 of the PRSA code highlights this issue, that a member should act in accord with "the public interest." Several other articles address the importance of the persuadee's freedom to disagree, by acknowledging that the withholding of important information violates a message recipient's freedom to evaluate the veracity of a message. As a result, the public relations practitioner is expected to "deal fairly" to "give due respect to the ideal of free inquiry and the opinions of others" (Article 3). The member must act with honesty and integrity (Article 2), communicate truthfully and accurately (Article 4), refrain from knowingly spreading false or misleading information (Article 5), refrain from representing conflicting interests (Article 10), and be prepared to identify publicly the client or employer on whose behalf public communication is made (Article 7). In addition, the practitioner may not corrupt the integrity of channels of communication or the processes of government (Article 6), or accept fees or other remuneration from anyone except clients or employers who must fully disclose facts (Article 12).

In simple language, the PRSA code means that persuasion must occur without resorting to lying or misrepresentation. Indeed, research shows that persuasion is more effective and has longer lasting effects when persuaders acknowledge and refute the other side of an issue. It should not be necessary to use dishonesty to persuade someone; after all, if the organization holds a particular view, its reasons for the view are real. The key to persuasion is to communicate successfully the reasons why a target public should share the organization's view on an issue or should want to participate in a behavior the organization thinks is a good idea.

In support of this perspective, a theory has developed based on research that has shown the most effective campaigns treat persuasion as a relational situation in which everyone can benefit, instead of as a contest in which the organization desires victory and the public must concede. Managers must not view a campaign as an attempt to push a public to accept something the organization wants distributed, such as a product or an attitude. Instead, the manager should view a campaign as an opportunity to demonstrate to a public that the organization has something from which it will want to benefit. Public relations calls this a receiver orientation; marketers call it a consumer orientation. A theory called *social marketing* illustrates the value of this perspective.

Social Marketing Theory

According to social marketing theory, purveyors of ideas need to think more like purveyors of products, who view a purchase as an equal exchange. The consumer deciding whether to buy a product must weigh the cost of the product against the benefits of having the product. If the benefits outweigh the costs, the consumer will buy the product. Similarly, the public deciding whether to embrace an idea must weigh the costs associated with embracing the idea with the benefits. For example, the cost of turning out to vote could include lost time, a missed opportunity to do something else, the need to go outside in bad weather, the need to move a car from a hard-won parking space, and so on. The benefits—the possibility of helping a favored candidate or proposal win at the polls—must outweigh those costs. This cost-benefit analysis is known as a profit orientation, and social marketing theory acknowledges that even the consumers of ideas evaluate the degree to which they will profit from the ideas.

Social marketing theory views the consumer as the center of the universe. As with product marketing, success hinges on a successful exchange relationship with the consumer. The marketing of ideas, however, presents a tougher challenge than does the marketing of products. In product marketing, the gain of a small market share can translate into large profits for a company. In social marketing, however, stakes often are much higher: the need for 51% of the vote, for example. Solomon (1989) listed several other differences:

1. Social marketing often targets the toughest audiences instead of the most easily profitable. A rule of thumb for persuasion is that on a continuum of support, persuasive efforts are most likely to reinforce positive opinions, crystallize neutral opinions to become more positive, and neutralize negative opinions. To move negative opinions to the positive side represents a huge, probably unrealistic, leap for a single campaign. Persuasion likely must take place in increments. As a result, social marketing often must acknowledge that change will take time.
2. Social marketing consumers often do not pay in dollars for services and products. The costs to them are perceptual, such as in time, reputation, ego, or guilt.
3. Political dimensions often exist in social marketing campaigns.
4. The products or services marketed often are not seen as valuable by the target public. It can be tough to sell the idea of a new school to the 80% of the public who do not have school-age children but will have to pay for it in taxes.
5. Social marketers often have small budgets and need to acquire both clients and funding sponsors.
6. Too much success can prove disastrous if the marketer cannot handle the demand. Colleges implementing new register-by-telephone systems have had entire telephone systems fail because of the sudden overload. An 800 number can be overwhelmed so that no one can get through. An organization can run out of brochures, or pizzas, if too many people show up.

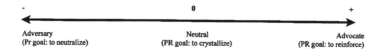

FIG. 13.4. The continuum of public support.

PRODUCT

PLACEMENT

PRICE

What is our goal?

How can we get our
message to them?

What do they see
as the costs?

Who is
our PUBLIC?

How is our product
unique to them?

What will they embrace
as the benefits?

POSITIONING   PROMOTION

FIG. 13.5. The marketing mix. Elements of the social marketing model as applied
to public relations. The marketing mix includes the six "Ps" of public, product, price, promotion,
positioning, and placement.

To apply social marketing theory successfully, the public relations
manager can refer to the model of the "six Ps" to answer the questions
that give the campaign focus. The six Ps encompass the traditional four
Ps of marketing—product, place, price, and promotion—but also include the public (instead of the consumer) and positioning. The combination of elements is known as the *marketing mix*. Managers
determine each element through research, given that each choice to
guide a campaign must respond to public perceptions.

1. Who is the *public*? Everything else in the campaign hinges on the
   public's needs, interests, and perceptions.
2. What is the *product*? The product is the focus of the transaction
   between an organization and a public. In social marketing, the
   product is the goal, whether this involves the embrace of an item,
   or an idea, or the adoption of a behavior.
3. What is the *price*? The price represents the cost of embracing the
   idea or behavior from the public's point of view. This can include
   time, sacrifices, cultural misgiving, and psychological discomfort.
4. What is the *promotion*? The promotion represents the benefits of
   the idea or behavior from the public's point of view. What benefits

outweigh or decrease the costs it associates with the behavior? Promotion does not mean a simple advertising slogan but represents a summary of the cohesive message strategies that are used in a campaign.

5. What is the *place*? The place refers to the distribution channels by which the public gains access to information about the product, service, or idea. Where can the public best get a message about the product?

6. What is the *positioning*? Positioning refers to what makes a product special or unique. What makes one event especially worthy of the public's attention? What will make yet another anti-drunk-driving campaign get noticed among the crush of other messages about driving, drinking, and safety? Positioning answers the "why should anyone care" question and distinguishes the idea, service, or product from competitors in ways the public appreciates.

Figure 13.6 illustrates a social marketing mix. The strategic planning ladder corresponding to this case appears in chap. 3. The goal was to maximize investments in the Colorado Prepaid Tuition Fund,

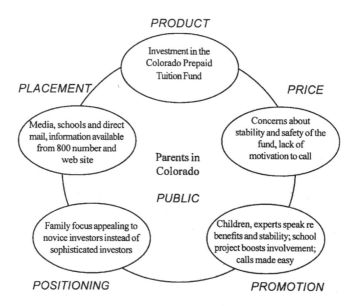

FIG. 13.6. Social marketing in action. From the Colorado Prepaid Tuition Fund's "Educate Our Kids" Campaign, implemented by the Colorado Student Obligation Bond Authority with Kostka Gleason Communications, Inc.

with the concern that contributions might drop off precipitously in the second year of the program. The product, therefore, was investment in the fund. Because research determined 39% of families initially heard about the fund from TV and 87% from newspapers, and parents had an interest in looking out for their children's secure education, the program planners chose a combination of media, schools, direct mail, an 800 number, and a web site as the places for promotion. Research also determined the barriers to investment: the price, which included the concern of 77% surveyed about the stability and safety of the fund, and a lack of motivation to call the 800 number. The research showed an opportunity for overcoming these barriers, known as the promotion: Parents would identify with children enrolled in the fund who speak to its benefits, they would find reassurance from financial experts who could emphasize the stability of the fund, and they might become more aware and motivated if their children became involved in a project that netted widespread publicity. The campaign, therefore, included a statewide school project in which children built a giant county-by-county puzzle with pieces gathered via media tour. The puzzle was then displayed in downtown Denver during the enrollment period. The overall positioning that made the campaign special and especially relevant to the target public was a family focus designed to appeal to novice investors instead of seasoned investors. This was a program for every family, not for a select group of savvy, higher-income individuals. The campaign was successful, exceeding all of its objectives and earning a Silver Anvil Award.

In another case demonstrating the importance of audience-centered and research-based communication, Publicis•Dialog, on behalf of Gardenburger, decided to position its veggie burgers as products for mainstream, omnivorous 25- to 54-year-old women instead of as a specialty product for funky vegetarians. They gambled on spending $1.5 million to put a 30-second advertisement on the last episode of *Seinfeld* on May 14, 1998. According to Kevin Bush (personal interview, 1999) who supervised the campaign, the investment represented one seventh of the company's advertising budget for the year and brought them considerable attention for taking such a risk. The advertisement could have given the product awareness that lasted an eyelash blink, but the strategy of a small player making such a big play attracted national media coverage—more than 400 news stories—that greatly increased public attention to the spot and to the product. The week after the spot aired, sales jumped 104%. Several months later, Gardenburger's share of the meatless burger market had increased from 35% to 54%. Although the social marketing approach cannot guarantee success, Gardenburger's success illustrates how the audience-centered approach can give clients the confidence to embrace unusual or seemingly risky strategies that will cut through a crowded marketplace of ideas.

Choosing a Level of Effect

Campaign designers must determine what type of effect they intend to achieve. As chap. 14 illustrates in more detail, it is much harder to change someone's attitudes or opinions than to change their level of awareness, and it is even more difficult to change their value system. Knowledge of the target public and the social environment is required for the communication manager to choose a realistic level of effect on which to base measurable objectives for a communication program. Organizations often make the mistake of trying to change people's values, which is usually unnecessary and unrealistic. Targeting values is a divisive strategy, whereas appealing to people's values is a more constructive approach.

Attacking the target public's values is especially common among single-issue advocacy groups, such as those focused on animal rights, gun rights and gun control, abortion, and environmental issues. As

FIG. 13.7. The level of effects pyramid. Outcomes at higher levels of the pyramid are progressively more difficult to change.

Plous wrote (1990), however, value-based campaigns often offend the people they aim to persuade. Some political analysts, for example, suggested that Republicans severely damaged their appeal to mainstream voters in their 1992 national convention when they attacked nontraditional families to embrace a traditional family values platform. The Democrats, on the other hand, used their convention to promote the alternative message, that family values should mean every family has value. The Democrats had economic issues in their favor, commonly considered a major political asset, which meant the Republicans could ill afford a strategy that alienated a large portion of the population.

Accusations that people who disagree with an organizations' preferred view hold substandard values make those people defensive and less willing to entertain other viewpoints. Demonstrating a shared value, on the other hand, as the Democrats did in 1992, can enable adversaries to find common ground on which to build understanding and, ultimately, consensus. It isn't easy and it takes time to build trust, but some foes on the abortion issue have demonstrated it can be done. With effort, they realized that both sides wanted to avoid unwanted babies. As a result, they collaborated to form the Common Ground Network for Life and Choice to focus on campaign goals with which they can agree. As one pro-choice activist said in a 1996 article, prevention is the goal they have in common: "No one that I know in the pro-choice camp is in support of abortion" (Schulte, 1996). Projects on which they collaborate include teen pregnancy prevention, the promotion of adoption, and the prevention of violence in the debate over the issue. The motto of the umbrella organization that helped bring them together, the Common Ground Network, comes from Andrew Masondo of the African National Congress: "Understand the differences; act on the commonalities" (Search for Common Ground, 1999).

FINAL THOUGHTS

Efforts such as the Common Ground Network's embody Plous's (1990) point that "activists will be more effective if they are able to understand and empathize with people whose views differ from their own" (p. 2). Even a pure advocacy campaign can benefit from a symmetrical theoretical perspective on public relations. This theoretical framework should guide goal setting and planning. Then, within this theoretical perspective, the manager can turn to more specific theories that explain the communication process and communicators themselves. An understanding of these theories can guide strategy development, give a program proposal credibility, and increase the probability of program success. They are the focus of chap. 14.

❧ 14 ❧
Theories for Creating
Effective Message Strategies

In the 1950s and early 1960s, communication experts noticed that mass communication campaigns were having little effect, and many believed the situation hopeless. One scholar caused an uproar with an article calling mass media campaigns essentially impotent, and another published an influential book asserting that information campaigns tended to reinforce existing opinions but rarely changed anybody's minds. These followed on the heels of two other scholars who blamed the receivers of messages for failing to be persuaded by them. This pessimistic view still prevailed a decade later, when a man named Mendelsohn shot back with a more realistic diagnosis and a more optimistic prognosis. His ideas have had an enormous impact on the communication field.

MENDELSOHN'S THREE ASSUMPTIONS FOR SUCCESS

Mendelsohn (1973) believed campaigns so often failed because campaign designers overpromised, assumed the public was going to automatically receive and be interested in their messages, and blanketed the public with messages that were not targeted properly and were likely to be ignored or misinterpreted. As McGuire (1989) wrote later, successful communication campaigns depend on a good understanding of two types of theories: those that explain how someone will process and respond to a message, and those that explain why someone will or will not respond to a message in desirable ways.

After nearly three decades, Mendelsohn's diagnosis still applies. Recent surveys and interviews with public relations professionals have shown consistently that one of the major reasons clients and superiors lose faith in public relations agencies and professionals is overpromising (Bourland, 1993). Overpromising often occurs when program planners do not have a good understanding of their publics and of the situation in which program messages will be received. People from varied backgrounds and with varied interests are likely to interpret messages differently. Moreover, a good understanding of the problem, the publics, and the constraints affecting the likelihood of change (remember social marketing's "price") helps the program planner set goals and objectives that can be achieved using the strategies available in the time allotted. Mendelsohn's (1973) trio of campaign assumptions are as follows:

1. Target your messages.
2. Assume your target public is uninterested in your messages.
3. Set reasonable, midrange goals and objectives.

On the one hand, Mendelsohn's admonition that message receivers will not be interested in a campaign and that campaigns setting ambitious goals are doomed to failure can cultivate pessimism. Mendelsohn's point, however, is that campaign designers who make his three assumptions can make adjustments in strategy that will facilitate success both in the short term and in the long run. The implication of Mendelsohn's tripartite is that research is necessary to define and to understand the target publics, and that an understanding of theory is necessary to develop strategies that acknowledge the public's likely lack of interest and that point to strategies that will compensate for it. Mendelsohn illustrated his point with an example from his own experience, which, depending on your perspective, could be viewed either as a major success or a dismal failure.

Mendelsohn's campaign tried to increase traffic safety by addressing the fact that at least 80% of drivers considered themselves good or excellent drivers, yet unsafe driving practices killed people every day. Long holiday weekends were especially gruesome. Meanwhile, most drivers ignored the 300,000 persuasive traffic safety messages disseminated each year in the print media.

Mendelsohn's team, in cooperation with the National Safety Council and CBS, developed "The CBS National Driver's Test," which aired immediately before the 1965 Memorial Day weekend. A publicity campaign distributed 50 million official test answer forms via newspapers, magazines, and petroleum products dealers before the show aired. The show, viewed by approximately 30 million Americans, was among the highest rated public affairs broadcasts of all time to that point and resulted in mail responses from nearly a million and a half viewers. Preliminary research showed that almost 40% of the licensed drivers who had participated in the broadcast had failed the test. Finally, 35,000 drivers enrolled in driver-improvement programs across the country following the broadcast. The producer of the program called the response "enormous, beyond all expectations." Yet no evidence was provided that accident rates decreased because of the broadcast, and the number of people enrolled in driver improvement programs reflected only about .07% of those who had been exposed to the test forms. How was this an "enormous" success?

Mendelsohn realized that bad drivers would be difficult to reach because of their lack of awareness or active denial of their skill deficiencies, and he realized that to set a campaign goal of eliminating or greatly reducing traffic deaths as the result of a single campaign would be impossible. As a result, Mendelsohn's team chose more realistic goals in recognition of the fact that a single campaign could not be expected to completely solve any problem. The goals of the campaign were as follows:

1. Overcome public indifference to traffic hazards that may be caused by bad driving (increasing awareness).
2. Make bad drivers cognizant of their deficiencies (comprehension).
3. Direct viewers who become aware of their driving deficiencies into a social mechanism already set up in the community to correct such deficiencies (skill development).

HOW PEOPLE RESPOND TO MESSAGES (MCGUIRE'S HIERARCHY OF EFFECTS OR "DOMINO" MODEL)

Evaluating Mendelsohn's success illustrates both the pitfalls of dependence on the traditional linear model of the communication process and the advantages of adopting a more receiver-oriented view, commonly known as the *domino* model or *hierarchy of effects* theory of persuasion. The domino model acknowledges that campaign messages have to achieve several intermediate steps that intervene between message dissemination and desired behavior changes.

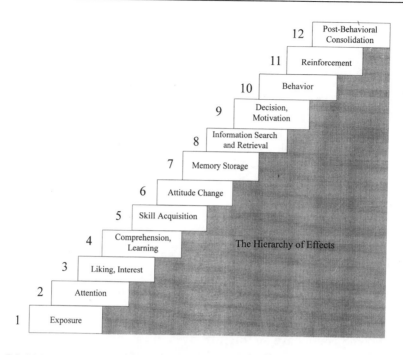

FIG. 14.1. McGuire's domino model. According to McGuire's (1989) model, message receivers go through a number of response steps that mediate persuasion and decision making. Managers setting program goals at the top of the hierarchy may be unrealistic.

According to McGuire, the originator of the domino model, effective campaigns need to acknowledge the following steps, which have been modified here to reflect recent research findings and the symmetrical public relations perspective. Each step is a repository for dozens, if not hundreds, of studies that have shown the importance of the step in people's decision making, along with the factors that enhance or compromise the success of campaign messages at each step.

1. *Exposure.* This, unfortunately, is where most public relations programs begin and end, with getting the message out. Obviously, no one can be persuaded by a message they have had no opportunity to receive. Simply placing a message in the environment, however, is not enough to ensure its receipt or acceptance. Recall that some 300,000 safe driving messages had been ignored consistently by the target public before Mendelsohn's campaign.

2. *Attention.* Even a paid advertisement broadcast during the Super Bowl will fail if the target publics have chosen that moment to head to the refrigerator for a snack, never to see or hear the spot os-

tensibly broadcast to millions. A message must attract at least a modicum of attention to succeed, and campaign designers should not forget the obvious: that complex messages require more attention than simple messages. Production values such as color can make a difference: Color can attract attention, communicate emotion and enhance memory ("Breaking Through," 1999; "The Cultural," 1998). Production values, however, do not guarantee success even if they do attract attention. Color must be used carefully, for example, because the meaning of color may vary with the context and cultural environment. Although orange may signify humor, Halloween, and autumn, it also can mean quarantine (United States) or death (Arabian countries). Red can mean danger (United States), sin (United States), passionate love (Austria and Germany), joy and happiness (China and Japan), and death (Africa). Quite a range! As a result, the International Red Cross, sensitive to this issue, uses green in Africa instead of red (Felton, 1998). According to the Y & R Brand Futures Group ("Survey Finds," 1998), blue has become a popular color to signify the future, because people across cultures associate it with the sky and water, signifying limitlessness and peace.

3. *Involvement (liking or interest).* Although research has shown people have an "orienting response" that instinctively draws their attention to sudden changes in sounds or visual effects, other research has shown they stop paying attention if a message seems irrelevant, uninteresting, or distasteful. Messages that seem relevant sustain people's interest, making people more likely to learn from the message. Social marketing theory acknowledges the importance of this step by its placement of the audience, or public, in the center of the planning profile. Everything about the campaign goal—its benefits, costs, and unique qualities—must be considered from the target public's point of view. They care much more about how a proposal will affect them than how it will affect your company. The City of Tacoma, Washington, for example, wanted to extend the life of its landfill and promote recycling. A 1995 survey of customers found that customers would recycle more if they did not have to sort and separate items. As a result, the city responded by offering a new commingle recycling program that enabled customers to throw all recyclables into the same bin. Recycling increased 300% to 400%, far exceeding the research-based objective of 200% to 300% and earning the city a Silver Anvil Award from PRSA.

4. *Comprehension (learning what).* Sustained attention increases but does not guarantee the likelihood of comprehension. Messages can be misinterpreted. As noted in chap. 4, a cereal promotion suggested over a dozen whimsical ideas for getting a cookie

prize, named Wendell and shaped like a person, to come out of the cereal box. Having a cookie for breakfast appealed to children, as did the silly ideas, such as telling him he had to come out because he was under arrest. Unfortunately, one if the ideas—call the fire department to rescue a guy from your cereal box—backfired when some children actually called 911, which confused, alarmed and irritated the rescue teams. The boxes had to be pulled from the shelves in at least one region of the country.

   5. *Skill acquisition (learning how).* Well-intentioned people may be unable to follow through on an idea if they lack the skills to do so. Potential voters without transportation to the polls will not vote; intended nonsmokers will not quit smoking without social support; interested restaurant patrons will not come if they cannot afford it; parents interested in a civic betterment program will not attend a meeting if they do not have child care. An effective campaign anticipates a target public's needs and provides the help they require. The National Fire Protection Association (NFPA), for example, found through a Burke Marketing survey that many people had a passive attitude about fire, believed they had much more time to escape than they really do, and only 16% had developed and practiced a home fire escape plan. As a result, NFPA's 1998 Fire Safety Week promotion focused on teaching students about fire escape planning and practice, with incentives to encourage them to participate in a documented practice drill with their families. Although the Silver Anvil Award-winning campaign generated an enormous amount of publicity, the most dramatic result was that at least 25 lives were saved as a direct result of the families' participation in the promotion.

   6. *Persuasion (attitude change).* Although McGuire listed this step following skills acquisition, attitude change often precedes skill development. People who lack the skills to follow through on an idea may tune out the details, figuring it is not relevant for them. Attitude change is another of the necessary but often insufficient steps in the persuasion process. Sometimes, however, attitude change is all that is necessary, particularly if the goal of a campaign is to increase a public's satisfaction with an organization to avoid negative consequences such as lawsuits, strikes, or boycotts. Usually, however, a campaign has an outcome behavior in mind. In that case, remember that people often have attitudes inconsistent with their behaviors. Many smokers believe smoking is a bad thing but still smoke. Many nonvoters say voting is important and they intend to vote, but they still fail to show up on election day.

   7. *Memory storage.* This step is important because people receive multiple messages from multiple sources all day, every day. For them

to act on your message, they need to remember it when the appropriate time comes to buy a ticket, make a telephone call, fill out a form, or attend an event. They need to be able to store the important information about your message in their memory, which may not be easy if other messages received simultaneously demand their attention. Key elements of messages, therefore, need to be communicated in ways that make them stand out for easy memorization.

8. *Information retrieval*. Simply storing information does not ensure it will be retrieved at the appropriate time. People might remember your special event on the correct day but forget the location. Reminders or memory devices such as slogans, jingles and refrigerator magnets can help.

9. *Motivation (decision)*. This is an important step that many campaign designers forget in their own enthusiasm for their campaign goals. Remember Mendelsohn's (1973) admonition that people may not be interested in the campaign? They need reasons to follow through. The benefits need to outweigh the costs. In addition, the benefits must seem realistic and, should be easily obtained. The more effort required on the part of the message recipients the less likely it is they will make that effort. If the message recipients believe a proposed behavior is easy, will have major personal benefits, or is critically important, they are more likely to act. The challenge for the program planner is to discover what will motivate the target audience successfully, an issue addressed later in this chapter. Elgin DDB of Seattle, when asked to help reduce Puget Sound curbside disposal of grass clippings by 5%, realized motivation would be an important focus. Focus groups and phone surveys indicated the target group, male homeowners aged 25 to 65, had an interest in grasscycling but needed the proper tools to make it easy and practical. As a result, they arranged to recycle consumers' old polluting gas mowers for free at a special event and sell Toro and Ryobi mulch mowers at below the normal retail price, with an additional rebate. With a goal of selling 3,000 mowers, they sold 5,000. They hoped to remove 1,500 gas mowers from the market and ended up recycling approximately 2,600. And, as for their original goal of reducing curbside disposal of grass clippings by 5%? They more than tripled the target amount, reducing grass clippings by 17%, winning a 1999 Silver Anvil Award.

10. *Behavior*. Success often is measured in terms of behaviors such as sales or attendance figures. Marketing experts, however, know that getting someone's business once does not guarantee long-term success. One study ("Building Customer," 1996) found that keeping customers loyal can boost profits up to 80%. As a re-

sult, the program planner needs to do everything possible to ensure that behavior attempts meet with success. Victoria's Secret, for example, wound up with hundreds of thousands of frustrated web browsers when it promoted an online fashion show following the 1999 Super Bowl only to have the technology crash. Anticipating demand and handling unsuccessful attempts in a positive way can help cement relationships for the long term.

11. *Reinforcement of behavior, attitude or both.* Most people are familiar with the term *buyer's remorse*, which is what people feel if they have second thoughts about a decision they made. Sometimes buyer's remorse results from a bad experience with an organization, such as an unresponsive telephone operator, quite unrelated to the product or idea that was the focus of a campaign. Program planners should anticipate possible reasons for buyer's remorse in a campaign and make follow-up communication part of the campaign to ensure targeted publics continue to feel good about the organization's products or ideas.

12. *Post-behavior consolidation.* This is the final step in a message receiver's decision-making process. At this point, the receiver considers the campaign messages, the attitudes and behaviors involved, and the successes or failures encountered in implementing the targeted attitudes or behaviors, to incorporate this new information into a preexisting world view. By attending a special event promoting both a company and a cause, such as feeding the homeless, a message recipient may develop a long-term connection with both the company and the cause. Alternatively, target publics may decide they had a fun time but these issues do not take higher priority for future decisions than they did before the campaign. Affecting a targeted public's world view is the most challenging goal for a public relations campaign, but for programs focused on building long-term, mutually beneficial relationships, this result also is the most coveted.

McGuire (1989) suggested a success rate of 50% at each stage in a typical mass media campaign would be improbably optimistic. Given that level of attrition, a campaign exposed to 1 million people would gain the attention of 500,000, would hold the interest of 250,000, would be understood as intended by 125,000, would address the necessary skills and needs of 62,500, would be persuasive to 31,250, would be remembered at the time of the communication by 15,625, would be recalled later by 7,813, would be sufficiently motivating to 3,907, would achieve behavior change among 1,954, would achieve repeat behavior among 977, and would gain long-term "consolidation" among 489. No wonder campaign designers in the 1950s and 1960s thought campaigns were doomed to failure. The good news, however, is that this pessimistic view assumes each step has an equal chance of success, each step is equally important to the campaign, and the steps must proceed in the order delineated by McGuire's matrix. Fortunately, these assumptions do not always apply.

If we think back to Mendelsohn's (1973) campaign, in which 50 million people were exposed to promotions regarding the CBS National Driver's Test, 30 million viewed the program to become aware of the hazards of unsafe driving, nearly 40% of licensed drivers failed the test, and approximately 35,000 drivers enrolled in driver improvement programs, should we consider Mendelsohn's campaign a success or a failure? The campaign achieved close to .1% success throughout the hierarchy of effects.

Given Mendelsohn's points about assuming the target is uninterested, the need for targeting the audience, and the need to set reasonable goals, we must consider the situation before assigning credit or blame. Bad drivers are not likely to be interested in being told their driving is deficient; indeed, they are likely to be defensive. Everyone thinks everyone else is the bad driver. In fact, Mendelsohn found that 80% of drivers thought they were good drivers, yet almost half of licensed drivers failed the National Driver's Test. That means that one of every two bad drivers either didn't know or would not acknowledge their deficiencies. So Mendelsohn was correct, even understated, on the first point. As for targeting the audience, the CBS National Driver's Test did not broadcast exclusively to bad drivers. It had to find them among all other viewers of the program, some of whom would not be licensed drivers, would not be old enough to drive, or would be safe drivers. As a result, the campaign could not reasonably expect, nor would it desire, all 50 million people exposed to the campaign to enroll in driver improvement programs. Indeed, if that many people signed up for class, there would not have been enough teachers to serve them all. If 40% of the drivers who watched the program took the test and failed it in the privacy of their own homes, many of them probably changed their attitudes about their own driving and perhaps took some extra precautions the next time they drove, regardless of whether they enrolled in a formal driver improvement program. Finally, the 35,000 drivers who did sign up for formal programs represented a 300% increase, in a 3-month period, over the previous annual enrollment in the programs.

Any public relations agency promising 50 million exposures and 50 million behaviors would be dismissed as naive and absurd. Any public relations agency promising a 300% increase in targeted behaviors, particularly for a challenging behavior to change, probably also would be dismissed as arrogant and unrealistic. So from Mendelsohn we can learn that the definition of success depends on the viewer's perspective. Defining success in terms of desired receiver-oriented outcomes is more appropriate than defining success in terms of source-oriented outputs such as reach or impressions. Promising clients huge exposure can tempt them to expect more impressive behavioral outcomes than would be realistic. With such dangers in mind, McGuire (1989) explained various fallacies that can doom a campaign, along with principles for counteracting challenges along the way.

Common Problems in Application of the Domino Model

McGuire (1989) noted three fallacies that dog campaign designers with an insufficient grasp of persuasion theory.

1. *The attenuated effects fallacy.* Clients and agencies alike want to assume that exposure will produce success in terms of reputation, sales, or other desirable outcomes. The likelihood of continued success along each successive decision-making step, however, is probably less than 50% in a mass market campaign, making the final outcome likely to be less than .1% of the original number exposed to the campaign, as demonstrated.

2. *The distant measure fallacy.* Sometimes program planners report results for attitude change as if they represent behavior change, or they may report changes in awareness as a representation of attitude change. If a program hopes to achieve behavior change, it must measure behavior, not attitudes, as an outcome. Using "clip counts" as an indicator of awareness, by collecting the amount of publicity accumulated, misrepresents campaign effects.

3. *The neglected mediator fallacy.* Well-meaning program planners can make unwitting mistakes if they assume elements that enhance success at one step will continue to enhance success at every step. For example, using Nancy Reagan as a spokesperson for the Just Say No antidrug programs of the 1980s helped the campaigns achieve tremendous exposure nationwide. But Nancy Reagan's credibility among the targeted audience of at-risk adolescents was not high. Likewise, having police officers deliver messages to school children in the DARE to Say No to Drugs campaigns might get the children's attention, but it would do little to provide them with the skills needed to face possible ostracization from their peers. A spokesperson more relevant to their own needs and interests is important to such a campaign.

McGuire also offered several recommendations designed to help maximize success at each step. Even if a campaign cannot achieve 300% increases in behavior, as Mendelsohn's campaign did, it probably can do better than .1% of those initially exposed to a program message if the designer successfully implements the following principles.

1. *The compensatory principle.* The good news is that sometimes things can balance out such that something working against your campaign at one step may work in favor of it at another step. If a simple, graphics-heavy message on television gets people's attention but communicates little information about a complex issue, a companion message, perhaps in a medium such as print or web-based technologies more amenable to careful consideration, can provide the necessary details. Not everyone will pursue the details, but if the initial message piques the public's interest, more people probably will pay deeper attention to the companion message than would have done so otherwise. If a political figure helps a campaign achieve exposure but is irrelevant to the ultimate target public, a campaign can include more appropriate message sources for different targeted publics.

2. *The golden mean principle.* Usually, a moderate amount of something, rather than extreme levels, has the maximum effect. This principle seems like common sense but can be difficult to apply because it can be challenging to determine what levels of humor or fear, for example, seem extreme to the target public. Similarly, the campaign designer needs to know what level of complexity makes a message incomprehensible, versus what level of simplicity makes the message boring. The golden mean principle, therefore, illustrates why pretesting is vital to message development.

3. *The situation weighting principle.* According to McGuire (1989), achieving the hierarchy of effects is not as difficult as it may seem at first glance, because some steps will probably be easier to achieve than others. For example, publicity campaigns continue to hold such popularity because they often reach enough people who already have the interest and motivation to follow through on a message about a new product or service opportunity. Most people will not be interested, but if enough interested people read a well-placed piece on a new restaurant, they will need little additional impetus to get them to the restaurant, as long as the location is easy to remember. They already may possess the skills (transportation and money), the attitude (liking to eat out at that type of restaurant), and the motivation (perhaps an anniversary or birthday dinner is coming up). Likewise, people who want to do something they never thought possible may jump at the opportunity if a campaign addresses their needs (the skill development step).

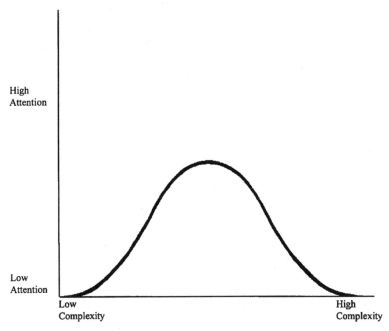

FIG. 14.2. The golden mean principle. According to the golden mean principle, moderate levels of production- or content-related strategies tend to have more effectiveness than extreme levels. The program designer's challenge is to determine more precisely what level is optimal for each target public and situation.

The result, according to the domino model and Mendelsohn's (1973) assumptions, is that a well-researched, carefully targeted campaign will make more dominos fall without going awry.

Limitations of the Domino Model—Acknowledging People Are Not Always Logical

Because the domino model is such a useful campaign planning tool, it is the most popular theory of persuasion among public relations program planners. In fact, Ketchum Public Relations has fashioned a Public Relations *Effectiveness Yardstick*. The Yardstick approximates the hierarchy of effects for easy application, by combining the steps of the domino model into three levels of effect.

The first level, called the *basic level*, measures *outputs*, or exposure in McGuire's (1989) terminology, such as total placements and number of impressions. The second level, called the *intermediate level*, measures *outgrowths*, such as whether target audiences have received

Level #1	Level #2	Level #3
Basic -- Measuring OUTPUTS	*Intermediate -- Measuring* OUTGROWTHS	*Advanced -- Measuring* OUTCOMES
Media Placements	Receptivity	Opinion Change
Impressions	Awareness	Attitude Change
Targeted Audience	Comprehension	Behavior Change
	Retention	

FIG. 14.3. The Ketchum Effectiveness Yardstick. The Ketchum Effectiveness Yardstick is a strategic planning tool that was developed by the Ketchum Research and Measurement Department. Used with permission from Ketchum Public Relations.

messages directed at them, whether they have paid attention to them, whether they have understood them, and whether they have retained them. This corresponds to the steps of attention, comprehension, interest and memory storage in McGuire's model. The third level, called the *advanced level*, measures public relations *outcomes*, such as opinion, attitude, or behavior change.

The domino theory, however, has one important limitation: It incorporates an assumption the recipients of campaign messages will process them in a logical way, carefully considering the veracity of campaign messages to evaluate whether they wish to perform the proposed behavior. The truth is people are not always logical, and we do some things not because they seem right but because they feel good. As a result, it is important to consider another theoretical perspective on persuasion that explicitly acknowledges our logical lapses.

The most popular alternative to the hierarchy of effects theory is called the elaboration likelihood model (ELM). Developed by Petty and Cacioppo (1986) using tightly controlled experiments with limited samples of college students, this theory has its detractors and should be applied with respect for its limitations (Chen & Chaiken, 1999). Its basic principles, however, provide a useful framework for public relations program application, regardless of how the scholars sort out the details. According to the ELM, people process messages differently depending on their level of involvement with the issue. In this way, the ELM dovetails with Grunig and Repper's (1992) situational theory of publics. People uninterested or uninvolved in a topic will not process messages deeply, but those more interested will be more likely to elaborate, or think more carefully about, the message.

The result is that the campaign designer can think broadly of two routes to persuasion. The first route is called the *central approach*, and emphasizes logic and careful consideration. The second route is called the *peripheral approach*, and forgoes logical arguments in favor of more emotionally or heuristic-based strategies. These strategies include elements such as likable, attractive, powerful, credible sources. According to the ELM, decisions achieved using the central approach are more likely to last, whereas decisions achieved using the peripheral approach are more likely to fade, or decay. The peripheral approach, however, can achieve changes more quickly because less thoughtful consideration is necessary from the message recipients. The central approach requires a larger investment of energy from the message recipient, making it more likely to succeed if recipients are highly involved or interested in the topic. If it succeeds it has longer lasting effects because people feel more invested in a decision that took more effort to make and that is based on facts instead of on surface cues. The peripheral approach is more appropriate for low-involvement issues or among target publics who do not care much about the issue. Again, it requires research to determine the extent to which target publics feel involved and ready to participate in thoughtful decision making.

McGuire (1989) called the ELM an alternative route to persuasion because the ELM model's central approach follows all the steps in the domino model, whereas the peripheral approach bypasses several steps, concentrating on elements such as attention, liking, and motivation to the exclusion of elements such as attitude change and skill development. Both the central approach and the peripheral approach require that the program planner understand what will attract and hold message recipients' attention, along with what will motivate them to follow through the hierarchy of effects necessary to achieve behavior change.

WHY PEOPLE RESPOND TO MESSAGES—FINDING THE RIGHT MOTIVATING STRATEGY

To help campaign designers sort through the possible strategies for motivating target publics, McGuire has created a matrix that summarizes hundreds of scientific studies on attitudes and persuasion into

Nature of Motivation		Need for Stability		Need for Growth	
State		Active	Reactive	Active	Reactive
Cognitive	Internal	1. Consistency (cognitive dissonance)	2. Categorization	5. Autonomy	6. Problem Solver
	External	3. Noetic	4. Inductional	7. Stimulation	8. Teleological
Affective	Internal	9. Tension-reduction (fear appeals)	10. Ego-defensive	13. Assertion	14. Identification
	External	11. Expressive	12. Repetition	15. Empathy	16. Contagion (bandwagon)

FIG. 14.4. McGuire' dynamic theories chart. McGuire's dynamic theories chart illustrates different types of motivations that affect the ways people respond to persuasive messages. Adapted with permission from Ronald E. Rice and Charles K. Atkin (Eds.), *Public Communication Campaigns*, Second Edition, Table 2.2, p. 54, copyright © 1989 by Sage Publications, Inc.

TABLE 14.1
The Central and Peripheral Routes to Persuasion

	Central Route	Peripheral Route
Type of strategy	More logic based	More emotion based
Effort required by recipient	Requires more thought	Does not require much thought
Appropriate target public	Best for highly involved message recipients	Best for low or uninvolved message recipients
Time required for results	Results more difficult to achieve, may take time	Results can be quicker to achieve
Long-term results	Results tend to be lasting	Results tend to decay

16 categories. A modified version of McGuire's matrix is presented here to help the public relations professional. Managers may notice that the top half of the chart, labeled cognitive theories, roughly corresponds to the central approach of the ELM theory, whereas the bottom half of the chart, labeled affective theories, roughly corresponds to the peripheral approach. The top and bottom halves of the chart are divided again, to acknowledge that sometimes people are motivated by the need for stability, because utter chaos would make life too unpredictable and uncomfortable, and sometimes people are motivated by the desire to grow, such as by the desire to become smarter, or more successful, or more independent, or more happy.

The most effective campaign probably will combine various strategies from the matrix to address the needs and interests possessed by different target publics or to address the challenges presented at different steps in the persuasion process. For example, a campaign might use an affective (emotionally based) strategy to pique the public's interest in an issue and follow that with a more logically based message to deepen the public's understanding of the issue. Remember that virtually no effective campaign will forgo emotional appeals as part of its strategic mix. A dry recitation of information attracts little attention, interest, or motivation except from the most dedicated target publics. Again, research and pretesting are required to determine which among the following strategies is most appropriate for a given public relations program or campaign.

Logical Strategies

The first half of McGuire's (1989) dynamic theories matrix focuses on primarily logic-based appeals. On the whole, logical appeals serve as useful strategies for publics who have an interest in a topic and some motivation to ponder it. For issues they care less about or feel defensive about, rational arguments may not work. Evan logic-based arguments include some affective elements, appealing in positive ways to make target publics think better of themselves or in negative ways to encourage them to avoid thinking less of themselves. As a result, they include a range of positive and negative strategies, as follows:

1. *Consistency*. People desire to have consistency in their lives. If campaigns demonstrate two conflicting beliefs (see Fig. 14.5), they will feel *cognitive dissonance*, meaning discomfort from the contradictions in their belief system, which they will want to resolve. The consistency-based message is one of the most popular campaign strategies, because it offers a straightforward way to communicate that the public is mistaken for disagreeing with the client's point of view. The Family Violence Protection Fund, for example, challenged its target public that "if the noise coming from next door were loud music, you'd do something about it," implying that if the noise is coming from something much more serious such as spousal abuse, there's no excuse for domestic violence and no excuse for failing to report it. The idea that the reader would intervene for something trivial but bothersome, yet not for something so serious, aims to create dissonance by making the reader feel selfish.

2. *Noetic or attribution*. Sometimes the campaigner prefers to take a more positive approach to people's desire for consistency. The noetic approach relies on highlighting an association that gives the target public and the organization some common ground on which to share their perspectives, to encourage the target public to

When some parents crave their favorite drug, they'll even use their own kids to get it.

When you tell your kids to get you a beer, are you unconsciously giving them permission to handle alcohol?

To kids, your most casual gestures involving alcohol can take on great importance. So examine any messages your behavior concerning this drug might be sending. And talk to them early about the responsibilities that go along with alcohol use.

Call **1-800-662-9111**, or send for our free guide, "Talking To Your Kids About Alcohol." And make sure what you're teaching your kids about alcohol is you want them to learn.

Washington State Substance Abuse Coalition
Talking to Your Kids About Alcohol Brochure
12729 N.E. 20th, Suite 18, Bellevue, WA 98005

FIG. 14.5. Example of a consistency appeal. This ad motivates behavioral change by pointing out the inconsistencies that exist between parents' inherent desire to parent well and their behavior when they do things like asking their children to get a beer for them. Courtesy of the Division of Alcohol and Substance Abuse, Department of Social and Health Services, Washington State.

view the organization or its proposed behaviors in a more favorable light. One use for attribution theory is to point out a simple association between two things the public may not have connected previously, such as CARE, a social assistance organization, and Starbucks coffee. Working Assets long distance service has used the strategy to appeal to consumers who favor nonprofit causes such as Greenpeace, Human Rights Watch, and Planned Parenthood. Of course, communication managers should use such strategies carefully. Appealing to consumers who favor Greenpeace and Planned Parenthood can alienate others who despise those organizations. Another use is to attribute the cause of a problem to a desired issue instead of an undesired issue. For example, some businesses might prefer to attribute the reason for a problem, such as diminished salmon runs, to dammed-up rivers instead of to a complex variety of environmental factors. In this way an organization can deflect blame from its own environmental practices to one cause.

3. *Categorization.* A popular strategy among political campaigners in particular, the categorization approach responds to people's desire to organize their world into sensible categories such as good and bad, or real and unreal. If the campaign designer can change the way people view a situation, it may change the way they evaluate issues relevant to the situation. For example, a moderate Republican challenging a Democrat for office may apply the label "liberal," or "tax and spend" to the Democrat to evoke a reliable response from targeted segments of the electorate, but the same Republican can fall victim to a more conservative Republican challenger who may relabel the moderate Republican as "too liberal" or as "tax and spend" to associate him or her more with Democrats than with Republicans. Such strategies, however, can stretch the truth or ethical boundaries and should be used with care. One candidate in a Pennsylvania Senate race, Rick Santorum, went so far as to relabel the "problem" for the state's gun-control opponents as his rival, Harris Wofford. Santorum's direct mail piece suggested Wofford should be "targeted" to rid Pennsylvania of the gun control problem. The piece, with Wofford's name imprinted in the center of a target, not only looked as if it was meant for real target shooting, but it even was offered for sale as such.

4. *Inductional.* This approach can be called the *coupon* approach because it endeavors to arrange a situation to induce the desired behavior without changing an attitude first. Instead, the campaign follows the behavior change with an appeal to change corresponding attitudes. For example, people might attend a rock concert benefiting the homeless out of a desire to hear the music and see

"Loser" is a harsh label for someone who isn't getting enough to eat.

Over 12 million children in America are suffering from hunger.
Hunger that is taking the energy they need to function every day.
 We can make it easier on them. Simply by feeding them.
Call Second Harvest, America's food bank network,
at **1-800-532-FOOD.**

SECOND HARVEST®
TOGETHER WE'RE
HUNGER'S HOPE

www.secondharvest.org

FIG. 14.6. Example of a categorization appeal. This ad cultivates a sympathetic response
from readers by pointing out that someone labeled a "loser" because they seem to have poor
athletic skills may be suffering from hunger instead.
Courtesy of the Ad Council.

the stars. Once at the concert, they might receive a pitch to support the targeted charity.

5. *Autonomy.* This strategy appeals to people's desire for independence. Particularly in the United States, individualist-minded publics do not want to be bossed around. Appealing to their desire to be self-sovereign sometimes can help an organization develop a convincing message. Organizations that believe their own sovereignty is under attack often resort to this strategy, hoping targeted publics will share their outrage. For example, Voters for Choice told readers of the *New York Times* that "you have the right to remain silent," displaying a tombstone with the name of Dr. David Gunn, who had been killed for practicing abortion, "but your silence can and will be used against you by anti-choice terrorists." Sometimes the strategy can work with an ironic twist, in an attempt to convince people that giving up some freedom, such as by following the rules in a wilderness park, actually will gain them more freedom by ensuring they can enjoy the peace and quiet themselves.

6. *Stimulation.* Sometimes the right thing to do seems boring, and some excitement makes it seem more appealing. As a positive type of appeal, stimulation strategies appeal to people's curiosity or their desire to help create or preserve something with an exciting payoff, such as a wilderness area that can offer outdoor adventures. A group of police officers in Washington state, for example, although visiting middle schools with a serious antidrug message, have transformed themselves into rap stars to deliver their message with rhythm instead of force. As they chant about things students should not do or "you're busted!" the students gyrate and yell the punch line back to the officers. The message gets through.

7. *Problem solver.* Another favorite campaign strategy, the problem solver approach simply shows a problem and demonstrates the favored way to solve the problem. Not enough people can afford to go to college; give to the United Negro College Fund. Not enough children have safe homes; be a foster parent. Use of this strategy assumes the target public will care enough about the problem to respond, which is a big assumption to make. Recall Mendelsohn's (1973) advice to assume the opposite, that the audience is uninterested. Campaigns that neglect to confirm this assumption through research risk failure. When the assumption holds, however, the results can be impressive. It worked for Beaufort County, South Carolina, which had to persuade voters to approve a 1% sales tax increase to pay for improving a dangerous 13-mile stretch of road and bridges when the measure had failed by a 2-to-1 margin twice before. The carefully coordinated Silver Anvil Award-winning cam-

MONEY CAN SEPARATE EVEN THE BEST OF FRIENDS.

The United Negro College Fund helps thousands of deserving students go to college. But for every one we help, there's one we can't. Not without the funds. With your generous donation you can help ensure that everyone who should go to college does, including the best of friends.

 Support The United Negro College Fund.
A Mind Is A Terrible Thing To Waste.

Call 1 800 332-UNCF.

FIG. 14.7. Example of a problem-solver appeal. This ad encourages donations by suggesting that the way to avoid separating friends is to give money to the United Negro College Fund. Courtesy of the Ad Council.

paign overwhelmed the vocal opposition in a 58% to 42% victory when White retirees, young workers, employers, and older African-Americans became familiar with the problem, that "The Wait Is Killing Us," and mobilized in support of the measure.

8. *Teleological.* Just as noetic theories (creating a positive association) offer the opposite strategy from consistency approaches (creating an apparent contradiction that requires resolution), teleological approaches offer the positive alternative to problem solver approaches. Teleological means heavenlike, and the approach relies on showing what the world would look like if a problem already had been solved. This is a useful strategy for incumbent candidates for political office who wish to show their service has made a positive difference for their constituents. In other cases, the target public is shown the ideal result of implementing a desired behavior, along with a script advising how to make the ideal result become reality.

Affective Strategies

The second half of McGuire's (1989) dynamic theories matrix focuses on more emotionally based appeals. On the whole, emotional appeals serve as useful nudges for undecided or uninterested target publics. For issues that require complex consideration, however, or for which a target public has a deeply held view that counters the sponsoring organization's view, emotional appeals can accomplish little or, even worse, backfire. They, too, include a range of positive and negative approaches, as follows:

9. *Tension-reduction (fear appeals).* This strategy attempts to produce tension or fear in the message recipient, which makes the target public uncomfortable and in need of a solution that will reduce the tension. It is the emotional parallel to the consistency-cognitive dissonance approach, which aims to create or highlight a contradiction in the target public's beliefs and behaviors they will want to resolve. The tension-reduction strategy is particularly popular among health campaigners, who try to scare the public into more healthy habits. The problem with fear appeals, however, is they can backfire badly if not applied with precision. One weakness in fear appeals is a failure to resolve the tension in the message. Threatening a target public with a dire outcome (usually death) linked to a behavior, such as drug use or eating habits, without showing how the problem can be fixed and how the situation might look with the problem resolved, can make the target public resent the message and the messenger. Another problem is the use of extreme or unrealistic levels of fear, such as the Partnership for a Drug-Free Amer-

SHE'S A DOCTOR TODAY BECAUSE HER ROLE MODELS WEREN'T MODELS.

She's delivered babies in rural South Carolina, performed surgery while on the Crow Indian Reservation in Montana and treated tropical diseases in The Gambia in West Africa. Dr. Nicole Lang is a role model for girls today thanks to the role models she had growing up — parents and a grandmother who were education advocates.

Show your daughter how achieving in math and science in school can open doors for her in the future.

Call 1-800-WCC-4-GIRLS. Or visit us on the Internet at http://www.academic.org.

Women's College Coalition

FIG. 14.8. Example of a teleological appeal. Instead of demonstrating a problem that needs a solution, this ad attempts to encourage involvement by demonstrating the positive results that can come from giving someone high expectations for themselves.
Courtesy of the Ad Council.

312

ica's admonition equating the use of marijuana with Russian roulette. Because the production of fear appeals is filled with so many pitfalls and the effects of fear appeals are so difficult to predict, they are best avoided. Although appropriate in some situations, such appeals must be well researched. Clients who cannot be dissuaded from using a fear appeal simply must build a large pretesting budget into the project.

10. *Expressive.* Just as noetic strategies take the opposite tack as consistency strategies and teleological approaches reflect the mirror image of problem-solver approaches, the expressive approach takes a positive twist on the tension-reduction approach. The expressive appeal acknowledges that a target public may find the organization's undesired behavior desirable. For example, many drug users perceive real benefits to the use of drugs, such as escape from reality or peer acceptance. From a social marketing point of view, these benefits are important to acknowledge, along with the real perceived costs of physical and mental discomfort associated with "saying no" to drugs. Expressive strategies probably have the greatest potential for making difficult behavior-change campaigns effective, but they are rarely used because they do not reflect the campaign sponsor's perspective. Various theories, however, ranging from co-orientation theory to excellence theory to social marketing theory, discussed in chap. 13, all lend strong support to the value of the expressive approach. Unfortunately, clients often design campaigns using strategies more persuasive to themselves than to their target publics.

11. *Ego defensive.* The ego-defensive approach sets up a situation in which the target public will associate smartness and success with the desired attitude or behavior, whereas failure is associated with the refusal to adopt the message. This approach can be used in both a positive and a negative application. For example, the Business Alliance for a New New York produced messages promising that "you don't have to be a genius to understand the benefits of doing business in New York. (But if you are, you'll have plenty of company.)" The Illinois Department of Public Health and Golin/Harris International focused on making safe-sex decisions "cool" in awkward situations. Research designed to ensure that the appeal would not backfire included mall intercepts of 200 teens, a 33-member teen advisory panel, feedback from high-risk adolescents via state-funded organizations, and message testing using quantitaive and qualitative methods. On the other hand, the Partnership for a Drug-Free America produced messages offering "ten ugly facts for beautiful young women," in an attempt to make use of cocaine seem

ego threatening. Again, the danger of ego-defensive appeals is they need to seem realistic to the target public and, therefore, require considerable pretesting.

12. *Repetition.* If you simply say the same thing over and over enough times, sometimes it will get through. According to McGuire (1989), three to five repeats can help a message get through, especially if the message is presented in a pleasant way. Many campaign designers interpret the three-to-five rule as a magic bullet guaranteeing a message will be successfully propelled into waiting target publics. Repetition, however, constitutes a useful supplemental strategy for an otherwise well-designed campaign, instead of a sufficient strategy in itself.

13. *Assertion.* The emotional parallel to autonomy appeals, the assertion strategy focuses on people's desire to gain power and status. A popular appeal for low-involvement issues or products, the assertion appeal promises increased control over others or a situation in return for adopting the proposed attitude or behavior.

14. *Empathy.* Empathy strategies appeal to people's desire to be loved. Although most applications of the empathic strategy focus on how target publics can achieve personal acceptance from others, this approach can appeal to people's altruism and desire to feel good for helping others they care about. A simple but eloquent American Red Cross appeal, for example, notes that "when you give blood, you give another birthday, another anniversary, another day at the beach, another night under the stars, another talk with a friend, another laugh, another hug, another chance."

15. *Identification.* People aspire to feel better about themselves and frequently aspire to be like someone else. Often they look to other role models who embody positive characteristics. Campaigns commonly use this to create positive associations between a proposed idea or product and a desirable personality such as Michael Jordan. Negative associations also can be made, but as with most negative appeals they require careful pretesting to avoid failure.

16. *Bandwagon.* Making an idea seem contagious can make the idea seem even better. If 2,000 community leaders and neighborhood residents have signed a petition favoring the construction of a new city park, shouldn't you favor it, too? Mothers Against Drunk Driving has made use of this strategy by encouraging people to tie red ribbons on their car antennas during the winter holidays to publicly state their support for sober driving. The strategy does not do much to change strongly held opinions, but it can sway the undecided and serve as a useful reminder and motivator for those in agreement with a campaign message.

Once this man dreamed of going to college. Today he finally made it.

For more than fifty years, The College Fund/UNCF
has helped thousands of young men and women achieve goals
their grandparents could only dream of. We are proud to
have made a critical difference in the lives of so many.
But our job is not done. With your help,we will continue
to bring many more dreams within reach.

SUPPORT THE COLLEGE FUND/UNCF.
A MIND IS A TERRIBLE THING TO WASTE.

1-800-332-UNCF

FIG. 14.9. Example of an empathy/identification appeal. This ad urges receivers to identify with
the grandfather and feel empathy both for him and his grandson. By giving to the fund, they can
feel fulfilled through someone else's achievement the way the grandfather has.
Courtesy of the Ad Council.

OTHER THEORIES THAT EXPLAIN SPECIAL SITUATIONS

Diffusion of Innovations

Another popular theory that is a variation on the domino model provides useful guidance for campaign designers hoping to promote the adoption of an innovation. Innovations can be products such as a new computing tool or ideas such as recycling or changing eating habits. According to diffusion of innovations theory (Rogers, 1983), people considering whether to adopt an innovation progress through five steps that parallel the hierarchy of effects in the domino model. The innovation-decision process follows the way an individual or decision-making unit passes from a lack of awareness to use of the new product or idea. The likelihood of someone making progress through the steps depends on prior conditions such as previous experiences, perceived needs, the norms of the society in which the target public lives, and the individual's level of innovativeness. The steps include knowledge, persuasion, decision, implementation, and confirmation. Innovations are evaluated on the basis of their relative advantages, which Rogers called compatibility, complexity, trialability, and observability. Simply put, an innovation is more likely to be adopted if it seems to have clear benefits that are not difficult to harvest, particularly if giving it a try is not especially risky. Diffusion of innovations theory teaches that most innovations occur according to a fairly predictable S-curve cycle. First, a few brave souls give the new idea a try, and then the innovation picks up speed and becomes more broadly accepted. Finally, most people likely to adopt the innovation do so, and the rate of change slows down again. Campaigns advocating relatively innovative ideas or products benefit from tailoring their messages according to where the innovation is on the S-curve.

Campaigns advocating adoption of an innovation should consider that people who are more innovative will have different needs and interests than people less innovative. According to diffusion of innovations theory, campaigners can think of five broad target publics: innovators, who are the first 2.5% to adopt a new product or idea; early adopters, who are the next 13.5%; the early majority, who represent 34% of the total potential market; the late majority, who represent another 34%; and laggards, who are the final 16%. People who fit in each of these categories have characteristics in common with each other. According to diffusion of innovations theory, people associate mainly with people who share key characteristics with them (called *homogeneous*), but they learn new things from people who are slightly different (called *heterogeneous*). People who are completely different will probably not be able to relate well with the target public and will have less persuasive potential.

Inoculation

Inoculation theory looks like the mirror image of diffusion of innovations theory. The idea behind inoculation (Pfau, 1995) is to address potential trouble before it starts so that potential problems never pick up speed to create a crisis. Just as a flu shot can prevent a full-blown attack of the flu bug, a small dose of bad news early can prevent an issue from turning into a full-blown crisis. For example, political candidates expecting bad news to hit the media can present the news themselves, from their own perspective. Taking away the element of surprise or confrontation makes the news less sensational and, therefore, less damaging.

FINAL THOUGHTS

Theories explaining how and why message recipients make decisions in various circumstances demonstrate that purely informational messages and messages that appeal mainly to the client instead of the message recipient can doom a communication program. Remember that if the target public already shared the organization's point of view perfectly, a communication program probably would not be necessary. Because the goal of a public relations program is to increase the degree to which a target public and an organization share common perspectives and priorities, the organization controlling the message needs to make overtures inviting collaboration with the target public, instead of expecting the target public to invite the organization's perspective into their lives. Making a change is not the target public's priority. Understanding how and why message receivers think the ways they do can greatly enhance the communication professional's ability to build constructive relationships with them by pinpointing the strategies target publics find relevant, credible, and compelling.

15

Practical Applications of Theory for Strategic Planning

About Sources
About Messages
About Channels
Which Channels Are Best
Media Advocacy (Guerilla Media)
Making Media Advocacy Work
Final Thoughts

The generalizations acquired from hundreds of studies about how communication programs work lead to some interesting conclusions about the parts of a communication program the manager can control. This chapter summarizes what research has demonstrated about sources, messages, and channels of communication. In general, the research has shown that, despite the complexities of communication program design, managers can follow some general rules to guide their planning. In fact, most successful practitioners intuitively take advantage of the lessons derived from formal social science research. The astute practitioner also realizes, however, that no rule applies to every situation, making a reliance on generalizations dangerous. As a result, managers should not consider the generalizations offered in this chapter an alternative to performing original program research. Instead, these principles can aid strategic planning preparatory to pretesting.

ABOUT SOURCES

Research has shown that one of the most important attributes of a source is its *credibility*. Some say it takes a long time to build credibility but only a short time to lose it, making credibility an organization's

318

most precious asset. Although various perspectives exist, experts generally agree credibility is made up of two main characteristics: *trustworthiness* and *expertise*. Some add a third characteristic called *bias*. Because credibility of the source exists in the mind of the receiver, it can be tricky to determine.

Despite the importance of credibility, some research has suggested that it matters more for short-term attempts at persuasion than for long-term campaigns. The reason for this is that, after a while, people can forget where they heard a bit of information although they still recall the information. For long-term campaigns, research suggests people rely more on aspects of the message than its source, considering factors such as how well the evidence presented in a message supports the viewpoint advocated.

A second characteristic of a source is perceived *similarity*. Both credibility and perceived similarity exist in the mind of the receiver. Similarity matters because people trust (that is, think more credible) people who seem to be like themselves in a relevant way. Message recipients may judge similarity on the basis of membership or attitudes. This is why presidents will go to work in a factory for a day, or presidential candidates will wear a flannel shirt or a t-shirt instead of a suit. They hope doing such things will increase their appeal to the average person.

This technique also can help persuade people to do things such as take their medicine, ride their helmets when in-line skating, or obey rules. For example, in the Seattle airport, an announcer advises that he has been a baggage handler for years "and I've never lost a bag." He continues on to admonish travelers that they will be more likely to hang on to theirs if they keep them close by and under constant supervision. The message, intended to reinforce airport policy, seems more personal than an anonymous disembodied voice threatening to confiscate unsupervised bags. Another announcer identifies himself as a smoker and tells travelers, in a cheerful voice, where he goes to smoke. In the first case, the announcer has identified himself as an expert who can be trusted on matters of baggage; in the second case, the announcer has established similarity by identifying himself as a member of the group he is addressing. Another announcer could establish similarity on the basis of attitudes by noting how much he hates long lines, just like other travelers, before encouraging them to get their tickets and identification out and ready before getting into line at a check-in gate.

A third characteristic of the source that can make a difference is *attractiveness*, which can refer to physical or personality traits. For example, although some communicators may find this unfortunate, research indicates that visually appealing sources hold more sway over a target public. Some scholars think this is because people want to imagine themselves as attractive, too, and so they establish similarity with an attractive source through wishful thinking. Because they do not want to seem unattractive, they don't want to do or think the same things that an unattractive source does or thinks. As with credibility and perceived similarity, attractiveness exists in the eye of the beholder, making audience-centered research essential for successful communication programs. Cultural differences, for example, can affect what seems attractive, and it is more important for a campaign to use sources that seem attractive to the target public than to use sources that seem attractive to the campaign sponsors (within limits). For example, a source with green hair, a myriad of pierced body parts, and a few tattoos will appeal to rebellious teenagers more than a dark-suited executive in a tie.

ABOUT MESSAGES

Much research provides managers with guidance on the development of messages. Just as the ELM assumes two possible routes to persuasion within a person's mind, the findings from message research focus on two aspects of meaning: logical aspects and emotional aspects. The basic theme behind these findings is that messages need to be accurate, relevant, and clear. Effective messages include the right mix (determined through research, of course) of evidence and emotion.

The Importance of Evidence

Evidence is important only to the extent that a target public will feel motivated to evaluate the authenticity of the evidence presented, but accuracy is a minimum requirement for any message. Messages with unintended inaccuracies communicate incompetence; messages with intentional inaccuracies are unethical and can be illegal, as well. Beyond accuracy, the most important generalization about evidence is that messages have more influence when they acknowledge and refute viewpoints that contradict the position advocated by a sponsoring organization. Consistent with inoculation theory (see chap. 14), scholars have found that two-sided messages are about 20% more persuasive than one-sided messages, provided the "other" side is refuted after having been acknowledged. If the message includes no refutational statement, the two-sided message is about 20% less effective than a one-sided message (Allen, 1991).

The Importance of Emotion

Emotion enhances the appeal of a message because it increases the relevance of the message. Through emotions, people can feel something as a result of a message even if they don't take the trouble to think about the information presented. Fear is probably the emotion most often elicited by campaign designers, but as noted in chap. 14, it also is the emotion most likely to backfire. Although fear appeals are popular for campaigns aimed at adolescents, such as to keep them off of drugs or out of a driver's seat when alcohol impaired, research has shown that fear appeals are more effective with older people than with children or adolescents (Boster & Mongeau, 1984). In addition, research has shown that people only respond favorably to fear appeals when they feel they have the power to deal effectively with the danger presented (Witte, 1992). As a result, campaigns that do things such as warning adolescents about the dire consequences of getting HIV without providing realistic ways for avoiding it will probably fail.

Another popular negative emotion among campaign designers is anger. Political ads in particular use anger, much like a variation on a fear appeal, to encourage voters to mobilize against a villainous enemy. Anger can be a powerful motivator because of people's instinctive desire to protect themselves against danger. As with fear appeals, however, attack strategies can backfire. Political candidates know, for example, that attacks that seem unfair will hurt the sponsoring candidate. Another danger arises from the possibility of cultivating cynicism and distrust in message recipients, which will reflect badly on the sponsoring organization and can dampen the target public's motivations and interest.

Positive emotions are easier to use effectively, provided people do not already have negative feelings about an issue or product. Positive emotions are particularly helpful when people are unfamiliar with a campaign topic, undecided, or confused. Feel-good messages are less apt to change strongly held negative attitudes. Two kinds of positive emotional appeals can be used by campaign managers. The first, the *emotional benefit appeal*, demonstrates a positive outcome to compliance with a campaign message. Positive emotional benefit appeals can be effective if they get people's attention, but they are not compelling unless they incorporate tactics such as attractive spokespeople and production features. These tactics, called *heuristics*, are the second kind of positive emotional appeal. They abandon logical reasoning and simply associate positive images or feelings with an attitude, behavior, or product (Monahan, 1995). Heuristic appeals sell a mood or a feeling instead of more rational benefits. Research has shown that positive heuristic appeals are effective attention getters, but they don't encourage deep involvement or thought on the part of the receiver. People tend to remember the good feeling the message produced rather than any information provided. As a result, positive heuristics have only short-lived effects on attitudes and cannot be depended on for behavioral change. Overall, a combination of positive benefits and positive heuristics garners the best success.

ABOUT CHANNELS

It may seem obvious that different communication vehicles lend themselves most effectively to different purposes. Mass communication vehicles have advantages and disadvantages that make them serve different purposes from interpersonal channels. In addition, managers find that mass communication channels are not interchangeable; similarly, interpersonal sources such as family members have advantages and disadvantages over other interpersonal sources such as teachers or religious leaders. New, interactive technologies are the subject of much recent study and seem to be characterized best as between interpersonal and mass communication, having some characteristics of each.

The Mass Media

The traditional definition of a mass medium is one that reaches many people at once but does not make immediate feedback possible. Increasingly, however, many forms of mass media reach many people at once but also allow varying degrees of feedback. Feedback is important because it makes it possible for message recipients to clarify information, and it makes it possible for organizations to understand how people are reacting to a message. Organizations must be able to adapt to feedback as well as encourage accommodations from others. Recall the co-orientation model illustrates that people need to agree and know they agree. To aid this process, radio offers talk shows; the Internet offers E-mail; television offers dial-in polling and purchasing; newspapers include reader editorials along with letters to the editor. Some generalizations based on the differences among traditional media types, however, still apply. For example, print media can carry more complex information than television or radio can, because people can take the time to read the material slowly or repeatedly to make sure they understand it. On the other hand, television can catch the attention of the less interested more effectively than newspapers or magazines can, because of the combination of visual and auditory production features that make it so entertaining. Radio, meanwhile, is accessible to people in their cars, in their homes, at work, in stores, and even out in the wilderness. This makes it possible to reach target audiences quickly, making it a particularly effective medium in crisis situations when news needs frequent updating. The drawback of radio, however, is that messages must be less complex than messages in print media or on television because people depend solely on their hearing to get the message. They cannot see pictures or printed reminders to reinforce or expand on the message, and it goes by quickly.

Additional generalizations can be made about mass media overall. First, they can reach a large audience rapidly, much more quickly than personally going door to door. As a result, they can spread information and knowledge effectively to those who pay attention. In terms of the hierarchy of effects or domino model, these characteristics make mass media appropriate for gaining exposure and awareness. The mass media also can combine a message with entertainment effectively, which helps message designers get people's attention.

Another benefit of mass media can be the remoteness of the source and situation portrayed from the receiver. Some things, such as scary or embarrassing topics (drug use), are better approached from a distance. Mass media can safely introduce such topics, which can be helpful to organizations ranging from hospitals to zoos. One experiment showed that people scared of snakes could overcome their fear by being introduced to snakes through media portrayals, gradually progressing to the real thing in the same room. Meanwhile, hospitals have found that videos explaining surgical techniques to patients before they experience the procedures can reduce anxiety. Something experienced vicariously often becomes less alarming in real life. One reason for this is the vicarious experience has removed the element of uncertainty from the situation. Research has shown that many of our fears come from uncertainty and from feeling a lack of control. Information, meanwhile, removes uncertainty and can provide more control. The results can be impressive: One study found that children who saw videos that took them through the process of having a tonsillectomy or other elective surgery—including visits to surgery, recovery, and some discussion of likely discomforts—actually got better more quickly, had fewer complications, and were more pleasant patients (Melamed & Siegel, 1975).

The mass media suffer from weaknesses, however. Anytime a message reaches a lot of people at once, it risks misinterpretation by some and provides less opportunity for two-way communication. The less feedback in a channel, the more potential there is for unintended effects to occur. In addition, people find it much easier to ignore or refuse a disembodied voice or a stranger who cannot hear their responses than to ignore someone standing in the same room or talking with them on the telephone. The ability to motivate people, therefore, is less strong with mass media than with interpersonal sources.

Interpersonal Sources

Real people can do many things mass media cannot. They can communicate by way of body language and touch, instead of only through sound and pictures. They also can receive questions and even can be interrupted when something seems confusing. As a result, interpersonal sources can help make sure messages get received without misinterpretation. They also can offer to make changes. For example, company presidents speaking with consumers threatening a boycott can eke out a compromise that satisfies both parties, whereas a mass-mediated message could make the consumers angrier.

Personal attention demonstrates that the target public's views have value. In addition, interpersonal sources can provide encouragement in difficult situations and can serve as models of a desired attitude or behavior. These abilities can be crucial for difficult behavior-change campaigns that require skill development and reinforcement. Thus, although interpersonal communication lacks reach, it often makes an excellent support strategy to a mass-mediated campaign, especially when targeting narrow audience segments. In terms of the hierarchy of effects or domino model, interpersonal sources can help with comprehension, skill development, attitude change, motivation, and reinforcement. This makes interpersonal sources especially important for communication programs addressing strongly held attitudes or challenging behaviors.

If communication programs cannot always include interpersonal sources, they can try to approximate them. For example, an antismoking program in Houston gained the cooperation of one television station and two local newspapers for a 3-month campaign. The media followed 10 ethnically diverse role models who quit smoking a few days ahead of schedule to allow for production requirements. They were shown participating in group counseling sessions, trying out various skills at home, going shopping, and relaxing. Viewers were invited

TABLE 15.1
Strengths and Limitations of the Mass Media as a Communication Vehicle

Strengths of Mass Media	Limitations of Mass Media	Benefits of Adding Interpersonal Communication
Reach large audience rapidly (exposure)	Unintended effects not controlled	Reinforce knowledge
Spread information, knowledge (awareness)	Persuasion to act (motivation) less strong	Provide models, examples, reinforcement, social support
Change weakly held attitudes	More difficult to target a specific audience	Make sure intended message is received
Combine message and entertainment effectively	Two-way communication usually absent	Provide two-way exchange of ideas and information
Provide vicarious consequences and experiences	Messages can be forgotten quickly	More likely to change a strongly held attitude

to imitate the role models, half of whom succeeded in maintaining their nonsmoking status. Donated newspaper space explained what the role models were doing, included instructions to those trying to imitate the models, provided self-tests, and contained motivational statements. Drug store and grocery store personnel, teachers, large employers and community groups handed out viewing guides and gave encouragement. Approximately 250,000 viewing guides were distributed by the interpersonal sources, and 1.34 million were disseminated via newspapers and 270,000 via company newsletters. Three months after the designated quit date, almost one third of Houston-area smokers had seen the programs. Over 10% of them had managed to quit for 3 months or more, meaning 3% of all smokers had quit during this period. The organizers estimated that the 20,000 to 40,000 new nonsmokers had gained an average of 1 to 2 years of life apiece, with a savings in medical costs averaging at least $1,000 apiece. They estimated the total return on investment, therefore, in a campaign that had cost about $100,000 per year, to be minimum of $5 million over 20 years, with associated savings of tens of thousands of years of life (McAlister, Ramirez, Galavotti, & Gallion, 1989).

WHICH CHANNELS ARE BEST

The information from these chapters should make it clear communication is a complex process that lends itself to few generalizations applicable to all situations. The search for the best solutions to a communication problem can tempt managers to draw broader conclusions from selected successes than are warranted, leading to risky, one-size-fits-all solutions. According to Chaffee (1982), communication experts sometimes assume that because interpersonal sources are more persuasive than mass media sources, or at least more difficult to rebuff, this means they also are more credible. And credibility is an extremely important attribute for a source. Chaffee, however, pointed out that studies have found interpersonal networks notoriously unreliable, and some studies have found people making up their minds based solely on information from the media, ignoring or rejecting interpersonal sources.

As Chaffee pointed out, it is silly to pit mass communication against interpersonal communication to determine which is more effective. The reality, according to Chaffee, is that opinion leaders—-the sources from which people seek information or find influential—depend on the context. For information about the quality of local day cares, local parents may be the expert sources. For information about peace negotiations in another country, professional reporters are more likely to be the experts. Nevertheless, Chaffee noted that a few generalizations can be made about communication that can help the program designer.

1. *People seek information from the most accessible source.* Research has shown that if people are highly involved in a topic, meaning deeply interested, they will go to the trouble to find information from the most credible sources available. In other cases, however, they rarely go out of their way. Some people develop habits of checking multiple sources of information, but others do not have the opportunity, ability, or desire to do so. This means communication programs should endeavor to make information easily accessible to target publics, instead of expecting them to seek it out.

2. *People give opinions more often than they seek opinions.* People like to make their opinions known. They do not like having other people's opinions foisted upon them. As a result, the most effective persuasion is *self-persuasion*, in which people reach their own conclusions, guided by information made available to them. To the extent communication programs can set the agenda for what people think about and provide the basis on which they evaluate issues, called framing, the more likely target publics will be to draw conclusions compatible with those of the sponsoring organization.

3. *People seek information more often than they seek opinions.* People search for information instead of for opinions. In fact, they often search for information to back up their existing opinions. If they succeed, they may try to convince others to agree with them. When a communication program can make information available while establishing a common ground of shared values or opinions with a target public, the public will be more likely to accept the information as credible and make use of it in ways consistent with the sponsoring organization's viewpoint.

4. *Interpersonal social contacts tend to be similar (homophilic).* This has various implications for the communication manager. People tend to associate with people who are like themselves because they share a frame of reference. Establishing similarity with a target public tends to enhance credibility. Credibility and closeness can motivate change, and people who are close can provide reinforcement when change takes place. This makes interpersonal sources critical for motivating and consolidating behavior changes.

5. *Expertise, followed by trustworthiness, are the most persuasive attributes of a source.* Both expertise and trustworthiness are aspects of credibility. Although similarity can help facilitate open communication and can enhance credibility, credibility itself is still more important. The key is to determine on what criteria message

recipients will be evaluating a source's expertise and trustworthiness. Remember that interpersonal sources are not necessarily more expert or trustworthy than mass communication sources, meaning they will not necessarily be more persuasive.

6. *The biggest effect of the mass media is more communication.* The previous generalizations necessarily lead to this conclusion. People get information from accessible sources, and mass media can make a message highly accessible. People like to receive information instead of opinions, so the media are more likely to spread credible information than to change opinions. People tend to associate with people similar to themselves and often use information received from the mass media to try to convince others to share their opinions. Finally, people can motivate others similar to themselves to act and can provide reinforcement of those actions. The biggest strength of the mass media, therefore, is that they can spread information and spark interpersonal communication that can change opinions and lead to action. Although this means mass media campaigns are unlikely to prove sufficient for a social marketing-style advocacy program, they are definitely good for something. This has inspired the development of media advocacy.

MEDIA ADVOCACY (GUERILLA MEDIA)

Changing people's minds is no easy task, and just getting their attention can be a challenge. As a result, social marketing campaigns intended to change attitudes or behaviors usually require funds that enable a long-term, gradual adjustment process. Sometimes organizations simply do not have the time or the money to underwrite such a campaign. Instead of giving up, however, they can address the issue from a different theoretical viewpoint, called *media advocacy*.

The media advocacy approach acknowledges the hierarchy of effects model, but it does so from a different angle from social marketing approaches, often striving more for shock value than for establishing common ground with the target public. Social marketing campaigns make three crucial assumptions that distinguish them from media advocacy campaigns:

1. Campaigns ultimately aim to change individual attitudes and behaviors.
2. Individuals ultimately have control over and are responsible for their own attitudes and behaviors.
3. Therefore, to change attitudes and behaviors, campaigns must convince and motivate individuals.

Media advocacy campaigns, on the other hand, make different assumptions:

1. People's attitudes and behaviors depend on environmental opportunities and constraints.
2. Organizations and governmental institutions control critical environmental factors.
3. Organizations and governmental institutions respond to the public's agenda.
4. The agenda for public opinion can be affected by the mass media.
5. Therefore, to change attitudes and behaviors, public opinion needs to force organizations and institutions to alter environmental factors such as public policy.

Both sets of assumptions have validity because human behavior is complex. The communication manager, however, must decide which theoretical strategy is most appropriate for a given situation. Both social marketing and media advocacy have advantages and disadvantages, and both have strengths and limitations. For example, because social marketing targets individuals, people who do change attitudes or behaviors will feel invested in the changes made. In addition, because social marketing tries to establish common ground with the target public through source and message strategies, social marketing is less likely than media advocacy to backfire (provided sufficient preprogram research and pretesting has been performed). Social marketing campaigns, however, are likely to require more time and funding than media advocacy campaigns because they strive for incremental changes that rarely happen quickly and can require a large investment of funds. People also resist change, particularly if they are made to feel defensive about their own attitudes or behaviors.

Media advocacy campaigns, meanwhile, focus on getting people's attention and motivating them to communicate further in some way, instead of on persuading people to change their own attitudes or behaviors. They encourage people to blame a company, public official or institution for a problem instead of accepting personal responsibility, which can eliminate a good deal of potential resistance among the target public. Media advocacy campaigns often use shock or anger to get people's attention and motivate them to turn on a perceived "enemy" under the assumption that public pressure may force the enemy to make a desired change.

Although media advocacy campaigns focus on mass media coverage, thriving on negative emotions and, therefore, on controversy, this also presents some drawbacks. As with any strategy based on negative emotions, the media advocacy strategy can backfire, with the public blaming the sponsoring organization. In addition, heated public debates rarely continue for long, and the media or target publics soon get bored and turn to another topic for discussion. The shorter time frame and strategy of creating newsworthy controversy can make media advocacy campaigns less expensive to run than social marketing campaigns, but they also mean the campaigns are shorter and changes can lack staying power. In other words, the attack strategy of media advocacy, sometimes called guerilla media because of the assault tactics used, makes it lower cost but higher risk.

Media advocacy, therefore, is the strategic use of mass media for advancing a social or public policy initiative, applying techniques for reframing public debate. Social marketing, in contrast, is the strategic use of mass and interpersonal channels to achieve change among individuals, applying techniques aimed at individual responsibility and motivations.

For example, contrast the two campaigns illustrated in Fig. 15.1 and Fig. 15.2, both of which target television as a cause of societal ills. The social marketing version targets parents, encouraging them to take responsibility for getting their children away from the television. The second appeals to people's anger and willingness to blame someone else for teenage pregnancy and violence in society. This ad, which appeared in major newspapers such as the *Wall Street Journal*, made news, attracted contributions (which bought more advertising), and helped spark congressional hearings.

MAKING MEDIA ADVOCACY WORK

Media advocacy recognizes the media are a primary forum for challenging policies. As a result, a successful media advocacy campaign depends on the sponsoring organization's ability to make news. An organization may buy advertising space, for example, but the goal often is for the ad to make news rather than for the ad to persuade many people itself. Organizations buying such ads usually have much less to spend than the companies or institutions they attack. For example, Kalle Lasn, president of a group that ran a parody of an Absolut Vodka ad that resulted in prominent coverage in the *New York Times*, has said, "Even though we're little, we take a big, large corporation, and we use these images to slam them on the mat like a judo move." To do this effectively requires several skills.

1. *Research.* It is essential when using swift and risky guerilla tactics to have confidence in their effectiveness. The media advocate needs to know what story angles will interest the media, what mes-

CAUTION: CHILDREN NOT AT PLAY.

Once, children spent their time running and playing. Today, they're more likely to be found in front of the TV. And that could mean trouble. Because lack of exercise can lead to weight problems and high blood cholesterol. Encourage your children to be more active. Fighting heart disease may be as simple as child's play. To learn more,

contact the American Heart Association, 7272 Greenville Avenue, Box 36, Dallas, TX 75231-4596.

You can help prevent heart disease and stroke. We can tell you how.

American Heart Association

FIG. 15.1. Social marketing example. This ad encourages parents to take responsibility for their children's health. Reproduced with permission, *Caution: Children Not At Play*, PSA Magazine Ad Kit Winter/Spring 1992, Copyright American Heart Association.

Shame on movies, records and TV!

Help us get one million petitions!

A GRASSROOTS PETITION TO BOARDS OF DIRECTORS OF ENTERTAINMENT INDUSTRY

We Are Outraged!

And We're Not Going To Put Up With It Any Longer!

We're a group of mothers, fathers, grandparents and other citizens who are outraged at how today's movies, TV programs, music videos and records are hurting our children, our families and our country.

We're **DISMAYED** that today 1.1 million girls between the ages of 15 and 19 get pregnant each year.

We're **SHOCKED** when we learn that two thirds of all births to 15 and 19-year-old girls are out of wedlock.

We're **FRIGHTENED** at the way violence and crime are spreading everywhere and threatening our children, our families and our homes.

SHAME on those in charge in Hollywood for an endless stream of films filled with **PROFANITY, NUDITY, SEX, VIOLENCE** and **KILLINGS**. For example, the recent giant movie hit features murders during sex, setting a new standard of perversion even for today's movies.

SHAME on TV directors for allowing the average child to see more than **200,000 ACTS OF VIOLENCE** and **33,000 MURDERS** by the age of 16 . . . even though directors **KNOW** that TV violence is implicated in **22% OF ALL JUVENILE CRIME AND HALF THE HOMICIDES** in America.

SHAME on the directors in the film industry which long ago stopped reflecting the values of most families and has now abolished the "X" rating, replacing it with "NC-17," so sex-filled, erotic, bloody films will no longer be barred from community movie houses.

We say the tragic price our children, families and country are paying demands something be done to end what's going on. Alone we can't stop it. But together we think we can.

The **REASON** for all the sex, violence, filth and profanity is with the writers, directors, producers, singers, actors, etc. But **THEY** can be controlled. All it takes is for the Boards of Directors of their companies to order them to stop! Remember when movies were wholesome family entertainment? We're going to insist that happen again.

Together We Can Make It Happen

We're asking every reader of this ad to help us run it all over America ... **AND** send in the petition on the right. Every 2 months we're going to send every member of the Boards of Directors of the entertainment companies a copy of the ad and tell them the total number of petitions received. They're going to **KNOW** American families are outraged.

Spare us the censorship lecture – you in the entertainment industry. And this is not an appeal for prudery. All we want is to get the movie, TV and record industries to act responsibly. Our children, our families and our country are being hurt too much for us to remain silent.

Right now mail the petition below. Please enclose a tax-deductible contribution to help pay for another ad like this. We'll do the rest.

A PETITION To The Members of The Boards of Directors of Every Major TV Network, Film, Music and Record Company

Mail To:

American Family Association, Dept. J70, P O. Drawer 2440/107 Parkgate Drive, Tupelo MS 38803

I want to be part of this Grass Roots petition drive and help run this ad all over America. You agree to notify the Directors of the entertainment companies every 2 months of the progress of this effort, and you agree all funds will be used for running additional ads. With this understanding I am enclosing a tax-deductible contribution of $________ to help pay for another ad and get those in charge to **SET STANDARDS** and **ENFORCE THEM.**

Please return this petition today!

It is the total number of petitions which come in that is important. This project is so important that even if you can't send a contribution please mail in this petition to add to the total number we receive. Thanks.

Please print legibly.

Name ______________________

Address ______________________

City/State/Zip ______________________

A Project of American Family Association
Dr. Donald E. Wildmon, President
Approved by The I.R.S. as a 501-c-3 not for profit organization

1-800-3BE-WISE

FIG. 15.2. Media advocacy example. This ad encourages the public to blame the media for a variety of health problems in society. According to Allen Wildmon, public relations director for the American Family Association, Inc., the ad generated almost 900,000 responses. Ad courtesy of the American Family Association, Inc.

sages will motivate the public, and what messages may backfire. Data are needed to demonstrate convincingly the extent of a problem, including whether some people are affected more than others (people respond when something seems unfair). Research can suggest useful solutions such as policy initiatives, regulations, or the elimination of regulations. Research also can guide efforts to build coalitions, which can make a small organization seem more powerful.

2. *Creative epidemiology.* Creative epidemiology is the use of inventive strategies to make dry information such as statistics more interesting. Often policy issues are complex, and statistics demonstrating the extent of a problem or the value of a solution can be boring. Big numbers can be convincing but hard to digest. As a result, media advocates need to make abstract data seem more relevant and interesting through vivid examples and sound bites. For example, antismoking advocates can draw yawns with the statement that some 350,000 people die each year from smoking-related causes. On the other hand, they can create a vivid image in people's minds if they say instead that "1,000 people quit smoking every day—by dying. That is equivalent to two fully loaded jumbo jets crashing every day, with no survivors," or 730 crashes per year.

Techniques for creating such vivid imagery abound. Media advocates can turn the abstract into the concrete by *localizing* information (such as indicating how many in a community have died from smoking, or AIDS, or drunk-driving accidents); using *relativity techniques*, recharacterizing numbers into a more meaningful form (such as saying the alcohol industry spends approximately $225,000 every hour of every day to advertise, instead of saying they spend more than $2 billion per year); and *showing effects of public policy*, by highlighting individuals who have been affected.

3. *Issue framing.* Usually media advocacy campaigns challenge the public's complacency on an issue. To jar people into listening to a perspective they have not heard before requires finding an angle that will attract attention. For this reason, media advocates often focus on industry practices instead of on individual behavior, or attempt to delegitimize the enemy by exposing their supposedly exploitative and unethical practices.

This requires using familiar symbols to create an advantage. Industries and organizations targeted by media advocates often have carved out a comfortable niche in society through the skilled use of symbols to associate themselves with values shared by the public. For example, tobacco companies often appeal to the public's desire for freedom by claiming censorship or an assault on the First Amendment. Increasingly, media advocates have found it more productive to co-opt the enemy's symbols than to use their often-meager resources to try to carve out their own. For example, People for the Ethical Treatment of Animals co-opted the "what becomes a legend most" catchphrase of the fur industry to turn it into "what disgraces a legend most" to push their Fur is Dead campaign. Similarly, Adbusters created a take-off on Kool cigarettes to create an ad that showed a smoker as an "Utter FOOL." An antismoking group called In fact created a Marlboro™ man imitation whose face was half turned into a skeleton.

4. *Gaining access to media outlets.* According to Wallack, Dorfman, Jernigan, and Themba (1993), reporters need a compelling story to tell that has something new. Newsworthiness "pegs" can include associating the issue with an anniversary, a season, or a milestone; localizing the story in some way; demonstrating irony, injustice, or a breakthrough of some sort; attaching a celebrity to the story; or creating controversy.

Media advocacy usually requires guerilla-style tactics. It requires more creativity to gain attention, make news, and mobilize public opinion without going negative. The trend toward negativity makes media advocacy a powerful but dangerous tool. The media advocate must bear in mind that once news has been created it can take on momentum in directions damaging to the sponsoring organization. The media advocate must be able to anticipate counterarguments from targeted organizations and be ready to handle a crisis situation should guerilla tactics go awry.

In short, communication managers considering the media advocacy approach must consider the risks against the potential payoffs. According to Wallack et al. (1993), an advocacy campaign will probably make enemies because "it points a finger, names names, and starts a fight" (p. 40). This means the communication manager must consider the likelihood of victory against the costliness of failure, and must remember that, above all, an organization needs to maintain its credibility in any communication program. If a guerilla-style campaign costs an organization its credibility, even a short-term victory will not be worth the cost. Advocacy campaigns still must operate in ways consistent with an organization's long-term mission.

Public relations managers must be prepared to defend their organizations against media advocacy campaigns waged by other groups. Media advocates target institutions that have power in a community. If an organization becomes a target of an advocacy campaign, it must fight back with its own guerilla tactics or somehow demonstrate the campaign has no merit. For example, American Forests found itself under attack for a promotion that used Dr. Seuss's environmentalist Lorax character, which cautions against cutting down Truffula trees. According to the Heritage Forests Campaign in Portland, American Forests advocated clearcutting, which made its campaign disingenuous. Focusing on the contradiction between the Lorax character and the company's policies provided an easy way for the anticlearcutting group to gain media attention on what would have been the 95th birthday of Dr. Seuss. Deborah Gangloff of American Forests responded in Seuss-like language: "Shame on you. Shame. Shame. You think publicity by deceit is a feat!" and then provided evidence that the group's congressional testimony on the subject had been misinterpreted, that it is not an advocate of clearcutting, and that the organization often disagrees with timber companies (Hughes, 1999). In doing so, American Forests managed to turn the attack into positive publicity. The ability to launch a credible defense in such crisis situations depends on an organization's relationship with media personnel and past performance. A history of honesty, openness, and accessibility makes reporters more amenable to an organization's side of a story.

With this in mind, remember that even though media advocacy can make enemies, successful media advocacy requires the cultivation of relationships, with gatekeepers such as reporters, as well as with potential collaborators or program cosponsors. Wallack et al. (1993) wrote that the best media advocacy campaigns build a sense of community and of community-based power. Media advocacy campaigns aim to enact change at the community level instead of at the individual level. This, in turn, can help individuals in the community. By shaping the public agenda, shaping the way the agenda gets debated, and advancing a policy-oriented solution, media advocacy can help improve the environment in which an organization and its key publics operate.

FINAL THOUGHTS

Communication research can contribute much to the professional's understanding of how people look for and make use of information. Decades of study have led to helpful generalizations about sources, messages, and communication channels that can help practitioners develop effective program strategies. The principles can help managers identify when a situation calls for an accommodation- or social marketing-oriented strategy and when a situation calls for an advocacy-oriented or even guerilla-style strategy. Many of the generalizations presented in this chapter come intuitively to the seasoned communication professional, but one lesson may seem less obvious. This lesson is the overarching rule of how communication works: It depends. No message, strategy, channel, or source has the same effect in every situation or for every person. This is why preliminary research and pretesting are such a vital part of effective program planning.

THE SUCCESSFUL PITCH
AND FOLLOW-THROUGH

❦16❧

The Campaign Plan

Public relations practitioners can expand their role in organizational decision making because of their important contributions to the organization's success, but they need to present their ideas effectively to do so. The public relations manager's ideas are only as good as they seem to those who must approve project plans, budgets and personnel decisions. Clients who cannot understand your research or who have not become convinced that your ideas will work will not hire you for the job. The campaign proposal, therefore, should be viewed as a kind of public relations campaign.

Every agency and organization will have its own customs and expectations for oral and written presentations. Some like a lot of detail in written form, and some prefer brief proposals in an outline format. This chapter presents a generic, detailed format, shown in Table 16.1,

TABLE 16.1
Elements of the Campaign Proposal

Title Page

(Include client's name, agency name, date, and title)

Cover letter

Table of contents

List of tables and figures

I. Executive Summary
- Problem statement
- Overview of method and results for research performed
- Overview of conclusions (recommendations)
  (about a sentence or two for each)

  length: 1 to 2 pages

II. Research Needs
- Problem statement
- Situation analysis
  - the issue (problem statement)
  - what was known about the client and the issue before research
    (internal and external opportunities and challenges)
  - assumptions
  - information needs (questions)

  length: usually 2 to 4 pages

III. Research Goals (What were you trying to find out?)
- Formal statement of research goals
- Further explanation of each goal, as needed

  length: usually 1 page or less

IV. Research Objectives   (i.e., how you found out, and by when)
- Formal statement of objectives

  length: usually 1 page or less

TABLE 16.1 (Continued)

V. Hypotheses and Research Questions (hunches, etc.)

- Anticipated answers to questions
- Reasoning for the answers anticipated

  length: usually 1 to 2 pages

VI. Research Strategies

- Explanation of methodology, sampling
- Operationalization of concepts (how ideas were measured)
- Procedures for data analysis
- Response rates
- Strengths and limitations of the strategies employed

  length: usually 2 to 4 pages

VII. Results

- Discussed as answers to research questions or hypotheses
- Includes tests of assumptions
- Includes surprises
- Includes explanatory tables and figures as necessary
- Can integrate findings from different methods or discuss sequentially

  length: usually several pages, plus illustrative material

VIII. Implications of the Results (Revised Situation Analysis)

- Overview of strategic recommendations with supporting evidence
- Identification of
  - target publics
  - media/communication vehicles
  - messages/themes
  - evaluation strategies

  length varies; parts may be in outline form with annotations for supporting evidence

(Continues)

TABLE 16.1(Continued)

IX. Proposed Public Relations Plan

- Goals

- Objectives

- Strategies

- Tactics

- Calendar (time line)

- Budget
  length varies; may be in outline form

X. Conclusion

- Summary of
  - original situation analysis and problem statement
  - revised situation analysis
  - recommended strategy
  - anticipated results
  - implications for a longer-term view

XI. References (as needed)

XII. Appendixes

- Research instruments

- Raw results

- Sample campaign materials

- Other relevant background materials

so that practitioners have guidelines for the most formal reports. The format can be modified to fit a specific organization's needs.

INTRODUCTORY MATERIAL

Plans often will include a brief cover letter, sometimes called a transmittal letter. The cover letter for an internal document, such as a report submitted to a CEO by a department, can take the form of a memo. The cover letter states that the proposal requested is being submitted. The letter provides an opportunity to express appreciation to clients for the opportunity to work with them. It also makes it possible to highlight unique, surprising, or especially notable findings or recommendations that should interest the client. Finally, the cover letter invites the client to contact the agency with questions or concerns and provides contact names, phone numbers, fax numbers, and E-mail addresses as appropriate. It should be constructed using the conventions of formal business style.

The plan includes customary introductory material, such as a title page that includes the client's name, the agency or department's name, the date, and a title identifying the purpose of the report. Giving the client's name more prominence than the agency on the title page gives a more service-oriented impression, consistent with social marketing's focus on the target audience. Emphasizing the agency or department producing the report can seem arrogant.

The introductory material also should include a detailed table of contents, along with separate lists of tables and figures so that clients can find material of special interest quickly. Items included in appendixes should be listed individually so the reader knows what is there and in what order. Appendixes, however, often do not have page numbers. Instead, each piece receives a different heading, such as Appendix A, Appendix B, and Appendix C along with a title that identifies the content more specifically, such as "community survey questionnaire." Some stylistic guidelines call for the tables of contents and illustrative material to appear before the executive summary, whereas others call for them to appear after the executive summary.

EXECUTIVE SUMMARY

The executive summary addresses the needs of busy clients and executives who want to get critical information at a glance. They may never have the motivation or opportunity to read a report all the way through. Indeed, committees evaluating a series of proposals may look first for reasons to weed out proposals as inappropriate, unresponsive, or impractical. As a result, managers must make a strong case for a credible proposal in just a few words.

Therefore, the executive summary usually serves as a special form of abstract. The executive summary is the business parallel to scientific papers that often have abstracts of 75 words to describe complicated procedures and findings. Companies, however, have different customs for executive summaries, with some organizations using the executive summary more as an overview chapter than an abstract. Such "executive summaries" can go on for 10 to 25 pages. Once an executive summary goes beyond two pages, however, it should be considered a summary chapter and not an abstract. Obviously, it cannot be read at a glance. In this case, an additional one- or two-page abstract may be helpful.

The purpose of the executive summary is to present the purpose of the report or proposal, the procedures used to evaluate and address the needs presented by the situation, the findings of research performed, the conclusions drawn from the research, and an overview of specific recommendations for action. A concise executive summary outlines every crucial section of the report or proposal, giving one or two sentences to each section. Some summaries include page numbers directing readers to the sections of the proposal that contain the details.

SITUATION ANALYSIS AND RESEARCH NEEDS

The situation analysis demonstrates the agency's understanding of the issue and situation under consideration. In some cases, this section presents the findings, but in other cases, this section provides an overview of how a situation appeared before research was performed. If an agency has performed research, this provides an opportunity to highlight the purpose of the research so clients can understand why it was necessary.

The section should open with a statement of the problem, just like the lead to a news story. It then summarizes everything known about the client and the issue. This includes the client's mission, history, personnel and decision-making structure, locations, facilities, and other projects. It also includes a history of the issue itself, such as whether it is an international problem of concern to many organizations or whether it is a problem only for the client. The description of the issue describes the extent to which the issue is emerging, declining, stable, or cyclical. As explained in chap. 2, the situation analysis provides a detailed explanation of the opportunities and challenges that exist within the organization and its environment. It also identifies what additional information is required to design a successful campaign. Agencies and organizations often have their own preferred format for presenting this information, such using the SWOT (strengths, weaknesses, opportunities, threats or challenges) analysis. Whether presented in narrative, outline or tabular form, background on the situation is an essential element for campaign planning. This section usually requires about four to five pages.

RESEARCH GOALS

The campaign proposal then turns to the presentation of research goals. If it is a proposal to perform research preparatory to the development of a campaign, this section must explain the purpose of the research. Although this section should present research goals in a formal style, the purpose of the goal statements is to explain what the agency or department was (or will be) trying to find out. Some explanation of the goals can be provided, but this section usually requires only a page or less, most often in an outline form.

RESEARCH OBJECTIVES

The research objectives should be presented in formal objective style, in an outline. These objectives state what research was (or will be) performed in response to the research goals. The goals and objectives can be presented in one interwoven section instead of two separate sections if doing so makes the purpose of the research more clear. This section usually requires only one page.

RESEARCH HYPOTHESES

Although public relations managers do not need to act like academic scientists, they still can present informed hunches to clients. These hunches guide both data collection and data analysis. In response to the questions that need answers (the research goals), this section provides insight into what answers the manager may expect to find, along with the reasons for these expectations. If a manager expects to present surprising or discomfiting results to the client, this section can help prepare the client by presenting possible results scenarios. This section usually requires one or two pages.

RESEARCH STRATEGIES

All research requires a thorough explanation of the methods used to collect data. For quantitative research, refer to the Standards for Minimal Disclosure of Opinion Polls (American Association for Opinion Research, 1986), contained in a sidebar to chap. 12, with further details available in the Appendix. Because every research project suffers from limitations of some sort, the client needs to understand what guided your decision making as you performed the research. For example, if you present a mail survey, the client may want to know why a telephone survey would not have been a better choice. If you surveyed residents of one town when the client operates in seven towns, the client will wonder why only one town was used.

This section should discuss the specifics of methodology, along with the reasons for making choices of method, sample, question design, and procedure. Steps made to ensure quality control throughout data collection also should be included. The wording of all questions used in surveys, focus groups and formal interviews should be described, although long data-collection instruments can be described briefly using examples, and complete details can be provided in the appendixes. This section also should include a discussion of the limitations of the research performed, as well as a defense of its usefulness given its limitations. For example, a telephone survey of individuals who have declined to donate to an organization during previous fund-raising campaigns could ask what might prevent a respondent from donating to an organization like the client's, instead of asking what has prevented the respondent from giving in the past. The disadvantage of such a strategy is the question is less direct, but the advantage is respondents may give a more honest, less defensive answer if they do not feel singled out for having refused to donate previously. This section should include information on response rates, refusal rates, and data analysis procedures, explained in chapter 12. This usually requires about two to four pages, depending on the scope of the project.

RESULTS (WITH MINIMAL INTERPRETATION)

This section presents a straightforward recitation of the research findings, putting each finding into the context of the research goals and hypotheses. It helps to restate each research goal and hypothesis before providing the results. This allows a client to read the results section independent of the rest of the document. Providing context ensures the results will make sense to the reader, so do not simply list results. The client will read to find out what questions have answers, what assumptions have support, and what surprises have emerged. Research for a client with a credibility problem, for example, may reveal that the client suffers from a lack of awareness rather than a lack of trust.

It helps to provide tables and figures to highlight particularly important findings. Too many tables and figures, however, overwhelm the reader and reduce their impact. Tables and figures should be integrated into the text instead of being relegated to the appendixes because most clients do not have the time or motivation to flip back and forth between the two sections. The length of this section depends on the scope of the research.

When reporting several research projects, such as a survey and a series of focus groups, the manager must decide whether the information will have the greatest effect presented as discrete sections (survey, Focus Group 1, Focus Group 2, Focus Group 3), or in a consolidated discussion format organized in terms of research questions and hypotheses. Often, the consolidated format works well. For example, a survey finding on low credibility can be supplemented by focus group responses (which should take the form of themes illustrated by specific quotes) describing impressions of the client's recent communication activities.

REVISED SITUATION ANALYSIS

This section discusses the implications of the research results. After the research has been performed, the public relations manager should have a more definite view of the reasons for a problem experienced by the client, along with directions to guide strategy development. This section summarizes the results, indicating how they change or confirm the original view of the situation. The section goes on to provide an overview of recommendations for a public relations program or communication campaign. Each recommendation must seem appropriate and realistic. To convince the client, each recommendation should be accompanied by reasons that describe why it is appropriate; why it will be effective; and why it is worth the cost, in time and money of implementation. Supporting evidence can take the form of findings from the research, public relations principles, and communication theory. Clients expect concrete reasons for action rather than esoteric discussions of theory, however, so keep it simple.

Coming after the summary of the situation and recommendations, this section should present a clear breakdown of the elements for the communication program. These include a discussion of appropriate target publics, communication channels, recommended messages and themes, and methods to evaluate program success. This section can be presented in outline form, provided each recommendation is explained and defended in a companion section. The length varies depending on the scope of the campaign.

PROPOSED PUBLIC RELATIONS PLAN

This section, frequently presented in outline format, presents the complete public relations program plan. This includes goals, objectives, strategies, tactics, a calendar for implementation and completion, and a proposed budget. Some managers prefer to present all of the goals, followed by the objectives, followed by strategies and tactics. Others integrate all components needed to achieve each goal with that particular goal, presenting strategies and tactics specific to each objective along the objective itself.

CONCLUSION

A brief conclusion should provide a summary of the problem, the discoveries, and the solutions. The conclusion can put the project into a larger context, showing how achieving the goals of this program will contribute to the organization's overall mission. A long-term view will demonstrate the public relations manager has a deep understanding of the client's needs and challenges, which can help build credibility both for the project proposed and for the long term. The conclusion should remain brief, rarely stretching beyond one or two pages.

REFERENCES AND APPENDIXES

Some public relations plans include references, but managers must determine the extent to which clients will appreciate background material as opposed to finding it distracting or, even worse, self-important. Appendixes, however, usually are essential. The appendixes should include copies of all research instruments used, a summary of the raw results, and other illustrative sample campaign materials such as brochures.

THE SUCCESSFUL WRITER'S MIND SET

One of the most important skills for the manager is the cultivation of a confident demeanor, both on paper and in person. Managers sell themselves short by appearing hesitant, because hesitance will appear to come from self-doubt. In writing, hesitance reveals itself through use of the first person to advance ideas. Using phrases such as "I believe" and "we recommend" signals to the reader that managers do not have evidence on which to base opinions. As a result, written reports and proposals should avoid using "I" and "we," which appear to advance tentative opinions instead of authoritative facts. A better strategy is to write in the third person stating ideas directly and plainly, remembering to back up every idea with evidence, such as public relations principles and theory, and data from research, a source, or experts. Assertions have much more credibility when the manager can demonstrate their veracity with facts and sources, instead of "believing" or "feeling" them to be true.

Reports and proposals also should avoid passive voice, which gives the appearance of hesitance or, worse, evasiveness. Passive voice makes it seem as if an action is being done to another thing by something, instead of something doing an action to another thing. In other words, it reflects reactive writing instead of proactive writing because it emphasizes the receiver of the action instead of the initiator. Active voice and active verbs, on the other hand, give power to communication efforts. Active voice appears authoritative.

Throughout the document, the manager must display confidence, expertise and empathy with the client. To communicate effectively, writing must be clear, interesting, and correct. As shown in *The Effective Writer's Mind Set* (in Austin & Pinkleton, 1995), writers should ask these questions:

1. *What do I want to get across?* Know your main communication objective. The opening argument or lead forms the foundation for a communication piece. A strong lead helps the rest of a piece fall into place and shows readers why they should continue to read. A good lead uses direct sentence construction and addresses who, what, where, when, how, and why. A main argument for a report or speech shows a commitment to the subject through a clear, strong position statement. A strong opening argument statement will inspire and focus your writing (and will inspire the reader as well).

2. *Can I visualize my audience?* Writing must target an audience. Try to imagine the audience and its expectations. Show an awareness of its interests and level of expertise. Show respect for audience members: Assume they are intelligent. But do not assume they know what you're talking about: Spell everything out using simple language. Tell them only what they care to know. If you want them to know something, make sure you show them why they should want to know it (demonstrate its relevance to them).

3. *Is my main point obvious?* Get to the point quickly. You do not have room or time to get wordy. Busy readers will not bother to wade through extra verbiage. Use active voice (not passive voice that relies on words such as "is" and "was" and "to be"), look out for lots of "little words" such as "then," "in," "to," "so," "as," etc. (they often signal clutter), and worry more about providing supporting statements for your arguments than about adding embellishments and description.

4. *Am I vague?* Get specific. Without sufficient support, even the best ideas remain generalizations. At worst, the reader will think the communicator is trying to hide something. Try to develop main ideas to their fullest extent; explore the areas of a subject in relevant detail. Do not just tell; instead, show, by using evidence and examples. Remember that you need to convince the reader with your argument, so avoid merely describing your position.

5. *Am I logical?* Make strong transitions. Written ideas should progress in a continuous, logical manner. Readers should see easily how every new bit information relates to what came before it. Do not assume any relationships are obvious; you have to make these connections obvious for the reader as you write. Present new news before old news.

6. *Do I provide enough (too much) explanation?* Use supporting evidence effectively. Use only what you need: the perfect example, the exemplary quotation, the clinching statistic. When using quotes, remember to introduce the quote and explain its significance or implications (i.e., what it shows or proves). Do not just drop it in. Readers need to know why you want them to read a quote.

7. *Am I interesting?* Vary sentence structure. Variety comes naturally to our thoughts and spoken words, so variety in your writing will read more naturally and will seem more interesting. How do you do it? Vary short and long sentences. Try mixing the order of subordinate clauses or subject and verb. Read your writing aloud to hear how it sounds. But avoid a lot of complexity, particularly in news items that generally have few embellishments.

8. *Does my writing read naturally?* Write as you would speak, but avoid conversational expressions. Good writing read aloud sounds like good conversation. In conversation, however, we use shortcuts and embellishments that appear sloppy in print. Avoid meaningless qualifiers such as "really," "very," "pretty," "so," "sort of," and "kind of." Also avoid colloquialisms and cliches. If you have original thoughts, they deserve original words to describe them! Make sure you follow the appropriate style guidelines for your piece: Associated Press style for news releases, newsletters, etc.; Chicago style for magazine articles; American Psychological Association style for scientific documents, and so on.

9. *Is my writing free of errors?* Eliminate mechanical and grammatical errors: Always proofread. No matter how good your ideas, no one will take them seriously if your writing includes basic errors. If in doubt of spelling or grammar, look it up or ask a colleague. Always proofread once just for grammar and spelling errors.

10. *What impression do I leave at the end?* Write a strong conclusion. In report, feature, proposal, and speech writing, your conclusion should make as strong an impact as your introduction. Here you sum up your evidence and show how it all inevitably validates your main argument. This also provides you the opportunity to take the reader the next step: You can expand on the topic, suggest where all this may lead, or show how it all contributes to an overarching mission.

11. *Am I my worst critic?* Revise and rewrite. Become your toughest critic. Do not fear multiple rewrites. Good writing appears deceptively easy, just like good gymnastics. It takes a lot of practice and wrong moves to get it right. Do not get discouraged!

ORAL PRESENTATIONS

Presentations themselves require research. Presentations differ depending on the size of the room and the number of people attending a presentation, for example. It helps to know as much about the audience as possible to understand their interests, their needs, and their expectations of formality. It also helps to know their competition and your own competition to put recommendations into a context that will maximize the presenters' credibility. Familiarity with room lighting and seating arrangements helps presenters construct a presentation with the appropriate degree of formality or intimacy. Always be ready to adapt, however, as timing, room locations, and other characteristics of the presentation situation may change on a moment's notice.

Oral presentations often take the form of a brief pitch, after which clients can ask questions. The sale of a project ultimately depends on the quality of its presentation. Effective presentations require substance more than bells and whistles, but some sizzle helps demonstrate professionalism and creativity. A successful pitch depends on effective organization, clarity, and completeness; clear illustration of key points; and a professional demeanor.

1. *Organization of ideas.* As with a written document, clients appreciate it if managers present ideas in a logical order. Clients who become confused will blame the communicator rather than themselves. They will look for another agency that makes more sense. In other words, if the presentation loses the client, the agency loses the job.

2. *Clarity and completeness of presentation.* Ideas need to seem concrete, efficient, and effective. They should build on each other to create a cohesive plan, without redundancy. A brief presentation can never present every detail of a proposal, so careful choices must be made. The client should think they have heard the key ideas, recommendations, and evidence. The manager's challenge is to demonstrate a deep understanding of the client that enables the agency or department to anticipate the client's priorities, concerns, and reservations about the project. The client should not have any nagging questions or doubts following the presentation. It helps to practice answering tough questions to anticipate dealing with reservations a client may have.

3. *Illustration of key points.* Presenters need visual aids to illustrate key points and to add interest to a presentation. Illustrations also can help relieve the presenter's nerves by providing clients with a focus other than the presenter. Illustrations such as outlines of key points can pull a presentation back on track if a presenter forgets the script or becomes distracted by questions or disturbances. Visual aids must serve an explanatory purpose, instead of seeming pointless. Pointless illustrations risk leading clients to believe agencies will recommend pointless program tactics as well. Because illustrations represent the presenters in a prominent way, they must be neat and free of errors. Charts, and tables require large type and

few words to be readable and easy to interpret. Give the audience at least 3 to 5 seconds to digest even the simplest visual aid. Clients often expect computer-aided presentations, but they aid a presentation only if they make sense. Keep in mind that equipment frequently malfunctions, and have a "low-tech" backup plan if you go "high tech."

4. *Presentation style.* Presenters need to look and act professional, which requires rehearsal. Most clients expect presenters to dress in business attire, but some agencies have success with a more avant garde approach that distinguishes them from the norm. This is a risky strategy, however. To demonstrate confidence and empathy, presenters should make eye contact with audience members. The presentation of bad news requires a gentle demeanor, and in some situations eye contact can seem overly aggressive: Avoid making clients feel defensive. It can help soften bad news to open with a bit of good news and presenting bad news in a way that gives the client realistic hope that problems can be resolved. Presenters should show enthusiasm for and confidence in their material. If something goes wrong during the presentation, the client probably won't worry about it if the presenters show good humor and continued confidence in their material.

FINAL THOUGHTS

The public relations plan serves as the manager's sales pitch. The manager demonstrating expertise at promoting an organization's mission should illustrate this expertise in the promotion of the public relations department or agency itself. Each public relations pitch constitutes a public relations campaign in miniature. The manager wants to appear confident, credible, enthusiastic and creative, but never hesitant, insincere, uninterested, or arrogant. Public relations and communication principles apply just as much to plan writing and presentation as to programming itself.

Appendix A

Code of Professional Standards
for the Practice of Public Relations

Public Relations Society of America

This Code was adopted by the PRSA Assembly in 1988. It replaces a Code of Ethics in force since 1950 and revised in 1954, 1959, 1963, 1977, and 1983. For information on the Code and enforcement procedures, please call the chair of the Board of Ethics through PRSA Headquarters.

Declaration of Principles

Members of the Public Relations Society of America base their professional principles on the fundamental value and dignity of the individual, holding that the free exercise of human rights, especially freedom of speech, freedom of assembly, and freedom of the press, is essential to the practice of public relations.

In serving the interests of clients and employers, we dedicate ourselves to the goals of better communication, understanding, and cooperation among the diverse individuals, groups, and institutions of society, and of equal opportunity of employment in the public relations profession.

We pledge:

To conduct ourselves professionally, with truth, accuracy, fairness, and responsibility to the public;

353

To improve our individual competence and advance the knowledge and proficiency of the profession through continuing research and education;

And to adhere to the articles of the Code of Professional Standards for the Practice of Public Relations as adopted by the governing Assembly of the Society.

Code of Professional Standards
for the Practice of Public Relations

These articles have been adopted by the Public Relations Society of America to promote and maintain high standards of public service and ethical conduct among its members.

1. A member shall conduct his or her professional life in accord with the public interest.
2. A member shall exemplify high standards of honesty and integrity while carrying out dual obligations to a client or employer and to the democratic process.
3. A member shall deal fairly with the public, with past or present clients or employers, and with fellow practitioners, giving due respect to the ideal of free inquiry and to the opinions of others.
4. A member shall adhere to the highest standards of accuracy and truth, avoiding extravagant claims or unfair comparisons and giving credit for ideas and words borrowed from others.
5. A member shall not knowingly disseminate false or misleading information and shall act promptly to correct erroneous communications for which he or she is responsible.
6. A member shall not engage in any practice which has the purpose of corrupting the integrity of channels of communications or the processes of government.
7. A member shall be prepared to identify publicly the name of the client or employer on whose behalf any public communication is made.
8. A member shall not use any individual or organization professing to serve or represent an announced cause, or professing to be independent or unbiased, but actually serving another or undisclosed interest.
9. A member shall not guarantee the achievement of specified results beyond the member's direct control.
10. A member shall not represent conflicting or competing interests without the express consent of those concerned, given after a full disclosure of the facts.

11. A member shall not place himself or herself in a position where the member's personal interest is or may be in conflict with an obligation to an employer or client, or others, without full disclosure of such interests to all involved.

12. A member shall not accept fees, commissions, gifts or any other consideration from anyone except clients or employers for whom services are performed without their express consent, given after full disclosure of the facts.

13. A member shall scrupulously safeguard the confidences and privacy rights of present, former, and prospective clients or employers.

14. A member shall not intentionally damage the professional reputation or practice of another practitioner.

15. If a member has evidence that another member has been guilty of unethical, illegal, or unfair practices, including those in violation of this Code, the member is obligated to present the information promptly to the proper authorities of the Society for action in accordance with the procedure set forth in Article XII of the Bylaws.

16. A member called as a witness in a proceeding for enforcement of this Code is obligated to appear, unless excused for sufficient reason by the judicial panel.

17. A member shall, as soon as possible, sever relations with any organization or individual if such relationship requires conduct contrary to the articles of this Code.

OFFICIAL INTERPRETATIONS OF THE CODE

Interpretation of Code Paragraph 1, which reads, "A member shall conduct his or her professional life in accord with the public interest."

The public interest is here defined primarily as comprising respect for and enforcement of the rights guaranteed by the Constitution of the United States of America.

Interpretation of Code Paragraph 6, which reads, "A member shall not engage in any practice which has the purpose of corrupting the integrity of channels of communication or the processes of government."

1. Among the practices prohibited by this paragraph are those that tend to place representatives of media or government under any obligation to the member, or the member's employer or client, which is in conflict with their obligations to media or government, such as:

   a. the giving of gifts of more than nominal value;

b. any form of payment or compensation to a member of the media in order to obtain preferential or guaranteed news or editorial coverage in the medium;

c. any retainer or fee to a media employee or use of such employee if retained by a client or employer, where the circumstances are not fully disclosed to and accepted by the media employer;

d. providing trips, for media representatives, that are unrelated to legitimate news interest;

e. the use by a member of an investment or loan or advertising commitment made by the member, or the member's client or employer, to obtain preferential or guaranteed coverage in the medium.

2. This Code paragraph does not prohibit hosting media or government representatives at meals, cocktails, or news functions and special events that are occasions for the exchange of news information or views, or the furtherance of understanding, which is part of the public relations function. Nor does it prohibit the bona fide press event or tour when media or government representatives are given the opportunity for an on-the-spot viewing of a newsworthy product, process, or event in which the media or government representatives have a legitimate interest. What is customary or reasonable hospitality has to be a matter of particular judgment in specific situations. In all of these cases, however, it is, or should be, understood that no preferential treatment or guarantees are expected or implied and that complete independence always is left to the media or government representative.

3. This paragraph does not prohibit the reasonable giving or lending of sample products or services to media representatives who have a legitimate interest in the products or services.

4. It is permissible, under Article 6 of the Code, to offer complimentary or discount rates to the media (travel writers, for example) if the rate is for business use and is made available to all writers. Considerable question exists as to the propriety of extending such rates for personal use.

Interpretation of Code Paragraph 9, which reads, "A member shall not guarantee the achievement of specified results beyond the member's direct control."

This Code paragraph, in effect, prohibits misleading a client or employer as to what professional public relations can accomplish. It does not prohibit guarantees of quality of service. But it does prohibit guaranteeing specific results which, by their very nature, cannot be guaranteed because they are not subject to the member's control. As an example, a guarantee that a news release will appear specifically in a particular publication would be prohibited. This paragraph should not be interpreted as prohibiting contingent fees.

Interpretation of Code Paragraph 13, which reads, "A member shall scrupulously safeguard the confidences and privacy rights of present, former, and prospective clients or employers."

1. This article does not prohibit a member who has knowledge of client or employer activities that are illegal from making such disclosures to the proper authorities as he or she believes are legally required.

2. Communications between a practitioner and client/employer are deemed to be confidential under Article 13 of the Code of Professional Standards. However, although practitioner/client/employer communications are considered confidential between the parties, such communications are not privileged against disclosure in a court of law.

3. Under the copyright laws of the United States, the copyright in a work is generally owned initially by the author or authors. In the case of a "work made for hire" by an employee acting within the scope of his or her employment, the employer is considered to be the author and owns the copyright in the absence of an express, signed written agreement to the contrary. A freelancer who is the author of the work and is not an employee may be the owner of the copyright. A member should consult legal counsel for detailed advice concerning the scope and application of the copyright laws.

Interpretation of Code Paragraph 14, which reads, "A member shall not intentionally damage the professional reputation or practice of another practitioner."

1. Blind solicitation, on its face, is not prohibited by the Code. However, if the customer lists were improperly obtained, or if the solicitation contained references reflecting adversely on the quality of current services, a complaint might be justified.

2. This article applies to statements, true or false, or acts, made or undertaken with malice and with the specific purpose of harming the reputation or practice of another member. This article does not prohibit honest employee evaluations or similar reviews, made without malice and as part of ordinary business practice, even though this activity may have a harmful effect.

AN OFFICIAL INTERPRETATION OF THE CODE AS IT APPLIES
TO POLITICAL PUBLIC RELATIONS

Preamble

In the practice of political public relations, a PRSA member must have professional capabilities to offer an employer or client quite apart from any political relationships of value, and members may serve their employer or client without necessarily having attributed to them the character, reputation, or beliefs of those they serve. It is understood that members may choose to serve only those interests with whose political philosophy they are personally comfortable.

Definition

"Political Public Relations" is defined as those areas of public relations that relate to:

    a. the counseling of political organizations, committees, candidates, or potential candidates for public office; and groups constituted for the purpose of influencing the vote on any ballot issue;
    b. the counseling of holders of public office;
    c. the management, or direction, of a political campaign for or against a candidate for political office; or for or against a ballot issue to be determined by voter approval or rejection;
    d. the practice of public relations on behalf of a client or an employer in connection with that client's or employer's relationships with any candidates or holders of public office, with the purpose of influencing legislation or government regulation or treatment of a client or employer, regardless of whether the PRSA member is a recognized lobbyist;
    e. the counseling of government bodies, or segments thereof, either domestic or foreign.

Precepts

    1. It is the responsibility of PRSA members practicing political public relations, as defined above, to be conversant with the various statutes, local, state, and federal, governing such activities and to adhere to them strictly. This includes, but is not limited to, the various local, state, and federal laws, court decisions, and official interpretations governing lobbying, political contributions, disclosure, elections, libel,

slander, and the like. In carrying out this responsibility, members shall seek appropriate counseling whenever necessary.

2. It is also the responsibility of the members to abide by PRSA's Code of Professional Standards.

3. Members shall represent clients or employers in good faith, and while partisan advocacy on behalf of a candidate or public issue may be expected, members shall act in accord with the public interest and adhere to truth and accuracy and to generally accepted standards of good taste.

4. Members shall not issue descriptive material or any advertising or publicity information or participate in the preparation or use thereof that is not signed by responsible persons or is false, misleading, or unlabeled as to its source, and are obligated to use care to avoid dissemination of any such material.

5. Members have an obligation to clients to disclose what remuneration beyond their fees they expect to receive as a result of their relationship, such as commissions for media advertising, printing, and the like, and should not accept such extra payment without their client's consent.

6. Members shall not improperly use their positions to encourage additional future employment or compensation. It is understood that successful campaign directors or managers, because of the performance of their duties and the working relationship that develops, may well continue to assist and counsel, for pay, the successful candidate.

7. Members shall voluntarily disclose to employers or clients the identity of other employers or clients with whom they are currently associated, and whose interests might be affected favorably or unfavorably by their political representation.

8. Members shall respect the confidentiality of information pertaining to employers or clients past, present, and potential, even after the relationships cease, avoiding future associations wherein insider information is sought that would give a desired advantage over a member's previous clients.

9. In avoiding practices that might tend to corrupt the processes of government, members shall not make undisclosed gifts of cash or other valuable considerations that are designed to influence specific decisions of voters, legislators, or public officials on public matters. A business lunch or dinner, or other comparable expenditure made in the course of communicating a point of view or public position, would not constitute such a violation. Nor, for example, would a plant visit designed and financed to provide useful background information to an interested legislator or candidate.

10. Nothing herein should be construed as prohibiting members from making legal, properly disclosed contributions to the candidates, party, or referenda issues of their choice.

11. Members shall not, through use of information known to be false or misleading, conveyed directly or through a third party, intentionally injure the public reputation of an opposing interest.

AN OFFICIAL INTERPRETATION OF THE CODE AS IT APPLIES TO FINANCIAL PUBLIC RELATIONS

This interpretation of the Society Code as it applies to financial public relations was originally adopted in 1963 and amended in 1972, 1977, 1983 and 1988 by action of the PRSA Board of Directors. "Financial public relations" is defined as "that area of public relations which relates to the dissemination of information that affects the understanding of stockholders and investors generally concerning the financial position and prospects of a company, and includes among its objectives the improvement of relations between corporations and their stockholders." The interpretation was prepared in 1963 by the Society's Financial Relations Committee, working with the Securities and Exchange Commission and with the advice of the Society's legal counsel. It is rooted directly in the Code with the full force of the Code behind it, and a violation of any of the following paragraphs is subject to the same procedures and penalties as violation of the Code.

1. It is the responsibility of PRSA members who practice financial public relations to be thoroughly familiar with and understand the rules and regulations of the SEC and the laws it administers, as well as other laws, rules, and regulations affecting financial public relations, and to act in accordance with their letter and spirit. In carrying out this responsibility, members shall also seek legal counsel, when appropriate, on matters concerning financial public relations.

2. Members shall adhere to the general policy of making full and timely disclosure of corporate information on behalf of clients or employers. The information disclosed shall be accurate, clear, and understandable. The purpose of such disclosure is to provide the investing public with all material information affecting security values or influencing investment decisions. In complying with the duty of full and timely disclosure, members shall present all material facts, including those adverse to the company. They shall exercise care to ascertain the facts and to disseminate only information they believe to be accurate. They shall not knowingly omit information, the omission of which might make a release false or misleading. Under no circum-

stances shall members participate in any activity designed to mislead or manipulate the price of a company's securities.

3. Members shall publicly disclose or release information promptly so as to avoid the possibility of any use of the information by any insider or third party. To that end, members shall make every effort to comply with the spirit and intent of the timely-disclosure policies of the stock exchanges, NASD, and the SEC. Material information shall be made available on an equal basis.

4. Members shall not disclose confidential information the disclosure of which might be adverse to a valid corporate purpose or interest and whose disclosure is not required by the timely-disclosure provisions of the law. During any such period of nondisclosure members shall not directly or indirectly (a) communicate the confidential information to any other person or (b) buy or sell or in any other way deal in the company's securities where the confidential information may materially affect the market for the security when disclosed. Material information shall be disclosed publicly as soon as its confidential status has terminated or the requirement of timely disclosure takes effect.

5. During the registration period, members shall not engage in practices designed to precondition the market for such securities. During registration, the issuance of forecasts, projections, predictions about sales and earnings, or opinions concerning security values or other aspects of the future performance of the company, shall be in accordance with current SEC regulations and statements of policy. In the case of companies whose securities are publicly held, the normal flow of factual information to shareholders and the investing public shall continue during the registration period.

6. Where members have any reason to doubt that projections have an adequate basis in fact, they shall satisfy themselves as to the adequacy of the projections prior to disseminating them.

7. Acting in concert with clients or employers, members shall act promptly to correct false or misleading information or rumors concerning clients' or employers' securities or business whenever they have reason to believe such information or rumors are materially affecting investor attitudes.

8. Members shall not issue descriptive materials designed or written in such a fashion as to appear to be, contrary to fact, an independent third-party endorsement or recommendation of a company or a security. Whenever members issue material for clients or employers, either in their own names or in the names of someone other than the clients or employers, they shall disclose in large type and in a prominent position on the face of the material the source of such material and the existence of the issuer's client or employer relationship.

9. Members shall not use inside information for personal gain. However, this is not intended to prohibit members from making bona fide investments in their company's or client's securities insofar as they can make such investments without the benefit of material inside information.

10. Members shall not accept compensation that would place them in a position of conflict with their duty to a client, employer, or the investing public. Members shall not accept stock options from clients or employers nor accept securities as compensation at a price below market price except as part of an overall plan for corporate employees.

11. Members shall act so as to maintain the integrity of channels of public communication. They shall not pay or permit to be paid to any publication or other communications medium any consideration in exchange for publicizing a company, except through clearly recognizable paid advertising.

12. Members shall in general be guided by the PRSA Declaration of Principles and the Code of Professional Standards for the Practice of Public Relations of which this is an official interpretation.

Appendix B
Code of Professional Ethics and Practices

American Association for Public Opinion Research

We, the members of the American Association for Public Opinion Research, subscribe to the principles expressed in the following code. Our goals are to support sound and ethical practice in the conduct of public opinion research and in the use of such research for policy and decision-making in the public and private sectors, as well as to improve public understanding of opinion research methods and the proper use of opinion research results.

We pledge ourselves to maintain high standards of scientific competence and integrity in conducting, analyzing, and reporting our work in our relations with survey respondents, with our clients, with those who eventually use the research for decision-making purposes, and with the general public. We further pledge ourselves to reject all tasks or assignments that would require activities inconsistent with the principles of this code.

THE CODE

I. Principles of Professional Practice in the Conduct of Our Work

A. We shall exercise due care in developing research designs and survey instruments, and in collecting, processing, and analyzing data, taking all reasonable steps to assure the reliability and validity of results.

1. We shall recommend and employ only those tools and methods of analysis which, in our professional judgement, are well suited to the research problem at hand.

2. We shall not select research tools and methods of analysis because of their capacity to yield misleading conclusions.
3. We shall not knowingly make interpretations of research results, nor shall we be tacitly permit interpretations that are inconsistent with the data available.
4. We shall not knowingly imply that interpretations should be accorded greater confidence than the data actually warrant.

B. We shall describe our methods and findings accurately and in Appropriate detail in all research reports, adhering to the standards for minimal disclosure specified in Section III.

C. If any of our work becomes the subject of a formal investigation of an alleged violation of this Code, undertaken with the approval of the AAPOR Executive Council, we shall provide additional information on the survey in such detail that a fellow survey practitioner would be able to conduct a professional evaluation of the survey.

II. Principles of Professional Responsibility in Our Dealings With People

A. The Public:

1. If we become aware of the appearance in public of serious distortions of our research, we shall publicly disclose what is required to correct these distortions, including, as appropriate, a statement to the public media, legislative body, regulatory agency, or other appropriate group, in or before which the distorted findings were presented.

B. Clients or Sponsors:

1. When undertaking work for a private client, we shall hold confidential all proprietary information obtained about the client and about the conduct and findings of the research undertaken for the client, except when the dissemination of the information is expressly authorized by the client, or when disclosure becomes necessary under terms of Section I-C or II-A of this Code.
2. We shall be mindful of the limitations of our techniques and capabilities and shall accept only those research assignments which we can reasonably expect to accomplish within these limitations.

C. The Profession:

1. We recognize our responsibility to contribute to the science of public opinion research and to disseminate as freely as possible the ideas and findings which emerge from our research.

2. We shall not cite our membership in the Association as evidence of professional competence, since the Association does not so certify any persons or organizations.

D. The Respondent:

1. We shall strive to avoid the use of practices or methods that may harm, humiliate, or seriously mislead survey respondents.
2. Unless the respondent waives confidentiality for specified uses, we shall hold as privileged and confidential all information that might identify a respondent with his or her responses. We shall also not disclose or use the names of respondents for non-research purposes unless the respondents grant us permission to do so.

III. Standard for Minimal Disclosure

Good professional practice imposes the obligation upon all public opinion researchers to include, in any report of research results, or to make available when that report is released, certain essential information about how the research was conducted. At a minimum, the following items should be disclosed:

1. Who sponsored the survey, and who conducted it.
2. The exact wording of questions asked, including the text of any preceding instruction or explanation to the interviewer or respondents that might reasonably be expected to affect the response.
3. A definition of the population under study, and a description of the sampling frame used to identify this population.
4. A description of the sample selection procedure, giving a clear indication of the method by which the respondents were selected by the researcher, or whether the respondents were entirely self-selected.
5. Size of samples and, if applicable, completion rates and information on eligibility criteria and screening procedures.
6. A discussion of the precision of the findings, including, if appropriate, estimates of sampling error, and a description of any weighting or estimating procedures used.
7. Which results are based on parts of the sample, rather than on the total sample.
8. Method, location, and dates of data collection.

March 1986

Appendix C
Guidelines and Standards for Measuring and Evaluating PR Effectiveness

The Institute for Public Relations Research and Evaluation

GETTING SPECIFIC: STANDARDS FOR MEASURING PR OUTPUTS

There are many possible tools and techniques that PR practitioners can utilize to begin to measure PR *outputs*, but there are the four that are most frequently relied on to measure PR impact at the *output* level: Media Content Analysis ... Cyberspace Analysis ... Trade Show and Event Measurement ... and Public Opinion Polls.

1. *Media Content Analysis*

This is the process of studying and tracking what has been written and broadcast, translating this qualitative material into quantitative form through some type of counting approach that involves coding and classifying of specific messages.

Some researchers and PR practitioners in the U.S. refer to this as "Media Measurement" and/or "Publicity Tracking" research. In the United Kingdom, the technique is often referred to as "Media Evaluation;" and in Germany as "Media Resonance." Whatever the terminology used to describe this particular technique, more often than not its prime function is to determine whether the key messages, concepts and themes that an organization might be interested in disseminating to others via the media do indeed, receive some measure of exposure as a result of a particular public relations effort or activity.

The coding, classifying and analysis that is done can be relatively limited or far-reaching, depending on the needs and interests of the organization commissioning the research. More often than not, Media Content Analysis studies take into consideration variables such as there:

Media Vehicle Variables, such as date of publication or broadcast ... frequency of publication or broadcast of the media vehicle ... media vehicle or type (that is, whether the item appeared in a newspaper, magazine, a newsletter, on radio, or on television) ... and geographic reach (that is, region, state, city, or ADI markets in which the item appeared).

Placement or News Item Variables, such as source of the story (that is, a press release, a press conference, a special event, or whether the media initiated the item on their own) ... story form or type (a news story, feature article, editorial, column, or letter to the editor) ... degree of exposure (that is, column inches or number of paragraphs if the item appeared in print, number of seconds or minutes of air time if the item was broadcast) ... and the story's author (that is, the byline or name of the broadcaster.)

Audience or 'Reach' Variables. The focus here usually is on total number of placements, media impressions and/or circulation or potential overall audience reached—that is, total readers of a newspaper or magazine, total viewers and listeners to a radio or television broadcast. The term "impressions" or "opportunity to see" usually refers to the total audited circulation of a publication. For example, if *The Wall Street Journal* has an audited circulation of 1.5 million, one article in that newspaper might be said to generate 1.5 million impressions or opportunities to see the story. Two articles would generate 3 million impressions, and so on. Often more important than impressions is the issue of whether a story reached an organization's target audience group, by specific demographic segments. These data often can be obtained from the U.S. Census Bureau or from various commercial organizations, such as Standard Rate and Data Services. In addition to considering a publication's actual circulation figures, researchers often also take into consideration how many other individuals might possibly be exposed to a given media vehicle, because that publication has been routed or passed on to others.

Subject or Topic Variables, such as who was mentioned and in what context ... how prominently were key organizations and/or their competitors referred to or featured in the press coverage (that is, were companies cited in the headline, in the body copy only, in both, etc.) ... who was quoted and how frequently ... how much coverage, or "share of voice" did an organization receive in comparison to its competitors ... what issues and messages were covered and to what extent ... how were different individuals and groups positioned—as leaders, as followers, or another way?

Judgment or Subjective Variables. The focus here usually is on the stance or tone of the item, as that item pertains to a given organization and/or its competitors. Usually tone implies some assessment as to whether or not the item is positive, negative or neutral; favorable, unfavorable or balanced. It is extremely important to recognize that measuring stance or tone is usually a highly subjective measure, open to a possibly different interpretation by others. Clearly-defined criteria or groundrules for assessing positives and negatives—and from whose perspective—need to be established beforehand, in order for stance or tone measures to have any credibility as part of Media Content Analysis.

"Advertising Equivalency" is often an issue that is raised in connection with Media Content Analysis studies. Basically, advertising equivalency is a means of converting editorial space into advertising costs, by measuring the amount of editorial coverage and then calculating what it would have cost to buy that space, if it had been advertising.

Most reputable researchers contend that "advertising equivalency" computations are of questionable validity. In many cases, it may not even be possible to assign an advertising equivalency score to a given amount of editorial coverage (for example, many newspapers and/or magazines do not sell advertising space on their front pages or their front covers; thus, if an article were to appear in that space, it would be impossible to calculate an appropriate advertising equivalency cost, since advertising could never ever appear there).

Some organizations artificially multiply the estimated value of a "possible" editorial placement in comparison to advertisement by a factor of 2, 3, 5, 8 or whatever other inflated number they might wish to come up with, to take into account their own perception that editorial space is *always* of more value than is advertising space. Most reputable researchers view such arbitrary "weighting" schemes aimed at enhancing the alleged value of editorial coverage as unethical, dishonest, and not at all supported by the research literature. Although some studies have, at times, shown that editorial coverage is sometimes more credible or believable than is advertising coverage, other studies have shown the direct opposite, and there is, as yet, no clearly established consensus in the communications field regarding which is truly more effective: publicity or advertising. In reality, it depends on an endless number of factors.

Sometimes, when doing Media Content Analysis, organizations may apply weights to given messages that are being disseminated, simply because they regard some of their messages as more important than others, or give greater credence (or weight) to an article that not only appears in the form of text, but also is accompanied by a photo or a graphic treatment. Given that the future is visuals, organizations are more and more beginning to measure not only words, but also pictures.

It should be noted that whatever groundrules, criteria and variables are built into a Media Content Analysis, whatever "counting" approaches are utilized to turn qualitative information into quantitative form, it is important that all of the elements and components involved be clearly defined and explained up front by whoever is doing the study. The particular system of media analysis that is applied and utilized by one researcher should—if a second researcher were called in and given the same brief and the same basic criteria pertaining to the aims of the study—result in broadly similar research findings and conclusions.

2. Cyberspace Analysis

Increasingly, a key measure of aq organization's image or reputation and of how that organization might be positioned is the chatter and discussion about that organization in cyberspace—specifically in chat rooms, forums and new groups on the Word Wide Web. The same criteria used in analyzing print and broadcast articles can be applied when analyzing postings on the Internet.

What appears in print is frequently commented about and editorialized about on the Web. Therefore, one component of *PR output* measurement ought to be a review and analysis of Web postings.

In addition, a second *output* measure of cyberspace might be a review an analysis of Website traffic patterns. For example, some of the variables that ought to be considered when designed and carrying out Cyberspace Analysis might include deconstructing "hits" (that is, examining the requests for a file of visitors to the Internet) ... a review of click-throughs and/or flash-click streams ... an assessment of home page visits ... domain tracking and analysis ... an assessment of bytes transferred ... a review of time spent per page .... Traffic times ... browsers used ... and the number of people filling out and returning feedback forms.

Best practices for this type of research are covered in "Getting Started On Interactive Media Measurement," available from the Advertising Research Foundation, 641 Lexington Avenue, New York, NY 10022, and "Hits Are Not Enough: How to *Really* Measure Web Site Success," prepared by *Interactive Marketing News* and available from Phillips Business Information, Inc., 1201 Seven Locks Road, Potomac, MD 20854.

3. Trade Shows and Event Measurement

Frequently, the intent of a public relations programs or activity is simply to achieve exposure for an organization, its products or services, through staging trade shows, holding special events and meetings, involvement in speakers' programs and the like.

For shows and events, obviously one possible *output* measure is an assessment of total attendance, not just an actual count of those who showed up, but also an assessment of the types of individuals present, the number of interviews that were generated and conducted in connection with the event, and the number of promotional materials that were distributed. In addition, if the show is used as an opportunity for editorial visits, one can measure the effectiveness of those visits by conducting a content analysis of the resulting articles.

4. Public Opinion Polls

Although most surveys that are designed and carried out are commissioned to measure *PR outcomes* rather than *PR outputs*, public opinion polls are often carried out in an effort to determine whether or not key target audience groups have, indeed, been exposed to particular messages, themes or concepts and to assess the overall effectiveness of a given presentation or promotional effort. For example, conducting a brief survey immediately following a speech or the holding of a special event to assess the short-term impact of that particular activity would constitute a form of *PR output* measurement.

GETTING SPECIFIC: STANDARDS FOR MEASURING PR OUTCOMES

Just as there are many tools and techniques that PR practitioners can utilize to begin to measure PR *outputs*, there also are many that can be used to measure PR *outcomes*. Some of those most frequently relied on include surveys (of all types) ... focus groups ... before-and-after polls ... ethnographic studies (relying on observation, participation, and/or role playing techniques) ... and experimental and quasi-experimental research designs.

Best practices for both qualitative and quantitative research are covered in the Advertising Research Foundation's two documents: "Guidelines for the Public Use of Market and Opinion Research" and the *ARF Guidelines Handbook: A Compendium of Guidelines to Good Advertising, Marketing and Media Research Practice*. Both are available from the Advertising Research Foundation, 641 Lexington Avenue, New York, NY 10022.

Ultimately, one intent of public relations is to inform and persuade key target audience groups regarding topics and issues that are of importance to a given organization, with the hope that this will lead those publics to act in a certain way. Usually, this involves four different types of *outcome* measures: Awareness and Comprehension Measurements ... Recall and Retention Measurements ... Attitude and Preference Measurements ... and Behavior Measurements.

1. Awareness and Comprehension Measurements

The usual starting point for any PR *outcome* measurement is to determine whether target audience groups actually *received* the messages directed at them ... paid *attention* to them ... and *understood* the messages.

Obviously, if one is introducing a new product or concept to the marketplace for the first time—one that has never been seen or discussed before—it is reasonable to assume that prior to public relations and/or related communication activities being launched, that familiarity and awareness levels would be at zero. However, many organizations have established some type of "presence" in the marketplace, and thus it is important to obtain benchmark data against which to measure any possible changes in awareness and/or comprehension levels.

Measuring awareness and comprehension levels requires some type of primary research with representatives of key target audience groups.

It is important to keep in mind that **Qualitative Research** (e.g. focus groups, one-on-one depth interviews, convenience polling) is usually open-ended, free response and unstructured in format ... generally relies on nonrandom samples ... and is rarely "projectable" to larger audiences. **Quantitative Research** (e.g. telephone, mail, mall, fax, and e-mail polls), on the other hand, although it may contain some open-ended questions, is far more apt to involve the use of closed-ended, forced choice question that are highly structured in format ... generally relies on random samples ... and usually is "projectable" to larger audiences.

To determine whether there have been any changes at all in audience awareness and comprehension levels, usually requires some type of comparative studies—that is, either a *before* and *after* survey to measure possible change from one period of time to another, or some type of "test" and "control" group study, in which one segment of a target audience group is deliberately exposed to a given message or concept and a second segment is not, with research conducted with both groups to determine if one segment is now better informed regarding the issues than the other.

2. Recall and Retention Measurements

Traditionally, advertising practitioners have paid much more attention to recall and retention measurement, than have those in the public relations field.

It is quite common in advertising, after a series of ads have appeared either in the print or the broadcast media, for research to be fielded to determine whether or not those individuals to whom the ad messages have been targeted actually recall those messages on both an unaided and aided basis. Similarly, several weeks after the ads have run, follow-up studies are often fielded to determine if those in the target audience group have retained any of the key themes, concepts, and messages that were contained in the original advertising copy.

Although recall and retention studies have not been done that frequently by public relations practitioners, they clearly are an important form of *outcome* measurement, that ought to be seriously considered by PR professionals. Various data collection techniques can be used when conducting such studies, including telephone, face-to-face, mail, mall, e-mail, and fax polling.

When conducting such studies, it is extremely important that those individuals fielding the project clearly differentiate between messages that are disseminated via PR techniques (e.g. through stories in the media, by work of mouth, at a special event, through a speech, etc.) from those that are disseminated via paid advertising or through marketing promotional efforts. For example, it is never enough to simply report that someone claims they read, heard or saw a particular item; it is more important to determine whether that individual can determine if the item in question happened to be a news story that appeared in editorial form, or was a paid message that someone placed through advertising. Very often, it is difficult for the "average" consumer to differentiate between the two.

3. Attitude and Preference Measurements

When it comes to seeking to measure the overall impact or effectiveness of a particular public relations program or activity, assessing individuals' opinions, attitudes, and preferences become extremely important measures of possible *outcomes.*

It needs to be kept in mind that "opinion research" generally measures what people say about something; that is, their verbal expressions or spoken or written points of view. "Attitude research," on the other hand, is far deeper and more complex. Usually, "attitude research" measures not only what people say about something, but also what they know and think (their mental or cognitive predispositions), what they feel (their emotions), and how they're inclined to act (their motivational or drive tendencies).

"Opinion research" is easier to do because one can usually obtain the information desired in a very direct fashion just by asking a few question. "Attitude research," however, is far harder and, often more expensive to carry out, because the information desired often has to be collected in an indirect fashion. For example, one can easily measure people's *stated* positions on racial and/or ethnic prejudice, by simply asking one or several direct questions. However, actually determining whether someone is *in actual fact* racially and/or ethnically prejudiced, usually would necessitate asking a series of indirect questions aimed at obtaining a better understanding of people's cognitions, feelings and motivational or drive tendencies regarding that topic or issue.

Preference implies that an individual is or will be making a choice, which means that preference measurement more often than not ought to include some alternatives, either competitive or perceived competitive products or organizations. To determine the impact of public relations preference *outcomes* usually necessitates some type of audience exposure to specific public relations *outputs* (such as an article, a white paper, a speech, or participation in an activity or event), with research then carried out to determine the overall likelihood of people preferring one product, service, or organization to another.

Usually, opinion, attitude and preference measurement projects involve interviews not only with those in the public at large, but also with special target audience groups, such as those in the media, business leaders, academicians, security analysts and portfolio managers, those in the health, medical and scientific community, government officials, and representatives of civic, cultural and service organizations. Opinion, attitude and preference measurement research can be carried out many different ways, through focus groups, through qualitative and quantitative surveys, and even through panels.

4. Behavior Measurements

The ultimate test of effectiveness—the highest *outcome* measure possible—is whether the behavior of the target audience has changed, at least to some degree, as result of the public relations program or activity.

For most media relations programs, if you have changed the behavior of the editor and/or reporter so that what he or she writes primarily reflects an organization's key messages, then that organization has achieved a measure of behavior change.

However, measuring behavior is hard because it is often difficult to prove cause-and-effect relationships. The more specific the desired *outcome* and the more focused the PR program or activity that relates to that hoped-for end result, the easier it is to measure PR behavior change. For example, if the intent of a public relations program or activity is to raise more funds for a nonprofit institution and if one can show after the campaign has been concluded that there has, indeed, ben increased funding, then one can begin to surmise that the PR activity had a role to play in the behavior change. Or, to give another example: For measuring the effectiveness of a public affairs or government relations program targeted at legislators or regulators, the desired *outcome*—more often than not—would *not only* be to get legislators or regulators to change their views, but *more importantly* to have those legislators and regulators either pass or implement a new set of laws or regulations that reflect the aims of the campaign. Behavior change requires someone to act differently than they have in the past.

More often than not, measuring behavior change requires a broad array of data collection tools and techniques, among them before-and-after surveys ... research utilizing ethnographic techniques (e.g. observation, participation, and role playing) ... the utilization of experimental and quasi-experimental research designs ... and studies that rely on multivariate analyses and sophisticated statistical applications and processes.

What is crucial to bear in mind in connection with PR *outcome* behavior measurement studies is that measuring *correlations*—that is, the associations or relationships that might exist between two variables—is relatively easy. Measuring *causation*—that is, seeking to prove that X was the reason that Y happened—is extremely difficult. Often, there are too many intervening variables that need to be taken into consideration.

Those doing PR *outcome* behavior measurement studies need to keep in mind these three requirements that need to exist in order to support or document that some activity or event caused something to happen: 1) Cause must *always* precede the effect in time; 2) there needs to be a relationship between the two variables under study; and 3) the observed relationship between the two variables cannot be explained away as being due to the influence of some third variable that possibly caused both of them.

The key to effective behavior measurement is a sound, well thought out, reliable and valid research concept and design. Researchers doing such studies need to make sure that study or test conditions or responses are relevant to the situation to which the findings are supposed to related, and also clearly demonstrate that the analysis and conclusions that are reached are indeed supported and documented by the fieldwork and data collection that was carried out.

QUESTIONS THAT NEED TO BE PUT TO THOSE ORGANIZATIONS THAT COMMISSION PR EVALUATION STUDIES

Here are some of the key questions that those who commission PR evaluations studies ought to ask themselves before they begin, and also the types of questions that those who actually carry out the assignment ought to ask their clients to answer before the project is launched:

- What are, or were, the specific goals and/or objectives of the public relations, public affairs, and/or marketing communications program, and can these be at all stated in a quantitative or measurable fashion? (e.g. To double the number of inquiries received from one year to the next? ... To increase media coverage by achieving greater "share of voice" in one year than in a previous year? ... To have certain legislation passed? ... To enhance or improve brand, product, or corporate image or reputation.)
- Who are, or were, the principal individuals serving as spokespersons for the organization during the communications effort?
- What are, or were, the principal themes, concepts, and messages that the organization was interested in disseminating?
- Who were the principal target audience groups to whom these messages were directed?
- Which channels of communication were used and/or deemed most important to use in disseminating the messages? (e.g., the media ... word-of-mouth ... direct mail ... special events?)
- What specific public relations strategies and tactics were used to carry out the program? What were the specific components or elements of the campaign?
- What is, or was, the timeline for the overall public relations program or project?
- What is, or were, the desired or hoped-for outputs and/or outcomes of the public relations effort? If those particular hoped-for outputs and/or outcomes could, for some reason, not be met, what alternative outputs and/or outcomes would the organization be willing to accept?
- How does what is or has happened in connection with the organization's public relations effort related to what is or has happened in connection with related activities or programs in other areas of

the company, such as advertising, marketing, and internal communications?
- Who are the organization' principal competitors? Who are their
  spokespersons? What are their key themes, concepts, and messages that they are seeking to disseminate? Who are their key target audience groups? What channels of communications are they
  most frequently utilizing?
- Which media vehicles are, or were, most important to reach for
  the particular public relations and/or marketing communications activities that were undertaken?
- What were the specific public relations materials and resources
  utilized as part of the effort? Would it be possible to obtain and review copies of any relevant press releases, brochures, speeches,
  promotional materials that were produced and distributed as
  part of the program?
- What information is already available to the organization that can
  be utilized by those carrying out the evaluative research assignment to avoid reinventing the wheel and to build on what is already known?
- If part of the project involves an assessment of media coverage,
  who will be responsible for collecting the clips or copies of broadcast material that will have been generated? What are the ground
  rules and/or parameters for clip and/or broadcast material assessment?
- What major issues or topics pertaining to the public relations undertaking are, or have been, of greatest importance to the organization commissioning the evaluation research project?
- What is the timeline for the PR evaluation research effort? What
  are the budgetary parameters and/or limitations for the assignment? Do priorities have to be set?
- Who will be the ultimate recipients of the research findings?
- How will whatever information that is collected be used by the organization that is commissioning the research?

QUESTIONS THAT NEED TO BE PUT TO THOSE RESEARCH SUPPLIERS, AGENCIES AND CONSULTING FIRMS THAT ACTUALLY CONDUCT PR EVALUATION STUDIES

Here are some of the key questions that ought to be put to those who
actually are asked to carry out a PR evaluation research project, before
the assignment is launched:

- What is, or will be, the actual research design or plan for the PR
  evaluation project? Is there, or will there be, a full description in

non-technical language of what is to be measured, how the data are to be collected, tabulated, analyzed and reported?

- Will the research design be consistent with the stated purpose of the PR evaluation study that is to be conducted? Is there, or will there be, a precise statement of the universe or population to be studied? Does, or will, the sampling source or frame fairly represent the total universe or population under study?

- Who will actually be supervising and/or carrying out the PR evaluation project? What is, or are, their backgrounds and experience levels? Have they ever done research like this before? Can they give references?

- Who will actually be doing the field work? If the assignment includes media content analysis, who actually will be reading the clips or viewing and/or listening to the broadcast video/audio tapes? If the assignments involve focus groups, who will be moderating the sessions? If the study involves conducting interviews, who will be doing those and how will they be trained, briefed, and monitored?

- What quality control mechanisms have been built into the study to assure that all "readers," "moderators," and "interviewers" adhere to the research design and study parameters.

- Who will be preparing any of the data collection instruments, including tally sheets or forms for media content analysis studies, topic guides for focus group projects, and/or questionnaires for telephone, face-to-face, or mail survey research projects? What role will the organization commissioning the PR evaluation assignment be asked, or be permitted, to ply in the final review and approval of these data collection instruments?

- Will there be a written set of instructions and guidelines for the "readers," the "moderators" and the "interviewers"?

- Will the coding rules and procedures be available for review?

- If the data are weighted, will the range of the weighs be reported? Will the basis for the weights be described and evaluated? Will the effect of the weights on the reliability of the final estimates be reported?

- Will the sample that is eventually drawn be large enough to provide stable findings? Will sampling error limits be shown, if they can be computed? Will the sample's reliability be discussed in language that can clearly be understood without a technical knowledge of statistics?

- How projectable will the research findings be to the total universe or population under study? Will it be clear which respondents or which media vehicles are underrepresented, or not represented at all, as part of the research undertaking?

How will the data processing be handled? Who will be responsible for preparing a tab plan for the project? Which analytical and demographic variables will be included as part of the analysis and interpretation?

- How will the research finding and implications be reported? If there are finding based on the data that were collected, but the implications and/or recommendations stemming from the study go far beyond the actual data that were collected, will there be some effort made to separate the conclusions and observations that are specifically based on the data and those that are not?
- Will there be a statement on the limitations of the research and possible misinterpretations of the findings?
- How will the project be budgeted? Can budget parameters be laid out prior to the actual launch of the assignment? What contingencies can be built into the budget to prevent any unexpected surprises or changes once the project is in the field or is approaching the completion stage?

References

Aday, L. A. (1989). *Designing and conducting health surveys: A comprehensive guide.* San Francisco: Jossey-Bass.

Adler, E. S., & Clark, R. (1999). *How it's done: An invitation to social research.* Belmont, CA: Wadsworth.

Allen, M. (1991). Meta-analysis comparing the persuasiveness of one-sided and two-sided messages. *Western Journal of Speech Communication, 55,* 390–404.

American Association for Public Opinion Research. (1986). *Ethics code* [On-line]. Available: http://www.aapor.org/ethics/code.html

American Dairy Association. (1999). *I love cheese what's new* [On-line]. Available: http://www.ilovecheese.com/survey.html.

Andrews, F. M., & Withey, S. B. (1976). *Social indicators of well being.* New York: Plenum.

Austin, E. W., & Pinkleton, B. E. (1995). *Writing for results: A workshop for effective communicators.* Pullman, WA: Washington State University.

Austin, E. W., Pinkleton, B. E., & Dixon, A. (in press). *Journal of Public Relations Research.*

Avoiding common errors in the production of prevention materials. (1990, June). *Technical Assistance Bulletin* [Brochure]. Bethesda, MD: Center for Substance Abuse Prevention.

Babbie, E. (1999). *The basics of social research.* Belmont, CA: Wadsworth.

Berelson, B. (1952). *Content analysis in communication research.* New York: The Free Press.

Blankenship, A. B., Breen, G. E., & Dutka, A. (1998). *State of the art marketing research* (2nd ed.). Lincolnwood, IL: NTC Business Books.

Boster, F. J., & Mongeau, P. A. (1984). Fear-arousing persuasive messages. In R. N. Bostrom (Ed.), *Communication yearbook 8* (pp. 330–375). Beverly Hills, CA: Sage.

Bottom-line orientation boosts PR measurement's success. (1999, November 1). *PR News, 55,* 1–6.

Bourland, P. G. (1993). The nature of conflict in firm-client relations: A content analysis of *Public Relations Journal*, 1980–89. *Public Relations Review, 19*, 385–398.

Breaking through the clutter: Color is a major tool, sometimes. (1999, May 31). *PR Reporter, 42*, 1–2.

Broom, G. M., & Dozier, D. M. (1990). *Using research in public relations: Applications to program management*. Englewood Cliffs, NJ: Prentice-Hall.

Building customer loyalty a little can double profits. (1996, June 3). *PR Reporter, 39*, 3.

Bush, K. (personal communication, January 15, 1999).

Cameron, G. (1997). Publics PR Research Software (Version 2.1b) [Computer software]. Athens, GA: The Right Brain.

Cameron, G. (1998, February 16). Professor: 2-way symmetrical PR doesn't always work. *PR Reporter, 41*, 1–3.

Campbell, B. A. (1981). Race-of-interviewer effects among southern adolescents. Public *Opinion Quarterly, 45*, 231–244.

Campbell, D. T., & Stanley, J. C. (1963). *Experimental and quasi-experimental designs for research*. Boston: Houghton Mifflin.

Can value of corporate reputation be quantified? (1996, April 15). *PR News, 52*, 7.

Cato, F. W. (1982, Fall). Procter & Gamble and the devil. *Public Relations Quarterly, 27*, 16–21.

Chaffee, S. H. (1982). Mass media and interpersonal channels: Competitive, convergent, or complementary? In G. Gumpert & R. Cathcart (Eds.), *Inter/media: Interpersonal communication in a media world* (2nd ed., pp. 57–77). New York: Oxford University Press.

Chen, S., & Chaiken, S. (1999). The heuristic-systematic model in its broader context. In S. Chaiken & Y. Trope (Eds.), *Dual-process theories in social psychology* (pp. 73–96). New York: The Guilford Press.

Chiagouris, L. (1998, Winter). Confessions of a Silver Anvil judge. *The Public Relations Strategist, 4*, 29–31.

Cline, C. G., & Toth, E. L. (1993). Re-visioning women in public relations: Practitioner and feminist perspectives. In P. J. Creedon (Ed.), *Women in mass communication* (pp. 183–198). Newbury Park, CA: Sage.

Cochran, W. G. (1977). *Sampling techniques*. New York: Wiley.

Converse, J. M. (1987). *Survey research in the United States: Roots and emergence, 1890–1960*. Berkeley, CA: University of California Press.

Culling lessons from Swissair crash: Across-the-board commitment needed. (1998, September 14). *PR News, 54*, 1, 7.

The cultural consequences of color. (1998, May 25). *Tips & Tactics* (supplement of *PR Reporter*), *36*, 1–2.

Cutlip, S. M., Center, A. H, & Broom, G. M. (2000). *Effective public relations* (8th ed.). Upper Saddle River, NJ: Prentice-Hall.

Czaja, R., & Blair, J. (1996). *Designing surveys: A guide to decisions and procedures*. Thousand Oaks, CA: Pine Forge Press.

Dahl, J., & Miller, L. (1996, July 24). Which is the safest airline? It all depends.... *Wall Street Journal*, pp. B1, B4.

Davids, M. (1987, March). Panic prevention. *Public Relations Journal, 43*, 18–21, 24, 43.

Dillman, D. A. (1978). *Mail and telephone surveys: The total design method.* New York: Wiley.

Dozier, D. M., Grunig, L. A., & Grunig, J. E. (1995). *Manager's guide to excellence in public relations and communication management.* Mahwah, NJ: Lawrence Erlbaum Associates.

Ehling, W. P. (1985). Application of decision theory in the construction of a theory of public relations management. II. *Public Relations Research & Education, 2,* 1, 4–22.

Feldstein, L. (1992, June 15). Balancing social responsibility with the bottom line. *Tips & Tactics* (supplement of *PR Reporter*), *30*, 1–2.

Felton, J. (1998, May 25). The cultural consequences of color. *Tips & Tactics* (supplement of *PR Reporter*), *36*, 1–2.

Fitzgerald, K. (1996, December 16). Publicity about toy shortages feeds the frenzy. *Advertising Age, 67*, 12.

Fowler, F. J., Jr. (1995). *Improving survey questions: Design and evaluation.* Thousand Oaks, CA: Sage.

Fowler, F. J., Jr., & Mangione, T. W. (1990). *Standardized survey interviewing: Minimizing interviewer-related error.* Newbury Park, CA: Sage.

Fraser, E. (1998, December 21). Corporate communication trends: What's hot for the millennium. *Tips & Tactics* (supplement of *PR Reporter*), *36*, 1–2.

Freedman, D., Pisani, R., & Purves, R. (1978). *Statistics.* New York: Norton.

Frey, J. H. (1989). *Survey research by telephone* (2nd ed.). Newbury Park, CA: Sage.

Gap research: Why & how it does what other methods don't. (1994, July 18). *PR Reporter, 37,* 1.

Geistfeld, R. E. (1995, August 17). What's the problem? That's the question. *This Thursday,* 2.

Groves, R. M. (1989). *Survey errors and survey costs.* New York: Wiley.

Groves, R. M., & Lyberg, L. E. (1988). An overview of nonresponse issues in telephone surveys. In R. M. Groves, P. P. Biemer, L. E. Lyberg, J. T. Massey, W. L. Nicholls, & J. Waksberg (Eds.), *Telephone survey research* (pp. 191–211). New York: Wiley.

Grunig, J. E. (1989). Symmetrical presuppositions as a framework for public relations theory. In C. H. Botan & V. Hazleton, Jr., (Eds.), *Public relations theory* (pp. 17–44). Hillsdale, NJ: Lawrence Erlbaum Associates.

Grunig, J. E., & Grunig, L. (1998, September 7). Does evaluation of PR measure the real value of PR? *Jim & Lauri Grunig's Research* (supplement of *PR Reporter*), *1*, 1–4.

Grunig, J. E., Grunig, L., & Ehling, W. P. (1992). What is an effective organization? In J. E. Grunig (Ed.), *Excellence in public relations and communication management: Contributions to effective organizations* (pp. 65–90). Hillsdale, NJ: Lawrence Erlbaum Associates.

Grunig, J. E., & Huang, Y. (in press). From organizational effectiveness to relationship indicators: Antecedents of relationships, public relations strategies, and relationship outcomes. In J. A. Ledingham & S. D. Bruning, (Eds.), *Public relations as relationship management: A relational approach to the study and practice of public relations.* Mahwah, NJ: Lawrence Erlbaum Associates.

Grunig, J. E., & Hunt, T. (1984). *Managing public relations.* New York: Holt, Rinehart & Winston

Grunig, J. E., & Repper, F. C. (1992). Strategic management, publics, and issues. In J. E. Grunig (Ed.), *Excellence in public relations and communication management: Contributions to effective organizations* (pp. 117–157). Hillsdale, NJ: Lawrence Erlbaum Associates.

Grunig's paradigm: Superb issue anticipation & planning tool. (1998, October 5). *PR Reporter, 41,* 3–4.

Harris, T. L. (1998). *Value-added public relations.* Lincolnwood, IL: NTC Business Books.

The health communication process. (1990, June). *Technical Assistance Bulletin* [Brochure]. Bethesda, MD: Office for Substance Abuse Prevention.

Holsti, O. (1969). *Content analysis for the social sciences and humanities.* Reading, MA: Addison-Wesley.

How Mondavi uses vision statement to drive company behavior. (1998, August 17). *PR Reporter, 41,* 1–2.

Hughes, J. H. (1999, March 2). Dr. Seuss figure caught in crossfire. *Columbian,* p. B2.

Hyman, H. H., & Sheatsley, P. B. (1947). Some reasons why information campaigns fail. *Public Opinion Quarterly, 11,* 412–423.

In focused philanthropy era, some don't even publicize gifts. (1996, June 10). *PR Reporter, 39,* 1–2.

Jackson, M. (1998, September 13). More companies nurture family-friendly culture. *Spokane Spokesman-Review,* p. A19.

Johnson, J. B., & Joslyn, R. A. (1986). *Political science research methods.* Washington, DC: Congressional Quarterly.

Just for fun: Is Japan ahead in public relations, too? (1994, November 28). *Tips & Tactics* (supplement of *PR Reporter*), 32, 1–2.

Kendall, R. (1996). *Public relations campaign strategies: Planning for implementation* (2nd ed.). New York: Harper Collins.

Kerlinger, F. N. (1973). *Foundations of behavioral research* (2nd ed.). New York: Holt, Rinehart & Winston.

Keys to world class publications. (1998, April 13). *Tips & Tactics* (supplement of *PR Reporter*), 36, 1–2.

Kish, L. (1965). *Survey sampling.* New York: Wiley.

Krueger, R. A. (1994). *Focus groups: A practical guide for applied research* (2nd ed.). Thousand Oaks, CA: Sage.

Lavrakas, P. J. (1993). *Telephone survey methods: Sampling, selection, and supervision* (2nd ed.). Newbury Park, CA: Sage.

Levine, R. (1989, October). Type A cities and your heart. *Psychology Today, 23,* 42.

Lindenmann, W. K. (1993, Spring). An 'effectiveness yardstick' to measure public relations success. *Public Relations Quarterly, 38,* 7–9.

Lindenmann, W. K. (1997). *Guidelines and standards for measuring and evaluating PR effectiveness.* Gainesville, FL: The Institute for Public Relations Research & Education.

Locander, W., Sudman, S., & Bradburn, N. M. (1976). An investigation of interview method, threat, and response distortion. *Journal of the American Statistical Association, 71,* 269–275.

A look at one solution: Family-responsive programs. (1997, January 6). *PR Reporter, 40,* 4.

M&As: Time for business communicators to prove their worth. (1998, August 24). *PR News, 54,* 1, 7.

Mangione, T. W. (1995). *Mail surveys: Improving the quality.* Thousand Oaks, CA: Sage.

Marlow, E. (1996). *Electronic public relations.* Belmont, CA: Wadsworth.

Marrow, A. J. (1969). *The practical theorist; the life and work of Kurt Lewin.* New York: Basic Books.

McAlister, A., Ramirez, A. G., Galavotti, C., & Gallion, K. J. (1989). Antismoking campaigns: Progress in the application of social learning theory. In R. E. Rice & C. K. Atkin (Eds.), *Public communication campaigns* (2nd ed., pp. 291–307). Newbury Park, CA: Sage.

McElreath, M. P. (1997). *Managing systematic and ethical public relations campaigns* (2nd ed.). Dubuque, IA: Brown & Benchmark.

McGuire, W. J. (1989). Theoretical foundations of campaigns. In R. E. Rice & C. K. Atkin (Eds.), *Public communication campaigns* (2nd ed., pp. 43–65). Newbury Park, CA: Sage.

McKeown, B., & Thomas, D. (1988). *Q methodology.* Newbury Park, CA: Sage.

McLeod, J. M., & Chaffee, S. H. (1972). The construction of social reality. In J. Tedeschi (Ed.), *The social influence process* (pp. 50–59). Chicago: Aldine-Atherton.

Melamed, B. G., & Siegel, L. J. (1975). Reduction of anxiety in children facing hospitalization and surgery by use of filmed modeling. *Journal of Consulting and Clinical Psychology, 43,* 511–521.

Mendelsohn, H. (1973). Some reasons why information campaigns can succeed. *Public Opinion Quarterly, 37,* 50–61.

Miller, M. M. (2000). *VBPro content analysis* [On-line]. Available: http://www.excellent.com.utk.edu/~mmiller/vbpro.html

Monahan, J. L. (1995). Thinking positively: Using positive affect when designing health messages. In E. Maibach & R. L. Parrott (Eds.), *Designing health messages: Approaches from communication theory and public health practice* (pp. 81–98). Thousand Oaks, CA: Sage.

Morgan, D. L., & Krueger, R. A. (1998). *The focus group kit.* Thousand Oaks, CA: Sage.

Nachmias, D., & Nachmias, C. (1981). *Research methods in the social sciences* (2nd ed.). New York: St. Martin's Press.

Nager, N. R., & Allen, T. H. (1984). *Public relations: Management by objectives.* Lanham, MD: University Press of America.

National Cancer Institute. (1999) *Making health communication pro-
grams work: A planner's guide* [On-line]. Available:
http://rex.nci.nih.gov/NCI_Pub_Interface/HCPW/HOME.HTM
The new math: Plotting PR's course on the measurement curve. (1999, No-
vember 22). *PR News, 55,* 1, 4.
Newcomb, T. (1953). An approach to the study of communicative acts.
Psychological Review, 60, 393–404.
O'Keefe, D. J. (1990). *Persuasion: Theory and research.* Newbury Park,
CA: Sage.
PR needs its own research modes, not borrowed ones. (1993, January 4).
PR Reporter, 36, 1–3.
PR pros content with their career choice but think profession is little un-
derstood. (1998, December 21). *PR News, 54,* 1–2.
PR pulse: For credibility, tie results to objectives; colleagues, experience
vital to growth. (1994, March 28). *PR News, 50,* 1, 2.
Palshaw, J. L. (1990). The fixation on focus groups. *Direct Marketing, 53,*
22, 58.
Personal competency and guts will prepare the future of PR. (1998, June
1). *PR Reporter, 41,* 1–2.
Petty, J. E., & Cacioppo, J. T. (1986). *Communication and persuasion:
Central and peripheral routes to attitude change.* New York:
Springer-Verlag.
Pfau, M. (1995). Designing messages for behavioral inoculation. In E.
Maibach & R. L. Parrott (Eds.), *Designing health messages: Ap-
proaches from communication theory and public health practice* (pp.
99–113). Thousand Oaks, CA: Sage.
Pinkleton, B. E., Austin, E. W., & Dixon, A. (1999). Orientations in public
relations research and campaign evaluation. *Journal of Marketing
Communications, 5,* 85–95.
Plous, S. (1990, January 15). Tips on motivating publics to act: Advice
from a psychologist. *Tips & Tactics* (supplement of *PR Reporter*), *28,*
1–2.
Professor: 2-way, symmetrical PR doesn't always work. (1998, February
16). *PR Reporter, 41,* 1–3.
Public Relations Society of America. (1995, October). *PRSA Research
Committee/National Conference questionnaire results.* Paper pre-
sented at the annual conference of the Public Relations Society of Amer-
ica, Seattle, WA.
Public Relations Society of America. (1999). *National credibility index*
[On-line]. Available: http://www.prsa.org/nci/nci.html
Reflections of an American guru: An afternoon with Peter Drucker. (1998,
Fall). *The public relations strategist, 4,* 8–15.
Reputation as a competitive asset. (1994, December). *Inside PR, 5,* 13–20.
Richmond, L. B. (1990). Putting the public in public relations. In D. G.
Rutherford (Ed.), *Hotel management and operations* (pp. 263–269).
New York: Van Nostrand Reinhold.

Riffe, D., Lacy, S., & Fico, F. G. (1998). *Analyzing media messages: Using quantitative content analysis in research.* Mahwah, NJ: Lawrence Erlbaum Associates.

Robinson, E. J. (1969). *Public relations and survey research.* New York: Meredith.

Rogers, E. M. (1983). *Diffusion of innovations* (3rd ed.). New York: The Free Press.

Rogers, E. M., & Kincaid, D. L. (1981). *Communication networks: Toward a new paradigm for research.* New York: The Free Press.

Salmon, C. T., & Nichols, J. S. (1983). The next-birthday method of respondent selection. *Public Opinion Quarterly, 47,* 270–276.

Saris, W. E. (1991). *Computer-assisted interviewing.* Newbury Park, CA: Sage.

Sarle, W. (1994). *Discussion on measurement scales* [On-line posted at Edstat-1 discussion group]. Available: Saswss@unx.sas.com

Schulte, B. (1996, May 28). Foes in abortion debate find common ground. *Spokane Spokesman-Review,* pp. A1, A6.

Schutt, R. K. (1996). *Investigating the social world: The process and practice of research.* Thousand Oaks, CA: Pine Forge Press.

Search for Common Ground. (1999). *Search for common ground* [On-line]. Available: http://www.searchforcommonground.org/

Selltiz, C., Jahoda, M., Deutsch, M., & Cook, S. W. (1959). *Research methods in social relations.* New York: Holt.

Settles, C. J. (1989, December). The tease that backfired. *Public Relations Journal, 45,* 40–41.

Shanks, J. M., & Tortora, R. D. (1985, March). *Beyond CATI: Generalized and distributed systems for computer-assisted surveys.* Paper presented at the first annual research conference of the U.S. Bureau of the Census, Reston, VA.

Solomon, D. S. (1989). A social marketing perspective on communication campaigns. In R. E. Rice & C. K. Atkin (Eds.), *Public communication campaigns* (2nd ed., pp. 87–104). Newbury Park, CA: Sage.

Stafford, L., & Canary, D. J. (1991). Maintenance strategies and romantic relationship type, gender and relational characteristics. *Journal of Social and Personal Relationships, 8,* 217–242.

To start the year, let's explore this major challenge together: Management's demand for proof of results & Wall Street's turn to non-financial indicators makes measurement and evaluation 2000's PR topic no. 1. (2000, January 3), *PR Reporter, 43,* 1–6.

Steeh, C. G. (1981). Trends in nonresponse rates, 1952–1979. *Public Opinion Quarterly, 45,* 40–57.

Stephenson, W. (1953). *The study of behavior.* Chicago: University of Chicago Press.

Stiff, J. B. (1994). *Persuasive communication.* New York: The Guilford Press.

Sudman, S. (1976). *Applied sampling.* New York: Academic Press.

Survey finds blue is the color of the millennium. (1998, September 7). *PR Reporter, 41,* 3–4.

Survey Sampling, Inc. (1994). *Unlisted rates of the top 100 MSAs for 1993.* Fairfield, CT: Survey Sampling.

Toth, E. L., & Grunig, L. A. (1993). The missing story of women in public relations. *Journal of Public Relations Research, 5,* 153–175.

Wallack, L., Dorfman, L., Jernigan, D., & Themba, M. (1993). *Media advocacy and public health: Power for prevention.* Newbury Park, CA: Sage.

Warwick, D. P., & Lininger, C. A. (1975). *The sample survey: Theory and practice.* New York: McGraw-Hill.

What trends are shaping public relations—as seen by the Dilenschneider Group. (1997, January 20). *Purview* (supplement of *PR Reporter*), (415), 1–2.

Williams, F. W. (1992). *Reasoning with statistics: How to read quantitative statistics* (4th ed.). Fort Worth, TX: Harcourt, Brace, Jovanovich.

Wilson, L. J. (1997). *Strategic program planning for effective public relations campaigns* (2nd ed.). Dubuque, IA: Kendall/Hunt.

Wimmer, R. D., & Dominick, J. R. (2000). *Mass media research: An introduction* (6th ed.). Belmont, CA: Wadsworth.

Witte, K. (1992). Putting the fear back into fear appeals: The extended parallel process model. *Communication Monographs, 59,* 329–349.

You can avoid common errors as you develop prevention materials. (1994, September). *Technical Assistance Bulletin* [Brochure]. Bethesda, MD: Center for Substance Abuse Prevention.

Author Index

Subject Index